ROMANTIC IMPRISONMENT

GENDER AND CULTURE

Carolyn G. Heilbrun and Nancy K. Miller, Editors

GENDER AND CULTURE   *A Series of Columbia University Press*
Edited by Carolyn G. Heilbrun and Nancy K. Miller

Nina Auerbach

Romantic Imprisonment

Women and Other Glorified Outcasts

COLUMBIA UNIVERSITY PRESS   New York

Columbia University Press
New York   Guildford, Surrey
Copyright © 1986 Columbia University Press
All rights reserved
Printed in the United States of America

c 10 9 8 7 6 5 4 3 2

Library of Congress Cataloging in Publication Data

Auerbach, Nina, 1943–
    Romantic imprisonment.

    (Gender and culture)
    Includes index.
    1. Women in literature—Addresses, essays, lectures.
2. English fiction—19th century—History and
criticism—Addresses, essays, lectures.   3. English
fiction—20th century—History and criticism—Addresses,
essays, lectures.   4. English fiction—Women authors—
History and criticism—Addresses, essays, lectures.
5. Women—Addresses, essays, lectures.   I. Title.
II. Series.
PR830.W6A93   1985   820'.9'352042   85-11005
ISBN 0-231-06004-1

This book is Smyth-sewn and printed on permanent and durable acid-free paper.

Contents

IV Women Acting

Illustrations

Acknowledgments

1. "Jane Austen and Romantic Imprisonment," *Jane Austen in a Social Context*, David Monaghan ed. (1981); reprinted by permission of Macmillan.   2. "Jane Austen's Dangerous Charm," *Jane Austen: New Perspectives*, Janet Todd ed. (1983); reprinted by permission of Holmes & Meier.   3. "O Brave New World," *ELH* (1972); reprinted by permission of Johns Hopkins University Press.

4. "Incarnations of the Orphan." *ELH* (1975); reprinted by permission of Johns Hopkins University Press.   5. "Women on Women's Destiny," *The Massachusetts Review* (1979); reprinted with their permission.   6. "Robert Browning's Last Word," *Victorian Poetry* (1984); reprinted with their permission.   7. "Dickens and Dombey," *Dickens Studies Annual* (1976); reprinted by permission of A. M. S. Press.   8. "Alice and Wonderland," *Victorian Studies* (1973); reprinted by permission of Indiana University.   9. "Falling Alice," *Soaring with the Dodo*, Edward Guiliano and James R. Kincaid eds. (1982); reprinted by permission of the University Press of Virginia.

10. "Artists and Mothers," *Be Good, Sweet Maid*, Janet Todd, ed. (1978); reprinted by permission of Holmes & Meier.   11. "Dorothy L. Sayers and the Amazons," reprinted from *Feminist Studies* (Fall 1975), 3(½):54–62, by permission of the publisher, *Feminist Studies*, c/o Women's Studies Program, University of Maryland, College Park, Md. 20742.   12. "Charlotte Brontë," *University of Toronto Quarterly* (1973); reprinted by permission of the University of Toronto Press.   13. " 'This Changeful Life,' " *Shakespeare's Sisters*, Sandra M. Gilbert and Susan Gubar, eds. (1979); reprinted by permission of Indiana University Press.   14. "The Power of Hunger," © 1975 by the Regents of the University of California; reprinted from *Nineteenth-Century Fiction* (September 1975), 30(2):150–171, by permission of the Regents.

16. All material from Ellen Terry's letters, journals, and acting scripts is quoted by permission of Dame Ellen Terry's estate, Bischoff & Co., London.

Figure 9.1. Dante Gabriel Rossetti, "Found"; reproduced by permission of the Delaware Art Museum.   Figure 9.9. Lewis Carroll, photograph of Evelyn Hatch; reproduced by permission of the Charles L. Dodgson Estate, A. P. Watt, Ltd.

Figure 16.1. William Holman Hunt, "The Lady of Shalott"; reproduced by permission of the Wadsworth Atheneum.   16.2. John Everett Millais, "Portia"; reproduced by permission of the Metropolitan Museum of Art, New York.   16.3. John Singer Sargent, "Ellen Terry as Lady Macbeth"; reproduced by permission of the Tate Gallery, London.   16.5. Unidentified French engraving of Ophelia from George William Norris' illustrated *Hamlet* (1907); reproduced by permission of the Furness Shakespeare Collection, University of Pennsylvania, Philadelphia.   16.6. Ellen Terry as Ophelia; reproduced by permission of the Furness Shakespeare Collection, University of Pennsylvania, Philadelphia.   16.7. George Frederic Watts, "Choosing"; reproduced by permission of the National Portrait Gallery, London.   16.8. "Portrait of Ellen Terry"; reproduced by permission of the National Portrait Gallery, London.   16.10. George Frederic Watts, "Ophelia"; reproduced by permission of the Watts Gallery, London.   16.11. George Frederic Watts, "Ophelia's Madness"; reproduced by courtesy of the Trustees of the British Museum.

Introduction

MY TITLE locks its subjects into irony: Romantics envision boundless self-making, but I see this glorious process occurring only within social prisons that adore what they arrest. Confined, expansive women abound in this book, but they are not alone in it: they share their power with the seemingly freer male figures—the orphans, patriarchs, and bards— who regularly move into the foreground. In these essays, oppression forces all its subjects to invent themselves. For women, romantic imprisonment is a familiar, often exhilarating condition. Men tend to deny its relevance to them, but I see the strong men I write about through a female prism: they renew themselves, sometimes murderously, through women's imprisoning power over their imaginations. This book is skeptical about freedom, but it believes wholeheartedly in male as well as female heroes. Like Ellen Terry, the glorious, shackled actress who concludes it, I celebrate pathetic and triumphant heroism, but I complicate these categories, finding the triumphant heroism that springs from pathetic postures.

In a sense, this collection represents my own romantic imprisonment, though from a happier vantage point it appears to me as a temporary stopping-place in a long, and I hope an expanding, pilgrimage. As I reread essays written over a period of seventeen years, I remember moving many times, both literally and psychically, and I also remember fearing each move, which may account for the Gothic sheen seemingly homely subjects acquire. In 1967, when I first wrote about Charlotte Brontë's two countries, I was a deferential graduate student venturing into a little-known novel called *Villette*. In 1983, when I wrote about Ellen Terry, I was a full professor abandoning the novels that were my stock in trade to share the life of an actress beyond academic (even respectably feminist) horizons. I like to think that the chronological poles of this collection—and even the climb up the academic ladder that came in between—represent a continuing trespass against what authorities thought it good to know in those years. Even if my images of trespass are only a galvanizing figment of my own romantic imprisonment, it is good to see these essays, written during many years, states, circumstances, and climates, brought together in a book. And it is good to begin to retrace the journeys they represent for me.

When I reread these essays together, I was pleased and surprised to meet Tennyson's Ulysses so often: I see that I use his hunger for continuing voyages, his individualism, his unashamed departure from family and family virtues, to gloss any number of female plots. Never, I see, did I evoke the homely Penelope, even after feminists began to valorize domesticity. Instinctively, I snatched for my women the hunger for experience, the egoistic wanderlust, of apparently unsympathetic men, in and out of literature. As he struts and boasts and voyages through these pages, Ulysses expands the boundaries of permissible womanhood as Carolyn Heilbrun alone among feminist critics exhorts her readers to do.[1] His unsought and unremembered presence reminds me, years later, of the trespass that was always, for me, the heart of scholarship.

Like Ulysses, feminist criticism itself is one hero-villain of these essays: the early ones await its coming, the later ones lovingly fight its constraints. These essays are infused for me with moves— from year to year, state to state, and professional rung to rung—but the most dramatic moves took place in the world around me, of which the history of criticism was a still more dramatic microcosm. As I wrote these essays in the 1970s, feminist criticism was born, fought for itself, proclaimed its methods and its goals, and (with a series of magnificent books) consecrated itself as an academic institution. For me, for many of us, the years when our first tentative and dangerous perceptions took flower—and power—as scholarly truth were thrilling beyond belief. The move from student to teacher, from apprentice to authority, has for women traditionally been fraught with deceit: the bridal veil we were trained to aspire toward in my day is not a commanding symbol of social maturity. But for my generation of female scholars, feelings that throughout our girlhood could be expressed only in guilty and seditious whispers suddenly became (in many circles) revered truths: we were hired to teach, paid to write about, the things we had never been allowed to know. For me, Lewis Carroll's Alice alone could express the wonder of these changes. Her searing, simple power—"You're nothing but a pack of cards"—seemed adequate to dissolve all the ideologies that had bullied us into silence.

Things seem less simple in 1984. Prisons have bred not only other prisons, but, perhaps, a new romantic consciousness. By now, for many of us and for our students, feminist criticism itself has hardened into a sort of dear prison, challenging us to create ourselves yet again. Some of these essays challenge the converted reader to do just that; others, written earlier, lack the assurance a community of imagined like-minded readers gives. I suspect that the changing rhetoric in these essays, their move from apology to authority, would tell the inquisitive historian of criticism a good deal about the changing ideological climate of those years. For this reason, I have decided to leave the earlier essays unedited, hoping that errors, diffidences, and ditherings will emerge as signs of the times. There is a point here, I think, when I as the implied author stop sounding vulnerable, and begin to declare myself. That point should come in the essays published after 1975.

A complete history of feminist criticism is impossible here, but two memorable books provide the context of this collection. To understand some of what follows, the reader needs to know something about Kate Millett's *Sexual Politics* and Ellen Moers' *Literary Women.*[2] The two books are polar opposites of each other: *Sexual Politics* is a rough and raw exposure of the enraged misogyny of the great men who create high culture in their image, while *Literary Women* celebrates the corporate strength, the imaginative autonomy, of the gifted women such men exclude. For me, each book colors an epoch. I read *Sexual Politics* when it appeared in 1970, the year I began my first fully fledged academic job; it provided evidence for my growing mistrust of a profession that claimed a noble immunity from all things female and a complacent deafness to all outcast voices. I read *Literary Women* when it appeared in 1976, just as I was finishing my own first book, *Communities of Women;* the hymnlike intensity of Ellen Moers' inspirational language endorsed my own growing faith that women have a strength of vision no patriarch can bestow or take away. The six fermenting years that separated these books formed my own assertions, as I think they did those of many writing women my age. Kate Millett ignited the spark that flared into feminist criticism; Ellen Moers gave the new field a local habitation and a creed.

These essays are not arranged chronologically, but in my head they fall into a post–Kate Millett group, and then into a post–Ellen Moers group. The earlier essays reach nervously toward a definition of female strength despite the disenfranchisements Millett rendered unforgettable; the later ones rise from the assurance of strength within a community of literary women, though they try as well to break the barriers that segregate that community from the larger world outside. The complementary limitations of *Sexual Politics* and *Literary Women* were from the beginning part of the impact of each book on my own work: each made me ache to transcend it. *Sexual Politics* offended me because there were no believable women in it, while *Literary Women* constrained me because it purged itself of men, and thus of the larger world of fun and power to which I hoped we aspired. Millett's radical thrust gives men absolute power over women's selfhood, while Moers' invigorating conservatism gives us back ourselves but denies us the world: its potent writing women are segregated from men, from power, from cultural cruelties and achievements. My own writing has always wanted to overcome both denials. I am made nervous when feminist critics insist that I am a helpless victim of powerful men; I am still more nervous when they instruct me to settle into a complacent separatist bower of womanhood, with no hope of citizenship in the dominant culture. The essays that follow are part of a continuing attempt to dissolve the prison of gender by showing men and women sharing a common consciousness within a common culture—though these inner and outer lives are often dark and turbulent.

I hope that my organization of these essays emphasizes my desire to transcend and to reconcile. My own development in exciting, changing times is probably more interesting to me than it is to the reader, but for convenience I will list the essays written after I read *Literary Women* and came to see myself as part of a community similar to Ellen Moers'. After I became aware of myself as a feminist critic rather than a solitary and embattled dissident, I wrote "Jane Austen and Romantic Imprisonment," "Jane Austen's Dangerous Charm"

"Women on Women's Destiny," "Robert Browning's Last Word," "Falling Alice," "Secret Performances," and "Ellen Terry's Victorian Marriage." The reader may judge whether the voice of these essays reveals the transformations I felt in myself, my writing, and my culture.

I have retained as cultural symptoms factual errors in some earlier essays that embarrass me now. "The Two Countries" dismisses in a footnote "trivial" emphases on sexual battles in Charlotte Brontë's work compared with loftier ideals of high culture. I can say only that I had imbibed such silly distinctions in graduate school and was trying to sound suitably lofty myself. Time has proved me a parroting fool; I hope it has taught my own teachers as well as myself that sexual battle is inseparable from "high" culture. My later essay on Dickens' *Dombey and Son* is in part a penance for this footnote: it argues that for Dickens, who in my graduate school days was a guru of high culture and a sacred well of Freudian insights, all issues pale beside the agonizing importance, both cultural and personal, of sexual battle. I am still unblushingly convinced that this is so.

Local misreadings embellish my discussions of Elizabeth Gaskell's *Cranford*, Charlotte Brontë's *Villette*, and Jane Austen's *Persuasion*. Today at least they look to me like misreadings, which I preserve as fossils of my earlier deference. A short discussion of *Cranford* in "Dorothy L. Sayers and the Amazons" maintains that Matty, its middle-aged heroine, fails at business until her long lost brother takes over her shop. In fact Matty succeeds incontrovertibly without him. Both "The Two Countries" and "Incarnations of the Orphan" see unmitigated despair in the ending of *Villette*. Lucy's lover dies: naturally she must be alienated and powerless. Now I find her quite powerful, professionally and politically, and undoubtedly exultant, at the end. I think that when I wrote these essays, my own fears of myself guided my diminution of heroines. At that time, too, it was not usual to define fictional heroines in terms of power; critics preferred to diagnose their emotions.

I apologized for these apologies by including in *Communities of Women* a long chapter, not reprinted here, on *Cranford* and *Villette*, affirming the power of their women in the teeth of my earlier pity for their pathos. For me, this turn on myself was a great exorcism and a rite de passage in my developing sense of life's possibilities; were

I to reread it now, though, I wonder whether I might apologize for making the women *too* powerful. As I hope I show by these fits and starts, the essays herein do not aim at immutable truths about their subjects; they are rather my own psychic translations of the cultural life I felt I was living during their composition.

My essay on *Persuasion*, "O Brave New World"—which I now see as a prophetic title, if a familiar one—is more enraptured about the Crofts' marriage than I now think right. Since this was my first published essay, and the only portion of my doctoral dissertation to survive in print, I reread it with particular trepidation. While I still like my celebration of Mrs. Croft as voyager away from the confinements of woman's prescribed world, I am amused at my blithe assertion that voyages *on her husband's ship* constitute "liberation." In those days it was beyond my imagination that a woman could aspire to a room, much less a ship, of her own. Since no female canon was easily available, I had not yet heard Margaret Fuller's challenge: "Let them be sea-captains, if you will." It is eerie to consider how much could not be imagined when I began these essays, and how much supposed scholars had forgotten or considered unworthy of being learned.

For all my authorial timidity in these early essays, I hope my elation of discovery still lives. When I heard the soft heroine of *Persuasion* scorning woman's supposed nature as the torturing creation of dictating men; when I saw the heroine of *Villette* traveling alone— as professional necessities forced so many of us to do in the 1970s— to teach alien students, engage in foreign intrigues, learn new, intricately professional sorts of love and fidelity; the taboos that were supposed to limit my own life lost their power. The assertions of *Persuasion* and *Villette* are now familiar landmarks in the feminist canon. Charlotte Brontë in particular has assumed inspirational centrality in what we have learned to call the female tradition;[3] her books have grown from secret discoveries into lessons. I fear they have even gained the authority to bore our present students. I hope that my halting early confrontations with them will remind the reader of the danger, the difficulty, even the brutality of books that are becoming enshrined. At that time, the very act of writing about them felt seditious, and so I piously diluted their power. Still, I am glad that I experienced so early the power of books that galvanize, not merely a segregated female tradition, but the larger culture women and men inherit jointly.

The categories into which I have arranged these essays, and the individual essays themselves, affirm what has always been an article of faith for me: women are not alone in the world. For Kate Millett, the promises of culture were a male lie; Ellen Moers compensated by giving us an inviolate and aloof female tradition, agreeing with Millett's patriarchs that good women were sequestered and self-complete. In contrast, my Jane Austen and my Emily Brontë, though they seem as sequestered as women could be, snatch at and twist the iconography the great male Romantics made their own; combative and individualistic, they take little sustenance from a female tradition. This collection deplores rigidly female traditions as freely as it does male ones, looking for what is boldly abundant in great authors, not what is exclusive. The symbol of the orphan, male and female by turns, inspires everything I wrote, for s/he is a reminder that culture takes inspiration from its outcasts. Apparent power cannot free itself from its myths of the powerless. All these essays are concerned with the sorts of power the apparently alien and excluded snatch from and wield over citizens who think they are safe.

These revolutionary rumblings may sound odd in a book whose first section is devoted to Jane Austen, a writer pious patriarchs adore and single-minded feminists mistrust: her narrow compass, her pedagogic heroes, her relentless marriage endings, should not win the place of honor in a book that makes ambitious claims. In fact, as I see her, Jane Austen is one hero of this book, as she has always been one of my own heroes, because her apparent conformity to the norms of her silliest readers frees her to laugh at us all. In her militant moods, Charlotte Brontë shouts at us. A silly person is licensed to shout back, but he has a harder time exorcising the pervasive laughter that exposes him and all he holds dear. Jane Austen's comic spirit transcends her formal obedience, illuminating the silliness of that obedience; this collection concludes with Ellen Terry laughing privately in much the same way at her own roles and the culture that determines them. Comedy alone cannot make the world saner, but a writer who helps us see that pious assumptions about our place and nature are ridiculous at heart has freed us to make our own nature and our own place. Jane Austen's duplicity, her freedom from enforced and narrowing allegiances, generate the capacious ambitions within her apparent modesty.

All three opening essays celebrate Jane Austen as immodest, acquisitive as a writer, a challenging member of her Romantic culture: my Jane Austen is neither ladylike nor sequestered, but part of an overweening and visionary age. The first essay reconstructs the "common cultural ambience" she shared with such bizarre and dark comic novelists as Maturin, Hogg, and Godwin; the second examines her most withheld heroine as type of the Romantic Hamlet and of kindred strangers and monsters of her age; the third brings Romantic paradoxes as well as Romantic feminism to bear on *Persuasion*, which was then generally considered to be her most movingly personal work. All evoke an Austen who saw herself as free to make and to unmake Romantic claims; this seemingly private woman allotted to herself a daringly public context. She sees beyond the limitations of her life, as Mary Wollstonecraft and Ann Radcliffe did, but she is not locked in their company, insinuating kinship with men as well as women. Finally, even her seemingly pallid Fanny Price can become a Romantic hero as well as a heroine of romance.

Jane Austen is a particular hero of this collection because, as I see her, she absorbed cultural currents forbidden to genteel women. Thus, when we read her books, we see more than these books, for they are points of interfusion for many Romanticisms—male and female; poetic and fictional; political and visionary—that are rarely explored together. She transcends the obedient quietude of her life and the formal obedience of her books, thereby helping us to reconcile what we usually force apart.

The first two essays in the section called "Men's Women" do not properly concern men's women at all: they deal with the intersections among men and women in a culture of beliefs to which we all have access. These two opening essays look sketchy to me now, but I look back on them as important events in my writing life, for they gave form to my vision of things and shaped everything that followed them.

"Incarnations of the Orphan" laid down my central plot, one that pervades my second book, *Woman and the Demon*, in particular, for it is full of potent outcasts, solitary wanderers destroying great houses, and self-transforming, magical protagonists. This article also led me to my persona as expositor of cultural myths, those compelling tales at the intersection of religion and fiction, history and dream. The myths I care about are topical rather than timeless, inspiring their believers to action rather than contemplation or conservation. I feel especially close to this article because its vision is still my vision, but I realize that it doesn't do justice to the orphan. There is a great deal more to say about this rich figure than I say here, though for some reason s/he has attracted little sustained attention.

I realize, too, that my readings here are fairly conventional, though since *Jane Eyre* is at present seen as a myth communicating only to women, I like the broadly cultural meanings it takes on here. I also like the way familiar readings renew themselves in conjunction: in the larger narrative of orphan fiction, there is no longer a need to fret about the sincerity of Moll Flanders and Pamela, or the double ending of *Great Expectations,* about which we were supposed to fret at that time. When I wrote about the orphan, I, like my contemporaries, had been trained to write self-contained analyses of single texts; younger scholars were experimenting with methods that broke this straitjacket. Many would embrace literary theory as a soaring release from textual prisons, while others, like myself, found cultural patterns that gave new contexts, letting a group of texts tell new stories. The fascinating apparition of the orphan made this method possible to me, though I now see that I have barely tapped the suggestive meanings of the orphan herself—and himself.

"Women on Women's Destiny," I am sad to say, looks prescient to me now. I wish I could apologize for the datedness of this little essay, and for my own impatience with the limitations of early feminist criticism, but at this writing self-pitying insularity still dogs us, despite many triumphs. Perhaps fortunately, this essay never attracted much attention, but for me it was the first, awkward emulation of Jane Austen's comic transcendence: in it, I play the gadfly, trying to goad my feminist colleagues from within in the name of the "flexibility, scope, and joy" a larger, reconciling vision promises. I still fear that narrow allegiances will bar us from "an open world of promise and power," whether or not we are feminists, but as some of the ensuing essays suggest, I have become less sanguine about entrusting women's heroism to male writers. As "Secret Performances" shows, the end of *Middlemarch* has come to look a bit better when lit with theatrical lighting, another example of the unexpected contexts that can open out familiar texts.

The four articles that make up the body of this section

show great male writers goaded by women to reveal the pain within their power. These men's women are not the pliable receptacles Christina Rossetti sees "In an Artist's Studio," "not as she is, but as she fills his dream"; they madden the benign dreams of patriarchy. Eight years separate the essays on Dickens and Browning, but I realize that they are interestingly similar: both are composite biographies (of Dickens and his daughters; of Robert and Elizabeth Browning) of the lives within texts; both, I hope, empathize with rather than excoriate their subjects; both subjects are tortured and trammeled by the expectations of patriarchy and the confusing reality of female claims, and this torment is their artistic spur. The article on *Dombey and Son* learned much from earlier male critics' witty exposure of the novel's lethal, loving heroine, but my own essay, fueled by research about nineteenth-century sexual ideologies, no longer laughs. The wounds of the paterfamilias have come to matter, just as (in earlier Dickens criticism) the wounds of money and class came to matter. These essays now seem to me to give new access to the lives of male artists as they wrote themselves and their age, working from the culture to the man in a more flexible and sophisticated manner than traditional Freudianism allows. Dickens and Browning may not offer the grand legacy of hope and joy I promise in "Women on Women's Destiny," but they do help us understand the import of our common betrayal.

Jane Austen is one surprising hero of this collection, Lewis Carroll, another. Unmarried, as she was, he, too, seems an outcast in a society entangled in families. Like her, Carroll unveils the nonsense within the pieties we are supposed to hold dear. Despite their innocuous claims, his comic fantasies free the reader to imagine the explosive transformations of our potential dream selves. As I read the *Alice* books, the disobedient women who lacerated Dickens and Browning are celebrated in all their complex and imperious hunger—though admittedly they wear the prim pinafore of that supposed Victorian sugarplum, the polite little girl.

Eight years separate the composition of my two *Alice* essays, but though I have changed my mind about Charlotte Brontë several times, I love these books unchangingly. The first essay delves into texts; I was still uneasy with larger contexts. The second, I think, roams around in the nineteenth century with an easy audacity I worked hard to possess. My celebration of a hidden, Lawrentian Carroll is much the same in both: hunger, eroticism, even violence, are native to his dream child, fueling an aggression few men want to see in their women, little or big. I cherish this unwomanly aggression wherever I find it, for it is rarely acceptable. It is easy to condemn pious patriarchs for dreaming that a woman's world consists of "nothing but love," but what can we make of sophisticated feminists who purge women of violence and desire with self-imprisoning alacrity? Feminists have condemned Carroll for both sentimentality and lust, but within his fantasies is laughter at the more pernicious fantasy of female purity so many realists embrace. I hope that my essays commemorate the dangerously wise adult within the children's friend, revealing Carroll's fitful and unexpected heroism without stripping away the charm of his nonsense.

The essays arranged under "Female Traditions" seem to me (with one exception) harsher than the essays that precede and follow them. Female traditions are often celebrated as a nurturing, even a swaddling, ambience for a woman writer supposedly unheard in patriarchy. I want to free these traditions from their potential for constricting cant and self-flattery, their hypocritical protestations of womanly feeling. Like violence, self-deception is a human, not a male, instinct. My exacerbated impatience with the self-deceit women practice to gain approval comes from long experience with myself as well as others; hence my impatience with canting female self-definitions in some of these essays. In the spirit of my praise of an aggressive, incipiently violent Alice, I praise Emily Brontë's A. G. A. for her avaricious capacity to seize the moment; I relish the cannibalism of George Eliot's Maggie Tulliver (which she shares with Austen's Fanny Price), as well as the defiant denial of maternal instincts in her Alcharisi. Only when I prepared this collection did I realize the consistency of my preference for heroines who express hungers they are told not to feel, look at what they are forbidden to see. Though I criticize some of the woman writers who have meant most to me, this criticism does not want to blame the victim, but to complicate, expand, and empower her.

"Artists and Mothers" is one of my favorite essays, in part because, to my surprised delight, there was a little controversy about it when it appeared. Christopher Ricks, distinguished father and Oxonian, went so far as to defend Jane Austen against my imputation that she was unresponsive to children. Since I have always feared my own Jane Austen—like temptation to charm my reader into ignoring what I say, it was a treat to learn that I had offended at last. This essay says only what I have experienced and observed: that motherhood is not a universal instinct among women, any more than writing is, and that these two specialized and intense activities have little to do with each other. Only after the essay was published did I learn that women are still most palatable as mothers of some sort; the sentimentality about motherhood that seems to be drenching the 1980s may make this little essay look more radical today than I ever thought it would be. The intense responses it inspired, positive as well as negative, teach me that the most dangerous prison facing women and all glorified outcasts cannot be banished by legislation: it is the prison of our belief that we are what we are told we are. Those who disentangle themselves from others' sentimentality about them, whether they are writers or not, deserve accolades for their courage, not for metaphorical conformity.

In this spirit, the article on Dorothy L. Sayers tries to disentangle the brave woman from the popular writer who wants to please. When I wrote it, Sayers was being rediscovered and lauded as a truth teller by all persuasions of right thinkers. Her *Gaudy Night* had accompanied my first move as a young teacher, irradiating the streets of Cleveland with reinforcement of my own high purpose. Her failures of nerve and of empathy looked darker to me in the light of this remembered inspiration. To soften my critical scrutiny, I experimented with various sorts of contexts; the Amazons led me into a first sketch of *Communities of Women*, while her old maids were my first introduction to the seditious voyagers who throng through *Woman and the Demon*. Even when *Gaudy Night* disappoints me, it retains its inspiration.

"Charlotte Brontë: The Two Countries" is, as I have said, the earliest piece in this collection, though it was not the first to be published: I wrote it as a graduate student, polished it as a young faculty member, in the days before *Jane Eyre* and *Villette* became canonical texts for women. I am not pleased with my lugubriously diagnostic tone, my insistently Freudian focus on "the self" in isolation from any surrounding cultural medium, my high-minded avoidance of a distinctively female voice. Women know how to read these novels now, perhaps too well, but my first fascinated evasions may remind

readers of their difficulty, their brutality, even their danger to the enthralled uninitiate.

"Emily Brontë's Anti-Romance" appeared in a collection
called *Shakespeare's Sisters*, but despite the feminist iconography of
encompassing sisterhood, as well as the facts of her life, my Emily
Brontë stands alone, revising a procession of male bards. Perhaps I
denied her a sustaining female tradition to highlight her stark awareness that men's gateways to salvation are often women's prisons. Today, I would force myself to resist the stirring image of the unaccom-
panied woman facing a pride of men. Emily Brontë did have sustaining
sisters, but the courage with which she broke nineteenth-century taboos is all her own.

"Demonism and Maggie Tulliver" appeared the year be-
fore Ellen Moers' *Literary Women* did, anticipating Moers' brilliant
analysis of the "female Gothic" that expresses everyday situations. My
analysis of George Eliot's female, Gothic vision—as opposed to the
"masculine mind" by which her power was incessantly explained—is a
harbinger of the sort of thing that after *Literary Women* became feminists' stock in trade: identifying the femaleness of literary texts was
our new imprimatur. I have not done this sort of study again, feeling
that George Eliot was at that time in need of special redemption through
the recovery of her femaleness; but I am now intrigued by interesting
differences between my idea of a female tradition and, say, Ellen Moers'.
Our dual, but different, considerations of *Frankenstein* as a female text
crystallize the difference in our feminisms.

In her famous account of the novel, Moers reads *Frankenstein* as a birth myth: Frankenstein's horror before his creature is the
suppressed horror of many mothers when confronted with the squirm-
ing fruit of that workshop of filthy creation, the delivery room. Mothers, she implies, know this obstetric horror intimately, but a culture
that exalts motherhood forces them to translate their instincts into
Gothicism. This devastating account naturalizes monstrosity; properly
understood, it rests in common experience. My account keeps monsters alive. "A demon with reproductive organs is more demonic still,"
I declare with a cool acceptance of demons on their own terms, terms
which are forever opposed to commonality. Moers tells more than I do
about ourselves, but I think that I remain truer to the scope of our
myths and fears. I do not search for a common female experience that

makes sense of all women and of the books they write. I want to stay
true to differences, to perceived dangers and real ones, to all anomalies.
For this reason, the demons I see in my women remain demons: little
is translated into familiarity or explained away. If the uncanny visions
of a *Frankenstein* or a Maggie Tulliver were translated into an experience common to all, they would be more successfully suppressed than
explained.

My allegiance to outcasts and anomalies may explain my
crowning interest in that "sacred monster," the actress: her constraints
and her capacities encompass those of all the glorified outcasts in this
book. My final section, "Women Acting," consists of two unpublished
essays with which I want to transcend the limitations of literary criticism: the diva George Eliot and the star Ellen Terry made of their
lives shimmeringly mobile works of art. In so doing, perhaps they possessed momentarily that comic freedom from imposed identities and
false allegiances that lures me to the novels of Jane Austen and the
fantasies of Lewis Carroll.

Even when she is a star, the actress personifies romantic
imprisonment: she creates herself incessantly, but only in the roles she
is given. Generally, she represents what conventional people want her
to be. She towers over them, she expands herself before them, she
forces them to be silent and still, but in the end she bows to them.
Without a script, she would be unable to unfurl and transform herself.
The heavily sincere-looking George Eliot was ingenious enough to cast
herself as the author of her own script; as I see her, she wrote herself
a variety of leading roles, from fallen woman to Madonna, until she
forced a bemused audience to pray to her. Ellen Terry transfigured the
subordinate roles women onstage and off were supposed to play, haunting
her adorers as a disturbing reminder of perishability and waste. Neither
shared what George Eliot called "the common lot of womanhood,"
but neither freed herself from the prison of cultural expectations. The
achievements of both were romantic, for their mobility led enthralled
audiences to the verge of discontent with common experience. I hope
the essays in this collection have some of the same power.

ROMANTIC IMPRISONMENT

I.

Jane Austen

1.

Jane Austen and Romantic Imprisonment

Was not the world a vast prison, and women born slaves?
Mary Wollstonecraft, *Maria*

"You are a much fitter inmate for your present abode than your last, and from hence there is no danger of your escaping."
"And where, then, am I?"
"You are in the prison of the Inquisition."
Charles Maturin, *Melmoth the Wanderer*

Like many women, Jane Austen has won praise for her limitations. The Victorian critic George Henry Lewes held her up for emulation because of the vast worlds she omitted: "First and foremost let Jane Austen be named, the greatest artist that has ever written, using the term to signify the most perfect mastery over the means to her end. There are heights and depths in human nature Miss

Mary Wollstonecraft, *Maria, or the Wrongs of Woman* (1798; reprint, New York: Norton, 1975), p. 27. Future references to this edition will appear in the text.
Charles Maturin, *Melmoth the Wanderer* (1820; reprint, Lincoln: Nebraska: University of Nebraska Press, 1961), p. 174. Future references to this edition will appear in the text.

Austen has never scaled nor fathomed, there are worlds of passionate existence into which she has never set foot; but although this is obvious to every reader, it is equally obvious that she has risked no failures by attempting to delineate that which she has not seen. Her circle may be restricted, but it is complete."[1] Over a hundred years later, we find Stuart M. Tave praising her in similarly double-edged terms for the many things she does not do. His introductory chapter, "Limitations and Definitions," implies that the two are equivalent in her world: "She does not fight for escape but makes the best use of the conditions, and if that's not the whole of art at least that is where it begins and where it ends."[2]

In this view, which still prevails among many readers, Jane Austen is the artist of contentedly clipped wings. Critics such as Lewes and Tave tend to display her as an exemplum in a cautionary tale directed at their readers, particularly their female readers, sternly recalling life's borders. As a novelist she becomes a plotter of modes of confinement for elastic imaginations like those of Catherine Morland, Marianne Dashwood, Emma Woodhouse, and the rest. Her novels come to function as traps for undisciplined expectations, as Austen metes out restrictions with some of the serene sadism of Blake's Urizen. For such readers as Lewes and Tave, Austen is both the ingenious conceiver and the placid inmate of her restricted and complete universe, taking her pleasure from lack of risks. No voyages of discovery entice her.[3]

Jane Austen's artistic world does indeed call insistent attention to its own limitations, but not, I feel, in the spirit of contented resignation these critics define. Such recurrent devices as its hot, crowded rooms, its claustrophobic courtship and proposal scenes, its exacerbated sensitivity to banal, interminable talk and to the chafing imagination force the reader's awareness toward forbidden spaces, the "worlds of passionate existence" Lewes evokes and denies. I think it would be helpful to look beyond the implicit virtue Tave finds in Austen's apparent refusal to "fight for escape," seeing it as something more painfully complex, and more embedded in Austen's own Romantic age, than an amiable adjustment to "conditions" suggests.

For as I read Jane Austen, the pinched horizons that suggest forbidden spheres beyond themselves create a divided perspective like that of Keats' "sick eagle looking at the sky," generating a torn awareness of spaces and powers denied. This awareness of inexorable denial mingles with the unimpeachable comfort of Austen's settings and, I believe, creates the unique tension that makes us keep returning to them. This continual tension between the security of a restricted world and its unrelenting imprisonment brings Austen into a special sort of agreement with her Romantic contemporaries.

It may still seem a desecration to some to place Jane Austen within a Romantic tradition, as if her perfection is somehow sealed off from time, or at least from the fluctuations of literary history. But definitions of "Romanticism" may be as wide and various as were the concerns of its writers,[4] and the conjunction of Austen's severe limitations with the various Romantic quests for infinity may reveal new facets of both. The phrase from *Emma* that seems most resonantly to define both the quietly miraculous and the oppressive qualities of Austen's world—"a crowd in a little room" (p. 249)—may be kin to the pervasive "shades of the prison-house" that fall over Romantic poetry with paradoxical effect.[5]

Wordsworth's canon defines a childhood condition that is open to eternity, only to explore in mingled tones the ramifications of childhood's imprisoning recession. Blake's "mind-forged manacles" determine the contortions of his best-known paintings, engravings, lyrics, and prophecies, a condition of imprisonment so fundamental that it alone can determine the intensity of release into visionary wholeness. Coleridge's psychic prison of dejection is the mental counterpart of the becalmed ship in *The Rime of the Ancient Mariner,* and perhaps the dark kin of the "stately pleasure-dome" of "Kubla Khan," with its later analogues, Keats' questionable "paradise" of Madeline's chamber in *The Eve of St. Agnes* and the delusive pleasure house in his *Lamia.* In all these works, closed-in space is the spirit's most appropriate, if most bitter, home.

All these states of incarceration are defined as intensely complex combinations of pleasure and pain, fulfillment and frustration, suggesting a fascination with gradations of imprisonment that is one ingredient of Romanticism: Prometheus unbound can be defined only by the mingled triumph and humiliation of Prometheus bound. Such diverse minor poems as Wordsworth's sonnet "Nuns Fret Not at Their Convent's Narrow Room" and Byron's *The Prisoner of Chillon* recreate the ironic but intense satisfactions of accommodation to imprisonment, a complex loss and gain of selfhood that may illuminate both Jane Austen's already well-lit interiors and her refusal to "fight for escape" from them. For even a cursory glance over Romantic poetry reveals its insistent awareness of states of imprisonment, as if from one point of view the great lesson of Romanticism was not the fall of the Bastille, but its survival in perpetuity.[6]

Judging from her surviving letters and from irreverent mentions in the later novels, Jane Austen regarded the poetry of her Romantic contemporaries with a certain lofty and sardonic mistrust, if she regarded it at all; in *Persuasion*, its lingered-over regret is an emotional luxury a sane person cannot afford. We cannot know how much she read, how much she shielded herself from, how much simply bored her, but it is safe to surmise that the "shades of the prison-house" that close over her fiction as well as their poetry come less from mutual influence than from a common cultural ambience.

One poem we know she did read, Byron's *The Corsair*,[7] rests on a structural irony which, as I will show, is very close to the imprisoning rhythms of Austen's own novels, and to one structural principle of Romantic narrative: the motif of the double prison, in which a journey of apparent liberation from captivity leads only to a more implacable arrest. In such a journey, "Romantic" concepts of freedom become a deeply ironic snare, as they do in *The Corsair*, which opens, like the Ancient Mariner's tale and Mary Shelley's *Frankenstein*, with the sea voyager's boast of escape and transcendence: "O'er the glad waters of the dark blue sea, / Our thoughts as boundless, and our souls as free, / Far as the breeze can bear, the billow foam, / Survey our empire, and behold our home!" (lines 1–4). But this rollicking possession of boundlessness is as empty a boast as the defiant elopements of such characters as Austen's Lydia Bennet and Maria Bertram, whose flights insure only a more pervasive entrapment: Conrad, Byron's dashing hero, is soon taken captive by the Turk. After some languishing in prison, the movement from liberation to intensified captivity is repeated: Conrad is rescued by the passionate and bloodthirsty Gulnare, "the Harem queen—but still the slave of Seyd!" As she has murdered the Seyd to effect Conrad's escape, Gulnare becomes invested with a horrible criminality that the men's casual and sporting homicide never approaches, but Conrad is ignominiously in her hands, having gone from free surveyor of a boundless empire to being the slave of a slave. His escape is thus at one with his most devastating captivity; he wilts out of life shortly after the death of the true love he has betrayed. The voyage to boundlessness has brought nothing but varieties of slavery.

Whether Austen adapted Byron's particular pattern or not, this ironic consummation of the Romantic quest is a suggestive gloss on, for example, Catherine Morland's sunny journey to Bath in *Northanger Abbey*, where she quickly falls captive to the mercenary stupidity of the Thorpes. Henry Tilney rescues her for a new liberation at Northanger Abbey, where she becomes a deeper prisoner of his father's tyranny, as it exists both within her imagination and without. Her last "rescue" by Henry Tilney may be said to make her the slave of a slave of a slave, since the pedagogic Henry is ruled by the whim of his autocratic father, who is himself the slave of money and propriety. As in *The Corsair*, three journeys of escape lead to three more resounding imprisonments. As I shall discuss at length below, particularly in her early novels, Jane Austen shares the Romantic sense of pervasive and inescapable imprisonment. But their looming enclosures which are both seclusion and dungeon become for Austen not just a matter of setting and atmosphere, but a recurrent pattern in the structure of her narratives. The kinship between Catherine Morland's journey and Conrad's is part of a wider kinship they both share with a bizarre series of novels that flourished in the late eighteenth and early nineteenth centuries, which group loosely under the rubric of Romantic fiction.

It seems to me that the particular claustrophobia so many readers uncover in Jane Austen—beginning with Charlotte Brontë's recoil, "I should hardly like to live with her ladies and gentlemen, in their elegant but confined houses"[8]—has been too easily disregarded as a mote in the eye of the beholder. As we have seen, the Romantic imagination is in large part an imagination of confinement. The prisons and imprisoning pleasure houses we have noted in Romantic poetry become in Romantic fiction not only an obsessive series of examinations of the prison as setting, but a preoccupation with thematic and formal structures which themselves imprison both reader and protagonist, barring all escape from the confines of the novel's world. If, for the purposes of this essay, we place Jane Austen among this embarrassingly lurid school of her literary contemporaries who have received so little critical attention, I think we will find a convergence of

vision and structure that brings to the surface the darkness that is part
of her comic refusal to fight for her own or her characters' escape.

I am not defining "Romantic fiction" as a purely chronological phenomenon.[9] Rather, I am struck by a group of common
themes, motifs, and structural devices in fiction ranging from the romances of Ann Radcliffe (*The Mysteries of Udolpho* was published in
1794) to the seemingly incoherent mélange of cannibalism, demonism, and torturing imprisonment in Charles Maturin's *Melmoth the
Wanderer* (which was published in 1820) and the invisible border between spiritual possession and madness in James Hogg's *The Private
Memoirs and Confessions of a Justified Sinner* (1824). In these extravagant novels, or anti-novels, all roads, even the most apparently open
and winding, lead ultimately to some sort of prison.

In all of them, the journey to prison is presided over by a
darkly ironic narrator. In all, the devil is in control, and like Melmoth,
he is a laughing sardonic devil whose jocularity is corrosive. The joke
he plays most often is the journey of the double prison we have traced
in *The Corsair,* where Conrad's liberation from the Turkish dungeon
by Gulnare becomes a still more horrible captivity. More insidiously,
the devil-author often uses as his material the most ecstatic and liberating images of Romanticism, such as its ultimate dream of escape
from "the prison-house" through the transfiguring marriage between
the natural and the supernatural. Wordsworth defines this boundlessly
expansive "marriage" in his fragment from *The Recluse:* "For the discerning intellect of Man / When wedded to this goodly universe / In
love and holy passion, shall find these [journeys to Paradise] / A simple produce of the common day" (lines 52–55).

But these bonds of epithalamium that provide transfiguring release in Romantic visions are often a demonic bondage in Romantic fiction, as is the dark, carnivorous marriage between the supernatural Melmoth and the mortal child of nature, Immalee, whose issue
is not renewed and transfigured life, but imprisonment and a prisoner's
death. Marriage in Romantic fiction is often a dark metaphor for the
pursuit of the doppelgänger, or nightmarish anti-self; the dark prophecy
of Frankenstein's monster—"Remember, I shall be with you on your
wedding-night"—echoes through all these works. Frankenstein's wedding night is a true, if diabolical, marriage, for after murdering his
creator's bride as his own had been murdered, the monster is as indis-

solubly married to Frankenstein as was the demonic-divine murderer Falkland to Godwin's Caleb Williams. John Polidori's elegant vampire, Lord Ruthven, similarly marries the tale's narrator by "glut[ting] his thirst" with his sister on their wedding night. In *Melmoth the Wanderer,* the lovers in "The Parricide's Tale" and the intimate domestic unit in "The Tale of Guzman's Family" literalize their bonds by eating each other under the pressure of starvation. The demonic marriage of the dead between Melmoth and Immalee is a recurrent pattern in Romantic fiction, whose weddings are almost invariably weldings of unnatural bondage and horror.

Many readers have been troubled by the shadowed epithalamia in Jane Austen's novels. In the early *Northanger Abbey,* "Henry and Catherine were married, the bells rang and every body smiled" (p. 252); in *Emma,* the narrator blandly consecrates "the perfect happiness of the union" (p. 484) between a vivid "imaginist" (p. 335), her heavily pedagogical guardian, and her parasitic father; and the epithalamium of the final *Persuasion* is inaugurated by a glimpse of "quick alarm" (p. 252). All these weddings seem to transmit dark signals beneath their comic reassurances. I think it will help us perceive them in their fullness if we recall the two faces of the Romantic epithalamium, the visionary bond and the unhuman bondage, the hope for liberty through transfiguration and the final reduction of aspiration to demonic cannibalism. Both manifestations of the spirit of her age are present in Jane Austen, troubling her marriages and enriching them.

In its twisting of other motifs as well, Romantic fiction appears a dark parody of Romantic visions, orchestrated by a laughing devil. In *Natural Supernaturalism,* his compendium of Romantic paradigms, M. H. Abrams defines as a frequent Romantic structure the "circular or spiral quest," whose protagonist undertakes a pilgrimage gradually leading him back to his point of origin, which he perceives from a higher, often transfigured plane of vision.[10] The ultimate coherence and transcendence of this circular quest in, for example, *The Prelude, The Rime of the Ancient Mariner,* and *Prometheus Unbound,* carries the same hope we found in Wordsworth's fragment from *The Recluse* of a liberating journey to visionary clarity.

But Romantic fiction is typically a structural labyrinth, in which there is no freeing rediscovery of origin, but only a passage to deeper interiors. The rhythms of perception of Godwin's Caleb Wil-

liams, as he broods over Falkland's narrative, embody the typical
structure of this fiction: "I turned it a thousand ways, and examined
it in every point of view. In the original communication it appeared
sufficiently distinct and satisfactory; but, as I brooded over it, it gradually became mysterious."[11] As with Frankenstein's scientific research, exploration results not in clarity, but in ever-intensifying mystery. The rationalistic documents with which James Hogg's *The Private
Memoirs and Confessions of a Justified Sinner* begins soon lead us into
the insane and miasmatic consciousness of the sinner himself, for whom
all events and actions are inscrutable, he himself emerging as the most
inexorable mystery of all.

The labyrinthine process of understanding is echoed in a
typical device of Romantic fiction: the tale within the tale, collapsing
into a series of increasingly claustrophobic vistas, a narrative series of
dark passageways in which the reader recedes increasingly from the
novel's point of origin. At one point in *Melmoth the Wanderer,* for
instance, we are treated to a tale within a tale within a tale within a
tale within a tale,[12] none of them providing the final closure that would
allow us to return over the ground we have passed endowed with the
higher, more perfect vision of the Romantic circular quest. The circular quest releases and completes us; the tale within the tale locks us
in and away from transcendence.

Jane Austen's novels seem superficially removed from this
endless series of dark passageways. They seem to end, like Abrams'
circular quest, with perfect clarity; all but two of the heroines begin
their novels with some degree of befuddlement, achieving illumination,
marriage, and closure virtually in one burst, and in the cases of Fanny
Price and Anne Elliot, who are fixed points of knowledge from the
beginning, the movement from perplexity to illumination is taken over
by the heroes. But the fascination and debate a novel such as *Emma*
engenders suggests the presence of dark passageways of a particularly
subterranean sort. A heroine like Emma, who, the first paragraph assures us, can be thoroughly "known" by a judicious observer, becomes,
like Godwin's Falkland, increasingly inscrutable the more she is brooded
about. The many ways in which Emma can be seen (is a spoiled child,
developing toward adult perfection? Is she insidiously powerful and de-
ceitful woman? Is she dynamic victim of patriarchal rules and enclosures?) embody the essential movement of Austen's novel from clarity

to obscurity, as she continues the tradition of Romantic fiction by enticing each reader to add another tale within a tale, no one of which can free us from Emma's essential mystery.

Romantic fiction, then, is the laughing denial of Romantic hopes for illumination. M. H. Abrams begins his guide to the latter by quoting from Shelley's *A Defence of Poetry:* "The literature of England has arisen as it were from a new birth." The hope for a new birth, for the perfect child who is symbol of the perfect human future, becomes in Romantic fiction a plenitude of abortions, miscarriages, and clownish monsters, such as the twisted child Immalee bears Melmoth (looking forward to such contemporary demon children as that in *Rosemary's Baby*), or that ultimate abortion, Frankenstein's monster.[13] This swarm of twisted progeny, including such doppelgängers as Hogg's chameleon-like devil in *Private Memoirs*, who functions at one time or another as every character's deformed and parodic self, may provide one explanation for a certain horror of children in Jane Austen that has troubled critics.

Certainly, as an artist, Austen has little sympathy with the Wordsworthian child as "mighty prophet," heralding a holy return to sanctified origins. But she does reveal a penchant for Romantic abortions, as in the following letter which has displeased so many Janeites: "Mrs. Hall, of Sherbourne, was brought to bed yesterday of a dead child, some weeks before she expected, owing to a fright. I suppose she happened unawares to look at her husband."[14] This unappealing tableau is as far from Wordsworth as it is from the Jane Austen many people want to see, but if we think of Romantic fiction, with its demon marriages that become claustrophobic bondages to the unnatural, its penchant for monstrous and aborted births, we can locate even Austen's seeming aberrations in the proclivities and fears of her time.

The prisons that pervade Romantic fiction are both a mockery of life's promises and life's ultimate reality. No escape is possible because in the corridors of these worlds no escape is available. The long frustration of "The Spanish Tale," with which *Melmoth the Wanderer* begins, defines the ironic rhythms with which we and the protagonist are confronted. As the result of an elaborate plot against his family, the parents of the speaker have forced the Spaniard Monçada into a monastery, though he despises the niggling hypocrisy and institutionalized mediocrity of monastic life. The horror he perceives there is the threat behind all community, the horror of encroaching littleness. His tones are not alien to those of Marianne Dashwood confronting Mrs. Jennings' evening parties, or of Emma Woodhouse surveying Highbury, as he excoriates "the petty squabbles and intrigues of the convent, the bitter and incessant conflict of habits, tempers, and interests, the efforts of incarcerated minds for objects of excitement, the struggles to diversify endless monotony, and elevate hopeless mediocrity" (p. 57). As Monçada perceives it, monastic life embodies all the distastefulness of the normal.

But a ray of hope enters: his loving brother has discerned the plot and sends word of a plan of escape. The promise held out here is that of fraternity as well as liberty, of a family bond that promises release rather than stagnation and bondage. Led by a figure known only as the parricide, Monçada descends into the bowels of the convent and they slip away. As they wind through an interminable series of dark corridors and fetid enclosures, the parricide whiles away time with a tale of illicit lovers imprisoned in one of the dungeons. In the crucible prison provides, the lovers confront the reality behind their tender bonds, "the disunion of every tie of the heart": "In the agonies of their famished sickness they loathed each other—they could have cursed each other, if they had had breath to curse. It was on the fourth night that I heard the shriek of the wretched female,—her lover, in the agony of hunger, had fastened his teeth in her shoulder;—that bosom on which he had so often luxuriated, became a meal to him now" (pp. 164–65).

The tale of imprisonment and cannibalism that embroiders their passage to freedom proves prophetic. Monçada's brother is killed, the plot has triumphed, and the tortuous dark journey leads only to the words quoted at the beginning of this essay: "The Superior consented to your attempt to escape, merely that he might have you more in his power. . . . You are in the prison of the Inquisition" (p. 174). The motif of the double prison, the painful journey from captivity that leads only to profounder bondage, is shown here in purest form. The narrative moves from the prison of others' mediocrity to a vision of the cannibalism inherent in all human bonds, and finally, to the prison of the mind itself.

As all of these novels perceive, in a manner that looks forward to the twentieth-century political allegories of Kafka, Orwell, and Koestler, the ultimate prison is acquiescence, even when acquiescence seems all life has to offer. In Jane Austen's two earliest novels, *Northanger Abbey* and *Sense and Sensibility*, I find a similar rhythm of a painful journey toward what looks like freedom but is in fact a deeper prison of the mind. Elizabeth Bennet, Fanny Price, Emma Woodhouse, and Anne Elliot will learn in the course of their novels to keep a quiet corner of their minds to themselves; but Catherine Morland's adoring acquiescence in the rationalistic pedagogy of Henry Tilney, which leaves so much of his own household unperceived, and Marianne Dashwood's acquiescence in her mother's and sister's prudential pressures, carry undertones of the sort of hopelessness only a Romantic vision can contain. In *Melmoth*, Monçada's bleak equivocation to his Superior forecasts the necessity of defeat: "I am what they have made me" (p. 131). In *Sense and Sensibility*, Marianne's penitential promise to her mother and Elinor prepares us for the lugubrious marriage she will make: "I wish to assure you both . . . that I see every thing—as you can desire me to do" (p. 349).

Like Monçada, Marianne begins her story in a prison of pervasive mediocrity and social lies. She adopts Willoughby as her guide in a journey to freedom from convention and the total honesty possible only between equals—metaphorically, the brotherhood for which Monçada also hopes—but his desertion abandons her to the deeper grip of convention, in the form of the damp presence of her ultimate husband, Colonel Brandon, whom even Elinor finds worthy but depressing. Like Monçada, the bruised Marianne adapts her identity to the vision of her conquerors and her aspirations to the illusory nature of her dream of escape. The prison of social lies becomes her ultimate truth.

This juxtaposition might seem incongruous when Jane Austen's sparse, commonplace interiors are compared with the grandiose settings of Romantic fiction. But this opulence of setting which tends to overwhelm even the central characters should not blind us to their ultimate similarities of structure. True, Austen's novels are not peopled by that personified Romantic liberator, Nature, which in Ann Radcliffe's *The Mysteries of Udolpho* and in Mary Shelley's *Frankenstein* provides the greatest snare of all; in both, the Alps, that traditional Romantic release for the soaring spirit, prove the nest of tyrants and dungeons (in *Udolpho*) and, in *Frankenstein*, of the monstrous antiself, who seems the spirit of crevices and glaciers as he nimbly makes his way among them, using Percy Shelley's sublime Mount Blanc as an appropriate setting for his insistence to Frankenstein on their monstrous bond. Similarly, in James Hogg's *Private Memoirs,* stalwart young George, who "could not endure confinement," escapes, like the Wordsworthian poet-climber, to the majestic peak of Arthur's Seat, only to be terrorized by the dreadful phantom of his murderous brother in a cloud. In all, like the pilgrimage of escape in *Melmoth,* communion with sublime nature carries only the lesson of dark bondage. Jane Austen's nature, like her interiors, carries no such promises or threats; Marianne's effusions over the picturesque seem mannered and effete in contrast. But her quest, her vertigo, and her ultimate incarceration echo those of our more intrepid Romantic mountaineers.

In all these works, terror lies in the reliability of sense. The dungeons and monsters are dreamlike, but insidiously, they are not dreams; they are implacably perceived, and cannot be made to vanish. In these worlds of terror and enclosure, the word "sense" has a less cozy meaning than it does for most interpreters of Jane Austen. It indicates not repose on a steady commonality of perception which is opposed to the private turbulence of "sensibility," but the most reliable organ of inescapable danger. William Godwin's *Caleb Williams* uses the word in this empirical, anti-Johnsonian fashion to verify the futility of escape from a world become a prison:

Escape from [Falkland's] pursuit, freedom from his tyranny, were objects upon which my whole soul was bent; could no human inequity and exertion effect them? Did his power reach through all space, and his eye penetrate every concealment? Was he like that mysterious being, to protect us from whose fierce revenge mountains and hills were told might fall on us in vain? No idea is more heart-sickening and tremendous than this. But in my case it was not a subject of reasoning or of faith; I could derive no comfort either directly from the unbelief which, upon religious subjects, some men avow to their own minds, or secretly from the remoteness or incomprehensibility of the conception; *it was an affair of the sense;* I felt the fangs of the tyger striking deep into my heart. (p. 240, my italics)

In Austen's novel, the "sense" Elinor endorses and inculcates in Marianne seems less general wisdom than this acute perception of "the fangs of the tyger." Though its concrete, empirical meaning in *Sense and Sensibility* is usually ignored, sense is less a medium of enlightenment than an organ of Romantic terror and confinement. For Austen as for these other novelists, "sense" is the lens through which we perceive the terror within "things as they are," the subtitle of Godwin's novel which could have been Austen's as well.

Like Jane Austen's art itself, the word "sense" cuts both ways: it both assuages our terrors and verifies them. Reminding readers that "the fangs of the tyger" are present in her world as well as those of her more extravagant Romantic contemporaries should not deny her geniality, her charm, her awareness of life's blessings; rather, I want to recall the persistent double vision that is the essence of Austen's and of all Romantic art. The doppelgänger, that persistent haunt of Romantic fiction, is our incessant reminder of literal doubleness, the fact that the self with whom we live in intimacy can become deformed and a stranger; and a sobering reminder as well of the mask of commonality that passes for family happiness. In Romantic fiction by women, however, including that of Jane Austen, the sense of doubleness tends to take on a narrower focus. Its pervasive philosophic awareness of the self's potential self-betrayal becomes a more concrete, if ambiguously shifting, vision of the double face of male authority.

In Ann Radcliffe's *The Mysteries of Udolpho,* for example, which, in the tradition of Romantic fiction writers, Austen both absorbed and parodied, Emily St. Aubert is endowed with twin fathers. The rule of her "true" father is all benevolence; everything associated with him cloaks his power over Emily, as he weeps incessantly, travels obligingly, and languishes in a sickness consummated in saintly death. Almost immediately, Emily is dispossessed and imprisoned by her autocratic anti-father, her uncle Montoni, whose villainy lies less in his nature than in his awareness of the absolute power he may exercise over women: " 'You shall be removed, this night,' said he, 'to the east turret: there, perhaps, you may understand the danger of offending a man, who has an unlimited power over you.' " [15]

Sense, as Caleb Williams uses it, endorses rather than minimizes the villainy of Montoni insofar as it rests on a parodic extension of the unlimited rights of parent over child, male over female, much the same sort of power General Tilney coolly exercises in *Northanger Abbey.* In *Udolpho,* the doubleness of the male protector is never resolved. Emily escapes Montoni at last, hoping to recover her dashing lover Valancourt, only to learn of his supposed betrayal. Meet-

ing him again, she perceives with irrevocable double vision the man
who blends saintly father with diabolical anti-father:

> In these the first moments . . . she forgot every fault, which
> had formerly claimed indignation, and beholding Valancourt such as he had
> appeared, when he won her early affection, she experienced emotions of only
> tenderness and joy. This alas! was but the sunshine of a few short moments;
> recollections rose, like clouds, upon her mind, and, darkening the illusive
> image, that possessed it, she again beheld Valancourt, degraded—Valancourt
> unworthy of the esteem and tenderness she had once bestowed upon him; her
> spirits faltered, and, withdrawing her hand, she turned from him to conceal
> her grief. (p. 624)

Though the plot resolves her scruples, her double vision never clears as
she accepts Valancourt's ambiguous protection.

Similarly, as much as he is Frankenstein's double and
monstrous child, Mary Shelley's monster is the dominant father figure
in her novel. Aside from assuming droit du seigneur over Frankenstein's bride, his most heinous acts are the removal of patriarchs as
benevolent and as full of sensibility as M. St. Aubert—De Lacey and
the "indulgent" father of Victor Frankenstein—to replace them, as
Montoni does, with his own tyrannical and regnant image. Monstrosity
is less an emanation from within than it is an outgrowth of the double
nature of all fathers and fatherly men.

Here we may remember the double eye Jane Austen casts
upon General Tilney, who simultaneously is and is not a Montoni, or
upon even the good Mr. Knightley, the vigorous benevolence of whose
power finds its analogue in the clinging, denying nature of Mr. Woodhouse's, both of whom Emma seems to marry at the end of her novel.
Jane Austen, too, casts upon her protecting patriarchs a relentless double vision, though she is so deft an artist that she may lead us to think
our own vision is slightly out of focus.

The novel that seems most to bridge the gap between Jane
Austen and Romantic fiction, using the conventional settings of the
genre for a specifically female indictment, is Mary Wollstonecraft's
fragment Maria, or the Wrongs of Woman, the unfinished legacy she
left at her death, which Godwin published in 1798. Like much Romantic fiction, Maria is set entirely in prison, recalling the patriarchal
dungeon/castle of Udolpho (Maria has been locked away from her child

by her vengeful husband), but this prison is a madhouse as well, that
is, a prison of the mind, looking forward to the monastery of *Melmoth
the Wanderer*, where mediocrity institutionalized was at one with the
prison of the Inquisition. This prison, then, is comprehensive—"Was
not the world a vast prison, and women born slaves?" (p. 27)—and
Wollstonecraft is more explicit than our other authors about its allegorical nature. In a sketchy and unfinished preface, she makes clear
her general intention, to use the trappings of Romantic fiction as an
emblem of women's history within "the partial laws and customs of
society": "In the invention of the story, this view restrained my fancy;
and the history ought rather to be considered, as of woman, than of
an individual." This allegorical aim removes *Maria* from the usual mode
of Romantic fiction, where the opulent setting dwarfs the human action. Wollstonecraft's conscious allegory brings her techniques close to
Jane Austen's, whose imprisoning medium springs from our pervasive
awareness of confinement rather than from its detailed, palpable representation.

Whatever structure we can discern in *Maria* seems to rest
on the central irony of Romantic fiction: the existence of a double
prison. Maria's incarceration is the result of her flight to escape the
prison of her marriage. "Marriage had bastilled me for life" (p. 103),
she writes, but her attempt to tear down the bastille and flee to the
Continent leads her into this final trap of her husband's. Once she is
in prison, the novel's central ambiguity rests on the nature of Henry
Darnford, her adoring suitor there. Their romance grows from the books
Darnford lends her; significantly, in view of Wollstonecraft's denunciation in *Vindication of the Rights of Woman*, they both palpitate to
Rousseau; in fact, like Willoughby in *Sense and Sensibility*, Darnford
seems to spring whole out of her feverish reading. Interestingly, at least
in the Norton edition, the manuscript becomes patchy and fragmented
every time Darnford enters the story, as if his identity and his role in
the plot were a knot Wollstonecraft could not cut through. Darnford
promises to free Maria under his protection, but in at least two projected endings (with three more hinted at), he abandons her to solitude
and the ultimate prison of suicide. Like Emily St. Aubert's dashing,
reading Valancourt, Darnford seems simultaneously a redeemer and a
jailer, Maria's guide from the bastille of legally defined marriage to a
profounder dungeon of romantic love.

Wollstonecraft creates her hero with the double vision we find so often in women's Romantic fiction. The fragmentary nature of the manuscript allows us to perceive more vividly the ambivalence with which she conceives him, a radical ambivalence which remains at the heart of Jane Austen's finished art, many of whose men can equally be perceived as redeemer/jailers, and whose gestures toward escape lead only to the ironic ubiquity of a double prison.

Seen in this context, it is possible to perceive Jane Austen's canon as one long, and always doomed, fight for escape. The early novels are most sharply aware of "shades of the prison-house." In its ambivalent parody of Romantic fiction, *Northanger Abbey* abounds in prison settings: not only the coach of John Thorpe's mock-captivity, or the ominous abbey itself, where, in true Romantic fashion, Catherine's greatest imprisonment is her humiliating expulsion thence, but what should be the fairy-tale glow of Catherine's first ball.

Catherine's first view of it from above seems a parody of the sublime ascents up Romantic mountains we have seen earlier: "Here there was something less of crowd than below; and hence Miss Morland had a comprehensive view of all the company beneath her, and of all the dangers of her late passage through them. It was a splendid sight" (p. 21). But, as in *Udolpho*, the splendor of ascent gives way to awareness of imprisonment: "She was tired of being continually pressed against by people, the generality of whose faces possessed nothing to interest, and with all of whom she was so wholly unacquainted, that she could not relieve the irksomeness of imprisonment by the exchange of a syllable with any of her fellow captives" (pp. 21–22). Romantic ascent dissolves into a prison of pressing mediocrity, suggesting both Maturin's great and petty tyrannies and Wollstonecraft's prison of woman's history.

These slight verbal connections recur in the larger structure of the novel, as Austen toys with three variants of the Romantic double prison, while General Tilney shifts imperceptibly between ordinary father and monster, until the two come to resemble each other, and Henry takes on the ambiguous role of redeemer/jailer, "torment[ing]" and "instruct[ing]" Catherine simultaneously (p. 109). The mechanical, even faintly zombie-like quality of the final epithalamium—"Henry and Catherine were married, the bells rang and every body smiled" (p. 252), in which the smiles seem as nonhuman as the bells [16]—recalls the darker, enforced marriages of the unnatural in Romantic fiction, whose contrivance (as in *Frankenstein* or *Melmoth*) murders the living nature marriage claims to perpetuate.

With the exception of its title, and of Marianne's early effusions, literary language falls away in *Sense and Sensibility*. We have seen the dark construction the title's "sense" can take on when aligned with William Godwin's appalled apprehension of the prison of "things as they are"; Elinor Dashwood's sense is equally a seismographic awareness of danger, of the reality of others' power, from which Marianne's sensibility is, initially, blithely free. Marianne's movement in the novel is one long fight for escape from the functional prison of Barton Cottage, symbol of a family cannibalism (embodied in the John Dashwoods) only less blatantly motivated than those of *Melmoth the Wanderer*. Like the parricide in *Melmoth*, Willoughby claims to inaugurate her to a freedom beyond the savagery of convention, but in the ambiguity of his motives and of his very identity, he is a perfect type of the redeemer/jailer we have seen so often. His consistent doubleness may explain the intensity of Elinor's reaction to his final confession, in their one, puzzling confrontation:

> She felt that his influence over her mind was heightened by circumstances which ought not in reason to have weight; by that person of uncommon attraction, that open, affectionate, and lively manner which it was no merit to possess; and by that still ardent love for Marianne, which it was not even innocent to indulge. But she felt that it was so, long, long before she could feel his influence less. (p. 333)

The potent ambivalence of Elinor's response is often seen as a symptom of the fragility of her sense in the face of Willoughby's vividness and passion. But if we define "sense" as Godwin does, this passage anatomizes its strength: Elinor's profoundly double perception is painfully true to the dual identity of the hero, and, perhaps, to that of all heroes.

If we limit ourselves to the six Austen novels completed and published, the novels following *Sense and Sensibility* attempt in various ways to move beyond the double prison of Romantic structural irony by aligning the heroines with the sources of social power. Elizabeth Bennet in *Pride and Prejudice* is the simplest case: she assumes power by marriage to it, and the novel arcs with her comic rise. Unlike Catherine Morland and Marianne Dashwood, she falls back only in a muted, vicarious fashion through her sister's humiliating elopement. The double prison quietly persists, however, in Darcy's radically double character, his ambiguous affinity with his tyrannical aunt making him as suggestive a redeemer/jailer as Willoughby was. His humanization is so undefined a process that we can see the "shades of the prison-house" closing on Elizabeth forever at Pemberley.[17]

In *Mansfield Park*, Jane Austen solves the problem of the heroine rising to power through marriage, and thus remaining vulnerable to its vagaries, by dissociating Fanny's increasing power at Mansfield from her later union with Edmund in an unspecified future. Perhaps so many readers find this novel unpleasant because Fanny gains power in silence and solitude, keeping her own counsel in a most disingenuous and ungirlish fashion; only after she supplants his own children in the confidence of the head of the house does she marry the vacillating son. The influence Fanny gains over the estate enables her to exclude her enemies, such as Mary Crawford, from it; and to include her allies, such as her sister Susan, within its lush confines. She rises alone from being the prisoner of Mansfield to the status of its principal jailer.

This assumption by the lone woman of the hero's role of redeemer/jailer prepares us for the greater complexity of *Emma*, whose heroine, like Byron's Gulnare, is both queen and slave, prime mover and victim, of the confinements of Highbury and of her father's house. This tension between power and prison is so great that *Emma* is almost stationary, suggesting less a progress (even if illusory) through a double prison than an exploration, as Wollstonecraft's *Maria* might have been, of the multitudinousness and richness of confinement.

For like the madhouse/prison of *Maria*, Austen's prisons are neither "abodes of horror" nor "castles, filled with spectres and chimeras, conjured up by the magic spell of genius to harrow the soul, and absorb the wondering mind" (*Maria*, p. 23). Austen's homely settings have no need for the exotic terrors of Maturin's Inquisition. But their inescapability is the same. Like Maturin's labyrinths, they are founded on the institutionalization of mediocrity, a tyranny of the normal which the determined heroine can come to dominate, but which she cannot transcend. Like Wollstonecraft's, Austen's meticulous double vision transplants this remote Romantic terror to the reassuring familiarity of the world we think we know.

In its imagination of a more seemingly open world and a cleansing, even a Utopian, society, *Persuasion* is repeatedly dubbed Austen's one Romantic novel.[18] But as I hope I have shown, both Romanticism and Jane Austen express a profound awareness that the questing spirit is bowed down by indelible manacles, of its own and its society's making. When we read Austen among her Romantic contemporaries, the implacable reality of limitation leads neither to comfort nor complacency, but to the delicate desperation of Maria Bertram's complaint in *Mansfield Park:* "I cannot get out, as the starling said" (p. 99).[19]

2.

Jane Austen's Dangerous Charm: Feeling as One Ought About Fanny Price

Alone among masters of fiction, Jane Austen commands the woman's art of making herself loved. She knows how to enchant us with conversational sparkle, to charm our assent with a glow of description, to entice our smiles with the coquette's practiced glee. No major novelist is such an adept at charming. Samuel Richardson, her greatest predecessor, disdained gentlemanly amenities in his revelations of the mind's interminable, intractable mixture of motives when it engages itself in duels of love; George Eliot, her mightiest successor, rejected charm as an opiate distracting us from the harsh realities her knobby, convoluted books explore. These majestic truth tellers could not write winningly if they tried, for they are too dismally aware of the dark side of enchantment; while even in her harshest revelations, Jane Austen is a maestro at pleasing.

Yet, from the cacophony of marriages with which it begins, to the depressed union which ends it, *Mansfield Park* is unlikable. When so knowing a charmer abrades her reader, her withdrawal from our pleasure must be deliberate. She herself studied the gradations of liking that *Mansfield Park* inspired, something she had not troubled to do with her earlier books, as we know from her meticulously compiled "Opinions of *Mansfield Park*": "My Mother—not liked it so well as P. & P.—Thought Fanny insipid.—Enjoyed Mrs Norris. . . . Miss Burdett—Did not like it so well as P. & P. Mrs. James Tilson—Liked it better than P. & P.,"[1] and so on. We do not know whether these carefully measured dollops of liking amused Jane Austen or annoyed her, but we do know that she was intrigued by the degree to which her unlikable novel was liked. Her apparent withdrawal from the reader's fellowship suggests a departure from the community and the conventions of realistic fiction toward a Romantic and dissonant perspective. If we examine this difficult novel, with its particularly unaccommodating heroine, in relation to contemporaneous genres beyond the boundaries of realism, we may better understand Jane Austen's withdrawal from a commonality of delight.

The silent, stubborn Fanny Price appeals less than any of Austen's heroines. Perhaps because of this, she captivates more critics than they. "Nobody, I believe, has ever found it possible to like the heroine of *Mansfield Park*,"[2] Lionel Trilling intoned in 1955, and few would contradict this epitaph today. Yet Trilling goes on to apotheosize this literary wallflower, transfiguring her into a culturally fraught emblem who bears on her scant shoulders all the aches of modern secularism. Such later interpreters as Avrom Fleishman similarly embrace Fanny as emblem if not woman, wan transmitter of intricate cultural ideals.[3] It seems that once a heroine is divested of the power to please, she is granted an import beyond her apparently modest sphere, for, unlike Jane Austen's other, more immediately appealing heroines, Fanny has been said to possess our entire spiritual history as it shapes itself through her in historical time. Elizabeth and Emma live for readers as personal presences, but never as the Romantic, the Victorian, or the modern zeitgeist. Failing to charm, Fanny is allowed in compensation to embody worlds.

But readers who have been trained to respect the culturally fraught Fanny still shy away from her as a character. Living in uncomfortable intimacy with her as we do when we read the novel, we recall Kingsley Amis' taunt that an evening with Fanny and her clergyman husband "would not be lightly undertaken."[4] We may understand our heritage through Fanny Price, but ought we to want to dine with her The question is important because, for theorists like George

Levine, the more bravely realism departs from the commonality of fellowship, the more radically it tilts toward a monstrosity that undermines the realistic community itself.[5] In the very staunchness of her virtue Fanny Price seems to me to invoke the monsters that deny the charmed circle of realistic fiction. Though she uses the word "ought" with unyielding authority, she evokes uncertainty and unease. Though we learn more about her life, and participate more intimately in her consciousness, than we do with Jane Austen's other heroines, the bothering question remains: How ought we to feel about Fanny Price?

Mansfield Park tilts away from commonality in part because it breaks the code established by Jane Austen's other novels. Few of us could read Pride and Prejudice, Persuasion, or even Emma, without liking the heroines enough to "travel with them," in Wayne Booth's charming phrase.[6] Mansfield Park embodies a wryer literary perception, one especially congenial to Jane Austen's poetic contemporaries: the creator of Fanny Price assumes that one may live with a character one doesn't like. One motive power of Romantic poetry is the fascination of the uncongenial. In "Resolution and Independence," Wordsworth can be possessed by a deformed and virtually nonhuman leech gatherer, although the poet is too remote from the old man to absorb a word of his exhortation; an unkempt sinner, Coleridge's Ancient Mariner, can snatch our imagination from a wedding, that great congenial sacrament of human community. These gnarled figures lure us out of fellowship to adopt the perspective of the monstrous and the marginal.

Fanny captures our imaginations in this same Romantic way, by welcoming the reader into her solitary animosity against the intricacies of the normal: "Fanny was again left to her solitude, and with no increase of pleasant feelings, for she was sorry for almost all that she had seen and heard, astonished at Miss Bertram, and angry with Mr. Crawford."[7] The compelling blighting power of Fanny's spectatorship at Sotherton is characteristic; morality dissolves into angry and unpleasant feelings whose intensity is an alternative to community. For while Fanny's Romanticism suggests itself in her isolating sensibility, her stylized effusions to nature, she is most Romantic in that, like Wordsworth's leech gatherer or Coleridge's Mariner, there is something horrible about her, something that deprives the imagination of its appetite for ordinary life and compels it toward the deformed, the dispossessed.

This elevation of one's private bad feelings into a power alternate to social life associates Fanny not merely with early Romantic outcasts, but with such dashingly misanthropic hero-villains as Byron's Childe Harold, Mary Shelley's Frankenstein, and Maturin's Melmoth. Their flamboyant willfulness may seem utterly alien to this frail, clinging, and seemingly passive girl who annoys above all by her shyness, but like them, she is magnetically unconvivial, a spoiler of ceremonies. During the excursion to Sotherton, the rehearsals of *Lovers' Vows*, the game of Speculation, her baleful solitude overwhelms the company, perhaps because it expresses and exudes their own buried rancor. In families ranging from Sir Thomas Bertram's stately authoritarianism to the casual disorder of her father's house, Fanny exists like Frankenstein as a silent, censorious pall. Her denying spirit defines itself best in assertive negatives: "No, indeed, I cannot act" (p. 168).

Fanny's credo resonates beyond her particular disapproval of staging *Lovers' Vows*, for, even when the play is not in question, Fanny refuses to act. Instead, and consistently, she counteracts; a creed which seems a high-minded elevation of her own honesty against the dangerous deceit of role-playing is also resistance to the comic, collective rhythms of realistic fiction itself. The joyless exercises of her delicate body tacitly condemn not only acting, but activity in general; Mary Crawford's elation at horseback riding is as antagonistic to Fanny as is her flair for acting. At Sotherton, Fanny stations herself beside the dangerous ha-ha as a still bulwark against the mutual serpentine pursuit of the other characters; playing Speculation, she alone will not take the initiative that will advance the game. Fanny's refusal to act is a criticism not just of art, but of life as well. Her timidly resolute denial of acting includes activity and play, those impulses of comedy which bring us together in ceremonial motions where fellowship seems all. Her refusals are her countercharm against the corporate and genial charm with which Jane Austen's comedies win love.

Fanny's role as counteractive genius and spirit of anti-play is anomalous in a romantic heroine, but not in a hero-villain. Like Frankenstein and his monster, those spirits of solitude, Fanny is a killjoy, a blighter of ceremonies and divider of families. It is precisely this opposition to the traditional patterns of romantic comedy that lends her her disturbing strength. Her misery amid the bustle of the play is the stigma of her power:

She was full of jealousy and agitation. Miss Crawford came with looks of gaiety which seemed an insult, with friendly expressions towards herself which she could hardly answer calmly. Every body around her was gay and busy, prosperous and important, each had their object of interest, their part, their dress, their favourite scene, their friends and confederates, all were finding employment in consultations and comparisons, or diversion in the playful conceits they suggested. She alone was sad and insignificant; she had no share in any thing; she might go or stay, she might be in the midst of their noise, or retreat from it to the solitude of the East room, without being seen or missed. (p. 180)

But though she is stricken in the midst of play, unable and unwilling to act, Fanny never retreats from activity. Finally, her "jealousy and agitation" seem to take concrete shape in the angry intruder, Sir Thomas Bertram, who lends authority to Fanny's bad feelings and ends the play. Sir Thomas' interruption seems only the culmination of Fanny's silent, withering power over performance, for before he appears she has already drawn control to her watching self. Backstage, she alone is in possession of each actor's secret grievance; watching and prompting from her isolation, she alone knows everybody's lines. A center of fierce inactivity, Fanny broods jealously over the play until she masters both its script and the secret designs of its actors, at which point Sir Thomas' return vindicates her silent obstructive power. Fanny abdicates from stardom to assume a more potent control over the action: she appropriates to her solitude the controlling omniscience of the rapt audience.

As her novel's sole and constant watcher, the controlling spirit of anti-play, Fanny relinquishes performing heroinism to become the jealous reader, whose solitary imagination resurrects the action and keeps it alive. In her own delicately assertive phrase, "I was quiet, but I was not blind" (p. 358). As quietly seeing spectator of others' activities, Fanny plays a role as ambiguous as the reader's own: like Fanny, we vivify the action by our imaginative participation in it, while we hold as well the power to obstruct it by our censure. The anomalous position of the watcher more than justifies Mary Crawford's perplexed question: "Pray, is she out, or is she not?" (p. 81). Withholding herself from play, Fanny ingests the play of everyone she silently sees. As omniscient spectator of all private and public performances, Fanny remains "out" of the action, while her knowledge seeps into its subtlest permutations. Our discomfort at her, then, may incorporate our discomfort at our own silent voyeurism; as a portrait of the reader as a young woman, she is our unflattering if indelible reflection. Her fierce spectatorship forces our reluctant identification.

As ominiscient watcher and anti-comic spirit linked in uncomfortable community to the solitary reader, Fanny possesses a subtler power than we find in brighter and livelier heroines of fiction. That dynamic misreader Emma Woodhouse is forced by her own misconstructions into the limited position of actor in the comedy she is trying to control from without, while Fanny's role as omniscient outsider thrives on her continued abstention. In her role as controlling, anticomic watcher, Fanny moves beyond the sphere of traditional heroinism to associate herself with a host of dashing British villains. Like them, this denying girl will not, perhaps cannot, eat; her abstinence makes her a spectral presence at the communal feast. Reunited with her family at Portsmouth, instead of feasting with them, as any of Dickens' or Charlotte Brontë's waifs would gladly do, she is repelled by the very suggestion of food, by "the tea-board never thoroughly cleaned, the cups and saucers wiped in streaks, the milk a mixture of motes floating in thin blue, and the bread and butter growing every minute more greasy than even Rebecca's hands had first produced it" (p. 428). Family food induces only a strangely modern nausea. Fanny's revulsion against food, along with her psychic feasting on the activities of others, crystallizes her somewhat sinister position as outsider who strangely and silently moves into the interior. Her starved incapacity to eat familial food is suggestive of that winsome predator the vampire, an equally solitary and melancholy figure who haunts British literature in his dual role as dark abstainer from a comic dailiness of which he is secretly in possession. Like Fanny, the vampire cannot eat the common nourishment of daily life, but he feasts secretly upon human vitality in the dark.

In adopting the role of traditional literary villains, Fanny infects our imaginations in a way that no merely virtuous heroine could do. Her hungry exclusion seems unappeasable and triumphant. Insofar as she draws sustenance from her role as omniscient outsider at family, excursion, wedding, play, or feast, she stands with some venerable monsters in the English canon. Not only does she share the role of Mary Shelley's creature, that gloomy exile from family whose vocation is to control families and destroy them, but there is a shadow on her even of the melancholy Grendel in the Anglo-Saxon epic *Beowulf*. An exile from common feasting, Grendel peers jealously through the window of a lighted banquet hall. He defines his identity as outsider by appropriating the interior; he invades the lighted hall and begins to eat the eaters. At the end of *Mansfield Park*, Fanny too has won a somewhat predatory victory, moving from outsider into guiding spirit of the humbled Bertram family. Fanny's cannibalistic invasion of the lighted, spacious estate of Mansfield is genteel and purely symbolic, but, like the primitive Grendel, she replaces common and convivial feasting with a solitary and subtler hunger that possesses its object. In this evocation of an earlier literary tradition, Fanny is Jane Austen's most Romantic heroine, for she is part of a literature newly awakened to ancient forms and fascinated by the monstrous and marginal. In the subtle streak of perversity that still disturbs readers today, she shows us the monsters within Jane Austen's realism, ineffable presences who allow the novels to participate in the darker moods of their age.[8]

Fanny's jealous hunger, which can be assuaged only by private, psychic feasting, isolates her in comedy while it associates her with such venerable predators as the Ancient Mariner, the vampire, the Byronic hero-villain, and, in a far-off echo, *Beowulf*'s Grendel. Her initiation is not that of the usual heroine, whose marriage reconciles us to the choreography of comedy; instead, like the hero-villain, she proclaims her uniqueness through possessive spectatorship. The implications of Fanny's refusal to act are more richly glossed in Romantic poetry and fiction than in early nineteenth-century realism, but Romantic criticism also illuminates the complex genesis of a Fanny Price: her stubborn creed, "I cannot act," recalls some problematic characters of Shakespeare, in whom such critics as Coleridge and Hazlitt discovered new significance.

Like *Mansfield Park*, Shakespearean drama characteristically pivots upon the performance of a play within a play; like Jane Austen, Shakespeare increasingly pushes to center stage the character who refuses to act. Thus, in his early *A Midsummer Night's Dream*, all the rustics lumber through their parts in the thoroughly comic "Pyramus and Thisbe," but by the time we reach *Twelfth Night*, the play is marred: the austere Malvolio is made to perform in a cruel drama not of his making, posturing for the delectation of the raucous plotters just as he thinks he is being most sincere. This humiliation of an upright, if unlikable, character by the cruelty of play anticipates the complex tone of *Mansfield Park,* though Fanny's sharper eye for traps forbids her seduction by the players.

Malvolio abandons his part in outrage, bellowing as he exits, "I'll be revenged on the whole pack of you!" Perhaps in his revenge he returns as Hamlet, our most famous star who refuses to act. Like Fanny, Hamlet casts himself as a jealous and melancholy death's head in a gay, if false, company. His stern creed—"Madam, I know not seems"—epitomizes, like hers, refusal to act. Nonactive in the complex political drama of his family life, Hamlet likewise takes no part in the microcosmic play within the play, though, like Fanny, he hovers hungrily around its periphery, knowing all the parts. His avid spectatorship ultimately upstages the actors and spoils the performance, replacing communal play with rage and slaughter; at the end of her novel, Fanny too reigns at Mansfield in consequence of a family havoc begun at the ruin of the play.

Of course, Fanny is not Hamlet, nor was she meant to be. She is not a doomed prince, but a pauper, a woman, and a survivor; she neither rages nor soliloquizes, revealing her power and her plans only haltingly and indirectly. Still, in her complex relation to the play which epitomizes her novel's action, Fanny has more in common with Hamlet than she does with the helpless women she excoriates when they cross his path. For Hamlet is Shakespeare's supreme antiactor and counteractor, the avid and omniscient spectator of the game, who fascinates us as Fanny does because he expresses his virtue by the characteristics of conventional villainy. Jane Austen's contemporaries were obsessed by this troubling sort of hero: Samuel Taylor Coleridge reconceived Hamlet as a paragon of nonactivity, deifying for the modern age a character too pure to act, whose doom and calling are the destruction of play. Fanny Price may be one feminized expression of this new, Romantic fascination with Hamlet as a modern type. As Jane Austen's Hamlet, scourge and minister of a corrupted world, the perfection of the character who won't play, Fanny Price in her unyielding opposition, her longing for a purified and contracted world, gains majesty if not charm. She is as sternly denying as Hamlet, banishing in turn her cousins Maria and Julia, her parents, and the rakish, witty Crawfords from her own finer sphere. These multiple banishments align her with one type of Romantic hero, while denying her the warmth readers want in a heroine. Confronted with so richly disturbing a figure, we would insult her to sentimentalize her when *Mansfield Park* itself does not. For, as we shall see, Fanny's anti-human qualities are stressed in the text of the novel as well as in its contexts. In her progress toward power, her charmlessness only increases her efficacy as Mansfield's scourge and minister.

"Nobody falls in love with Fanny Price," Tony Tanner warns us (introduction to *Mansfield Park*, p. 8). We have seen that few readers have done so; Jane Austen further confounds our emotions by making clear that none of the characters within the novel falls in love with her either, though most heroines exist to win love. She wins neither the affection nor the interest of her parents, though they are not always unresponsive; the charm of a Henry Crawford evokes an answering charm in them, but when Fanny's penitential visit to Portsmouth is over at last, her parents seem as relieved to see her leave as she is to go. Kinship is equally unappetizing to all.

Within Mansfield, the gracious adoptive family to which Fanny returns with such ardor, she wins love in proportion to her cousins' shame, receiving emotional interest they failed to earn. Fanny, despised by all, is embraced as a last resource when Sir Thomas' natural children disgrace themselves in turn. Jane Austen is coolly explicit about the cannibalistic undercurrents of this, and perhaps of all, requited love:

My Fanny indeed at this very time, I have the satisfaction of knowing, must have been happy in spite of everything. She must have been a happy creature in spite of all that she felt or thought she felt, for the distress of those around her . . . and happy as all this must make her, she would still have been happy without any of it, for Edmund was no longer the dupe of Miss Crawford.

It is true, that Edmund was very far from happy himself. He was suffering from disappointment and regret, grieving over what was, and wishing for what could never be. She knew it was so, and was sorry; but it was with a sorrow so founded on satisfaction, so tending to ease, and so much in harmony with every dearest sensation, that there are few who might not have been glad to exchange their greatest gaiety for it. (p. 446)

In this redemption from her usual depression, Fanny's only available happy ending is the predator's comedy; surely there is deliberate irony in Jane Austen's pitiless repetition of "happy" amid this household of collapsed hopes. Never in the canon is the happy ending so reliant upon the wounds and disappointment of others; though we leave Fanny ministering avidly to these wounds, they will never heal. The love she wins from her adoptive family is not a free tribute to her beauty, her character, or her judgment, but the last tender impulse of a stricken household.

The love of her two suitors, Henry and Edmund, is similarly undermined. Everything about Henry Crawford, that mobile and consummate actor, calls his sincerity into question. He stages his love scenes before select audiences, all carefully chosen to put the greatest possible pressure on Fanny, only to humiliate her flamboyantly by his elopement with Maria once she has begun to respond. As Fanny and we know, his passion for her repeats more grandly his pattern of behavior with her silly cousins, so that only the most sentimentally credulous reader could find this new performance credible. The watcher Fanny knows his love is play, and thus by definition the medium of her humiliation; but in exposing the ardor of the romantic hero as a sadistic game, Jane Austen undermines the reader's own impulse to fall in love with Fanny by undermining love itself.

Readers of *Sense and Sensibility, Pride and Prejudice,* and *Emma* expect Edmund Bertram, Fanny's proper husband and sober soul mate, to redress the balance; the probity of this good suitor's love should define the sham of Henry's. But if for Henry love is another variant of private theatricals, a series of ritual attitudes staged for an audience, Edmund's love is so restrained as to be imperceptible. Like Mr. Knightley, he is exemplary as Fanny's tender mentor, proud of his pupil's right feelings and right attitudes, but he has none of Mr. Knightley's life as an incipient lover. Sexual jealousy fuels the latter's sternly protective manner and his indignant disapproval of Frank Churchill, while Edmund hints of no passions beyond what we see, showing not a glimmer of jealousy when Henry Crawford makes demonstrative love to Fanny. Edmund's impeccably clerical conscience interprets his future wife's prospective marriage as a convenience to facilitate his own engagement to Henry's seductive sister. Jane Austen is a sharp observer of men struggling with powerful feelings; like

Knightley, Darcy and Wentworth fight to repress, through prudence
or anger, a love that proves too strong for them; but she withholds
from Edmund Bertram any feelings worth denying. The unlocated and
undramatized conversion that leads to his marriage carries as little
emotional weight as it could do: "I only intreat every body to believe
that exactly at the time when it was quite natural that it should be so,
and not a week earlier, Edmund did cease to care about Mary Crawford, and became as anxious to marry Fanny, as Fanny herself could
desire" (p. 454).

 This clipped, perfunctory summary, together with the fact
that no earlier hints have prepared us for an outbreak of passion on
Edmund's part, seems deliberately designed to banish love from our
thoughts. The final marriage is as stately and inevitable as Edmund's
ordination will be; the ritual is performed, though neither love nor
guardianship quite joins the marrying couple. The narrator's reiterated
appeal to nature—"What could be more natural than the change?"—
is a further symptom of the hopelessness of love, for, as we shall see
below, nature is a feeble contender in the manipulated world of *Mansfield Park*. Though Edmund marries the woman he ought, the stern
hope he husbands is a loveless strength.

 A romance from a writer of marriage comedies that so
unremittingly denies love to its heroine is a brave novel indeed, particularly when this heroine is ready to love both her emotionally desiccated suitors. If two wooing men cannot manage to love Fanny, with
the true suitor proving as hollow as the false, then surely the reader
never will. Austerely alone in a community of fictional heroines for
whom love is their chief talent and reward, Fanny is further isolated
from affection by her radical homelessness. This waiflike attribute may
lead us to associate *Mansfield Park* with such Victorian orphan myths
as *Jane Eyre:* Jane, like Fanny, is a unprepossessing orphan, "a dis-
cord" in her corrupted foster family, who grows into an iron-willed
little savior. But like most of her orphaned analogues in Victorian
fiction, Jane is baptized into strength by the recovery of family: it is
not her love for Rochester, but her healing interlude with her recovered
cousins, the Rivers family, that allows her identity and her destiny to
cohere.[9] The more radical Fanny similarly recovers her family during
a romantic crisis, only to discover her total absence of kin. Her ideal
home is her utter homelessness. She belongs everywhere she is not:

"When she had been coming to Portsmouth, she had loved to call it her home, had been fond of saying that she was going home; the word had been very dear to her; and so it still was, but it must be applied to Mansfield. *That* was now the home. Portsmouth was Portsmouth; Mansfield was home" (pp. 420–21).

The word may be very dear, but the thing eludes her as she eludes it. Victorian orphan fiction typically begins with the loss of home and ends with its recovery, but here, home is palpable to Fanny only by its absence. Mansfield itself is no true home. The vacuum at its heart is evident not only in the flights of all its members except the supine Lady Bertram, but in the chilling ease with which it can be transformed into a theater. Upon her return, Fanny compels the gutted Mansfield to be her home by an act of will, but in its shrunken regenerate state it bears little resemblance to the place in which she grew up. Fanny's dual returns, to her natural and then to her adoptive origins, prove only the impossibility of self-discovery through return. Thus, though she may resemble later orphan heroes, Fanny is a more indigestible figure than these wistful waifs, for whom embracing their kin is secular salvation. In the tenacity with which she adheres to an identity validated by no family, home, or love, she denies the vulnerability of the waif for the unlovable toughness of the authentic transplant. Her fragility cloaks the will to live without the traditional sanctions for life. Underlying her pious rigidity is a dispossession so fundamental that, among nineteenth-century English novelists, only the tact of a Jane Austen could dare reveal it in a lady.

Readers are right, then, to find Fanny a relentlessly uncomfortable figure in a domestic romance and to wonder nervously where Jane Austen's comedy went. This uncompromising novel never dissolves its heroine's isolation; she merely passes from the isolation of the outcast to that of the conqueror. Her solitude is rarely alleviated by pathos; instead, she hones it into a spectator's perspective from which she can observe her world and invade it. In this above all, she is closer to the Romantic hero than to the heroine of romance: her solitude is her condition, not a state from which the marriage comedy will save her. In her relentless spectatorship, Fanny may be Jane Austen's domestic answer to Byron's more flamboyant and venturesome Childe Harold, exile from his kind, passing eternally through foreign civilizations in order to create elegies to their ruins. Though Fanny travels only to Sotherton and Portsmouth, her role, too, is alien and elegiac, as it is at Mansfield itself; like Byron's persona, she is a hero because she is sufficiently detached to see the death of worlds. Fabricating an identity from uprootedness, she conquers the normal world that acts, plays, and marries, through her alienation from it. In the text of her novel, she is a being without kin, but in its context, she exudes a quiet kinship with the strangers and monsters of her age.

Like other literary monsters, Fanny is a creature without kin who longs for a mate of her own kind. The pain of her difference explains a longing in *Mansfield Park* that is common to much Romantic literature and that, in its obsessed exclusiveness, may look to modern readers unnervingly like incest: the hunger of sibling for sibling, of kin for kind. Seen in its time, the ecstatic, possessive passion Fanny divides between her brother William and her foster brother Edmund, her horror at the Crawfords' attempt to invade her emotions, seem less relevant to the Freudian family romance than to the monster's agonized attempts to alleviate his monstrosity. Mary Shelley's monster asks only that Frankenstein create for him a sister-wife; Bram Stoker's Dracula experiences his triumphant climax when turning his victims into fellow members of the Undead, thus making of them sisters as well as spouses. Fanny yearns similarly in isolation for a brother-mate, repelling the Crawfords above all because they are so different as to constitute virtually another species: "We are so totally unlike . . . we are so very, very different in all our inclinations and ways, that I consider it as quite impossible we should ever be tolerably happy together, even if I *could* like him. There never were two people more dissimilar. We have not one taste in common. We should be miserable" (p. 345).

This rage of self-removal extends itself to Mary Crawford as well, above all perhaps in the emotional spaciousness with which Mary reaches out to Fanny as her "sister."[10] Mary's quest for sisters of gender rather than family, her uncomfortably outspoken championship of abused wives, her sexual initiative, and her unsettling habit of calling things by their names all suggest the pioneering sensibility of her contemporary, Mary Wollstonecraft; but Fanny cannot endure so universal an embrace, clutching only the shreds of kinship. The novel ends as it ought, with Mary's expulsion into a wider and sadder world, while Fanny, still isolated, clings jealously to her conquered family.

Fanny as Romantic monster does not dispel our discomfort in reading *Mansfield Park*, but may explain some of it. Until recently, critics have limited their recognition of the monsters that underlie Jane Austen's realism to the peripheral figures whose unreason threatens the heroine, while the heroine herself remains solidly human.[11] yet Fanny excites the same mixture of sympathy and aversion as does Frankenstein's loveless, homeless creature, and the pattern of her adventures is similar to his. Frankenstein's monster begins as a jealous outcast, peering in at family and civic joys. His rage for inclusion makes him the hunted prey of those he envies, and he ends as the conqueror of families. Fanny too is a jealous outcast in the first volume. In the second, she is besieged by the family that excluded her in the form of Henry Crawford's lethal marriage proposal; finally her lair, the chilly East room, is hunted down like Grendel's and invaded by Sir Thomas himself. In the third volume, Fanny, like Mary Shelley's monster, becomes the solitary conqueror of a gutted family. This movement from outcast within a charmed circle to one who is hunted by it and then conqueror of it aligns Jane Austen's most Romantic, least loved heroine with the kin she so wretchedly seeks.

Modern readers may shun Fanny as a static, solitary predator, but in the world of *Mansfield Park* her very consistency and tenacity are bulwarks against a newly opening space that is dangerous in its very fluidity: even Sir Thomas Bertram's solid home is made vulnerable by economic fluctuations in far-off Antigua.[12] Though the large and loveless house that gives it its name has made many readers feel that *Mansfield Park* is Jane Austen's most oppressive novel, its dominant emotional atmosphere induces a certain vertigo, evident in the apparent rocklike solidity, but the true and hopeless elusiveness, of the word "ought." "Ought" tolls constantly, its every sound bringing a knell of absolutism, and nobody uses it with more assurance than the hero and heroine. Fanny can dismiss Henry Crawford simply because "he can feel nothing as he ought," while Edmund freights the word with religious and national authority: "As the clergy are, or are not what they ought to be, so are the rest of the nation" (p. 121). As a barometer of feelings, morals, and institutions, the word seems an immutable touchstone, but in fact it has no objective validation. Its authority in the novel is entirely, and alarmingly, self-generated. The great houses Mansfield and Sotherton scarcely institutionalize the "ought" that resounds in the novel's language; the Portsmouth of the Prices and the London of the Crawfords are equally ignorant of its weight. It has no echo in the world of households and institutions.

Yet this lack of official authority does not prevent the novel's misguided characters from using the word with the same assurance as Fanny and Edmund do. Sir Thomas says of a Fanny who is brewing rebellion, "She appears to feel as she ought" (p. 230); for Mary, the party with which Maria Rushworth inaugurates her miserable marriage finds everything "just as it ought to be" (p. 406); Maria herself avoids only the word in seeing her mercenary marriage as "a duty" (p. 72). Even Edmund, who has transmitted its value to Fanny, abuses the word throughout the novel, beginning with his myopic pressure on Fanny to live with her hated Aunt Norris: "She is choosing a friend and companion exactly where she ought" (p. 60). The incoherence underlying Edmund's authoritative vocabulary tells us that the word recurs anarchically, for there is no objective code to endow it with consistency. Fanny, for example, longs for a loving reunion with her indifferent mother, hoping that "they should soon be what mother and daughter ought to be to each other" (p. 366), but as usual the novel provides no objective image of this "ought": in *Mansfield Park* and throughout Jane Austen's canon, mothers and daughters are at best indifferent and at worst antagonistic, depriving the commanding word of validation. Fanny is repeatedly hymned as the only character who feels consistently as she ought, but in a world where the word changes its meaning so incessantly, her role as a walking "ought" merely isolates her further. Whatever authority Fanny has comes magically from herself alone. Though she can control the inchoate outside world, it is too lacking in definition to claim kinship with her.

For though Fanny possesses a quasi-magical power over the action, she represents less a moral than s shaping principle, assuming the author's prerogatives along with the reader's: the novel's action happens as she wills, and so her emotions become our only standard of right. In its essence, the world of *Mansfield Park* is terrifyingly malleable. Jane Austen detaches herself from her Romantic contemporaries to reveal both inner and outer nature as pitifully ineffectual compared to what can be made. Mrs. Price grows listless toward Fanny because the "instinct of nature was soon satisfied, and Mrs. Price's attachment had no other source" (p. 382). The gap between Mrs. Price and Mrs. Bertram can never heal because "where nature had made so little difference, circumstances [had] made so much" (p. 400). Mary Crawford's nature, like Maria's and Julia's, is similarly helpless against the constructive, or the deconstructive, power of her medium: "For where, Fanny, shall we find a woman whom nature had so richly endowed?—Spoilt, spoilt!" (p. 441). By contrast, we know that Susan Price will survive, not because of her natural qualities, but because she is "a girl so capable of being made, every thing good" (p. 409). Nature's insufficiency may explain the deadness of Fanny's effusions to stars, trees, and "verdure," for though she laments improvements, Fanny is the most potent of the novel's improving characters. In so malleable and so defective a world, Fanny is polite to the stars, but she turns her most potent attention on the vulnerable, that which is "capable of being made."

In Mary Shelley's *Frankenstein* as well, family, nature, and even the Alps pall before the monster who is capable of being made. The monstrosity of *Mansfield Park* as a whole is one manifestation of its repelled fascination with acting, with education, and with landscape and estate improvements: the novel imagines a fluid world, one with no fixed principles, capable of awesome, endless, and dangerous manipulation. The unconvivial stiffness of its hero and heroine is their triumph: by the end, they are so successfully "made" by each other that he is her creature as completely as she has always been his. The nobility and malleability of *Mansfield Park* is a dark realization of an essentially Romantic vision, of which Fanny Price represents both the horror and the best hope. Only in *Mansfield Park* does Jane Austen force us to experience the discomfort of a Romantic universe presided over by the potent charm of a charmless heroine who was not made to be loved.[13]

3.

O Brave New World:
Evolution and Revolution
in *Persuasion*

An analysis of the symbolism in Jane Austen's *Persuasion* ma
lead us to discover stirrings of revolution underneath the quie
surface of the novel. To define the revolution of *Persuasion*, w
should begin by examining the laws of its created world in relation t
those governing Jane Austen's earlier novels.

It may be helpful in this connection to think of *Persua*
sion as Jane Austen's *Tempest*, another final work that reprises an
transforms themes and motifs introduced earlier in the author's canon
The plots of both are determined to a great extent by the movement
of the sea. Written during Jane Austen's last illness and not publishe
until after her death, *Persuasion* is defined by its blended tone of ele
giac departure and the "senseless joy" of renewal and reconciliation
Its action touches extremes of loss and desolation, but out of eacl
desolation comes the grace of recovery and enrichment of what wa
lost.

Like *The Tempest*, *Persuasion* is brooded over by the threa
of loss and death. Seen in these terms, the marriage of Louisa an
Benwick is more than a mechanical contrivance to free Wentworth fo

Anne Elliot. It is a lighthearted exemplification of the law that governs *Persuasion*, a law oriented to the fulfillment of human desire, in close association with nature and natural rhythms.

The union of Louisa and Benwick comes only after each has been brought close to loss and death. Benwick is suffering after the death of his fiancée, "a very superior creature"; Louisa's fall on the Cobb threatens her for a time with death or derangement. Wentworth defines the rhythm of the union clearly: " 'It was a frightful hour,' said he [speaking of Louisa's fall], 'a frightful day!' and he passed his hand across his eyes, as if the remembrance were still too painful; but in a moment half smiling again, added, 'The day has produced some effects however—has had some consequences which must be considered as the very reverse of frightful.' "[1]

The iron law of consequences is suspended in *Persuasion*; the seeds of apparent tragedy produce unexpected joy. The surprising union of Benwick and Louisa is a half-parodic repetition of the central reconciliation of Wentworth and Anne after "so many, many years of division and estrangement"; they are "more exquisitely happy, perhaps, in their re-union, than when it had been first projected" (p. 240).

Like *The Tempest*, *Persuasion* transforms tragedy into the profoundest comedy, and, also like *The Tempest*, it closes with a glimpse of a sea voyage, which will be explored more fully later on. At this point, we should examine some of the tragic motifs more closely, because almost all of them are reprises of events in Jane Austen's earlier novels. This transformation of material from earlier works relates *Persuasion* most intimately to *The Tempest*: it introduces for the last time motifs and events that have furnished the author's universe from the beginning, but which are joyfully transformed in the crucible of a brave new world.

In one important sense, *Persuasion* looks back as far as *Northanger Abbey*, which Jane Austen may have been revising during its composition: there is another journey to Bath. In *Northanger Abbey*, we regarded Bath with double vision. The inexperienced heroine, Catherine Morland, was dazzled by its excitement, but Henry Tilney's monologues subtly equated it with an oppressively inhuman spiritual climate. Phrases and incidents recurred in the narrative which associated Bath with imprisonment, further undermining Catherine's early innocent vision of it. When the Tilneys liberated Catherine from Bath, she found herself enclosed in the more obvious, if more genteel, prison of Northanger Abbey, which was governed by the same unnatural values that presided over the world of Bath. The apparent alternative to Bath provided by the Tilneys melted into a more insidious extension of it, and the disillusioned Catherine was cast out of both worlds after her journey of initiation into "actual and natural evil."

But Anne Elliot has no such lesson to learn. She knows from the beginning that she cannot endure "the white glare of Bath" (as Jane Austen could not). There are no subtle undercurrents needed to modulate our responses: Bath is equated from the beginning with the inhuman ostentation of Sir Walter and Elizabeth Elliot, and explicitly defined by Anne as a prison: "Anne entered [Bath] with a sinking heart, anticipating an imprisonment of many months, and anxiously saying to herself, 'Oh! when shall I leave you again?' " (p. 137).

But Wentworth and the naval group arrive in Bath almost immediately, and the alternative they provide is genuine. The Elliots have no power to oppress their joyful fellowship, although at first they may appear to: "The door was thrown open for Sir Walter and Miss Elliot, whose entrance seemed to give a general chill. Anne felt an instant oppression, and, wherever she looked, saw symptoms of the same. The comfort, the freedom, the gaiety of the room was over, hushed into cold composure, determined silence, or insipid talk, to meet the heartless elegance of her father and sister" (p. 226).

The Tilneys in *Northanger Abbey* were, like the Elliots, a motherless family presided over by a cold father; General Tilney was able to oppress his children's gaiety and freedom much as the Elliots do momentarily here. But in *Persuasion,* the world of heartless elegance is defeated on its own terms by the world of feeling. The new power of the navy forces Elizabeth Elliot to invite Wentworth to a select evening party, and Anne's knowledge of her secret engagement thaws her vision even of her father's house in Bath:

It was but a card-party, it was but a mixture of those who had never met before, and those who met too often—a common-place business, too numerous for intimacy, too small for variety; but Anne had never found an evening shorter. Glowing and lovely in sensibility and happiness, and more generally admired than she thought about or cared for, she had cheerful or forbearing feelings for every creature around her. Mr. Elliot was there; she avoided, but she could pity him. The Wallises; she had amusement in understanding them. Lady Dalrymple and Miss Carteret; they would soon be innoxious cousins to her. She cared not for Mrs. Clay, and had nothing to blush for in the public manners of her father and sister. With the Musgroves, there was the happy chat of perfect ease; with Captain Harville, the kind-hearted intercourse of brother and sister; with Lady Russell, attempts at conversation, which a delicious consciousness cut short; with Admiral and Mrs. Croft, every thing of particular cordiality and fervent interest, which the same consciousness sought to conceal;—and with Captain Wentworth, some moments of communication continually occurring, and always the hope of more, and always the knowledge of his being there! (pp. 245–46)

The infiltration of the naval group into Sir Walter's exclusive Bath soirée is able to nullify the power of Sir Walter's society, in Anne's eyes at least, and she is our guiding consciousness. When Anne is liberated from Bath, there is no imprisonment in an imperfectly restored medieval abbey: she is carried into the world of the future, and to sea.

It has often been noticed that *Persuasion* is an inverted *Sense and Sensibility*.[2] In many ways, Anne Elliot is a mellowed and fully accepted variant of Marianne Dashwood with the world restored. Marianne's solitary walks and bursts of poetry were cruelly parodied at the beginning of *Sense and Sensibility,* and in the last volume of her story, they almost led to her death by bringing on an attack of putrid fever. Anne also escapes into solitary walks and poetic musings, but hers are sanctified. Their potential preciosity and affectation are drawn off into Jane Austen's parody of Benwick, just as the potential danger of Anne's abandonment to feeling is contained in Louisa Musgrove's fall on the Cobb. Mrs Musgrove's "large fat sighings" over the death of her unworthy son contain all the potential insincerity and ludicrousness of Anne's protracted mourning over the death of feeling. These flat, comic characters siphon off our subversive impulses toward the romantic heroine, and probably Jane Austen's subversive impulses as well. They allow a full acceptance of Anne's emotional world, and they allow Jane Austen to posit an ethic of feeling purified of "sensibility": "How eloquent could Anne Elliot have been,—how eloquent, at least, were her wishes on the side of early warm attachment, and a cheerful confidence in futurity, against that over-anxious caution which seems to insult exertion and distrust Providence!—She had been forced into prudence in her youth, she learned romance as she grew older—the natural sequel of an unnatural beginning" (p. 30).

Jane Austen's final admonition to Lady Russell is an unequivocal repudiation of the attempt of "sense" to counsel feeling:

[Lady Russell] must learn to feel that she had been mistaken . . . ; that she had been unfairly influenced by appearances . . . ; that because Captain Wentworth's manners had not suited her own ideas, she had been too quick in suspecting them to indicate a character of dangerous impetuosity; and that because Mr. Elliot's manners had precisely pleased her in their propriety and correctness, their general politeness and suavity, she had been too quick in receiving them as the certain result of the most correct opinions and well regulated mind. There was nothing less for Lady Russell to do, than to admit that she had been pretty completely wrong, and to take up a new set of opinions and of hopes. (p. 249)

In *Sense and Sensibility*, nature and feeling were dangerous and productive of disease; one could survive in a chilled society only by avoiding both. The passages cited seem to be clear and conscious signposts, indicating how far Jane Austen has traveled since then. In *Persuasion*, prudent accommodation gives way in a world guided by emotion and vision. A contrast of the villains in each novel seems to be another signpost:

Elinor saw nothing to censure in [Willoughby] but a propensity, in which he strongly resembled and peculiarly delighted her sister, of saying too much what he thought on every occasion without attention to persons or circumstances. In *hastily* forming and giving his opinion of other people, in sacrificing general politeness to the enjoyment of undivided attention where his heart was engaged, and in slighting too easily the forms of worldly propriety, he displayed a want of caution which Elinor could not approve in spite of all that he and Marianne could say in its support.[3]

Mr. Elliot was rational, discreet, polished,—but he was not open. There was never any burst of feeling, any warmth of indignation or delight, at the evil or good of others. This, to Anne, was a decided imperfection. Her early impressions were incurable. She prized the frank, the open-hearted, the eager character beyond all others. Warmth and enthusiasm did captivate her still. She felt that she could so much more depend upon the sincerity of those who sometimes looked or said a careless or a *hasty* thing, than of those whose

presence of mind never varied, whose tongue never slipped. (p. 161, my ital-
cs)

The contrast is clear. But the point is not simply that Jane
Austen has discarded an ethic of prudence and repression for an ethic
of emotional release: she has shifted the axis of her created world. The
characters in *Persuasion* must accommodate themselves to a different
set of laws. Its world is governed by nature and by human desire, and
characters who cannot accommodate themselves to these laws, like the
Elliots and Lady Russell, are threatened and deprived of power as unequivocally as Marianne Dashwood was in Jane Austen's earlier world.

When we open *Persuasion* we see staring at us from the
first page in capital letters: ELLIOT OF KELLYNCH HALL. Sir
Walter's identity is inseparable from his title, from his crest, above all
from Kellynch Hall; he is identified with the apparatus and accoutre-
ments that encompass him. This apparatus of identity lends resonance
to the early description of Anne: "She was only Anne" (p. 5).

But the power of Kellynch Hall is no longer supported by
the power of money: the Elliots cannot keep their house, just as the
Bennets in *Pride and Prejudice* could not. Elizabeth was forced out of
her childhood home by Mr. Collins, a horrible embodiment of the
power of form to stifle humanity, and her problem in the book was to
find a house she could live in. Wickham's "unhoused free condition,"
his world of impulse and feeling, was an illusion, easily dissolved by
the power of money. Nature, growth, freedom, could survive only in
the heavily fortified atmosphere of Pemberley, presided over by the
equivocal figure of Mr. Darcy.

Admiral Croft and his wife, Wentworth's sister, encroach
upon Anne's home in a similar way, but unlike the threat of Mr.
Collins, their encroachment is a liberation. The navy in *Persuasion* is
associated with nature, openness, hospitality, romance; but, as Marvin
Mudrick points out in *Jane Austen: Irony as Defense and Discovery*, it
is also associated with income, Jane Austen's central symbol of social
power. Power has passed from those who oppress and chill feeling to
those who represent it, and this is symbolized by the dispossession of
the Elliots. If there has been a revolution of values in Jane Austen's
mind, she depicts a similar revolution in her society. Only *Persuasion*

endows the representatives of nature and feeling with the superior social power income symbolizes and bestows. Anne, our moral and emotional barometer, recognizes the justice of the change: "She could have
said more on the subject; for she had in fact so high an opinion of the
Crofts, and considered her father so very fortunate in his tenants, felt
the parish to be so sure of a good example, and the poor of the best
attention and relief, that however sorry and ashamed for the necessity
of the removal, she could not but in conscience feel that they were
gone who deserved not to stay, and that Kellynch Hall had passed into
better hands than its owners" (p. 125). Admiral Croft symbolically
strips away Sir Walter's mirrors, thus purifying Kellynch of its stagnant self-enclosure:

"I have done very little besides sending away some of the large looking-glasses
from my dressing-room, which was your father's. A very good man, and very
much the gentleman I am sure—but I should think, Miss Elliot" (looking
with serious reflection) "I should think he must be rather a dressy man for
his time of life.—Such a number of looking-glasses! Oh Lord! there was no
getting away from oneself . . . now I am quite snug, with my little shaving-
glass in one corner, and another great thing that I never go near." (pp. 127–
28)

In *Pride and Prejudice*, the threat of dispossession was an additional
threat to Elizabeth's security and independence. An influx of liberating
energy might be indicated at the end of *Emma*, when Mr. Knightley
moved into Hartfield, but the implications of this move were ambiguous; perhaps his own energy was boxed in. In *Persuasion*, the implications of the move are unshadowed: a decaying sector of the petty
aristocracy is dislodged from its sanctuary by the purifying force of a
new world.

    Mansfield Park and *Persuasion* are often grouped together
as Jane Austen's "Cinderella novels," but Fanny Price's alienation at
Mansfield was the result of her social inferiority; she was removed from
the Bertram family by her lower social and financial status. Anne, on
the other hand, is an Elliot in all but spirit. It is her "elegance of
mind and sweetness of character" that isolate her among the Elliots
of Kellynch Hall: "She was only Anne." As her isolation is interior-
ized into a quality of mind and feeling, so are her silent observations
of the world around her. Fanny's moralizing judgments are trans-

formed into Anne's sympathetic emotional projection. She defines a situation not by its propriety, but by the emotional vibrations it contains. Furthermore, her own emotional life is so rich and constant that it often interferes with her role as spectator, as here, for instance: "[Wentworth's action] produced such a confusion of varying, but very painful agitation, as she could not recover from, till enabled by the entrance of Mary and the Miss Musgroves to make over her little patient to their cares, and leave the room. She could not stay. It might have been an opportunity of watching the loves and jealousies of the four; they were now all together, but she could stay for none of it" (p. 80).

Fanny had little to distract her from observing the sword dance of other peoples' loves and jealousies. Only Anne is provided with a significant and autonomous inner world, which is strong enough to pull her from the incessant conflicts around her.

When William Price entered Mansfield, the sea wind blew through Jane Austen's world for the first time, but it was not strong enough in *Mansfield Park* to provide an alternative to Fanny's oppressive existence at Mansfield; William sailed off again, and the sea became associated in Fanny's mind with the "noise, disorder, and impropriety" of her father's house at Portsmouth. This new element in Jane Austen's novels shrinks into a dirty puddle in *Mansfield Park*. Only in *Persuasion* do we become aware of the enormous revolutionary potential it contains, as it brings mobility to a static society and emotional release to a suppressed heroine. Wentworth is William Price transformed into a lover and able to offer the dispossessed heroine citizenship in a fresh community, full of vitality and promise.

The role of the sea in Jane Austen's last three novels, and perhaps in *Sanditon* as well, is a subject which has not been sufficiently examined. With the growth of her sailor brothers, a new world and new possibilities come into Jane Austen's novels. When William Price enters, there is a new emotional excitement in *Mansfield Park*, and the relationship between Fanny and her sailor brother is the vivid heart of the book. But later on, the sea becomes equated with a world in which Fanny cannot live, and she shrinks back into the bosom of Mansfield. Emma, Jane Austen's most powerful heroine, has never seen the sea: her father is afraid of it. Her honeymoon will be two weeks at the seashore under Mr. Knightley's protection, but then she will move back to Hartfield, where there will now be two fathers instead of one. Only in *Persuasion* is the sea world allowed to dominate and take control of the book and carry off the heroine, with all its romantic excitement, and all its attendant danger.

In *Persuasion*, Jane Austen's world is transformed, in its details as well as its larger structure and tone, by the influx of a revolutionary force: the world symbolized in the sea, which for the first time gives a home to values that had to struggle for survival on land. The passage of money from land to sea guarantees the power of these values. This sea change, symbolized by the transfer of Kellynch Hall at the beginning and the transfer of Anne Elliot at the end, suggests a hope that a purified community will be able to flourish in the "real" world. In freeing the navy of any trace of incompetence or corruption—even the incorrigible Dick Musgrove conveniently dies soon after his induction—Jane Austen is not simply echoing her brothers' probable chauvinism: she is symbolizing utopian hopes suggesting peculiar affinities to Shelley's in *Prometheus Unbound*, begun in 1818, the year of *Persuasion*'s publication.

The role of Wentworth as hero is interesting in relation to Jane Austen's new utopianism. Wentworth has been called the first of Jane Austen's heroes who is a self-made man, and he is also the first hero to represent the world of the future rather than the past. As Anne's lover, Wentworth can initiate her into the brave new world that is so radically transforming the structure of the old. The warmth and generosity that were chilled by the old society can flourish in the new. Before her reconciliation with Wentworth, Anne attends a naval officer's dinner party, and becomes aware that naval society thrives on everything aristocratic society suppresses: "There was so much attachment to Captain Wentworth in all this, and such a bewitching charm in a degree of hospitality so uncommon, so unlike the usual style of give-and-take invitations, and dinners of formality and display, that Anne felt her spirits not likely to be benefited by an increasing acquaintance among his brother-officers. 'These would have been all my friends,' was her thought; and she had to struggle against a great tendency to lowness" (p. 98).

To find this generosity of feeling, Elizabeth Bennet, Fanny Price, and Emma Woodhouse retreated into the past: Elizabeth ensconced herself in Pemberley, Fanny in Mansfield, and Emma was

protected by the sheltering values of Mr. Knightley, whose relation to
an older tradition of English life was symbolized in part by his name.
But there were oppressive and equivocal elements in this protective
world of tradition. Darcy's resemblance to his aunt, Lady Catherine de
Bourgh, pointed to elements in his character of the antihuman pride
of his class, although at times Jane Austen ignored Darcy's unpleasant
side with skillful sophistry in order to maintain the light and bright
and sparkling tone of the book. Mansfield was the home of vanity and
oppression throughout most of *Mansfield Park:* only when the greater
cruelty of the new was made apparent did it begin to loom large as a
refuge. Even Emma and Mr. Knightley were not able to share the rich
fruitfulness of Donwell. They had to move into Hartfield, another home
of constriction and oppression, governed by Mr. Woodhouse's fear of
marriage, procreation, food, and the elements. It is significant that in
Persuasion we are placed on the fringes of the aristocracy from the
beginning. The hero of this book breaks into the equivocal shelter of
England's past, and links the heroine with forces of future hope and
change.

In an interesting article, "Luck and Fortuitous Circumstance in *Persuasion:* Two Interpretations," Paul Zeitlow provocatively
discusses the role of fortune in the novel, which is associated particularly with Wentworth's rise.[4] I would disagree only with Zeitlow's
"darker" interpretation, which argues that the role of luck places the
characters in a contingent universe. The world of *Persuasion* operates
according to a coherent pattern, to which each instance of luck contributes: the novel becomes contingent only if we insist on comparing
its autonomuous laws with those of our own universe. The "providential" interpretation does not seem incompatible with intimations of
tragedy; in fact, like the providential structure of *The Tempest,* it depends on them. The element of chance in Wentworth's career, particularly the favorable weather without which he would have been drowned
on his first sea voyage, suggests an equation between his life and the
rhythms of the elements: he is a man in harmony with the spirit of
the sea, who lives in conjunction with the elements and their motions.

Wentworth's career brings us to another important element in *Persuasion* which has been merely hinted at in Jane Austen's
earlier novels: the new importance of productive labor as fulfillment in
itself. The importance of natural rhythms in the book, and the ideal-

ization of the navy as a life conjoined with them, are never equated
with a passive yielding to external ebbs and flows. The relation between
nature and human exertion is embodied in a beautiful emblem near
the beginning of the novel, during the Uppercross party's walk to
Winthrop: "After another half mile of gradual ascent through large
enclosures, *where the ploughs at work, and the fresh-made path spoke
the farmer, counteracting the sweets of poetical despondence, and meaning
to have spring again,* they gained the summit" (p. 85, italics mine).

The labor of the farmer harmonizes with and even anticipates the natural processes. As the farmer works with the rhythm of
the seasons, so the sailors work with the rhythm of the sea. The luck
guiding Wentworth's career indicates a healthy kinship to natural processes and laws similar to that of the farmer. The ideal of labor in
harmony with nature is especially important if we compare it to the
fear of the weather shown by so many of Jane Austen's earlier characters, a fear which many patronizing critics have attributed to Jane
Austen herself. Moreover, this ideal is not limited to obviously "out-
door" professions such as farming and sailing: the social-climbing Mrs
Clay, of all people, makes a useful extension when she connects the
idea of exposure with *all* the professions:

"Soldiers, in active service, are not at all better off; and even in the quieter
professions, there is a toil and a labour of the mind, if not of the body
which seldom leaves a man's looks to the natural effect of time. The lawyer
plods, quite care-worn; the physician is up at all hours, and travelling in all
weather; and even the clergyman;—" she stopt a moment to consider what
might do for the clergyman—"and even the clergyman, you know, is obliged
to go into infected rooms, and expose his health and looks to all the injury
of a poisonous atmosphere." (p. 20)

With simple irony, Jane Austen invites us to reverse Mrs
Clay's meaning by linking work to wholesome exposure to the weather
even to a "poisonous atmosphere" of the kind Marianne Dashwood so
rashly ventured into years before. The opposite of the man who labors
is the beautiful and youthful Sir Walter, says Mrs. Clay; and Sir Walter, says Jane Austen, represents the death-in-life of a man who escapes into his own mirrors. In *Emma,* Mr. Knightley the gentleman-
farmer was permitted to stand as an ideal because we were always aware

of William Larkins' and Mr. Knightley's own activities in attending to the business of the estate. But in *Persuasion,* this compromise is no longer possible. The world of gentlemen and fine ladies shrinks into the symbol of Sir Walter Elliot's mirror, and although there is some talk at the end of a reconciliation between Wentworth and Lady Russell, the landed world of the gentry is shown to be pretty much unredeemable and decaying. Money and the world of the future lie in work, of which the sea is the chief emblem.

But ideas of exertion and exposure are not linked exclusively to men. The first chapter of *Persuasion* describes Elizabeth Elliot's barren existence, "the prosperity and the nothingness" of her life. She is not barren only, or even primarily, because she is still unmarried at twenty-nine. She is barren because she has nothing to do: "Such were Elizabeth Elliot's sentiments and sensations; such the cares to alloy, the agitations to vary, the sameness and the elegance, the prosperity and the nothingness, of her scene of life—such the feelings to give interest to a long uneventful residence in one country circle, to fill the vacancies which there were *no habits of utility abroad, no talents or accomplishments for home, to occupy*" (p. 9, my emphasis).

Her married sister Mary, whose attachment to her imaginary illnesses is as profound as Sir Walter's to his mirrors, is scarcely better off. Mrs. Croft, the first wholly admirable and likable married woman in Jane Austen's novels, makes a remark that casts an indirect light on Mary's illnesses:

Thank God! I have always been blessed with excellent health, and no climate disagrees with me. . . . The only time that I ever really suffered in body or mind, the only time that I ever fancied myself unwell, or had any ideas of danger, was the winter that I passed by myself at Deal, when the Admiral . . . was in the North Seas. I lived in perpetual fright at that time, and had all manner of imaginary complaints *from not knowing what to do with myself, or when I should hear from him next.* (p. 71, my emphasis)

If the navy is Jane Austen's vision of a brave new world, Mrs. Croft is her tactful and subtle portrait of the "new woman." The Crofts are the first happily married couple in Jane Austen's novels to receive more than peripheral treatment. But this does not mean that Jane Austen was mellowing in a sentimental way toward marriage as she had seen it on land. Their marriage is a naval marriage, different in kind from any other in Jane Austen's books, and it will set a hopeful pattern for Anne and Wentworth's.

"[Mrs. Croft] had bright dark eyes, good teeth, and altogether an agreeable face; though her *reddened and weather-beaten complexion, the consequence of her having been almost as much at sea as her husband,* made her seem to have lived some years longer in the world than her real eight-and-thirty" (p. 48, my emphasis). Although Jane Austen never trumpets on about "fulfilling careers for women," in the Crofts' exemplary marriage, the wife shares her husband's life of exertion and exposure; she no longer lives in a woman's world, and she has no children. Later on in the book, we see Mrs. Croft "looking as intelligent and keen as any of the officers around her." As an emblem of this good marriage, Jane Austen inserts a slyly feminist note:

"My dear Admiral, that post!—we shall certainly take that post" [says Mrs. Croft].

But by coolly giving the reins a better direction herself, they happily passed the danger; and by once afterwards judiciously putting out her hand, they neither fell into a rut, nor ran foul of a dung-cart; and Anne, with some amusement at their style of driving, which she imagined no bad representation of the general guidance of their affairs, found herself safely deposited by them at the cottage.

(p. 92)

Mrs. Croft's view of women, which her life gives her freedom to practice, is summed up in her cry to Wentworth: "But I hate to hear you talking so, like a fine gentleman, and as if women were all *fine ladies,* instead of *rational creatures.* We none of us expect to be in smooth water all our days" (p. 70, my emphasis).

To appreciate the triumph of this assertion, we must turn back to Mr. Collins' proposal in *Pride and Prejudice,* and to Elizabeth's truly desperate plea: "Do not consider me now as an *elegant female* intending to plague you, but as a *rational creature* speaking the truth from her heart."[5] Mr. Collins' and his society's disjunction between the elegant female and the rational creature was perhaps the most severe threat to Elizabeth's life, and this disjunction has persisted as an undercurrent throughout Jane Austen's novels. In the quiet urgency of its insistence, we may even hear echoes of voices like Mary Wollstonecraft's: "My own sex, I hope, will excuse me, if I treat them like rational creatures, instead of flattering their *fascinating* graces, and viewing them as if they were in a state of perpetual childhood, unable to stand alone."[6] In Jane Austen's canon, only the heroine of *Persuasion* is able to achieve the freedom to be rational, and therefore human, that Mary Wollstonecraft had envisioned twenty-five years before.

For the gentle Anne herself is not immune from such a topic. It arises in what is perhaps the most consistently misread scene in all of Jane Austen's novels: the dialogue with Captain Harville at the White Hart Inn, which Jane Austen substituted for a more conventionally contrived love scene after she had finished the novel. Therefore, if we define *Sanditon* as a sketch and a fragment, we may regard this scene as Jane Austen's last fully realized piece of writing. In the undercurrents of Anne's romantic lyric, Jane Austen's vaunted "realism" is given its fullest expression. If, in one side of the mirror, Anne's speeches are a simple lyric cry, a nineteenth-century provincial version of the "patience-on-a-monument" motif, a glance through the looking-glass shows us their unromantic foundation. Women feel, quite simply, because they are given nothing else to do: "We certainly do not forget you, so soon as you forget us. *It is, perhaps, our fate rather than our merit. We cannot help ourselves. We live at home, quiet, confined, and our feelings prey upon us. You are forced on exertion.* You have always a profession, pursuits, business of some sort or other, to take you back into the world immediately, and continual occupation and change soon weaken impressions" (p. 232, my emphasis).

Only a rather cruel male supremacist would define intense suffering as the "merit" of women rather than their "fate." But many critics have done so, both in their reading of this scene and in their sentimentalization of one side of Anne Elliot's character. She does not sentimentalize herself, and she is right not to. Her modest and simple tone should not blind us to what she is saying: women do not pine for love and suffer over men because they are by nature more sensitive and emotionally refined, and thus, as it were, "created to suffer." They suffer because their social role creates for them a life without exertion, in which state one's feelings become a torment. Once again, Mary Wollstonecraft may help us to read Jane Austen, by defining a similar condition, though less sympathetically: "Their senses are inflamed, and their understandings neglected, consequently they become the prey of

their senses, delicately termed sensibility, and are blown about by every
momentary gust of feeling. . . . Ever restless and anxious, their over-
exercised sensibility not only renders them uncomfortable themselves,
but troublesome, to use a soft phrase, to others. . . . Miserable, indeed, must be that being whose cultivation of mind has only tended
to inflame its passions!" (*Vindication*, p. 67).

Anne shifts this theme into another key in her next speech:
" 'You have difficulties, and privations, and dangers enough to struggle with. You are always labouring and toiling, exposed to every risk
and hardship. Your home, country, friends, all quitted. Neither time,
nor health, nor life, to be called your own. It would be too hard indeed'
(with a faltering voice) 'if woman's feelings were to be added to all
this' " (p. 233). Anne's own emotional situation is leading her to take
an elegiac, even a tragic, view of all human affairs, men's doing as well
as women's suffering. Her characteristic richness of sympathy may also
obscure her basic statement: the life that women are expected to live
is conducive primarily to anguish. We do not expect a radical definition of woman's nature from Anne Elliot, and putting such words in
her mouth is a supreme example of Jane Austen's ability to bury her
most significant statements in contexts that allow complacent readers
to accept her without dismay.[7]

But readers who want Jane Austen to be a defender of the
status quo will have to skip Anne's next speech entirely. Harville has
substituted for his initial interpretation of her words another male cliché
about woman as "la belle dame sans merci." He supports his statement
by citing poetry, songs, and proverbs, to which Anne replies, "If you
please, no references to examples in books. Men have had every advantage of us in telling their own story. Education has been theirs in so
much higher a degree; the pen has been in their hands. I will not allow
books to prove anything" (p. 234).

This is Anne's only complaint that is directed specifically
against society. It is mild, but telling. Society's conventional view of
women is dictated by men, because better education allows men to
write all the books. Only unequal education prevents women from writing
as many books as men do, and presumably, books that are as good; if
they were allowed to make themselves heard, the conventional view of
women would be radically altered. This emphasis upon unequal education rather than inherent inequality once again recalls Mary Woll-

tonecraft's central thesis in *Vindication of the Rights of Woman;* [8] and n fact, Jane Austen did write the books whose lack Anne Elliot delores. How profoundly they subvert the conventional picture of the 'elegant female," of the "fine lady," is something that only our own century has begun to see. In Jane Austen's most famous and emotionally charged love scene, the heroine speaks obliquely for her right to exist in something more than love. These speeches reveal Anne as worthy not only of Wentworth, but of Mrs. Croft as well.

Anne's life after her marriage seems to be forecast for us n the dialogue between the Crofts and Wentworth which has been cited above. Wentworth is holding forth vehemently on the evils of women at sea: "I hate to hear of women on board, or to see them on board; and no ship, under my command, shall ever convey . . . ladies anywhere, if I can help it" (p. 69). "Women . . . have no *right* to be comfortable on board" (p. 69, Jane Austen's emphasis). Admiral Croft reminds Wentworth that once he marries, his feelings will change, and his sister berates him for seeing women only as "fine ladies." The irony is simple and cheerful. Once exposed to the sea air at Lyme, Anne will begin to "bloom" again. This word, which is applied to Anne throughout the novel, hints at her renewed conjunction with the processes of nature. Like Mrs. Croft, Anne will be "liberated" after her marriage. She will go to sea.

To end a discussion of *Persuasion* on a note of triumph and cheer, however, is to falsify another side of the sea world. Death is not associated only with the land. It is a continual presence on the sea, and the book is always reminding us that great disaster is the other side of great achievement. Wentworth's description of his triumphant voyage on the *Asp* strikes a note that is sounded throughout: "I knew that we should either go to the bottom together, or that she would be the making of me" (pp. 65–66).

Like *The Tempest* again, *Persuasion* does not end with a chorus of reconciliation and joy, but with a glimpse of "quick alarm." As in *The Tempest*, the sea is threatening as well as merciful. "His profession was all that could ever make [Anne's] friends wish [her] tenderness less; the dread of a future war all that could dim her sunshine. She gloried in being a sailor's wife, but she must pay the tax of quick alarm for belonging to that profession which is, if possible, more distinguished in its domestic virtues than in its national importance"

(p. 252). Danger is the other side of romance. The sense of liberation does not nullify the sense of fear: it contains it. As in Tennyson's "Ulysses," the triumph of the sea over the land contains the possibility of violent death, but to die violently is better than to rust away on land in stagnant enclosure.

This final union of fear and joy strikes the emotional heart of the book. The pervasive tone of *Persuasion* is a tone of neither triumph nor tragedy; it is a paradoxical mixture of pleasure and pain. A description of a paradox of intense contrasting emotions is repeated over and over again. It is almost savored. "[Anne was] grieving to forego all the influence so sweet and so sad of the autumnal months in the country" (p. 33). "Anne walked up at the same time, in a sort of desolate tranquility" (p. 36). "It was a proof of his own warm and amiable heart, which she could not contemplate without emotions so compounded of pleasure and pain, that she knew not which prevailed" (p. 91). "Internally [Lady Russell's] heart revelled in angry pleasure, in pleased contempt" (p. 125). "All the overpowering, blinding, bewildering, first effects of strong surprise were over with her. Still, however, she had enough to feel! It was agitation, pain, pleasure, a something between delight and misery" (p. 175). "When pain is over, the remembrance of it often becomes a pleasure" (p. 184). "There was no delay, no waste of time. She was deep in the happiness of such misery, or the misery of such happiness, instantly" (p. 229). And so on. Emotional extremes meet and marry in an intensity of feeling.

This blended tone of *Persuasion* brings us close to the elegiac lyrics of Jane Austen's contemporaries, Shelley and Keats, whose poetry dwells on the inward complexities that accompany a release of passion and vision. The revolutionary vision of *Persuasion* encompasses both the polemics of a Mary Wollstonecraft and the subtleties of later Romantic art. Jane Austen was a provincial spinster who did, perhaps, spend most of her life indoors, but she was not encased in the eighteenth century; she felt and recorded the vibrations of her age as the Romantic poets and prophets did, but, like the lady that she was, she spoke more softly.

II.

Men's Women

4.

Incarnations of the Orphan

The figure of the wandering orphan, searching through an alien world for his home, has fascinated generations of novelists. The loneliness and the license of his point of view shake the solid foundations of English fiction. His isolation is a counterpoint to the view of the English novel given us by such critics as Wayne Booth, Ian Watt, and, most recently, David Goldknopf, who see it as a form in which consciousness is born into self-knowledge only in and through a fully realized social medium. The orphan is born to himself and establishes his own social penumbra. An examination of the forms he has taken in novels of different periods may give us another perspective on the English novel, both as a genre in itself and as a reflection of the culture it simultaneously embodies and repudiates.

Of course, artists have always been pulled toward visions of the self utterly dispossessed and exposed, trying to construct out of solitude a house that will shelter it and attract visitors. But only in the novel do we find the orphan emerging as the primary metaphor for the dispossessed, detached self. In a sense, the orphan can be thought of as a metaphor for the novel itself: a faintly disreputable and possibly bastardized offspring of uncertain parentage, always threatening to lose

I should like to thank Avrom Fleishman, Roger Sale, and Jan Van Meter, for the invaluable suggestions they made while I was writing this essay.

focus and definition, but, with the resilience of the natural victim, always managing to survive; a particular product of the modern world.

At the very least, the orphan seems to represent a vital strain in the novel, a vein of inchoate creative energy necessary for the continued healthy growth of the form. For it is an easy sentimental mistake to think of the orphan as fragile. He seems composed of alternate layers of glass and steel, and sends out stingrays at those who try to adopt him. He first appears in the eighteenth century as a slyly potent underground figure, who does not show himself as a waif until the early nineteenth century. But even the Romantic waif is brimming with a certain equivocal energy that threatens the world he is homeless in. His solitude energizes him as visionary, artist, and silent schemer, his appearance of winsome fragility feeding into his power of survival.

In an important sense, this figure always remains himself, an archetype that continually impels novelists to him. But he is able to split his being according to the culture that contains him, his mutability becoming an important facet of his survival. His passage through three centuries of novels, and the different shapes he takes on, can almost be said to constitute a myth with shifting emphases; a myth that was particularly important in the nineteenth century, the great age of the English novel, but which began to germinate earlier, and which still has offshoots today. Although this study will follow him through some of his incarnations, it is a mistake to separate his various appearances too rigidly from each other. The criminal always contains aspects of the waif, and even in his relative powerlessness, the orphan maintains a good deal of his former subterranean energy. The cultural scheme that follows is an enforced splitting of something that should be whole, just as the orphan is able to retain his wholeness by splitting himself.

In the eighteenth century, the mixed nature of the orphan reflects both the picaresque and the practical origins of the English novel. The orphan is a rogue with unroguish dreams of gentility, a picaro who uses his ability to manipulate lies and appearances for uncharacteristically respectable ends. In the nineteenth century, the shady picaro is refined into the spiritually energized figure of the orphan, whose freedom from a past he still somehow carries within him endows him with religious and revolutionary energy. He has the power to transform at a touch the decaying houses that he enters, to dispel their lingering pasts, to destroy and recreate: the social climber becomes supernatural scourge. He fades into pathos when this power wanes, and the dark houses he enters threaten increasingly to engulf or extinguish him. Finally, he is cast out altogether, and with the revival of the picaresque mode in the twentieth century, he takes to the road again, this time with no dreams of gentility to shape his being or his life. Though to some writers he is still trailing clouds of his nineteenth-century glory,[1] the grace he embodies may be just a projection of critics' wishes and his own self-consuming art. In the twentieth century, the orphan is more estranged and brutalized than he has ever been, and we identify with him all the more potently because, in our quiescent lives, we are the more engulfed.

THIS AMPHIBIOUS CREATURE:
MOLL FLANDERS

Perhaps because it has been found such a difficult novel to classify, *Moll Flanders* seems to me to be the best place to begin a quest for the orphan. Critical discussion of it has concentrated on the radical question of what exactly the thing *is:* Is it a novel or not a novel?[2] Is it picaresque or not?[3] The fascination of the book, and its importance for this study, lie in its very amorphousness. Its indeterminacy of being suggests that of the orphan himself, who has no past, no social identity, often no name, to give him contour. Moll herself is the very type of the eighteenth-century orphan: an "amphibious creature,"[4] half whore, half gentle (wo)man, fighting desperately in silence to manipulate a social identity out of a hostile world.

Moll's escapades are the continental picaroon's transplanted to the English climate. As the picaroon traditionally is, Moll is radically alone throughout the novel. She trusts no one, cloaking her identity even from Jemy and her "governess," whom she claims to love. In her solitary and suspicious whoredom, there is none of the comradeship between outcasts which Robert Alter defines as a leaven in the picaresque tradition. Instead, her wariness isolates her even from herself.

Like the picaroon, as well as Keats' chameleon poet, Moll

seems finally to have no organizing center of self. She seems endlessly protean, slipping in and out of her environment, changing her name, her costume, and her identity, with each episode she participates in. Of course, this shiftiness and mutability of being are staples of the traditional episodic picaresque plot, in which the picaroon keeps things spinning by assuming many roles; but Defoe uses the device brilliantly to characterize Moll. In her compulsive, many-lived secrecy, she seems to have internalized her orphanhood, having no past to give her shape.

But unlike the picaroon's, Moll's identity does not fly apart into a series of disguises: she shapes herself by her overriding ambition to be a gentlewoman. The rigidity of this obsession is the other side of the protean Moll, creating a further amphibious dimension in her nature. This simultaneous mutability and rigidity of being may be the source of an amusing critical controversy, in which some critics see Moll as having no character at all, while others find in her a triumph of characterization.[5] Money and social position may seem mundane determinants to us, but in Defoe's world, they provide not only external security, but the only integrity of being the orphan can know.

Given nothing, this orphan imposes an identity on herself by adopting—and adapting—the ambiguous terminology of genteel society. "Gentlewoman" is only the most overriding of the many terms with which she tries, somewhat pedantically, to label herself. When her first seducer persuades her to marry his brother, she seems particularly irate at his refusal to categorize her:

"You shall be my dear sister, as now you are my dear—and there he stop'd.
"Your dear whore, says I, you would have said, and you might as well have said it; but I understand you."

(p. 36)

She always has particular trouble with the distinction between the categories of "whore" and "wife," though she never loses her awareness of it: "I found presently that whether I was a whore or a wife, I was to pass for a whore here, so I let that go" (p. 141). Even as a thief, she scrupulously stops to categorize herself: "Lord, said I, what am I now? a thief!" (p. 167). Even the book's title reflects her attempt to bestow an identity on herself. "Moll Flanders" is not her real name; it is an appellation bestowed on her by thieves; but, presumably with the help of her "editor," she selects it as the title of her memoirs, relegating all her other names to an "etc." In choosing to define herself as a thief, Moll is reinforcing her amphibious identity as a gentlewoman, since the basis of her gentility at the end of the novel rests on the stolen goods she has retained despite her supposed "penitence." In defining herself as a thief, she is also defining herself as an artist, in a special sense that belongs to eighteenth-century orphanhood.

  Of course, her triumph as a thief is the apex of her career, which consisted all along of secret manipulations to accumulate money, and thus gentility, and thus an identity, out of a hostile world. Her late emergence as a thief—she is forty-eight when she begins—suggests a characteristic that is peculiar to the orphan, though it is particularly apparent in his picaresque incarnation: his capacity for perpetual rebirth, his continual ability to shuck off the past and begin life anew, a lonely freedom appropriate to a being who is without a past to begin with. We are reminded of Joyce Cary's Sara Monday, Moll's cousin in the twentieth century, who is not born into her roguish identity until she is well into middle age; she, like Moll, is always able to be born, her identity remaining always *Monday*. Moll is born and reborn continually, as she shucks off or is dispossessed of each life to begin another one, but her brilliant career as a thief includes and epitomizes all her previous roles. It is frequently noticed that she reveals her capitalist orientation by referring to thievery as her "business," but it is also important that she refers to it as an "art": "I grew the greatest artist of my time" (p. 186). Of course, in 1722 "art" still retained its old meaning of "skill," and had not yet assumed the special aura it took on in the nineteenth century and retains today. It also carried unsavory connotations, among which the *OED* lists "skillful, crafty, or artificial conduct. An artifice, contrivance, stratagem, wile, trick, cunning device. Studied conduct or action, especially such as seeks to attain its ends by artificial, indirect, or covert means; address; cunning, artfulness." In this sense, Moll is a supreme artist, and this is the sense we must use to define the art of *Moll Flanders* itself.

  Claudio Guillen's suggestive definition of the picaresque novel as "the fictional confession of a liar"[6] defines the narrative voice of *Moll Flanders* in a manner that settles the old critical question of whether or not Defoe intended irony in his delineation of Moll. In the world of *Moll Flanders*, artistry and thievery are one, and the pseudo-confession itself becomes a strategem, a wile, to attain its ends. Early in the novel, Moll uses a doggerel poem composed of half-truths as a counter in the marriage game—though in this case, her stratagem backfires, since the prize she wins is her third husband who turns out to be her brother as well. Her narrative itself is similarly a stratagem, a counter in a game rather than a "sincere" confession. Here, Moll reveals her kinship to Richardson's Pamela, whose memoirs constitute a somewhat later "confession of a liar," or at least, as B. calls her, an "equivocator." Effectively orphaned in the "evil, great house," Pamela writes patently disingenuous letters to her parents, which, like Moll's doggerel, function primarily as a counter in the marriage game rather than as sincere confession: she never admits in them the salient fact of her growing love for and desire to marry B., nor her obvious disinclination to return home. In their omissions and self-projections, Pamela's letters, like Moll's life, constitute a series of roles adopted as strategems to gain an identity through the assumption of gentility. The eighteenth-century novel is not confessional; we need only remember the contortions of *Tristram Shandy*, which are designed to reveal the impossibility of true confession, of finding, to use Booth's terminology, a "reliable narrator." Moreover, the eighteenth-century orphan, amphibious and at bay as he is, has no self to confess. He is attempting to manufacture a self by assuming social definition, insufficient as this may seem to our own post-romantic, post-Freudian labyrinths of introspection.

   Like Pamela, Moll lives in a tangle of shadows, of equivocations and stratagems, but she is more aware than Pamela of the orphan's plight: besieged as he is outwardly and amorphous as he is inwardly, he is perpetually unable to confess. She repeatedly expresses her fear that the unnatural silence in which she lives will drive her to expose herself in sleep or in delirium, and defines the loneliness of a life hemmed in by secrets: "For let them say what they please of our sex not being able to keep a secret, my life is a plain conviction to me of the contrary; but be it our sex, or the men's sex, a secret of moment should always have a confident, a bosom friend, to whom we may communicate the joy of it, or the grief of it, be it which it will, or it will be a double weight upon the spirits, and perhaps become even insupportable in it self; and this I appeal to human testimony for the truth of" (p. 282). But Moll will admit no such friend, not even the "reader" so dear to Victorian narrators. Her essential silence envelops us as well as her comrades in her bottomless suspicion.

Moll's coming into her inheritance at the end of the novel, after her final rebirth in the "new world," does not constitute an integration of her shadowed identity. We need only contrast the device with its use in Victorian novels, in which the attainment of the inheritance fulfills the character's being and causes all his relationships to cohere. As an heiress, Moll is still multi-lived, slipping back and forth between Jemy's home and her son's, hiding each from the other. Her "penitence" is always a slippery thing, and at "almost seventy," she still contains the orphan's potential for reformation and rebirth. The book ends in all the openness of the future tense: "My husband remain'd there some time after me to settle our affairs, and at first I had intended to go back to him, but at his desire I alter'd that resolution, and he is come over to England also, where *we resolve* to spend the remainder of our years in sincere penitence for the wicked lives we have lived" (p. 297, my italics). Amorphous and incoherent as her being still is, her story can end, for she has achieved lasting gentility and thus social definition.

Throughout the eighteenth century, the orphan is a shadowy, manipulative, cloaked figure who finally achieves possession of an identity through the social category he attains.[7] For this reason, many eighteenth-century orphan novels have an amphibious quality. There is a positive disjunction in *Roderick Random,* whose orphaned hero simply changes character in the last third of the book, going from rogue to romance hero before coming into his inheritance. But the disjunction in Smollett's novel hints at a slight fissure inherent in the attempt to blend criminality and gentility, the multiple picaresque self with the unilateral social being, the unshaped orphan with the structure of his society.

The games the orphan must play in order to manufacture a self seem to me most chilling in Richardson's novels, perhaps because their games are exclusively sexual. Pamela and Clarissa are both self-induced orphans. They have left their parents' houses, from which they become radically exiled, so they must fight self-annihilation with wile and stratagem. Cunning and flexible as she is—the perfect picaresque servant—Pamela wins the game and is born into selfhood, which

is equated with social power and respectability. Before her marriage, in
true picaresque tradition, she is adept at disguise: when she comes to
B. dressed enticingly as a poor country girl, she is no longer expressing
her identity—like all orphans, Pamela knows you can't go home again—
but dramatizing a dead self to attain an end, as she does in the letters
themselves. B., who always knows her well, defines the bottomless paradox of the picaresque self: "For though you are as innocent as a
dove, yet you are as cunning as a serpent."[8] After the marriage, like
Roderick's, her character changes utterly. She becomes a frozen model
of pure Being poor B. must struggle to emulate: "I want you to be
nothing but what you are, and have been. You cannot be better, and
if you could, it would be but filling me with despair to attain the awful
heights of virtue at which you have arrived" (p. 432). But she does,
to our horror and his, grow better and better. With gentility, Pamela's
selfhood evolves from an enigma to an absolute. Clarissa, on the other
hand, has abandoned the selfhood bestowed on her by orphaning herself, and can attain no other. Estranged from both her parents' world
and Lovelace's, her only option is to fade away and die. Whatever
apotheosis she may achieve, her earthly identity dissolves in the violated limbo of orphanhood. Without social definition, it seems, the
self must vanish utterly.

   Whereas in most of these novels, orphanhood seems equated
with moral and psychic chaos searching for social form, Tom Jones'
orphanhood seems the opposite: a guarantee of integrity. Our first
vision of Tom as a baby is of a self-generated embodiment of innocence, lovingly brooded over by Squire Allworthy and by Fielding himself.
As a young man, Tom is infallibly "sincere" as Lionel Trilling defines
the initial use of the word in Sincerity and Authenticity: he is honest,
open, and whole, unlike the mutable rogue. His innocence is appealing
because it is in no way self-contained. His free-flowing sexuality is a
metaphor of his being. He spends himself as lavishly and generously as
he does his seed, with little regard for the character of the recipient.
In a paradoxical way, his spontaneous overflow of sexual energy guarantees his purity, much as that of Hardy's Tess will do later on. His
willingness to spend himself makes of him a kind of sexual saint, the
apparent opposite of Moll and Pamela, who fiercely hoarded themselves until the moment was advantageous for investment.

   But the orphan's seed is a dangerous growth, to no one

more than to the orphan himself. Although Fielding assures us from the beginning that Tom is "innocent," the very flow of his purity is an emblem of guilt: he is "certainly born to be hanged" by the world he lives in. The sin of imprudence he learns to correct is the sin of lavishness. Not only does he copulate too freely, but, perhaps more dangerously, he also talks too freely, to the wrong people. At Squire Allworthy's recovery, at the inn on the road to Bristol, and at many other points, he is fatally voluble and expansive. Surrounded by a network of spies and schemers, with protective benevolence embodied only by the naive Allworthy, Tom must learn to control and direct the torrent of his mouth and his hormones: "To be direct and honest is not safe." The book's action forces the picaresque lesson on him. His banishment from Paradise Hall and his journey to London constitute a picaresque rite de passage as Robert Alter defines it: experience teaches the picaro to dissolve his identity by manipulating it, to be multiple rather than sincere, to take on the color of his surroundings, wear a mask. The flood of pure energy with which Tom's orphanhood seemed to endow him must sink into underground channels.

By the time he reaches London and Lady Bellaston, Tom has learned the rules of the picaresque game. In the last third of the book, he is closer to Moll and Pamela than to the gush of boisterous energy he was at the beginning. Rather than being a dark excrescence in a sunny book, Tom's whoredom with Lady Bellaston is the nexus to which the entire action tends: it demonstrates his ability to manipulate his sexuality rather than being swept away by it. As befits the picaro, Tom meets Lady Bellaston at a masquerade and proceeds to play sophisticated games with her involving money and marriage. He has learned, as the picaro must, to lie and equivocate rather than speaking out directly. It is no accident that Tom begins to write only after submerging himself in picaresque disguise: his letter of proposal to Lady Bellaston is a masterly piece of equivocation, worthy of Moll or Pamela. The early Tom was too open and sincere to be an artist telling his own story; he had to be presented to us in the ironic curlicues of the narrator's rhetoric. His cagy letter of proposal allows him to be, briefly, an artist and his own creator. It also essentially frees him for his Sophia, but before attaining her, he must touch the abysses that Moll had known throughout most of her life: he is thrown in Newgate and forced to confront the possibility of incest in himself. Unlike Moll's,

Tom's association with Newgate and with incest are only accidental, not radical—they do not constitute the stuff of his being—but he, too, is amphibious, and must submerge himself in whoredom before emerging into gentility.

As we have seen, the orphan novel itself is amphibious in the eighteenth century. It represents a graft of the old picaresque genre onto a new genre which is a perennial middle-class favorite: the how-to book. *Pamela*'s origins as a how-to book are well known, but *Moll Flanders* is equally informative. Moll's detailed descriptions of her artistry as a thief provide as good instruction as Fagin's will do later on, although as usual the instruction cuts both ways, for Moll's avowed intent is to teach gentility how to guard itself against criminality. The orphan becomes a tarnished but exemplary figure for a class on the way up; the infinite open-endedness of the picaresque novel is sacrificed in favor of its practical edification. Like how-to books today, from Norman Vincent Peale's to Norman Podhoretz's, the eighteenth-century orphan novel teaches the reader how to make it by learning the rules of the game.

The amphibious nature of the eighteenth-century orphan novel is appropriate not only to the needs of a rising capitalist class, but to an age of deism, whose universe was a magnificent act of construction. The eighteenth-century orphan literally makes himself; he is his own Frankenstein. He has no social origins to give him shape, and (in these novels) there is no God to give him soul. He stands supreme and a little monstrous, the great artificer, the self-made man. Human ingenuity is the great fact of his world; his identity is a creation of "art" in its old sense. In the early Victorian novel, he will touch the sun by establishing his connection to God.

THE OUTLAW WITH THE BROOM: FROM JANE EYRE TO PIP[9]

It is common to say that the picaresque novel disappears in the nineteenth century to resurface in the twentieth. As Claudio Guillen speculates: "The picaresque novel prepares for or follows, apparently, periods of full novelistic bloom."[10] I would say rather that in his infinite adaptability, the picaro mutates again in the nineteenth century in obedience to his cultural climate, as we have already seen him do in the eighteenth. This time, he shucks off his roguish nature and retains only his orphanhood, which becomes his glory. In the eighteenth century, orphanhood meant nullity of self. In the nineteenth century, it comes to stand for something like pure selfhood, Being in the Wordsworthian sense, Coleridge's "infinite I AM."

Given at best an amphibious being, Moll used her artistry to construct a functional one. Her memoirs were a paradox, the confession of a liar, of a being perpetually denied confession. In her preface to the second edition of *Jane Eyre,* defending the novel from Victorian pharisees, Charlotte Brontë gives Jane's fictional confession a different status: "[Self-righteousness and religion] are diametrically opposed: they are as distinct as is vice from virtue. Men too often confound them: they should not be confounded: appearances should not be mistaken for truth: narrow human doctrines, that only tend to elate and magnify a few, should not be substituted for the world-redeeming creed of Christ."[11] In Moll's twilight world, half-lies blended with half-truths to create endless ambiguities. In biblical cadences, Charlotte Brontë rigidly differentiates lies from truth, deception from revelation. Jane's confessions are not a strategem, but a vehicle of revelation. That which she reveals is the intact and imperious purity of her selfhood, which she asserts at key moments:

> "Do you think I can stay to become nothing to you? Do you think I am an automaton?—a machine without feelings? and can bear to have my morsel of bread snatched from my lips, and my drop of living water dashed from my cup? Do you think, because I am poor, obscure, plain, and little, I am soulless and heartless? You think wrong!—I have as much soul as you,—and full as much heart! . . . I am not talking to you now through the medium of custom, conventionalities, nor even of mortal flesh—it is my spirit that addresses your spirit; just as if both had passed through the grave, and we stood at God's feet equal,—as we are!"
>
> (p. 222)

Unlike the eighteenth-century orphan, who is always on the verge of it, it is impossible for Jane to "become nothing." This is because, unlike the eighteenth-century orphan, she is not an artifact ("an automaton"), but a "soul": she is supernaturally sanctioned. With a series of doggerel equivocations, Moll enticed her third husband into marriage; but the surreal drawings with which Jane first attracts Rochester are art in its later sense, no longer "wile," but self-expression and truth. Similarly, the portraits she sketches throughout the novel are compelling vehicles of truth for all who see them. Unlike Moll and Pamela, she recoils from Rochester's attempt to dress her as a lady; his attempt to disguise her seems more a violation than the projected bigamy would be.

This metamorphosis is startling, because the plot of *Jane Eyre* so much resembles those of the eighteenth-century picaresque how-to books, especially, of course, *Pamela:* Jane too rises from obscurity to wealth and gentility. Pamela became a "lady"; Jane becomes, more solidly, an "independent woman," her new status sanctioned not by God alone, but by her inheritance of a fortune and position as a baronet's wife. Like Pamela, Jane is revolutionary in her quiet, dutiful way: once she has gained power in the "evil, great house" she was a servant in, she reforms its license, banking its lusts and replacing them with religion and duty. But Jane has none of Pamela's honest worldliness, her equation of gentility and divinity; though she does for a while confuse Rochester with God, she soon recognizes this as a sin. Moreover, she rises, not by wiles and gamesmanship, but by the honesty and potency of the Being she is endowed with, which, in the structure of the novel, becomes equated with inspiration.

For the Gothicism Charlotte Brontë employs throughout *Jane Eyre* is woven into the fabric of Jane's character. Jane can legitimately cry with Rochester, "I know my Maker sanctions what I do" (p. 225). This antinomianism is a sin on Rochester's part primarily, it seems, because it isn't true—a fact which God quickly lets him know by splitting the chestnut tree. Jane, on the contrary, *is* close to the supernatural; being truly inspired, of course, she would never try to trespass on a sacrament, as Rochester does.

"God is a friend to the poor orphan child"—the words of Bessie's conventionally pious hymn at the beginning of the novel come startlingly and literally true in the course of it. Jane's first brush with the supernatural comes in the red room when she is a child, and it terrifies her: "I thought the swift-darting beam was a herald of some coming vision [of her uncle Reed] from another world. My heart beat thick, my head grew hot; a sound filled my ears, which I deemed the rushing of wings: something seemed near me; I was oppressed, suffocated: endurance broke down; I rushed to the door and shook the lock in desperate effort" (p. 14). This childish experience is laced with qualifications ("I thought," "I deemed") which disappear in her mature supernatural encounters. Later on, she has no doubt that her mother's spirit appears, commanding her to "flee temptation," in a manner that recalls her childish intimation of her hovering uncle. The coincidence that deposits her at her relatives' door when she is starving is only one of a series of intimations that a supernatural force guides her in her wanderings and at times, works through her. "I never laughed at presentiments in my life; because I have had strange ones of my own. Sympathies, I believe, exist . . . whose workings baffle mortal comprehension" (p. 193). At another time, Jane says more dryly, "God directed me to a correct choice: I thank His providence for the guidance" (p. 316). St. John seems to sense the supernatural charge to her, and, cruel and awesome as he is, there is nothing in the novel to question the authenticity of his spiritual vocation; he dies a true prophet, not a pharisee, whose apotheosis Jane never doubts. As he is not merely her cousin, but her namesake as well, St. John seems to represent Jane's own potential sanctification. The marriage he offers her can be described only in the language of Revelation: "The Impossible—i.e. my marriage with St. John—was fast becoming the Possible. All was changing utterly, with a sudden sweep. Religion called—Angels beckoned—God commanded—life rolled together like a scroll—death's gates opening, showed eternity beyond: it seemed, that for safety and bliss there, all here might be sacrificed in a second. The dim room was full of visions" (p. 368). These visions seem no less legitimate than the ensuing, and more famous, miracle of Rochester's call and Jane's answer. God reveals to his divinely inspired orphan that martyrdom and sanctification are indeed "Possible" for her, but then informs her through the nature that she loves that he does not require them of her.

The visions with which Jane is inundated might serve only to characterize her as either conventionally pious or deranged if others in the novel did not continually perceive her as a supernatural being or agent. Rochester is drawn despite himself, not to her beauty or her manner—Charlotte Brontë deliberately endows her with neither—but to her otherworldliness. He frequently refers to her as ambiguously "elfin," a creature sometimes angel, sometimes witch, giving the plain little governess an aura of "la belle dame sans merci." Mrs. Reed, too, is terrified of the uncanny child, and even the innkeeper near Thornfield says she has "bewitched" Rochester. Throughout, others are more aware of her eeriness than she is; for Jane, it is natural to live swimming in visions and presentiments. She is not a Wordsworthian child, whose visionary dread redounds largely on himself; we are made most aware of Jane's supernatural potency through the intensity of its effect on the surrounding world.

The ambiguity of the novel, she talks oddly about her "powers." She conquers every environment she enters, but her powers are most dramatically evident at Thornfield, one of the great bleak houses of nineteenth-century English fiction, bastion of feudal authority and the past. It is Jane who unwittingly releases the banked fires of madness there in the form of the incarcerated Bertha, who stands for one proclivity in Rochester himself and in the tradition he represents: his passion to possess is as anarchic as B.'s in *Pamela*, and like B.'s, it is inflamed and tamed by the little orphan. The fire Jane's spell catalyzes is both destructive and purifying. When Rochester's opulent estate is reduced to rubble and his opulent body to a charred shell, Jane can return to him as little wife rather than little witch, tending the ruins of the house she has passed through, cleaned up, and helped to bring down.

The ambiguity of the supernatural aura surrounding Jane— she is called a witch at least as often as she is called an angel, and many critics have pointed out that the book's symbolism also links her to the thoroughly demonic Bertha—suggests that the Victorian orphan has retained some of his roguish characteristics in transcendentalized form. This is connected to the fact that in nineteenth-century supernatural literature, the demonic and the divine tend to merge: in an age possessed by faith but deprived of dogma, *any* incursions of the supernatural into the natural become ambiguously awful because unclassifiable. The nineteenth-century orphan, then, retains some of his amphibious nature, but in early Victorian literature, instead of being gentleman-whore, he becomes angel-demon.

Jane Eyre's pattern is repeated by two other orphans of the 1840s, Thackeray's Becky Sharp and Emily Brontë's Heathcliff. Becky, actress and schemer, is truer to her picaresque origins than Jane was, as Thackeray remained always half-submerged in his nostalgia for the eighteenth-century novel. Unlike Jane, Becky appears to her best advantage in costume, relishing all the duplicity her artistry demands. If Moll Flanders was in part an embodiment of the eighteenth-century artist-thief, Becky raises the artist's thievery to all the glory and the fun of Keats' chameleon poet. Like Moll's, Becky's orphanhood results in a flashing mutability of being, and this very mutability impels her rise: she is able to act all things for all men, turning herself into the woman they want to see. The men in her life are indistinguishable to her; acting with a profound grasp of the wife/whore question, she seems indifferent as to which selfhood she will finally adopt. Like Moll, she sees money and position as the only real determinants of identity, speculating that she could be a good woman on five thousand a year. But in fact, financially and psychically, she lives on nothing a year, her identity disappearing in a dazzling play of surfaces and roles. Looking forward to the artist-heroes of the 1890s, Becky turns her life into a work of art, and finally loses herself in the game. The narrator's ambivalent irony toward her reinforces our sense of Becky's indeterminacy; finally, all the moralizing puppeteer can do is to shake his head in wonderment at his creature and ask, "Was she guilty or not?" She is so flashingly mobile in her artifice that even her creator, the novel's God, is unable to impale her.

Thackeray's portrait of the orphan-artist and his concern with endless mirrors of artifice seem worlds away from Charlotte Brontë's Puritan reliance on "soul" and "Truth." Given this difference of emphasis, it is remarkable how closely Becky follows Jane Eyre's pattern: in her own way, this tiny governess with the odd eyes is also a social climber translated into supernatural scourge. Thackeray's language loosely, and perhaps inappropriately, supernaturalizes her. He defines her amphibious nature by linking her in a famous passage to a mermaid, and surrounds his enchantress with divine-demonic imagery throughout the novel. Becky's selfhood is less absolute than Jane's, but her powers are the same: she transforms every great house she enters, and by the end of the novel has become an inadvertent catalyst of social revolution. Her marriage to Rawdon loses Rawdon his aunt's inheritance, which passes instead to his stuffy brother Sir Pitt, who uses it to renovate the estate of Queen's Crawley, gone to seed in the dissolute old baronet's time; by the end, Becky's impact has driven out Regency misrule, and the estate will flourish once again. She precipitates a similar destruction and renovation in the Sedley's house: she kills Joseph, its silly fat scion, but pushes its frail flower Amelia away from memories of the dandified George and into the arms of noble Captain Dobbin, whose idealism, though somewhat rigid and deluded, is preferable to Joseph's and George's selfish flaccidity. By the end of the novel, Becky has directly or indirectly killed off all the dominant Regency bucks who obstructed the coming of the new Victorian era. Thackeray does not emphasize this cultural passage, insisting that his novel rides only "the skirts of history," but if we look closely, we see that it is there, pushed out of the foreground like the momentous events in Brueghel's paintings. Though Becky herself is relegated to the outer rim of Vanity Fair, the orphan, with all her dangerous magic, has functioned as the agent of benevolent change.

Heathcliff, too, is a divine-demonic creature. His ambiguously supernatural aura is proclaimed on Mr. Earnshaw's first appearance with the child: "You must e'en take it as a gift of God, though it's as dark almost as if it came from the devil." [12] He, too, enters a great house, destroys and renovates it, simply, it seems, by his "soul," seeming to represent, in his supernatural magnetism, a soul naked and exposed within the social medium. More explicitly than the other Victorian orphans, he exerts a pull toward unknown sources of being; like them, he catalyzes a social change he cannot fully participate in. His seed cannot take in this world: his son Linton is described as a mutant who must die off, and his love for Catherine must pass through the window beyond this world, but from it, Hareton and Cathy's secularized community flourishes. [13]

Heathcliff embodies the mystical undercurrents latent in Jane Eyre and Becky Sharp, who pass into houses and exert a powerful destructive effect which gives birth to a new civilization out of the ashes. In these novels of the 1840s, the strange cunning power of the orphan is yoked to forces of social evolution; in his turbulent passage through a household, he carries with him history's mysterious sources, brought with him from another world. His social rise no longer "makes" him, as it did in the eighteenth century, but establishes him as the agent of a providential spirit working through history. The parents of the orphan become equated with the mysterious home of destiny and the soul.

The transcendentalizing of the orphan and the yoking of

him to a mysterious Providence working through history reflect Victorian cultural needs. It was easy for Victorian readers to see in the orphan a symbol of incendiary revolutionary energy; like the French Revolution which haunted Victorian England, the orphan is a dangerously unknown quantity because he is a being without precedent or visible sanction. Just as Carlyle's *French Revolution* transcendentalizes the revolution into a providential scourge, so do these novels transcendentalize the orphan. At the end of the three novels we have looked at, a calmer new society emerges out of the whirlwind the orphan has inadvertently sown. The Victorians fervently hoped that Providence remained to meld revolutionary energy into evolutionary shape.

Moreover, the recurrent religious crises of the nineteenth century suggest the incarnation the orphan takes on in the works of the Brontës: a symbol of the detached human soul. Haunted as they were by their fears and dreams of another world which seemed rapidly evaporating, obsessed with possible mysterious connections between God and man, it is not surprising that the Victorians emphasized the supernatural nimbus surrounding the orphan's loneliness. He is finally fixed for us by a theologian, John Henry Newman, as an irrefutable emblem of the dismembered soul:

Did I see a boy of good make and mind, with the token on him of a refined nature, cast upon the world without provision, unable to say whence he came, his birth-place or family connexions, I should conclude that there was some mystery connected with his history, and that he was one, of whom, from one cause or another, his parents were ashamed. Thus only should I be able to account for the contrast between the promise and the condition of his being. And so I argue about the world;—*if* there be a God, *since* there is a God, the human race is implicated in some terrible aboriginal calamity. It is out of joint with the purposes of its Creator.[14]

The orphan stands at the center of Newman's vision of bereft Victorian man, shining with both the link to and the disjunction from his supernatural home, the last weak embodiment of the soul God proudly bestowed on man.

For despite the revolutionary surge he manifests in novels of the 1840s, a turbulent and revolutionary decade in Victorian England, the orphan's power wanes as the century wears on. When we think of the Victorian orphan, we think first of all the lost boys wan-

dering through Dickens' London, embodying in their pathos all the
Victorians' self-pity and terror in the mazes of the new world the
nineteenth century had inaugurated. Industrialism, religious conflict,
and scientific discoveries had orphaned the Victorian age of its sense
of its own past; the other side of the orphan's freedom was his fear,
his need of guidance in a world without maps. Massive as its achievements were, an important facet of the age's self-image is expressed in
Tennyson's lines in *In Memoriam:* "An infant crying in the night, /
And with no language but a cry." The Victorians responded in kind
to Dickens' diminished orphans, making of them culture heroes, responding to their martyrdoms with "no language but a cry"; a tendency W. S. Gilbert satirized in *The Pirates of Penzance* when his crew
of pirates sobs in chorus at Major-General Stanley's somber declaration that he is an orphan.

   All Dickens' novels constitute variations on the theme of
orphanhood, but only in *Great Expectations* is he able to confront it
without false pathos, in all the dread it held for him and his age. Pip's
confessions both recapitulate and comment on those of previous orphan novels we have looked at, and show, too, why the myth of the
orphan—which at its high point practically constituted orphan worship—was losing its efficacy as the century drew to a close.

   Like *Jane Eyre, Great Expectations* shows the mutation of
the eighteen-century picaresque success story into the nineteenth-century orphan myth. Pip, like Moll, yearns for gentility and attains it,
and like hers, his being and destiny are a tangle of criminality and
gentility, lies and truth. But he is burdened with modern self-con-
sciousness. His very being does not constitute "truth," as Jane Eyre's
did, but he is more aware than Moll of the extent to which he is
counterfeit. In short, he is a true confessional artist, whispering his
shame to the world: "All other swindlers upon earth are nothing to
the self-swindlers, and with such pretences did I cheat myself. Surely
a curious thing. That I should innocently take a bad half-crown of
somebody else's manufacture, is reasonable enough; but that I should
knowingly reckon the spurious coin of my own make, as good money
An obliging stranger, under pretence of compactly folding up my bank-
notes for security's sake, abstracts the notes and gives me nutshells
but what is his sleight of hand to mine, when I fold up my own nut-

shells and pass them on myself as notes!" [15] The honesty of Pip's voice cannot be equated with Jane's inspiration; it is the spiritual nausea of a man constantly aware of his own bad faith, the voice of self-loathing which constitutes modern "sincerity."

Pip's story repeats mechanically the paradigm of the orphan myth established in the 1840s.[16] Like Jane Eyre, Pip brings down by fire the great house he enters as "a kind of servant," destroying and purging it of the banked embers of its past. The power Pip acquires over Miss Havisham is not Jane's quasi-supernatural spell over Rochester, but the power of his sincere emotion, which to Dickens is always magical. In a key scene, Miss Havisham kneels to him: " 'Until you spoke to her the other day, and until I saw in you a looking-glass that showed me what I once felt myself, I did not know what I had done. What have I done! What have I done!' And so again, twenty, fifty times over, What had she done!" (p. 411). Miss Havisham's yielding to the power of Pip's emotion seems somehow to ignite the fire that destroys her and Satis House, a destruction that Pip, like Jane again, has foreseen in odd premonitory visions. So the vision of the orphan passing through a great house which his influence destroys and restores retains its potency. But we do not think of this as we read the novel.

For one thing, its point of view makes us aware not of Pip's power over his world, but the power of his world over him. His early perspective—that of "the small bundle of shivers growing afraid of it all and beginning to cry"—is never really lost. His adult life is still pervaded by his childhood terrors, so that he does not convey to us his powers even when he commands them. Of course, Dickens' specialty is the worm's-eye perspective of a monstrous world looming large over a helpless child, but in *Great Expectations* the terror is not simply a trick of "camera angle," as it sometimes is in Dickens. It is inherent in Pip's situation: he really is alone. For the first time in the novels we have looked at, the orphan's parents are implacably dead, equated only with their tombstones. Father figures though generations of critics have rightly called them, neither Magwitch nor Joe is really Pip's father, making Pip's alienation all the more terrifying when Magwitch looms out of his parents' graves. Moreover, there is no God in *Great Expectations* to give sanction to Pip's identity. God withdrew from Dickens' world in *Bleak House*, when the "distant ray of light" that fell on the orphan Jo was finally extinguished in Jo's death. Pip's selfhood is contained not in his social definition, as Moll's was, nor in his soul, as Jane's was, but in a more fragile thing: his name.

For Pip's identity is self-bestowed; he names himself before the novel begins. His childish naming of himself recalls the eighteenth-century orphan as self-made man, but it is the last act of autonomy Pip is permitted. When Magwitch stipulates that Pip keep his name upon accepting his tainted inheritance, his fear is prophetic, for this is the one thing Pip can't do: from that moment, a bewildering variety of names is bestowed on him by everyone he meets, even his friend Herbert christening him "Handel." The crowning erosion of his identity is Joe's schizophrenic slipping back and forth between "Pip" and "sir." This is a cannibalistic inversion of the plenitude of names Moll assumed in her escapades. In her picaresque mutability, Moll was simultaneously all these selves and no-self. Pip has only one identity, which is Pip, and when others gnaw away at it, they gnaw away at him.

Just as the many names Pip is given employ a picaresque device to invert it, so does the motif of costume. Instead of being a master of disguise, Pip is tormented by his clothes, which become embodied in the humiliating nemesis of Trabb's boy. His social rise itself inverts the picaro's. Instead of being a brilliant improviser, succeeding by the spontaneous manipulation of chance events, Pip mechanically obeys commands to succeed. He does not inveigle his way into Miss Havisham's house; he is ordered there. He plays grimly when she says "Play!"—no picaro, with his love of games, would require such a command!—loves Estella when she commands him to "love her," and yearns for gentility as she programs him to. Moll's desire for gentility was spontaneous; Pip's is conditioned. Once Pip is "made" a gentleman, all his moves are charted for him according to stipulations delivered by Jaggers. Never once does he act independently; even his adherence to Magwitch is as much a reaction to the influence of another as his love for Estella is. The legacy he bestows on Herbert and forces Miss Havisham to maintain is his one autonmous act, and here, he is "making" another as he has been "made." Estella, whose automaton-like qualities are only an exaggeration of Pip's, acts as his chorus: "We have no choice, you and I, but to obey our instructions. We are not free to follow our own devices, you and I" (p. 285). The repetition of "you and I" is mechanical, sepulchral, emphasizing the identities they lack by insisting on them. Even more chilling are the words she intones to Miss Havisham: "I am what you have made me" (p. 322). This zombie-like creature is the opposite of the early Victorian orphan, whose mysterious origins were suggestive of infinite Being. Having no soul, the orphan in *Great Expectations* has become a thing.

The eighteenth-century orphan has been turned around, having become manipulated by rather than manipulator of events. He has gone from self-made man to made man. In an odd inversion of the Frankenstein image, Pip returns to the eighteenth-century idea of the orphan as artifact, but emphasizes his loss of power: "The imaginary student pursued by the misshapen creature he had impiously made, was not more wretched than I, pursued by the creature who had made me, and recoiling from him with a stronger repulsion, the more he admired me and the fonder he was of me" (p. 354). The idea of Pip as artifact is further emphasized by the fact that none of the people who manipulate him are his parents. His being is not organically shaped by inheritance, however hidden. His parents are tombstones; he is infinitely conditioned. The convict image that always follows him seems more suggestive of this incessant coercion than it is of guilt, despite the emphasis of Dorothy Van Ghent's brilliant essay.[17] After all, Pip sins only in thought or by omission. He wishes to run away from the forge, and later from Magwitch, but never actually does so. He avoids seeing Joe and Biddy, but when he does, he never actively cuts them, responding to their love with love as he responds to everybody's emotions. The most terrifying part of *Great Expectations* is Pip's lack of the initiative to sin. Like Alex, Anthony Burgess' clockwork orange, he is a made man even when he hugs his own evil to himself. In a state of infinite conditioning, there is no room for the fruit of the soul growing on the tree of God. The protective coloring of the orphan was always a sham.

The double ending of *Great Expectations* constitutes a strange variation on or repudiation of the 1840s orphan myth. In the "happy" ending, Satis House is demolished and Estella, too, is stripped of her money and power. This stripping of Estella reaffirms the power of the orphan: not only has he precipitated the destruction of Miss Havisham and her house, but also of Estella, her creature. In Dickens' original ending, a depleted Pip looks up at Estella in her carriage; she is chastened, perhaps, but still a lady. The "sad" ending is the truer one, not primarily because it deprives Pip of Estella's hand—the two are as literally "made" for each other as Frankenstein's monster and his bride were—but because it deprives Pip of any lasting effect on Satis House, whose chief product still survives. Lacking Jane Eyre's inspiration, he must lack her "powers," and so he and Estella cannot be reborn in the ruins of the great house as Jane and Rochester were.

Charlotte Brontë too strips the orphan of divine sanction in her last orphan novel, *Villette*. Living alone and desolate in Brussels, hopelessly in love with two men who are unattainable to her, Lucy Snowe has none of Jane's transforming magic. The emphasis is on the city's power over her, a city whose inhabitants speak a strange language and worship strange gods. Madame Beck, the headmistress of the school at which Lucy is a teacher, is spinning a plot which Lucy is unable to unravel or control. Here, too, the emphasis is on a world which dwarfs the orphaned heroine, over which she can exert no transforming power: she is caught in a web, unable to weave one of her own. The increasing helplessness of the orphan in later Victorian novels is a portent of the withdrawal of God from the world. Lucy lacks the incantatory magic of art, and her austere Protestant deities are defeated by Catholic craft. Like *Great Expectations, Villette* has a dual ending, as if Charlotte Brontë were unable to fully relinquish the orphan myth the logic of her novel demanded she abandon. M. Paul and Lucy's establishment of a school of their own would strip and defeat Madame Beck's *pensionnat:* once again the orphan would have the power to destroy and create a society. But in the sad and truer ending, Lucy is as desolte and powerless as she began, with M. Paul dead and her enemies thriving, alone in a world she has been unable to redeem.

Robbed of his nimbus as faith ebbed and many Victorians even forgot they had lost it, the orphan, too, ebbs out of late Victorian novels. When he does appear, he is no longer the icon he was; there is no band of pirates to weep for him. George Eliot's Daniel Deronda is a rather grotesque late mutation of him; as imperialist fervor was on the rise, Daniel, like the Victorians, now looks east for salvation, and finally departs altogether from an unredeemed England.[18] In George Gissing's *The Odd Women,* weak and silly Monica presents the orphan primarily as social statistic. Monica is torn between the bleak independence of spinsterhood and a horrible, though prosperous, marriage.

She marries and is destroyed; to Gissing, the orphan should not enter the evil great house at all, so pitifully reduced is her power. Perhaps the last great efflorescence of the myth is Barrie's excruciatingly nostalgic *Peter Pan,* the strength of which lies in its yearning for the myth, not in the myth itself. Of course, Tinker Bell's light had been extinguished long ago, perhaps when Jo died in *Bleak House.* Even Peter, anachronistic as he is, has no power over the great house he enters. Rather, he provides the children with a brief vacation from it, and it takes revenge on him by its adoption and absorption of all his lost boys. Peter does well to get out before he too is adopted and absorbed. His ineffable fairy dust is no substitute for Jane Eyre's incendiary magic.

SILENCE, EXILE, AND CUNNING:
THE ORPHAN TODAY

In our own century, the orphan abandons the great house and takes to the road again, assuming once more a picaresque coloration. His perambulations as a "picaresque saint" are too complicated and perhaps too close to us to explore fully here, but I should like to touch on his incarnation as a picaresque artist.

In "The Failing Center: Recent Fiction and the Picaresque Tradition,"[19] W. M. Frohock suggests that critics abandon the picaresque category, and thus by implication the orphan novel: in its overuse, the term has been stretched out of shape. But it is important that contemporary authors and critics do cling to the idea of the picaresque. Although we are now "all orphans," alone and free and dispossessed of our past, we yearn for origins, for cultural continuity. In our continual achievement of paradox, we have made of the orphan himself our archetypal and perhaps only ancestor.

The orphan embraces his own roots by resuming his artistry in the twentieth century, but his art is no longer a siren song exorcising his culture of its past, as it was in the nineteenth century. It is a device with which to create himself, as it was in the eighteenth century, but in a less defined and durable manner.

In *A Portrait of the Artist as a Young Man,* James Joyce

seems to resurrect the old vision of the orphan-savior, or at least he lets Stephen do it. Stephen's heroic movement in the book is his attempt to transcendentalize himself into an artist by making of himself an orphan. When he casts off his boozy father, he adopts the mythical "old artificer" Daedalus as his spiritual father, a "soaring impalpable imperishable being" whose flight Stephen will save his race by emulating. But in the itinerant Stephen of *Ulysses,* Joyce seems to debunk the orphan myth. Seen from outside, Stephen has none of the pure power of the savior; instead, he is dirty, unkempt, and lonely, thirsty for salvation himself. His transforming power over the Bloom household is uncertain. He and the Blooms touch each other briefly and Stephen passes into the night; perhaps their family and his art have been redeemed by the encounter, but perhaps not. Stephen's art obsesses Stephen, but we can no longer be certain whether it is sufficient to destroy and preserve a household. Yet the artificer Joyce struggles throughout *Ulysses* to make of this self-aggrandizing waif a figure of myth after all, as the mid-Victorians mythicized the orphan by their tears. The orphan as self-made man, as demonic-divine savior, and as artificially made man surface in turn in Stephen, joining the stockpile of myths Joyce plays with for his own ends. At the end of the journey, we have seen Stephen in multiple, cubist perspective; we remain as uncertain as he of who and what this creature is.

Gully Jimson, the protagonist of Joyce Cary's *The Horse's Mouth,* also resurrects the orphan as rogue, artist, and visionary. Gully has the orphan's power of perpetual rebirth: "Yes, every day's my birthday. Often twice a day. Due to art."[20] Like Stephen, Gully is a failed picaro: his attempts at rogueries continually turn against him, shattering his life rather than shaping it. His visionary art also lacks shaping and transforming impact. He is always searching for a house to live and work in, and he finds three: the shack on the wharf, the Beeders' mansion, and the crumbling chapel on whose walls he wants to paint his *Creation.* All three houses absorb and demolish his art, and thus, by implication, his selfhood. Coker takes over the shack on the wharf and uses Gully's *Fall* to repair the roof; the havoc Gully reaps in the Beeders' mansion with his *Lazarus* seems silently swept up, and the fresco, of course, disappears; his *Creation* is destroyed in the demolition of the tottering chapel, a fall which kills Gully as well. The destructive and creative power of the orphan has turned inward to

become momentary and incomplete, leading only to a series of demolished structures. The freshness of a daily rebirth is yoked to the terror
of perpetual death.

In the landscape of the Cary trilogy as a whole, we see the
two main constituents of the 1840s orphan myth: the great house and
the destructive-creative orphan. The magisterial estate of Tolbrook
presides over the second volume of the trilogy, *To Be a Pilgrim*, freighted
with the degenerate power of the English past. Old Mr. Wilcher, who
is dying there, is a modern variant of B. in *Pamela*, Rochester, and
Miss Havisham, embodying both the authority of tradition and the
poison of sexual madness. In *The Horse's Mouth*, the third volume of
the trilogy, we want Gully to enter Tolbrook, destroy and purify it by
covering the walls with his visionary frescoes: once more, we want the
orphan to enter the great house in order to confront, exorcise, and
transform the past. But Gully never goes near Tolbrook; the furniture
of the myth is there, but never used. Only Sara Monday is large enough
to straddle Mr. Wilcher's world and Gully's, happily sleeping with,
serving, and cheating both of them, but never bringing about a confrontation.

Gully is more brutalized, estranged, and dispossessed than
any orphan we have yet looked at, and in defiance, the selfhood he
creates through art is joyfully solipsistic and amorphous, yoking fragments from Blake to a mélange of colors without shape. He apotheosizes only the unfinished painting, the almost unbegun one:

Certainly an artist has no right to complain of his fate. For he has great
pleasures. To start new pictures. Even the worst artist that ever was, even a
one-eyed mental deficient with the shakes in both hands who sets out to
paint the chicken-house, can enjoy the first stroke. Can think, By God, look
what I've done. A miracle. I have transformed a chunk of wood, canvas, etc.,
into a spiritual fact, an eternal beauty. I am God. Yes, the beginning, the
first stroke on a picture, or a back fence, must be one of the keenest pleasures
open to mankind. It's certainly the greatest that an artist can have. It's also
the only one. And it doesn't last long—usually about five minutes."

(p. 161.

He celebrates art, not as a shaping process, but as a faint intimation
of possible shape that dies almost as soon as it is born. His ruminations are formless smears of color: "Sun all in a blaze. Lost its shape.

Tide pouring up from London as bright as bottle ale. Full of bubbles and every bubble flashing its own electric torch" (p. 3). Though he idolizes Blake, Gully shares none of Blake's insistence on the "bounding line," his recoil from the formless colors of Rubens. Gully's attempt to create his identity through art is the opposite of that of the eighteenth-century artificer, the self-made man. Through art, Gully makes himself by unmaking himself daily, his being an inchoate wash of color, a painting that decomposes faster than it is composed. We have reached some kind of end with Gully, as well as some kind of beginning. He is our first orphan to embrace rather than fear his own nonbeing, the vitality of perpetual incoherence and loss.[21]

5.

Women on Women's Destiny:
Maturity as Penance

In searching for wings for women, feminist criticism may inadvertently be building new prisons. Three of our soundest and most searching feminist scholars have produced divergent books based on a single assumption: that properly understood, women writers create and inhabit an exclusively female context, out of which a "female tradition" can be extracted.[1] A corollary to this quest for a female literary tradition is that in these days of shifting trends and conflicting expectations, a perplexed female reader can turn only to other women to define her experience and evaluate it.

Literary men dare not cross these critical thresholds. Though Spacks, Moers, and Showalter have pruned angry rhetoric out of their scholarship, in their tacit exclusion of men from their cross-fertilizing sisterhoods, they are obeying the warning of an earlier, more bellicose generation of feminist critics. Kate Millett's *Sexual Politics* was our first and most urgent rallying cry,[2] warning its female readers away from the monsters which "classic" male writers had made of them. The gauntlet Millett flung at the traditional syllabus led easily to a sweeping dismissal of all fictional women created by men: "Our literature is not about women. It is not about men and women equally. It is . . .

[about] not women but images of women [who] exist only in relation to the protagonist (who is male)."[3]

But in accepting too obediently the tenet that men mutilate their heroines to suit their own myopic needs, while even minor women writers reflect a certain truth of our experience, feminist criticism may itself be mutilating the women whose lives it wants to expand. For in excluding male visions from its canon, it may also be dismissing a faith in growth, freedom, and fun, of which women's worlds, in literature at any rate, are in general sadly deprived.

For from Fanny Burney's day to our own, women novelists have tended to cast a lugubrious and punitive glower over the lives of their heroines, lives into which male writers, no matter how overtly disapproving, often infuse a sense of option and power. Thackeray may insist intermittently that his Becky Sharp is a vixen to be shunned, but he endows her with the mobility to elude his definitions and to laugh at her own boundless role-playing with a freedom Jane Austen's similarly mobile Elizabeth Bennet is forbidden. Possibly because men have traditionally been raised to shape their own lives, while women are traditionally admonished to adjust to theirs; because a hero's vision of his life may be boundless, while a heroine's, conventionally, is predetermined by marriage, motherhood, and home; psychic and social boundaries tend to close quickly and ruthlessly in women's novels. Oddly, the omnipresence of feminism has only increased this pervasive literary entrapment.

Writing of a group of prize-winning stories by women, a recent critic "feels a kind of narrowing-down. The pure woman-on-women story can eventually become an exercise in solipsism. The reader suspects that this intensive genre is on the way to creating new stereotypes of its own . . . a composite [of which] might look something like this": the author goes on to describe an educated and immobilized protagonist, trapped by men, children, and "irrelevant details" that obsess her. "Sometime back there, she has chosen the wrong life and now she doesn't know how to get out of it. . . . When she moves to take revenge on her life, she finds a self-destructive (often sexual) method."[4] One hopes this is not the only literary reflection to which our feminism will let us turn. Nor does this gloomy immobilization spring from women's new consciousness of discontent with old norms. Written in 1961, May Sarton's The Small Room poses a rhetorical

question about an unorthodox life: "Is there a life more riddled with
self-doubt than that of a woman professor, I wonder?" As a woman
professor whose profession has been my most dependable cure for self-
doubt, I can only meet this mournful definition of my life by pounding
out "No! in thunder" with Leslie Fiedler, despite the fact that as a
man, Fiedler is supposed to be incapable of defining my experience.

Of course we needed to turn to ourselves for a definition
of ourselves; but at this point, I fear that one effect of feminist literary
separatism will be our incarceration in a small room with an inflated
specter of self-hate. Revealing and illuminating as women on women
so often are, as a group, women writers tend to deny the flexibility,
scope, and joy that are a vital dimension of all human life: the missing
dimension that feminism first promised to restore. But now, the fem-
nist ideal of the "woman-defined woman" threatens too often in our
iterature to turn into the "woman-destroyed woman" as well.

If one contemporary paradigm in women's literature is de-
ined by immolation, paralysis, and madness, her Victorian counterpart was endowed with an often monstrously outsize nobility that led
to her extinction, generally in the anonymity of an ambivalently de-
ined marriage. Though contemporary critics have turned fruitfully back
to the great Victorian women writers as role models, we need to remember the world they do not allow us: the world that makes possible
a self-definition which male writers so often, and so enviably, assume.

Antigone, George Eliot's favorite heroine, seems to hover
over our literary image of rebellious Victorian womanhood. Monumental in her rigid visionary insistence, her magnitude insures her defeat
by the triviality of life-as-it-is—in contrast to such actual moral au-
tocrats as Florence Nightingale and Queen Victoria, whose rigid self-
nsistence triumphed over surrounding pettiness. But art allows less
than life might have to two of the most famous Victorian heroines:
George Eliot's Dorothea Brooke in *Middlemarch* (1871–72) and Louisa
May Alcott's Jo March in *Little Women* (1869–70). Both are endowed
with all the fervor in their worlds, and both mature to renounce their
early powers through penitential marriages which subdue them to
commonality, although both Eliot and Alcott stubbornly fashioned
unorthodox lives whose honor sprang out of defiance. As with so many
women writers, the inevitability of defeat seems more literary than actual: the writer appropriates to herself all the joy of achievement, in

life and in art, leaving her failed self to infect her heroines and edify
her readers.

Though like the other characters in *Middlemarch*, Dorothea Brooke is "spiritually a-hungered," her destiny is defined exclusively by her two marriages and by the images of the prison and the
maze that the book flings round her, hedging in her nobility and stature until "Dodo" seems a provincial female Minotaur immured in the
labyrinth that is her novel. Though each marriage seems at first to
promise purpose and meaning, each enmeshes her further and more
finally: in its effects, her entombing marriage to the pedant Casaubon
repeats itself in her subsequent marriage to his dashing cousin, Will
Ladislaw. We learn early that Dorothea "likes giving up," and her
marriages display this one talent she exercises fully.

The marriages are perceived, though with increasing delicacy, in reiterated images of entombment. Dorothea's marriage to Casaubon is an incarceration which is literal, social, and spiritual at once,
as "the still, white enclosure which made her visible world" where "her
blooming full-pulsed youth stood . . . in a moral imprisonment which
made itself one with the chill, colourless, narrowed landscape, with the
shrunken furniture, the never-read books, and the ghostly stag in a
pale fantastic world that seemed to be vanishing from the daylight."[5]

Mercurial and mobile, Will Ladislaw seems initially "like
a lunette opened in the wall of her prison," and many critics still
assume that Eliot intended, however unsuccessfully, to liberate Dorothea from her multiple crypts through a better marriage. Thus generations of female students have been admonished against immaturity
by their male teachers when they chafe against her destiny; but the
unmistakably elegiac tone of the novel's finale provides Dorothea with
her final, and total, entombment, and the coffin is closed by George
Eliot in her mask of the sibylline Wise Woman.

The finale's mournful emphasis on waste and erosion blends
Dorothea's disastrous marriage to Casaubon with her supposedly
triumphant marriage to Ladislaw, showing the common closure beneath their surface differences. As she submerges her ardor in "the
common yearnings of womanhood," Dorothea loses even the mantle
of grand defeat, embodying only "that element of tragedy that lies in
the very fact of frequency": "But we insignificant people with our daily
words and acts are preparing the lives of many Dorotheas, some of

which may present a far sadder sacrifice than that of the Dorothea whose story we know" (p. 612). The ultimate burial of this Antigone is her assumption of the anonymity of Ismene: "Her full nature, like that river of which Cyrus broke the strength, spent itself on channels which had no great name on the earth. But . . . that things are not so ill with you and me as they might have been, is half owing to the number who lived faithfully a hidden life, and rest in unvisited tombs" (p. 613).

In her final revision, George Eliot banned Dorothea's uniqueness from survival even in the reader's memory, replacing it with her last, all-encompassing entombment. In manuscript, the final words had none of the implacability of "unvisited tombs," but restored Dorothea's most persistent attribute: "And that things are not so ill with you and me as they might have been is owing to the many of those who sleep in unvisited tombs, having lived a hidden life nobly."[6] This revision from "nobly" to "tombs" denies Dorothea's essence in perpetuity, forcing her into a common limbo touched only by the narrator's pitying, pervasive resignation. The turn of a phrase makes of her energy a forgotten irony, soothing the reader into agreeing that this last enclosure is the way of all aspiring flesh.

The lulling dreariness of Eliot's finale has often been used to epitomize her wisdom. It evokes more accurately a certain lugubrious pall that spreads over women writers when they create women's lives, even at the expense of its own material: for example, one wonders why Dorothea's many children neglect to visit her tomb. Moreover, though male Victorian writers similarly immolate their spirited heroines in marriage, they do not always let them go gentle into that good night. Hardy's Sue Brideshead must cope with the thundering wrath of Jude when she sacrifices herself to marriage: "That a woman-poet, a woman-seer, a woman whose soul shone like a diamond—whom all the wise of the world would have been proud of, if they could have known you—should degrade herself like this! I am glad I had nothing to do with Divinity—damn glad—if it's going to ruin you in this way!"[7] In *Middlemarch,* only the narrator has so exalted a vision of Dorothea's soul, and it is the narrator at the end who snuffs it out.

Similarly, in Henry James' *The Portrait of a Lady,* Ralph Touchett is the vehicle whereby Isabel Archer is reminded, not of life's constriction, but of its boundlessness. Like that of Hardy's Sue, her self-sacrifice in marrying Osmund is a free decision in a multitudinous world, while Dorothea's ultimate sacrifice is made to seem inevitable to the wise reader. Though women's heroines are repeatedly "ground in the very mill of the conventional," as Isabel is, few of them receive her bequest of the possibilities of space: " 'You seemed to me to be soaring far up in the blue—to be sailing in the bright light, over the heads of men. Suddenly some one tosses up a faded rosebud—a missile that should never have reached you—and down you drop to the ground. It hurts me,' said Ralph audaciously, 'as if I had fallen myself!' "[8] I would argue, sadly, that there is something singularly unfemale in the joy of this vision, at least as far as fiction is concerned. A hundred years later, it seems our wings have still been clipped; but it remains a "perversity," to use both Hardy's and James' word, to deny the imagination of an open world of promise and power.

Though Hardy's Sue and James' Isabel both "fall" into grinding convention, their authors bestow on them some of the majesty of tragic choice; moreover, both are endowed with choric suitors to insist on their lambent possibilities had their vision been as large as life's promises. The potential buoyancy of the lives they abandon might seem to be embodied in Louisa May Alcott's stories for girls. For despite the tempering presence of Marmee and other cautionary adults, Alcott's tomboys are boisterously, joyfully ambitious, their hunger for games merging into plans for a triumphant future of "sailing in the bright light, over the heads of men." No doubt this insistence on life's promise and scope continues to make athletic, artistic Jo March in *Little Women* an idealized self for girls today: Jo's scribbling, her impatience, her slang, above all her "romping," provide one of our few literary assurances that talent in a woman can burgeon out of sturdy good health.

The energy and fun of the first half of *Little Women* remove it from the ambience of *Middlemarch,* where "blooming full-pulsed youth" can move only from tomb to tomb. But the half-grotesque renunciation of Jo's marriage, together with the sense of inevitability that accompanies it, recalls the sacrificial consummation of Eliot's elegiac finale. Finally, Jo's romping and writing become embodied in her impossible wish to be a boy. She will not run off to Washington—seat of governmental power as well as escape from home—with her dashing comrade Laurie because the dream is inappropriate for "a miserable girl."[9] Shortly thereafter, she refuses Laurie himself and ultimately marries Professor Bhaer, the most Teutonic of Teutons, whose Spartan life is bare of the art, money, and vibrant physicality which life had seemed to promise Jo. His portliness precludes romping, and his Puritanism precludes writing: in deference to his horror at their effect on the young, she burns her published stories and denounces writing as "selfish." Destiny indulges her sacrifice equivocally: she becomes matriarch of her husband's boarding school, indefatigably tending the boys she can't be and indulging in secret her yearning love for the wildest ones.[10] In the final chapter, "Harvest Time," Marmee blesses her girls, who are now themselves chastened little mothers. This last emphasis on the seasonal cycle insists on the inexorability of Jo's destiny as strongly as had George Eliot's narrative voice of soothing, brooding wisdom. As in *Middlemarch,* the heroine is deprived of a fulminating Jude, or a visionary Ralph Touchett, to comment on the unnatural tragedy of her fall.

The adult and the adolescent classic concur in the message of their heroines' destinies: life, and the marriage with which it ends, are inevitable snuffings-out to which the strong submit. Both Dorothea and Jo are different characters at the end of their novels, more generalized and less vivid than they were. The end of their stories is less a ripening than a blurring into a common penitential destiny, whose assumed universality takes the edge from its betrayal. The traditional comic conclusion that Northrop Frye defines,[11] in which the flexibility of marriage and spring supplant winter's rigid authority, is streaked with tragedy in many women's novels, but the note of tragedy is secret, uncertain, rarely emerging to define itself as it does in corresponding novels by men. The rarity of Antigone's tragic fall is dubiously welded to the commonality of Frye's comic mythos, so that consummation unobtrusively turns to punishment, and the apparent liberation of life's continuity becomes its subtlest prison. The unstated yet implacable resignation which is so pervasive a part of women's literary voice rarely recomposes into heroic rebirth. Dorothea's nobility is extinguished in the final reality of her tomb. In the novel's vision, the closing epithalamium generates death rather than renewal of the spirit, a denial of the heroine's promise more profound than that in *The Portrait of a Lady,* where Ralph Touchett makes a final bequest of Isabel's rebirth, not vicariously through children, but in herself: "You will grow young again." Rarely do women endow their heroines with this resilience, or even with a prayer for it. They are doomed to grow up and leave the stage, though their author may play on till the end.

Today, women do seem as a class to be growing young again, going to school in life's promises as well as its prohibitions. In a decade of expansion, it seems needlessly, even wantonly, restrictive for us to reject what has at times bountifully been offered by literary men. But often to our loss we do. In George Gissing's late Victorian novel *The Odd Women* (1893), Rhoda Nunn rejects love to be a leader of women, her feminism exemplifying one of the few islands of elation in Gissing's dispirited novels. When she makes her final entrance there is no mention of tombs. Instead she exults: "The world is moving!"

For all her resolute anti-romance, Rhoda is one of the few women in fiction to be allowed a heroic identification of herself with her sweeping world. Her boundless identification of herself with space recalls the fluidity of Tennyson's Ulysses in his heroic boast: "I am a part of all that I have met." Though I can find no reason why this unity between the self and its world should be a masculine vision alone, in 1974 it was unequivocally rejected by one of Rhoda's literary descendants: the solitary, self-distrustful Jane Clifford in Gail Godwin's highly regarded novel, *The Odd Woman.*

Alone in a bleak world, trying to cling to an alien family, a self-absorbed lover she rarely sees, and a job whose slightest demands intimidate her, Jane combs desperately through Gissing's novel for a guide to life. But she ends up rejecting everything in it, last of all the heroine herself: "That left 'The world is moving!' 'How are you, Jane?' 'Oh, the world is moving!' She thought of Gerda [a caricatured feminist friend] burning her black candle, signing the death warrant for romantic love, now signing income tax forms for the employees of *Femme Sole.* She crossed off 'SUBLIMATION OF PERSONAL DESIRES AND FURIES INTO A "CAUSE." ' "[12]

Depicted in Gissing's novel as a difficult triumph, Rhoda's breakthrough into the public sphere is sheer loss for Jane Clifford, who dismisses the achievement in knowing pseudo-Freudian jargon as "sublimation." But finally, entombed in her small room and her hopeless daydreams, Jane is a far grimmer and more static character than

Rhoda was; moreover, her stubborn self-paralysis seems a more drastic
insult to a contemporary woman's psyche than were Rhoda's mobility
and courage. But as she sits alone with her notebook, scratching off
one male-created woman after another by turning them into dismissive
stereotypes, Jane Clifford is one image of our time, rejecting a literary
endowment from men that might prove a rich inheritance in favor of
the willed constriction of a very small room.

6.

Robert Browning's Last Word

Were the Brownings really married? This may seem an odd question in light of popular legends about their bliss, but it is a question scholars have been asking with increasing frequency. William Irvine and Park Honan, and more recently Clyde de L. Ryals, find a Browning increasingly estranged from his wife's moralism, political radicalism, and occultism. In their view, Robert Browning's marriage entailed the sacrifice of his deepest convictions and of the irony native to his poetic voice.[1]

Meanwhile, such feminist scholars as Helen Cooper, Dorothy Mermin, Dolores Rosenblum, and Sandra M. Gilbert are reconstructing Elizabeth's spiritual and artistic biography; all find Robert an accidental and ancillary presence as they recover an Elizabeth in quest of an authorizing poetic mother, one who will restore a woman abandoned in patriarchy to her proper legacy of a female culture and a woman's tradition.[2] Along with the jailer/father who once loomed so large in Freudian reconstructions of Elizabeth Barrett's life, the redemptive husband is diminishing to a mere distraction in the woman poet's quest for her lost female inheritance.

Female and male scholars alike are coming to doubt the authenticity of this marriage of poets. Only Flavia Alaya keeps faith, arguing eloquently that politically and poetically, the Brownings were as fully married as they appeared to be.[3] Otherwise, contemporary scholars dismiss the romance that once seemed so enthralling.

Nobody, though, has yet looked closely at the poetry that resulted from this marriage of poets. If, as Phyllis Rose believes, the essence of marriage is storytelling, what stories do the Brownings tell? In examining five Victorian marriages, Rose is struck by

the way in which every marriage was a narrative construct—or two narrative constructs. In unhappy marriages, for example, I see two versions of reality rather than two people in conflict. I see a struggle for imaginative dominance going on. Happy marriages seem to me those in which the two partners agree on the scenario they are enacting, even if . . . their own idea of their relationship is totally at variance with the facts.[4]

Rose avoids the political and literary complications of the Brownings' marriage, but this union of narrative poets exemplifies her theory of married storytelling. As Browning proclaims in his initial letter of invading adoration, their love story was read before it was experienced: "I do, as I say, love these books with all my heart—and I love you too" (quoted in Irvine and Honan, p. 147). Both Elizabeth and Robert Browning were ardent storytellers who felt that the books they produced were bodies. For Elizabeth's Aurora Leigh, "Poems are / Men, if true poems."[5] For Robert, the "pure crude fact" of the Old Yellow Book is "secreted from a man's life when hearts beat hard."[6] The breathing, beating humanness of these books allows us to catechize these narratives as if they were people to discover whether they are congruent or conflicting.

Despite the passionate ambition of *Casa Guidi Windows,* Elizabeth's major work during their life in Florence was her immensely popular epic *Aurora Leigh* (1853–56); Browning's volume *Men and Women* appeared in 1855, during the composition of *Aurora Leigh.* When he returned to England a widower, he transmuted Italy and Elizabeth into his own, fractured epic, *The Ring and the Book* (1868–69). This essay will examine the degree to which Robert Browning's dramatic monologues collaborate with Elizabeth's epic in the creation of a single story, the primary interest being biographical only insofar as poems are alive.[7] The tensions these poems reveal when explored together transcend the perishable, and perhaps happier, lives of the

people who composed them. To use Phyllis Rose's terms, we shall look
at the poems to see whether they agree on a unified story, or whether
they embody two versions of reality in tacit but radical conflict.

Before their marriage, Robert Browning described their
contrasting poetic voices with characteristic deference to Elizabeth's:
"You *do* what I always wanted, hoped to do, and only seem now likely
to do for the first time. You speak out, *you*,—I only make men &
women speak—give you truth broken into prismatic hues, and fear the
pure white light, even if it is in me."[8] In fact, in the "married" poems
this essay considers, the voices were more closely allied than this often-
quoted letter suggests. Elizabeth, if anything, seems to move toward
Robert. In *Casa Guidi Windows*, the poet's "I" announces itself boldly
and often—"I love all who love truth," she proclaims unabashedly—
but in *Aurora Leigh* she forfeits her own voice, for the epic authority
is herself a dramatic character. The glorious free-spirited Aurora has
little in common with the frail, family-beleaguered Elizabeth Barrett,
who lived as the broken daughter her creature escaped becoming.

Aurora Leigh seizes possession of the truth via its author's
abdication of the right to speak out directly: Elizabeth Barrett Browning grants her heroine an authority she herself never claims. In *Men
and Women* and *The Ring and the Book,* Robert Browning abandons
whatever attempt he once had made to "speak out": both volumes are
a cacophony of obscure voices from an exotic past, "tell[ing] a truth /
Obliquely" ("The Book and the Ring," ll. 855–56) as they contradict
each other. Both Robert and Elizabeth claim "the truth," but neither
dares utter it directly. Their methods in this period are more similar
than different. The truths they tell are very different indeed.

Aurora's boast, at the center of her poem, has thrilled
women readers from her day to our own:

> Never flinch,
> But still, unscrupulously epic, catch
> Upon the burning lava of a song
> The full-veined, heaving, double-breasted Age:
> That, when the next shall come, the men of that
> May touch the impress with reverent hand, and say
> "Behold,—behold the paps we all have sucked!"
> This bosom seems to beat still, or at least

> It sets ours beating: this is living art,
> Which thus presents and thus records true life."
>   (V. 213–22)

Through its heroine, *Aurora Leigh* celebrates its epic self audaciously as a grand female body who takes contemporaneity into herself. Nineteenth-century epics abounded in giant female personifications, though few of them had such moist and palpable breasts: Coleridge's Life-in-Death, Byron's Catherine the Great and her controlling female avatars in *Don Juan,* Keats' Moneta, Shelley's Asia, Tennyson's Vivien, Emily Brontë's A. G. A., Swinburne's Atalanta, and on a slighter scale Robert Browning's Pippa are all grand women who in some sense, like Britannia herself, personify their age. But its vaunted contemporaneity sets *Aurora Leigh* apart from other nineteenth-century attempts at epic. The younger Romantics and their Victorian followers set their long poems in a remote and mythic past; *Aurora Leigh* turns scornfully away from work that "trundles back . . . five hundred years. / Past moat and drawbridge, onto a castle-court" (V. 191–92). It decrees that the "sole work [of poets] is to represent the age, / Their age, not Charlemagne's" (V. 202–3).

   In scorning the past and claiming its time, *Aurora Leigh* scorns virtually all present poetry. Taking as its inspiration novels like *Jane Eyre,* which also glorifies the imperious "I" of a heroine with an irrefutably topical career, it seizes the age male bards have shunned. The epic present is personified as a full-breasted woman because, among poets, only insurgent women dare to claim it, just as in *Casa Guidi Windows* and *Poems Before Congress,* only a woman dare embody the revitalized Italy male politicians fear and betray (see Alaya, pp. 14–17). Aurora's denunciation of poets who "flinch from modern varnish," withdrawing into "Roland with his knights at Roncesvalles" (V. 208, 207), may even be a furtive swipe at Robert's great dark "Childe Roland to the Dark Tower Came," though Elizabeth does allow her husband his lizards and toads:

> I do distrust the poet who discerns
> No character or glory in his times,
> And trundles back his soul five hundred years,
> Past moat and drawbridge, into a castle-court,

To sing—oh, not of lizard or of toad
Alive i' the ditch there,—'twere excusable, . . .
[But] dead must be, for the greater part,
The poems made on their chivalric bones.
                                           (V. 189–98)

Nothing in *Aurora Leigh* qualifies this opposition between triumphant
female present and desiccated male past. The brazen "I" who proclaims herself "the Age" reduces to corpses the rich history reanimated
in *Men and Women*, which was published the year before Elizabeth
wrote scathingly about "poems made on . . . bones."

In "Old Pictures in Florence," one of the few nondra-
matic monologues in *Men and Women*, the "I"—is Robert Browning
speaking out at last?—embraces and restores the dead things Aurora
Leigh kicks away. Musing "that Old and New are fellows," the speaker
champions a past that is constantly obliterated:

Their ghosts now stand, as I said before,
    Watching each fresco flaked and rasped,
Blocked up, knocked out, or whitewashed o'er
    —No getting again what the church has grasped
The works on the wall must take their chance.[9]

Aurora's "full-veined, heaving, double-breasted Age" is supplanted by
a past of crumbling plaster, each square of which once blazoned a
vision as ephemeral as the long-dead men and women themselves. The
truth in *Men and Women* expresses itself through the poet's trick of
animating ghosts. The past is its terrain, specifically the male past,
despite a few interpolated utterances by nameless women ("A Woman's Last Word," "Any Wife to Any Husband"). Even the rapturous
tribute to Elizabeth in "One Word More"—"yourself my moon of
poets!" (st. 19, l. 2)—is shadowed ominously by Andrea del Sarto's
sardonic apotheosis of his promiscuous Lucrezia: "My face, my moon,
my everybody's moon" (l. 29). Women may gaze celestially, but the
past Browning animates throngs with male artists, seers, and spiritual
questers of all sorts, engaged not in Aurora's triumphant appropriation
but in the thwarting process of missing their moment.

The failure of the past to survive bestows on it Robert
Browning's seal of authenticity. His "contemporary"—who is of course

no longer contemporary with Victorian readers—is singularly myopic.
In "How It Strikes a Contemporary," a worldly man frets about a poet
who cloaks himself in silent anonymity:

> He took such cognisance of men and things,
> If any beat a horse, you felt he saw;
> If any cursed a woman, he took note;
> Yet stared at nobody,—they stared at him,
> And found, less to their pleasure than surprise,
> He seemed to know them and expect as much.
>   (ll. 30–36)

Elizabeth Barrett Browning imagines the contemporary poet
as public and female. Aurora Leigh snatches at her vocation by crowning herself; in her later aesthetic, her grand self-image crowns herself
not with a wreath but with her age. Like a fountain spouting in the
middle of a park, she cannot but be noticed. Robert's contemporary
exudes spying, staring, and secrecy. His poet is the most cloaked and
private of men, whose contemporaries exist to be known, not to know
him. Aurora is the seen, while Robert's obliquely perceived poet is the
seer. She takes life from contemporaneity; his provisional life comes
only after he has crumbled into the past. These different visions are
not so much at war as they are mutually exclusive. For each poet, the
world of the other is unreal, inhabited by the half-alive.

Moreover, in Keats' terms, Elizabeth Barrett Browning's
epic celebrates the egotistical sublime, even if the ego is not directly
the poet's own, while Robert's volume displays the virtuosity of the
chameleon poet. From the first page, *Aurora Leigh* assaults us with a
torrent of "I"'s and "my"'s. At the end, the power of the "I" is, if
possible, intensified, for Aurora's godly lover, blinded and abased, per-
mits her to "shine out for two" (IX. 910). Robert's speakers never
claim such paramount authority. The vociferousness and copiousness
of the volume allow them to elbow each other aside; the robust "Zooks!"
of Fra Lippo Lippi means more to us with the "dust and ashes" of
Galuppi's toccata echoing in our ears. The delicate orchestration of
the volume prevents any single speaker from achieving full authority,
while it gives each the authority to undermine the claims of the rest.

Moreover, the form of the dramatic monologue undermines by its very nature the claims of the epic. Robert Langbaum's

influential study emphasizes what we would now call reader response
to the dramatic monologue as it suspends us tantalizingly between
sympathy and judgment.[10] On the face of it, though, the dramatic
monologue makes fewer demands on the reader than the epic does.
The epic concerns itself with our acquiescence. If, after reading *Paradise Lost*, we do not feel that the ways of God have been justified, the
bard has failed, though the poem may have succeeded wonderfully. If
after reading *Aurora Leigh*, we fail to accept Aurora as the capacious
spirit of her turbulent age, the poem has insufficiently captivated us.
In dramatic monologues, the speakers turn their designs away from us,
directing their insistence to a generally skeptical listener. We hear and
observe the speaker not in full face, but at an angle, through a glass
darkly, relieved of the full force of his or her obsessed attention. Unlike the epic bard, the speaker is at no great pains to persuade us.

The unbelieving auditor, not the pressure of truth, dictates the dramatic monologue. The unseen authoritarian husband in
"A Woman's Last Word" orchestrates his wife's utter, and utterly
disingenuous, collapse; the ham-handed, torch-waving guard dictates
for that moment who Fra Lippo Lippi is, just as Lucrezia's scorn gen
erates Andrea's self-scorn, or Saul's soul-sickness, David's prophetic
self-glorification. Not only are the selves of these speakers denied absolute authority, but they are in the process of continual and convoluted formation according to the auditors' unspoken demands. "So
free we seem, so fettered fast we are," sighs Andrea for all these lux-
uriantly loquacious speakers. He is, in Browning's world, right, but
God does not lay down the fetters: they arise from the constraint
imposed by those unsympathetic others who dictate to the malleable
self what it should be. The dramatic monologue celebrates self-creation, but it is a self-creation enforced by the power of skepticism over
the insecurity of being. Other listeners would probably dictate other
poems. In its essence, the dramatic monologue asks of us neither sympathy nor judgment. Rather, it strikes home to us the impurity of our
own tale telling, the ways in which our own truth has been adjusted
not to a remote and acquiescent audience, but to our intimates who
don't believe us.

Browning's dramatic monologues, then, are an oblique
defense of the "prismatic hues" of his poetic truth, exposing the fat-
uousness of accusations like F. J. Furnivall's, in 1881:

The interest of [Browning's "Essay on Shelley"] lay in the fact that Browning's "utterances" here are *his*, and not those of any one of the "so many imaginary persons" behind whom he insists on so often hiding himself, and whose necks I for one should continually like to wring, whose bodies I would fain kick out of the way, in order to get face to face with the poet himself, and hear his own voice speaking his own thoughts, man to man, soul to soul. Straight speaking, straight hitting, suit me best.[11]

For Browning, there is no single "face to face" revelation, but only faces, each one of which imprints a different soul, and thus a different truth, on its interlocutor.

For Elizabeth, on the other hand, face to face revelations were an absolute experience of epiphany and salvation. As Dolores Rosenblum puts it, "Looking into the mirror face of a mother-sister marks Aurora's discovery of an integrated self and a poetics" (p. 335). The spiritual authorities Elizabeth holds dearest dissolve mockingly in Robert's *Men and Women* to a pageant of distorted refractions. We are not seen by others with the grandiosity we see in ourselves, Robert's volume reminds us. The self is embarrassingly adjustable, contemporaneity embarrassingly obtuse. The corrosive power of Robert's poems over Elizabeth's iconography may have determined the sudden violence that ends *Aurora Leigh:* Aurora's mocking lover/cousin Romney is struck blind, and so can be married without danger. Aurora's eyes alone will see, thus retaining the power to make of all faces what Rosenblum calls "mirror faces." The integrity of her vision will never be undermined by skeptical reflections in another's eyes.

So far, in looking at *Men and Women* in conjunction with *Aurora Leigh,* we find, as in our own arms race, explosive material each poet is afraid to use. The vision in each book could be lethal to the other one, so they sit side by side, never quite in contact. Perhaps Robert speaks for both poets when he defines the nervous truce of "A Woman's Last Word":

> What so false as truth is,
>   False to thee?
> Where the serpent's tooth is,
>   Shun the tree—
>
> Where the apple reddens
>   Never pry—

Lest we lose our Edens,
Eve and I!
(ll. 13–20)

Once the worst had happened—Elizabeth's death and the
loss of his Italian exile—Robert freed himself to transplant her material and her legend into his own poetic territory. During her life, she
had regarded his fascination for the Old Yellow Book with some horror (see, for instance, Irvine and Honan, p. 409); when he melded its
violence and intrigue into *The Ring and the Book,* he must at last have
known she was dead. To be safe, though, he killed her again. His
absorption of Elizabeth's iconography—particularly the glorification of
Marian Erle in *Aurora Leigh* as a holy twin of the supreme woman
poet who personifies her age—resurrects his sainted wife in order to
butcher her in the person of Pompilia. His most radical butchery is
spiritual. *The Ring and the Book* erodes Elizabeth Barrett Browning's
cherished systems of salvation, a devastation over which he makes her
preside in the attenuated person of "Lyric Love."

Lyric Love has little in common with the vibrantly physical poet evoked in book V of *Aurora Leigh.* Since she is "half angel
and half bird," she has no breasts and little blood to speak of; since
"heaven [is her] home," she has evaporated helplessly out of her age,
passing from cynosure to spectator, forced to gaze on a bloody past
she cannot affect. *Aurora Leigh* dismissed the "ghosts" *Men and Women*
restored. Now, Elizabeth herself is relegated to ghostliness, while Robert reanimates the seventeenth century in all its confused vitality. The
woman who claimed to embody her age has been pushed into a past
more remote than Italy's, forced to become the Muse of a tale she
never would have told.

Moreover, Elizabeth Barrett Browning's most cherished
material is part of the base metal out of which Robert forges his ring.
Aurora Leigh celebrates the choric power of female community: its
triumphant achievement is not Aurora's marriage to the diminished
Romney, but her union with the victimized seamstress, Marian Erle.
In the best tradition of fairy tale princes, the wealthy Romney has
reached down to "save" Marian from her abased class and gender, only
to be rejected twice; Aurora does save her, not by elevating her, but by
recognizing and ratifying her absolute truth. Together, Aurora and

Marian exemplify the mystic interdependence of the female victim and queen, an interdependence which (as I have argued elsewhere) is a resonant presence in Victorian iconography.[12] *The Ring and the Book* mutes this vibrant union to the solitary whisper of the moribund Pompilia, whose truth is heard only by the pure of heart and the dying. This pale, isolated heroine drains from female truth its clarion authority.

In *Aurora Leigh,* both Aurora and Marian tell stories that have an instantaneous impact. Aurora's stories—her poems, and the poem we are reading—are validated by their immediate success; her age crowns her truth. Marian's two stories have a similar authoritative impact on their sole hearer, Aurora herself. When they first meet, she tells the initially skeptical Aurora the sad story of her life. Most of Robert Browning's auditors would remain skeptical, thus squeezing Marian's tale into that embarrassed compound of lies and semitruths that constitutes the dramatic monologue. Aurora, on the other hand, is instantly converted, authenticating Marian's history by blending it into her own:

> She told me all her story out,
> Which I'll retell with fuller utterance,
> As coloured and confirmed in after times
> By others and herself too.
>
> (III. 827–30)

Our bard Aurora confirms Marian's truth without question by transmuting it into her own, utterly reliable language.

Later, a chastened Aurora and a Marian purified by humiliation meet again in Paris. This time, Marian's wildly implausible tale of abduction, rape, and miraculous motherhood needs no validation: Aurora allows her to tell it at length, in her own voice. Its truth is instantaneously apparent. Without hesitation or attempts at confirmation, Aurora writes to a powerful friend:

> "Dear Lord Howe,
> You'll find a story on another leaf
> Of Marian Erle"—what noble friend of yours
> She trusted once, through what flagitious means,
> To what disastrous ends;—the story's true."
>
> (VII. 235–39)

The truth of Marian's stories echoes and reinforces the truth Aurora
claims for herself as the self-crowning bard of her own life history.
The embodiments of truth know each other instantly in *Aurora Leigh*,
as the good people do in Dickens' novels, because their very beings are
illuminated. Thus, when Marian finds her mission in motherhood, we
must not doubt that God has taken her shape:

> For, Romney, angels are less tender-wise
> Than God and mothers: even *you* would think
> What *we* think never. He is ours, the child;
> And we would sooner vex a soul in heaven
> By coupling with it the dead body's thought,
> Than, in my child, see other than . . . my child.
> We only never call him fatherless
> Who has God and his mother.
>   (IX. 407–15, Elizabeth Barrett Browning's eli-
>   sion)

Even the best of men are excluded from this God-endowed authority
of true womanhood: God obligingly abdicates his conventional father-
hood to legitimize a mother's self-completeness. As Marian is to her
child, so is Aurora to her poem. Both women are the only begetters
the sole, self-consecrating authorities in a world with no other legitimate storytellers. Their affinity with God irradiates their spiritual power
In *The Ring and the Book*, Pompilia's intimacy with God assures that
she will be silenced for 170 years.

In recasting his wife's epic into his own, Robert Browning
compressed these two powerful women into a single, dying young girl
he also modulated the elation of inspiration into the agony of sanctification. Pompilia's large eyes, her fineness of perception, her aesthetic
and pictorial instinct, all look back to Aurora Leigh, as well as to
Elizabeth Barrett Browning; the ordeal of her victimization is Marian
Erle's. But Pompilia's truth rests in her martyrdom, not in the story
she barely articulates. The inspired utterances of Aurora and Marian
become the Christ-like wounds displayed involuntarily by a saint whose
seal of purity is her illiterarcy.

Aurora's quasi-allegorical name announces her; even when
she marries Romney, she need never change it. By contrast, Pompilia'
ornate names martyr her with lies:

'T is writ so in the church's register,
Lorenzo in Lucina, all my names
At length, so many names for one poor child,
—Francesca Camilla Vittoria Angela
Pompilia Comparini,—laughable!
("Pompilia," ll. 3–7)

In fact, of course, Pompilia's final name is legally "Franceschini." Her wishful omission of her husband's patronym does her no good: the marriage for which she is murdered and martyred is the salient fact of her life. Names do not express Pompilia, but oppress her. Her inexorable weight of names indicates her marginal position in her age: in her militance as well as her martyrdom, she is a hallowed spirit of anticultural life. It is impossible to imagine seventeenth-century Rome personified as a giant, heaving-brested Pompilia; the spirit of the age is embodied in the men who shout and dissemble and display themselves as she lies dying. The authenticity of Pompilia's truth lies in her very removal from the turbulent contemporary life Aurora Leigh embodied. The spiritual authority of Elizabeth Barrett Browning's women is thrust to the margins of the social and political life her poetry of the 1850s celebrated.

It may be Robert Browning's ultimate victory over his celebrated wife that he robs Pompilia of a public voice. Aurora Leigh's glory was more bardic than moral, a glory she shared with the oral poet Marian. Robert Browning is at pains to bless Pompilia, his own victim/queen, with illiteracy, though the Old Yellow Book proves that the historical Pompilia could both read and write.[13] Pompilia herself uses illiteracy as a badge of distinction opposed to her falsifying weight of names. Aurora Leigh's writing exalted her as the spirit of her age, while Pompilia's inability to write exalts her by isolating her from that age:

How happy those are who know how to write!
Such could write what their son should read in time,
Had they a whole day to live out like me.
Also my name is not a common name,
"Pompilia," and may help to keep apart
A little the thing I am from what girls are.
(ll. 82–87)

"'The thing I am" removes her utterly from the life of her culture, almost from humanity itself; like Lyric Love, "half angel and half bird," Pompilia forfeits human privileges. The Pope's soliloquy authorizes her by blessing her most un—Aurora Leigh—like silence: after apotheosizing her as "perfect in whiteness," the Pope muses:

> It was not given Pompilia to know much,
> Speak much, to write a book, to move mankind,
> Be memorized by who records my time.
> ("The Pope," ll. 1019–21)

Because she is neither the author nor the spirit of her age, Pompilia shines as the "one prize" in the secret ruminations of the lone, dying Pope.

Her silence is rewarded with a fittingly secret benediction: like Pompilia, the Pope speaks in soliloquy.[14] The purity of both is immunized from the ambiguous entanglements of the dramatic monologue. Pompilia is spoken about incessantly in street and court, but she speaks only to an indeterminate audience in the privacy of her deathbed, and her death is more speaking than her words. Pompilia's glory is her secret, fitted only for the intimacies of soliloquy and death. Had she dared to glorify herself in public, as Aurora Leigh did, Browning's poem assures us that no one would have noticed.

Since the trial does in fact vindicate Pompilia's innocence, *The Ring and the Book* might well have ended with general recognition of the dead saint. Instead, it ends in a tangle of dark and unregenerate activities with the bitter refrain "Let God be true, and every man a liar." The lawyer who had "sainted" her plans to indict her as a "person of dishonest life," allowing the Convertite nuns to claim her property; and these presumably are the very nuns who heard her deathbed soliloquy. Far from being instanteously converted, as Aurora Leigh was by Marian Erle's tales, the Convertites repudiate her truth and proceed on their hale if unglorified way.

Pompilia may be "perfect in whiteness," at least in the Pope's somber account, but her words have no more authority than the other words that fly around in this poem, whose "tongue" proves indeed "a two-edged sword" ("The Book and the Ring," l. 708). Like Marian Erle before her, Pompilia exalts the absolute and divine power of her motherhood, claiming kinship with a mothering God who expunges male violence:

> Let us leave God alone!
> Why should I doubt He will explain in time
> What I feel now, but fail to find the words?
> My babe nor was, nor is, nor yet shall be
> Count Guido Franceschini's child at all—
> Only his mother's, born of love not hate!
> ("Pompilia," ll. 1759–64)

Pompilia asserts her divinely sanctioned self-sufficiency only to have the poem destroy it. Even the fitfully omniscient narrator corrects her and puts her in her place:

> Well, proving of such perfect parentage,
> Our Gaetano, *born of love and hate,*
> Did the babe live or die?—one fain would find!
> What were his fancies if he grew a man?
> Was he proud,—a true scion of the stock,—
> Of bearing blason, shall make bright my Book—
> Shield, Azure, on a Triple Mountain, Or,
> A Palm-tree, Proper, whereunto is tied
> A Greyhound, Rampant, striving in the slips?
> Or did he love his mother, the base-born,
> And fight i' the ranks, unnoticed by the world?
> ("The Book and The Ring," ll. 812–22, my
> italics)

Browning's narrator is unyielding: Pompilia is allowed no mitigation of her invisibility and silence. Gaetano's inheritance from her is not glory, but the distinction of being consistently unnoticed. U. C. Knoepflmacher has explored ways in which, under Elizabeth's influence, Robert Browning gives a voice to the martyred women his earlier poems had silenced.[15] This is so, but *The Ring and the Book* is ruthless in insisting that if the saving poet had not descended to give Pompilia his own versatile voice, she would have been forever unheard. Elizabeth Barrett Browning's "unscrupulously epic" claims for absolute authority in her age are in *The Ring and the Book* suppressed with loving brutality. The story of Pompilia, who is perfect in whiteness and exemplifies truth, suggests that a woman speaks with purity only by dying unheard.

Having survived a poet who made epic claims for herself, Robert Browning perpetuated her voice by turning it into his own; he "married" Elizabeth Barrett one more time when he appropriated her after her death, weaving her declarations into the corrosive fabric of his dramatic monologues. According to Irvine and Honan, she had found from the first something sinister in his ability to read her: "She had been frightened of him at first. She felt he had a power over her, that he could read her thoughts as he might read a newspaper" (p. 192). This initial ability to read Elizabeth ripened into an ability to write her and finally, with love and reverence, to silence her.

Having lived beyond his marriage, Robert Browning had a man's last word. Characteristically, his final tribute to Elizabeth twisted the promise that was, in "A Woman's Last Word," a wife's'

> Teach me, only teach, Love!
> As I ought
> I will speak thy speech, Love,
> Think thy thought.
> (ll. 25–28)

Robert Browning ended up by speaking his wife's speech and thinking her thought, but in muting them to a dying whisper among dramatic monologues, he drained them of authority. Initially, he had praised Elizabeth enviously for her capacity to "speak out"; finally, he spoke out for her, making her voice one of many testimonies to the superior survival power of a poet who could "make men & women speak." In his crowning work, he added his wife to the chorus of his creations.

7.

Dickens and Dombey:
A Daughter After All

Dickens' daughter's indictment—"My father did not understand women"[1]—continues to gain momentum, until for some readers, it has threatened to obliterate his entire achievement.[2] His heroines are regularly dismissed as "so many pale-pink blancmanges, in the same dutiful mold";[3] he is placed historically as "not so much the recorder of Victorian womanhood as the dupe or the exploiter of its ideal."[4]

But if Dickens dreamed the Victorian dream of "wooman, lovely wooman" diffusing rarefied conjugal salvation to man in his besotted worldliness, his life and his novels quietly dramatize its component human loss. The "two nations" into which his England was divided defined the worlds of the sexes as well as those of Disraeli's rich and poor. Men and women were allotted different boundaries, different dreams, different vices and virtues; the ideal woman revolved alone in her unique "sphere," suggesting a cosmic dimension to the home she created and purified as an intermittent refuge for men from the machinery of their lives. Despite the wedding bells that clang manically through Dickens' novels, there is a note of sexual sadness and loss of the heart of all his work that suggests the isolation inherent in this sexual division, looking forward to such formulated feminist com-

plaints as that of Elizabeth Wolstenholme: "Of the saddest results of
the separate education and life of the sexes, it is impossible here to
speak; as a slighter, but still mischievous result, it is sufficient to notice
the profound ignorance of each other's real nature and ways of thinking common to both men and women. . . . Many a life has been
wrecked upon mistakes arising out of this ignorance."[5]

As *Great Expectations* is Dickens' most definitive indictment of his own earlier dream of miraculous metamorphosis from waif
into gentleman, so *Dombey and Son* seems to me his most thorough
exploration of his own and his contemporaries' doctrine of the "two
spheres," with each sex moving in a solitary orbit inaccessible to the
other one. The distance between the icy merchant, Paul Dombey, Sr.,
and his boundlessly loving daughter, Florence, and the incessant need
of each for the other, disclose more intimately one reality behind Victorian sexual relationships than does the transfiguration of Dickens'
forgettable lovers when the plot forces them together. Unable to sit
easily together in the same room, father and daughter illuminate a
cultural abyss which is reflected in the stereotyped gestures toward bliss
of Dickens' husbands and wives.

Throughout his novels, Dickens' dream of love is inseparable from his dream of kinship. Even Pip's obsession with Estella,
which is usually considered the most sustained and adult passion in
the canon, is revealed at the end to be effectively the love of brother
for sister. After his own separation from his wife, Dickens tried to
stave off rumors about his affair with Ellen Ternan in conventional
language with ambiguous overtones: "I know her to be innocent and
pure, and as good as my own dear daughters."[6] As in Freud's Victorian paradigm of emotional development, the language of love is at one
with the language of family. But among the novels, *Dombey and Son*
alone stays within the family walls and reveals the emotional waste
beneath its institutional pieties. In most of Dickens' novels, "home"
is "an intimate and emotion-laden word,"[7] a vague haven of love and
light waiting to embrace the wandering protagonists. But in *Dombey*,
Dickens writes: "Oh for a good spirit who would take the house-tops
off, with a more potent and benignant hand than the lame demon in
the tale, and show a Christian people what dark shapes issue from
amidst their homes, to swell the retinue of the Destroying Angel as he
moves forth among them!" (p. 648).[8] The novel's narrator, who is

himself the "good spirit' hovering over the action and exposing it, reveals the pestilence hidden in "home," rather than reassuring us at the end with its glow.

The rift of home in *Dombey and Son* is defined by the rift between Mr. Dombey and Florence, who spend much of the novel haunting their solitary rooms in the great dark house and brooding about each other. They are the polar deities of this polarized novel, and the tension between them generates the tension of the book. They exist as absolutes, memorable less for their individual psychologies than for their magnitude as embodiments of masculinity and femininity as these were conventionally perceived. According to Sylvia Manning: "In his work Dickens reveals a certain consciousness, though never articulated, of a polarity between the male and female that is both physiological and psychological and of this duality of the sexes as a reflection of metaphysical realities."[9] Dombey and his daughter are scarcely plausible as physiological and psychological beings alone; in the novel's scheme, they seem less to reflect than to embody the "metaphysical realities" Manning defines, as the iron force of Dombey's masculine will gives way before Florence's quietly irresistible magnetic field. In Victorian terminology, the power of the man who controls the world gives way before the influence of the woman who controls the mind. A popular conduct book of the day demarcates the spheres in which power and influence, respectively, exert their sway:

[Man's] power is principally exerted in the shape of authority, and is limited in its sphere of action. [Woman's] influence has its source in human sympathies, and is as boundless in its operation. . . . We see that power, while it regulates men's actions, cannot reach their opinions. It cannot modify dispositions nor implant sentiments, nor alter character. All these things are the work of influence. Men frequently resist power, while they yield to influence an unconscious acquiescence.[10]

Men and women possess the world and the self, respectively, and their holdings do not touch. Seen in the light of these radically separate spheres, *Dombey and Son* tells the story of male and female principles who can neither evade nor understand each other, whose tragedy and whose force come from their mutual exclusiveness.

In the first chapter of the novel, the postures and the rhythms of the central characters introduce us to the warring worlds they embody. Stiff and erect as always, Dombey jingles his "heavy gold watch-chain" over his newborn son and heir. Meanwhile Florence clings to her dying mother, her hair spreading over the pillow as Mrs. Dombey's consciousness ebbs away on "the dark and unknown sea that rolls round all the world" (p. 10). The ticking of Dombey's watch fights the silence of birth and death, seeming to speed up incessantly in a senseless race with that of Dr. Peps, until, in Florence's embrace, his wife cuts herself loose from time.

The loud watch which is so inseparable a part of Dombey is the voice of the civilization which gives him his power. The implacable, arbitrary dominance of clock time counterpoints his wife's equally implacable diffusion into death and space; time here is masculine; space, feminine. The tendency of his watch to accelerate is an emblem of his own attempt to force natural processes to march to the imperious rhythm of his manufactured ticking: "Therefore he was impatient to advance into the future, and to hurry over the intervening passages of [Paul's] history" (p. 91). "Dear me, six will be changed to sixteen, before we have time to look about us" (p. 138), he insists as he sends Paul to Dr. Blimber's "great hothouse" in which "all the boys blew before their time" and 'Nature was of no consequence at all" (p. 141). Captain Cuttle, who lives near the sea's cycle, has a ritual formula to prevent his own treasured silver watch from outrunning nature—"Put it back half an hour every morning, and about another quarter towards the afternoon, and it's a watch that'll do you credit" (p. 269)—but Dombey, with his network of power, seems to have no reason to check the time he carries with him in his pocket.

The new reliance on watches, with their arbitrary and manufactured measurement of arbitrary and manufactured time units, was a reality in the 1840s and 1850s: England was in the process of attuning itself to the railroad and its schedule. Later in the novel, the loud ticking of Mr. Dombey's watch will swell into the railroad's prefabricated roar, in a manner which is anticipated beforehand:

Wonderful Members of Parliament, who, little more than twenty years before, had made themselves merry with the wild railroad theories of engineers, and given them the liveliest rubs in cross-examination, *went down into the north with their watches in their hands,* and sent on messages before by the electric telegraph, to say that they were coming. Night and day the conquering engines rumbled at their distant work, or, advancing smoothly to their journey's end, and gliding like tame dragons into the allotted corners grooved out to the inch for their reception, stood bubbling and trembling there, making the walls quake, as if they were dilating with the secret knowledge of great powers yet unsuspected in them, and strong purposes not yet achieved. (pp. 218–19, my italics)

As the railroad and the watch came to demarcate the day, the agricultural calendar, with its seasons and ceremonies of growth and harvest, receded into a picturesque anachronism: natural rural time was out of joint with most men's lives.[11] But its organic and cyclical rhythms are still a powerful reality in *Dombey and Son:* in the sea that "rolls round all the world" which Dombey tries to wind up like his watch; in the "odd weedy little flowers" in the bonnets and caps of Miss Tox, and the "strange grasses" that are "sometime perceived in her hair"; and in the agricultural immortality with which Polly Toodles comforts Florence for the loss of her mother:

> "Died, never to be seen again by any one on earth, and was buried in the ground where the trees grow."
> "The cold ground?" said the child, shuddering again.
> "No! The warm ground . . . where the ugly little seeds turn into beautiful flowers, and into grass, and corn, and I don't know what all besides. Where good people turn into bright angels and fly away to Heaven!" (p. 24)

To Dombey, who lives by progression, events are completed by the ceremonies which define them: funerals, christenings, and weddings. At the same time, the females are the custodians of the natural cycle of eternal return, guarding its unwilled comings and goings with their somewhat ominous ability to wait.

To Dombey, this other, revolving world is invisible: he "intimated his opinion that Nature was, no doubt, a very respectable institution" (p. 289). He is as single-minded an artifact of civilization as his watch is. Early in the novel, we see him "turning round in his easy chair, as one piece, and not as a man with limbs and joints" (p. 15). His identification of himself with the machinery of his civilization is at one with his emphatic masculinity. Throughout the book, he is referred to in terms of his stiffness, rigidity, unbendingness, which at times seem to make him less a phallic symbol than the thing itself: "The stiff and stark fire-irons appeared to claim a nearer relationship than anything else there to Mr. Dombey, with his buttoned coat, his white cravat, his heavy gold watch-chain, and his creaking boots" (p. 52). "He is not 'brought down,' these observers think, by sorrow and distress of mind. His walk is as erect, his bearing as stiff as ever it has been" (p. 240). Toward the end of the novel, Mrs. Brown reduces his perpetual erectness to one unconquerable attribute: "Oh, hard, hard, hard!" (p. 725). This almost incantatory insistence upon a single set of traits makes Mr. Dombey seem the appropriate male divinity of an iron world.

His ethos is at one with his inveterate phallicism. Though he is supposed to be the Victorian businessman par excellence, reducing everything to financial terms, his outlook is more fundamentally sexual than it is monetary; he is more aware of his firm's thoroughgoing maleness than of its profits. His vision is cosmic and complete. He will not bring the flowing Polly Toodles into contact with his son until he has masculinized her by forcing on her the name of "Richards." His firm is the masculine axis at the turning of the world: "The earth was made for Dombey and Son to trade in, and the sun and moon were made to give them light. Rivers and seas were formed to float their ships; rainbows gave them promise of fair weather; winds blew for or against their enterprises; stars and planets circled in their orbits, to preserve inviolate a system of which they were the centre. Common abbreviations took new meanings in his eyes, and had sole reference to them. A. D. had no concern with anno Domini, but stood for anno Dombei—and Son" (p. 2). Unlike other overweening institutions in Dickens' novels—Chancery in *Bleak House,* or the Circumlocution Office in *Little Dorrit*—Dombey and Son is defined in terms that are sexual and metaphysical rather than social. It exists as a gigantic end, the source and destination of all motion, all order, the center not so much of its society as of its universe.

Implicit in this religion is its sense of the female as defective because she is out of tune with the basic masculine rhythm of the cosmos. "But what was a girl to Dombey and Son! In the capital of the House's name and dignity, such a child was merely a piece of base coin that couldn't be invested—a bad Boy—nothing more" (p. 3). Dombey's devaluation of the lovely Florence is the first hint of his lack of business skill, his obsession with gender rather than profits, for in fact a girl is an excellent investment if she is equipped to marry well: Mrs. Skewton knows this as she hawks her accomplished and exquisitely groomed Edith, Mrs. Brown as she sells her Alice. Dombey's inability to see beyond his inviolate masculine "system" into the female business of love is the flaw that will bring down his House. His vision of a girl as nothing more than "a bad Boy" recalls the sick spleen of Tennyson's narrator in *Locksley Hall,* published four years before *Dombey:*

> Weakness to be wroth with weakness! woman's pleasure,
>   woman's pain—
> Nature made them blinder motions bounded in a shallower
>   brain:
> Woman is the lesser man, and all thy passions, matched
>   with mine,
> Are as moonlight unto sunlight, and as water unto wine—
>   (ll. 149–52)

Like Dombey, Tennyson's speaker judges woman by himself, refusing to recognize her as unique and discrete. The lesson of *The Princess* will correct him: "For woman is not undevelopt man, / But diverse" (VII.259–60). From the recognition of incompatibility comes conversion into love. This vision of love predicated on divergence is inherent in the titles of the two lectures that form John Ruskin's *Sesame and Lilies,* "Of Kings' Treasuries" and "Of Queens' Gardens." His strictures in the latter admonish many Dombeys: "We are foolish, and without excuse foolish, in speaking of the 'superiority' of one sex to the other, as if they could be compared in similar things. Each has what the other has not: each completes the other, and is completed by the other: they are in nothing alike."[12] But this sweet ideal of mutual completion scarcely takes place in the torn *Dombey* world. As Dombey becomes increasingly aware of Florence as something more potent than "a bad Boy," he is also increasingly—and, it seems, justly—aware of her as his antagonist, exposing rather than completing him by her unlikeness: "Who was it whose least word did what his utmost means could not! . . . She was leagued against him now. Her very beauty softened natures that were obdurate to him, and insulted him with an unnatural triumph" (p. 561). As Sarah Lewis writes in her conduct book: "Men frequently resist power, while they yield to influence an unconscious acquiescence."

Dombey himself, who is all power, seems at first imper-

vious to any influence whatever: "It seemed as if its icy current, instead of being released by this influence [of his schemes for his son]
and running clear and free, had thawed for but an instant to admit its
burden, and then frozen with it into one unyielding block" (p. 47)
But the influence equipped to thaw this unyielding block of power is
expressed prophetically in Polly Toodles' first words about Florence:
"I never saw such a melting thing in all my life!" (p. 23). Florence
herself is literally melting in that she weeps incessantly, but she is most
important as an almost disembodied influence that causes the melting
of others around her. Unlike her father's power, her influence is unwilled: she will never "make an effort," as her aunt Louisa bemoans.
Its operation is unconscious, almost psychic: "[Mr. Dombey] almost
felt as if she watched and distrusted him. As if she held the clue to
something secret in his breast, of the nature of which he was hardly
informed himself. As if she had an innate knowledge of one jarring
and discordant string within him, and her very breath could sound it"
(p. 29). In contrast to her father's rigidity, Florence is, like George
Eliot's Dorothea Brooke, "incalculably diffusive," almost shapeless,
seeming to seep into the recesses of the mind. Her genius for presiding
over sickbeds has seemed ghoulish to some readers; [13] the avidity with
which she nurses her dying brother, and seems almost to leap at her
father whenever he is sleeping, injured, or ill, reminds us that to many
Victorians, woman's true sphere was neither the kitchen nor the bed-
room, but the sickroom. [14] Yet a sickroom needs a patient, and Florence's melting influence needs her father supine; she can touch him
only at the end, when she can nurse him. As Moynahan puts it,
"Florence wants to get Dombey's head down on the pillow where she
can drown him in a dissolving love." [15] Her "woman's mission" is to
make the stiff and erect spreading and diffuse in a manner ungraspable
by definition: women's influences "act by a sort of moral contagion,
and are imbibed by the receiver as they flow from their source, without
consciousness on either side." [16] If Dombey is so rigid that he seems
to lack joints, Florence, the novel's undiluted woman, seems to have
liquidity as her essence: she, too, is less a body with limbs and joints
than purely a "melting thing."

 The kinship between Dombey and Florence lies in the
single-minded obsessiveness of their approaches to life. If "the one
idea of Mr. Dombey's life" is the House, an inviolate masculine sys-

em of regulated enterprise, "nothing wandered in [Florence's] thoughts
ut love—a wandering love, indeed, and cast away—but turning always
o her father. There was nothing . . . that shook this one thought,
r diminished its interest" (pp. 254–55). As these absolute ideas can-
ot coexist in a single universe, father and daughter can only try to
bliterate each other. After his son's death, Dombey hands to the
tatuary his inscription for the monument:

> "Will you be so good as read it over again? I think there's a
> iistake."
> "Where?"
> The statuary gives him back the paper, and points out, with his
> ocket rule, the words, "Beloved and only child."
> "It should be 'son,' I think, Sir?"
> "You are right. Of course. Make the correction." (p. 241).

And when Florence is struck by her father: "She only knew that she
ad no Father upon earth, and she said so, many times, with her
uppliant head hidden from all, but her Father who was in Heaven"
o. 681). This radical denial is in part a result of the distance between
Kings' Treasuries" and "Queens' Gardens"—that "profound igno-
ance of each other's real nature and ways of thinking" that Elizabeth
Volstenholme was to see as one of the tragedies of the age, and which
1 *Dombey and Son* is the blight of the family.

For despite their distance from each other, Dombey's power
nd Florence's influence are alike in their potentially murderous seeds:
[Mr. Dombey] stood in his library to receive the company, as hard
nd cold as the weather; and when he looked out through the glass
oom, at the trees in the little garden, their brown and yellow leaves
ame fluttering down, as if he blighted them" (p. 52). Florence seems
t times an equally blighting force: "As the image of her father whom
he loved had insensibly become a mere abstraction, so Edith, follow-
ig the fate of all the rest about whom her affections had entwined
hemselves, was fleeting, fading, growing paler in the distance, every
ay" (p. 652). The language of this passage implies that, like that of
he vampire, Florence's love drains its objects into ghosts. In this she
esembles the child described by Paul's lugubrious nurse, Mrs. Wickam:
She took fancies to people; whimsical fancies, some of them; others,
ffections that one might expect to see—only stronger than common.

They all died" (p. 106). Florence's love seems as secretly lethal as Dombey's ambition is overtly life-withering. Their very isolation in their own absoluteness, whereby they contain nothing of each other, is the only bond between father and daughter, and, it seems, between the sexes in general. In part, they kill because "they are in nothing alike."

This schism between masculine and feminine spheres seems more fundamental to the novel's world than the usual division critics make between the "money world" of the firm and the "water world" of the Wooden Midshipman group. Gender links these inviolate male systems together against the depredations of the Mrs. MacStingers of the earth. In *Dombey and Son* and throughout Dickens's other novels, money is ultimately fluid and plentiful, and class lines are illusory and easily crossed. The real, and absolute, barrier is sexual, and it separates not merely individuals, but the landscape of the novel itself.

The two main symbols that dominate *Dombey and Son* can be divided equally into male and female poles which exclude each other. We have seen the link between Dombey's accelerating watch and the new rhythms of the railroad, between the incessant flow of Florence's tears and that of the sea. Each can generate life, but, untempered by the other, each becomes the reaper of its own kind of death.[17]

Like Mr. Dombey, the railroad is an artifact of civilization, the sphere of the mechanical and masculine rather than the organic and feminine. It, too, is part of a closed and regulated system, without flowing and diffusing beyond one. Like Dombey on a grand scale, the railroad embodies phallic force; and like clock time's, its progress is implacably linear. Dombey is always wishing for time to end in the apocalypse of Paul's development from self into Son: a boy has "a destiny" as the train has a preordained destination, to which terminus its violent movement is directed. The train, like the man again, has no private language; its voice is deafeningly public; its speech is "a shriek, and a roar, and a rattle," "a shrill yell of exultation." Dombey's careful periodic eloquence is meant only to be heard by all ears. In chapter 1, he can scarcely lower his voice to say "my dear," and later he forces Carker to intervene between himself and Edith, so repugnant is private conversation to him. The railroad pulls together all the values of his masculine sphere.[18] Its shrieking linear progress makes us turn with relief to the secret, private sphere of feminine dissolution.

Florence's realm, the sea, exists independent of the mechanized products of civilization. It is natural and eternal: Paul's dying vision relates it both to Brighton and to the River of Life, flowing through Paradise. Like the ebb and flow of the female cycle, its cyclical ebbs and flows bear no relation to the human will; its rhythms are involuntary and unconscious, related to the flow of emotion and dream; lacking a destination to shape its movements, it has all the interminable attraction of a world without end. Unlike the railroad's shriek, its voice is quiet and its language is private: only Paul can hear "what the waves are always saying," and that only when he is on the edge of death. The mindlessness of its repeated motions reminds us of Florence's incessant returns to the unyielding breast of her father until it melts for her. Her persistence seems more plausible in geological than in psychological terms: throughout most of the novel, her movements are as involuntary and unwilled as the sea's are. Her kinship with the sea is appropriate to her role as vessel of woman's influence, which is "imbibed by the receiver as [it] flows from [its] source, without consciousness on either side."

Opposed as they are in every way, the railroad and the sea have similar effects: both are simultaneously fertile and murderous. Our first awareness is of the lively, generative power of the railroad: it brings prosperity to the good and prolific Toodleses, and gives birth to the bursting community of Stagg's Gardens. But on Dombey's long journey to Leamington, it snakes into an engine of death, plowing through a wasteland, its iron will the final blind extension of the Dombey creed of "making an effort": "The power that forced itself upon its iron way—its own—defiant of all paths and roads, piercing through the heart of every obstacle, and dragging living creatures of all classes, ages, and degrees behind it, was a type of the triumphant monster, Death" (p. 280). The waste and sterility with which its power is finally associated erupt symbolically in Carker's "mutilated fragments"; retributive though his death is, the explosion of his body and Dombey's swoon suggest the train's unnatural, annihilating arrival at its final destination. The last words in the chapter describe "some dogs" "[sniffing] upon the road, and [men soaking] his blood up, with a train of ashes" (p. 779). The "conquering engines" have become "a train

of ashes," whose accelerating progress, like Dombey's, destroys more
life than it conceives.

The sea, too, seems full of vitality at first. Its power underlies the thriving firm of Dombey and Son itself, as well as its raucous and kindly analogue, the Wooden Midshipman's, with its chan-
teys and sea tales and toasts. Yet Mrs. Dombey and Paul ebb away on
the sea, which, like the railroad, becomes a type of "the old, old fashion—Death!" Florence's loving influence is itself a sweet drowning
and dissolution. In its boundless sweep toward eternity, the sea carries
the danger of loss of contour, of sanity, of life itself, until the living
and the dead reach to interpenetrate:

> "As I hear the sea," says Florence, "and sit watching it, it brings
> so many days into my mind. It makes me think so much—"
> "Of Paul, my love. I know it does."
> Of Paul and Walter. And the voices in the waves are always
> whispering to Florence, in their ceaseless murmuring, of love—of love, eternal
> and illimitable, not bounded by the confines of this world, or by the end of
> time, but ranging still, beyond the sea, beyond the sky, to the invisible coun-
> try far away! (p. 811)

As Florence seems to preside over the sea, traditional mysticism comes
together with a ravenous hunger for death. This sense of life "not
bounded by the confines of this world," but spilling over to touch
death, gives the tone to Dombey's cathartic rebirth at the end of the
novel, as Florence succeeds at last in encircling his prone head in her
oceanic arms. Moynahan is right to see a loss of will, of contour, of
intelligence and strength, in Dombey's final conversion into a weeping
old man dripping love at the seashore: "Ambitious projects trouble
him no more. His only pride is in his daughter and her husband"
(p. 873). Carker's iron death was an abrupt explosion into an ending;
Dombey's baptismal death is more of an interminable ebb. But the
shrieking "train of ashes" and the "ceaseless murmuring" of the waves
both produce the vitality of loss, not of growth. The masculine and
the feminine, the mechanical and the vital, the temporal and the spa-
tial, untempered by each other's qualities, become destroyers. The separation between railroad and sea metaphysically extends the separation
between Mr. Dombey and Florence at the heart of the novel's split
world.

Many of the secondary characters in the novel play variations on the idea of the two spheres. The separation between the sexes
that prevails in *Dombey and Son* reminds us over and over that "they
are in nothing alike"; but certain bizarre and equivocal mutations lead
to a suggestion of what we now call an androgynous vision, or to Emily
Davies' stubborn insistence in Dickens' own time that "there is a deep
and broad basis of likeness between the sexes." Perhaps the likeness
that glimmers sometimes in *Dombey and Son* will lead to a reconciliation that the central movement of the book does not provide.

Like Dombey, Major Bagstock lives in a sphere inhabited
exclusively by men and manliness: the "systems" at the center of his
world are the army and his club, although he does peer vindictively
through his telescope at his faded neighbor Miss Tox, as Dombey peers
under his handkerchief at Florence. His explosive wheezes that he is
"tough, sir, tough" seem an inflammatory variant of Dombey's icily
self-sustaining pride; and despite his toadyism and treachery, his spon-
sorship of Dombey is a more compatible relationship than either of
Dombey's marriages. Indeed, at his second wedding, Dombey seems to
be marrying the Major rather than Edith, so firmly are the two knit
together at that point. The Game Chicken, whose life consists of eating and hitting, is a similar parody of manliness rampant. He glues
himself to Toots as Bagstock does to Dombey, in a sad alliance of
sportsmanlike celibacy against the depredations Florence has made in
Toots' heart and wardrobe.

In a sense, the novel's hell and heaven are found in communities of men. Dr. Blimber's Academy is an inviolate male system
like the Dombey firm, although it admits the unfeminine Cornelia,
who has been classically educated like a boy, and tolerates as chorus
the effusions of her mother. With its remorselessly ticking clock and
its pale reading boys, the "forcing apparatus" of Blimber's establishment is made to bear responsibility for the loss of Toots' wits and
Paul's life. The blighting male "system" Dombey worships finds its
most potent incarnation at Blimber's.

But at the blessed masculine unit of the Wooden Midshipman, Toots and Paul—in the form of the resurrected Walter,
Florence's sturdy brother-lover—are to some degree restored. The domestic habits and rituals of Sol Gills, Captain Cuttle, and Walter Gay
are dwelt upon at great length, being in fact the only domesticity we

are allowed to see in the novel. As a result, we are inundated with their curiosities of housekeeping and the logistics of cooking with a hook. Captain Cuttle's early injunction to Walter seems one of the novel's few genuine sacraments: " 'Wal'r!' he said, arranging his hair (which was thin) with his hook, and then pointing it at the Instrument-Maker, 'Look at him! Love! Honour! And Obey! Overhaul your catechism till you find that passage, and when found turn the leaf down. Success, my boy!' " (p. 41).

The "marriage" between the three of them, and their consecrated home, are given purpose and solidarity by absent women: by the dreadful vision of Mrs. MacStinger, drowning the men in her washing day and snatching the Captain in wedlock, and by their collective aspiration to Florence, who offers a less overtly coercive baptism. The dependence of this home on the sea, and the tears that are shed so copiously there, link it with Florence's "melting" world. When she escapes to it from her father's house, there is a subtle, involuted suggestion that there, at least, the sexes may be in something alike:

Unlike as they were externally—and there could scarcely be a more decided contrast than between Florence in her delicate youth and beauty, and Captain Cuttle with his knobby face, his great broad weather-beaten person, and his gruff voice—in simple innocence of the world's ways and the world's perplexities and dangers, they were nearly on a level. . . . A wandering princess and a good monster in a story-book might have sat by the fireside, and talked as Captain Cuttle and poor Florence thought—and not have looked very much unlike them. (pp. 684–85)

The mutual housekeeping Cuttle and Florence perform for each other in chapters 48 and 49, where each outdoes the other in dexterity, is the novel's only sustained description of the sexes working and thinking in a single sphere; and as the language above demonstrates, the Wooden Midshipman is a fairy-tale world and these similarities may be fairy-tale transformations. Gills and Cuttle are sanctified, in a somewhat saccharine manner, by their exemption from manhood. Cuttle is literally maimed, and Gills is saved from bankruptcy only by Dombey's icy magnanimity; like a woman's, their sphere is self-possessed in being dispossessed. As the hero, Walter must conventionally "succeed" in a nebulous way and leave the Wooden Midshipman once he grows up; but as character actors, Gills and Cuttle exchange loss of power for female selfhood. Their all-male system becomes a domestic idyll whose table can at the end accommodate both Dombey and Daughter.

Failure and poverty can create a childlike haven where men are free to melt toward womanhood, but little Paul Dombey, forced into power, is not so lucky. His life begins when his father jingles a watch chain at him, and it ends in Florence's arms, rushing from the river to the sea which is Death. Since Paul *is* the child of which Captain Cuttle is the facsimile, one might hope that his presence would reconcile the antinomies of Dombey and Florence. But though he does his best, even suggesting to his father's horror that Florence be allowed into the firm, he is finally wrenched between the two worlds and destroyed in his passage from one to the other. His postures in the first scene in which we see him foreshadow the rhythm of his short life. At five, he is his father's eerie parody:

They were the strangest pair at such a time that ever firelight shone upon. Mr. Dombey so erect and solemn, gazing at the blaze; his little image, with an old, old, face, peering into the red perspective with the fixed and rapt attention of a sage. Mr. Dombey entertaining complicated worldly schemes and plans; the little image entertaining Heaven knows what wild fancies, half-formed thoughts, and wandering speculations. Mr. Dombey stiff with starch and arrogance; the little image by inheritance, and in unconscious imitation. The two so very much alike, and yet so monstrously contrasted. (pp. 91–92)

As in the tableau of Florence and Captain Cuttle above, union springs out of "monstrous" differences. Though Paul's participation in the stiff, erect posture of his father's sphere is inherited and instinctive, it is unnatural as well: his inheritance withers him, giving the child "an old, old, face." When Florence comes, he melts back into nature, with "a countenance so much brighter, so much younger, and so much more child-like altogether," but in his passage to his sister's sphere he sinks back toward a state of prebirth. When she takes him in her arms, he seems almost to dissolve: "She was toiling up the great, wide, vacant staircase, with him in her arms; his head was *lying* on her shoulder, one of his arms *thrown negligently* round her neck. So they went, toiling up; she singing all the way, and Paul sometimes crooning out a *feeble* accompaniment" (p. 95, my italics). Dombey's stiff Paul and Florence's boneless one look almost like two different boys. The moral of his transition might be "damn braces, bless relaxes"; but from another perspective, Paul moves from unnatural alertness to tender debility: enervated by his father's world, he drowns in his sister's. Little Paul Dombey passes in the book from a harbinger of a new, androgynous whole to a victim of his House's unhealed division.

So far, it seems as though only children and childlike men can incorporate the feminine into their natures; the Wooden Midshipman thrives because of it, and Paul dies in part because of it. But Carker, the villain of the novel, is in one sense farthest of all from Dombey's stiff and erect masculinity, despite the fact that, unlike Gills and Cuttle, he never weeps, never loves, and seems never to have been innocent. This "sleek, hushed, crouched" man works on those around him, not with the direct authority of Dombey's male power, but with the indirect insinuation of female influence.

Carker seems at first an exaggerated shadow of the stiffness and rigidity of his master. But we soon learn that he is quite the opposite of that upright public man: he is infinitely flexible and secret, and he is *acting* Mr. Dombey for his own private amusement. Like Florence's, his medium is silence. He does not make his power felt directly through language, but telegraphs sympathy in his "voiceless manner of assent" that makes his statements rather felt than heard. He communicates with Florence in a manner eerily close to telepathy: "Confused, frightened, shrinking from him, and not even sure that he had said those words, for he seemed to have shown them to her in some extraordinary manner through his smile, instead of uttering them, Florence faintly said that she was obliged to him, but she would not write; she had nothing to say" (p. 352). Carker's occultly revealed words and the "nothing" that Florence has "to say" to her father seem to rise out of the same quasi-magical source. In their conjunction, the silence of Cordelia meets that of the Cheshire Cat.

According to Sarah Lewis, indirection is one of the defining characteristics of female influence: it is never asserted, but diffuses unconsciously into the breast of the other. Dombey's fear that Florence is in uncanny possession of "something secret in his breast" is repeated in Edith's fear of Carker's equally wordless knowledge: "But, does Edith feel still, as on the night when she knew that Mr. Dombey would return to offer his alliance, that Carker knows her thoroughly, and reads her right, and that she is more degraded by his knowledge of her, than by aught else? Is it for this reason that her haughtiness shrinks beneath his smile, like snow within the hand that grasps it firmly, and that her imperious glance droops in meeting his, and seeks the ground?" (p. 444). Like Florence's, Carker's influence causes its object to melt and droop. But the possession of such influence seems to make of a woman a heroine, a man a villain.

Florence creeps stealthily through the house at night to crouch before her father's rooms; alone in his office, Carker plays secret games that bring the House down. Mr. Dombey can play no games and has no affinities with these silent, secret characters, though ironically, he might have been a better businessman if he had: "feminine" flexibility and love of play may be part of the remunerative virtue Florence would have brought into the firm had Paul been permitted to include her. Instead, Carker's feminine indirection destroys firm and family. Their fall is Florence's ascension, but Carker, who is so much like her, seems to be destroyed by all the vengeful masculine power of the universe (chs. 54, 55). Edith stands before him with a knife; [19] the enraged Dombey is at the door, and suddenly, Carker is swept into a frenzy of linear motion. Night and day flash past each other on his stagecoach journeys, repeating the inhuman acceleration of Dombey's watch in chapter 1. His flight recapitulates the furious noisy plunge of Dombey's railroad journey to Leamington until the final explosion of death, a giant eruption of the maleness he had tried to soften with his wiles. Carker's death inverts little Paul's, who had reached toward the feminine and disappeared into it: the recreant Carker is destroyed in a phallic roar. The good Toodles speaks what could be his epitaph in the voice of the train: "You see, my boys and gals . . . wotever you're up to in a honest way, it's my opinion you can't do better than be open. If you find yourselves in cuttings or in tunnels, don't you play no secret games. Keep your whistles going, and let's know where you are" (p. 534). Feminine tears may flow, but feminine secrecy and silence cannot temper the "shriek, and the roar, and the rattle" of the book's iron masculinity.

Like the men in the novel, the women range from being elaborate embodiments of their sexual essence to incorporating traits of the other sex that strengthen and doom them. Miss Tox, who is repeatedly described as being about to evaporate, follows Dombey around with a shadowy submissiveness that parallels Florence's. When we see "poor excommunicated Miss Tox water[ing] her plants with her tears" (p. 419), we are taken back to Florence's liquid essence and her solitary alliance with the natural cycle. But neither Florence nor Miss Tox is infected by the vituperation that expels them from Dombey's system. They transmit a "moral contagion," but they receive none: "There was no such thing as anger in Miss Tox's composition" (p. 532).

The moral contagion transmitted by Mrs. Skewton is the degenerate parody of the "womanly influence" celebrated in Florence's eventual triumph. Mrs. Skewton is "wooman, lovely wooman" in all her tendency to decay. Her arch romanticism, her invocation of "nature" and "heart," and even her tendency to dissolve—she literally comes apart every night, in a corrupt female foreshadowing of Carker's "multilated fragments"—suggest the cloying underside of the "melting thing" and the values attached to it. "New Voices in the Waves," the chapter in which her hideous death is described, adds an ugly sound to the "ceaseless murmuring" of Florence's liquid sphere. In repudiating her mother's values, Edith repudiates more than the humiliation of the marriage market: she seems to rebel against the novel's entire notion of a womanhood in which "heart" and "nature" melt together with "no such thing as anger" in its composition.

Opposed to the lachrymose and decomposing elements in Mrs. Skewton and Miss Tox are a forbidding bevy of "anti-women," in Sylvia Manning's phrase: Louisa Chick, Cornelia Blimber, Mrs. Brown, and Mrs. Pipchin. Louisa's martial creed of "making an effort," Cornelia's spectacles and books and worship of precision, make them the unnurturing opposite of Florence's crooning love. Mrs. Brown, chewing on her pipe as she forces Florence into her own daughter's rags, is the visionary ogre of a mother Florence may be lucky to have lost, of whom Polly Toodles is the endlessly bountiful and one-dimensional inversion. Mrs. Pipchin, too, is an "ogress and child-queller," monstrous in part because she has relinquished wetness and grafted on to herself the hardness and dryness of the novel's male sphere: she has a "hard grey eye, that looked as if it might have been hammered at on an anvil without sustaining any injury"; "one was tempted to believe . . . that all her waters of gladness and milk of human kindness had been pumped out dry, instead of the mines" (p. 99). Mrs. Pipchin has some kinship with the mutilated Captain Cuttle, in that both suggest the hybrid that may be the other side of the triumphantly reconciling androgyne. But the dangerously self-aware Edith Grainger gives us an anti-heroine who blurs together the two extremes of decomposing "wooman" and arid anti-woman.

As Carker insinuated "feminine" privacy and fluidity into the masculine sphere of Dombey and Son, so Edith brings "masculine" pride and professionalism to the female sphere of home. From the beginning, Edith preempts Dombey's masculine language. She is "handsome," rather than "beautiful" or "pretty," and in her pride, she is equally "hard, hard, hard": "So obdurate, so unapproachable, so unrelenting, one would have thought that nothing could soften such a woman's nature, and that everything in life had hardened it" (p. 624). But her basic affinity with Dombey lies in the fact that she, too, is a merchant, and she knows it. The insistent connection between Edith and her "shadow," the fallen woman Alice Marwood, points to the anomalous position of the Victorian woman on the marriage market, displaying her accomplishments like a merchant hawking his wares. Society, economics, nature, and God combined to define the real business of a woman's sphere as Esther Summerson's quest in *Bleak House:* "to win some love to myself if I could." In practice, the purposeful pursuit of love was a woman's "trade," a word which is the meeting place of "profession" and "barter." Thus, sentiment combines with ironic plausibility in Florence's early dream of her new mother: "And now Florence began to hope that she would learn, from her new and beautiful Mama, how to gain her father's love; and in her sleep that night, in her lost old home, her own Mama smiled radiantly upon the hope, and blessed it. Dreaming Florence!" (p. 407). Motherless as she is, Florence's education in enticing accomplishments has been neglected, and Edith might plausibly teach her the tricks of the trade of winning some love. The professionalization of femininity by "a world of mothers" created an uneasy liaison between lady and whore which is dramatized in *Dombey and Son* and fully exposed in Eliza Lynn Linton's notorious article "The Girl of the Period," written over twenty years later.[20] Eliza Lynn Linton brought to her readers' conscious awareness Dickens' insight that respectable young women were neither shunning nor saving their fallen sisters, but emulating their style in order to catch men. Lady and whore were one, not by virtue of a sanctified bond of sisterhood—which Dickens burlesques as a "free-masonry in fainting" in chapter 29—but by virtue of their similar trades.

Sisterhood is a tenuous thing in *Dombey and Son*, easily snapped because it is not institutionalized as male fellowship is, and exalted only between such remotely connected beings as Alice and the chaste Harriet Carker, or Edith and the innocent Florence. The genuine kinship between Edith and Alice is in no way elevated by the narrator, because of its masculine, professional nature: "[Alice] caught her arm, and drawing it before her own eyes, hid them against it, and wept. Not like a woman, but like a stern man surprised into that weakness; with a violent heaving of her breast, and struggle for recovery, that showed how unusual the emotion was with her" (p. 482). "[Edith] had changed her attitude before he arrived at these words, and now sat—still looking at him fixedly—turning a bracelet round and round her arm; not winding it about with a light, womanly touch, but pressing and dragging it over the smooth skin, until the white limb showed a bar of red" (p. 565).

In a series of pantomimic gestures, Edith and Alice reveal their essential masculinity. Like Dombey, whose stiffness is his soul, their bodies reveal their essences. But the ultimate masculine trespass of both women—the analogue of Carker's "secret games"—is the rage which removes them irrevocably from Miss Tox, who waters her plants with her tears, her lachrymose nourishment containing "no such thing as anger." "*I* am angry. I have been so, many years," says Alice to Dombey (p. 725). Edith almost repeats her words to Carker: "My anger rose almost to distraction against both [Dombey and Carker]. I do not know against which it rose higher—the master or the man!" (p. 761).

At one important point, this rage seems even to scar Florence, the book's paradigm of femininity. After her flight, she finds her inheritance written on her breast as a brand of a female Cain: "Then she knew—in a moment, for she shunned it instantly—that on her breast there was the darkening mark of an angry hand." But her response to this masculine stain is characteristically Tox-like, looking forward to the baptismal rhythm of the end: "Her tears burst forth afresh at the sight; she was ashamed and afraid of it; *but it moved her to no anger against him*. Homeless and fatherless, she forgave him everything; hardly thought that she had need to forgive him, or that she did; but she fled from the idea of him as she had fled from the reality, and he was utterly gone and lost. There was no such Being in the world" (pp. 680–81, my italics).

Love washes the angry mark of masculinity out of the universe. The death of Alice, a fallen woman who is more erect than the heroine, seems the death of a personified metaphysical principle in the novel's world: "Scorn, rage, defiance, recklessness, look here! This is the end" (p. 823). And so it is. Before she is banished to Italy, Edith seems to melt under Florence's forgiveness: "Edith, as if she fell beneath her touch, sunk down on her knees, and caught her round the neck" (p. 868). As Carker must be dismembered, the angry women must dissolve so that an increasingly ghostly Florence can preside: " 'No, [I am] nothing, Walter. Nothing but your wife.' The light hand stole about his neck, and the voice came nearer—nearer. 'I am nothing any more, that is not you' " (p. 789). Drained of her anger and aggression, she seems as close to evaporating as Miss Tox was at the beginning. Having become "a light hand," "a voice," and nothing more, she is ready to mount her throne as the womanly woman triumphant.

"Dombey and Son is a daughter after all." Miss Tox and the indefatigably maternal Polly Toodles return to close the great house that had banished them both. The entire world seems to melt into the feminine sphere, which is now "Chiefly Matrimonial." Susan Nipper, whose defiant fury was a comic analogue of Edith's and Alice's, follows her mistress into bustling marriage to a transformed Toots who has begun to talk like a more reverent Mr. Dombey. Miss Tox's suddenly potent influence redeems Rob the Grinder, the victim of Dombey's charitable system, into penitent respectability. The chapter concludes as Mrs. MacStinger drags Bunsby to the altar, leaving Captain Cuttle prey to horrible matriarchal visions of an eternal proliferation of daughters in a world without men: "One of the most frightful circumstances of the ceremony to the Captain, was the deadly interest exhibited therein by Juliana MacStinger; and the fatal concentration of her faculties, with which that promising child, already an image of her parent, observed the whole proceedings. The Captain saw in this a succession of man-traps stretching out infinitely; a series of ages of oppression and coercion, through which the seafaring line was doomed" (p. 857).

Dombey himself seems less to succumb to Florence than

to become her; by the end of the novel, he *is*, literally, "a daughter after all." Louisa Chick accuses him of the same sin of which she had accused Florence at the beginning: "If my brother will not make an effort, Mrs. Pipchin, what is to become of him? I am sure I should have thought he had seen enough of the consequences of *not* making an effort, by this time, to be warned against that fatal error" (p. 834). When Florence finds him, he is drifting through the empty house in a dream, just as she herself had done after his departure for Leamington. In their union, that part of civilization represented by Mr. Dombey seems to devolve back into her waiting sea, which destroys as much as it nourishes. The last chapter finds Dombey as faded as Miss Tox and as enfeebled as the dying Paul, weeping on his granddaughter at the seashore. The great system of which he was the center is replaced by a relationship remarkable for its privacy and secrecy. "He hoards her in his heart," having moved from total exteriority to total interiority. The end is something like that of *Idylls of the King*, with the sea waiting to swallow the last relics of a burnt-out civilization; in both, the ocean and the women that belong to it are placidly antagonistic to the efforts of a masculine civilization which excludes them. The ocean watches the fall of empires with a dead face. If we read *Dombey and Son* carefully, we can feel the rage that underlies its quiet rhythms.

I do not think that Dickens ever moved beyond the polarized vision delineated in *Dombey and Son*, and never afterward does he explore so thoroughly the schism between masculinity and femininity as his age defined them. Despite those forced happy marriages that look so much like deaths in his novels, his treatment of sexuality is infused with a troubled, tragic awareness of the gulf between the sexes. Its veneer may be complacency, but its essence is loss, as a famous letter expresses: "Why is it, that as with poor David, a sense comes always crushing on me now, when I fall into low spirits, as of one happiness I have missed in life, and one friend and companion I have never made?"[21] Life never produced the dream of love he willed so hard to believe, and his best writing is true to this sense of deprivation. It seems callow to denounce Dickens as a patriarch when his exploration of a patriarchy can produce the sexual laceration of a *Dombey and Son*, and I think it is misleading to overemphasize the change in his books that resulted from the furtive, apparently unhappy liaison with Ellen Ternan. His later heroines are still strangers, of a different species from the male characters, insulated in a sphere so much their own that they can never reach over to become "friends and companions." Born in the same year as his daughter Katey, Ellen seems to have remained a stranger to Dickens as well: " 'I had it,' said Canon Benham, 'from her own lips, that she loathed the very thought of the intimacy.' "[22]

Though "Nelly" was so much like the ingenue daughter he wrote about, who saves the wicked old man from his sins by loving him at the last minute, she denied Dickens after his death. But he had real daughters as well, who eerily resembled the daughter he created in *Dombey and Son* when they were children. Mamie apparently remained as true as Florence to the memory of her father stage-managing Christmas: "My love for my father has never been touched or approached by any other love. I hold him in my heart of hearts as a man apart from all other men, as one apart from all other beings."[23] Writing on her deathbed, Mamie preserved her father in the remote and solitary sphere which on her own deathbed Katey puncutred in the name of their mother: "I loved my father better than any man in the world—in a different way of course. . . . My father was a wicked man—a very wicked man. . . . Ah! We were *all* very wicked, not to take her part."[24] Kate Perugini's posthumous corroboration of the gossip about Dickens and Ellen may finally have broken through the silence between father and daughter. Like Florence, she used her indirect influence to redeem her mother by wearing away the armor of her father's reputation. In so doing, she gave us our present Dickens, the haunted man, and took away the memory of Christmas.

8.

Alice and Wonderland: A Curious Child

"What—is—this?" he said at last.
"This is a child!" Haigha replied eagerly, coming in
front of Alice to introduce her. . . . "We only found it
today. It's as large as life, and twice as natural!"
    "I always thought they were fabulous monsters!" said the
Unicorn. "Is it alive?"

For many of us, Lewis Carroll's two *Alice* books may have provided the first glimpse into Victorian England. With their curious blend of literal-mindedness and dream, formal etiquette
and the logic of insanity, they tell the adult reader a great deal about
the Victorian mind. Alice herself, prim and earnest in pinafore and
pumps, confronting a world out of control by looking for the rules and
murmuring her lessons, stands as one image of the Victorian middle-
class child. She sits in Tenniel's first illustration to *Through the Look-*

Lewis Carroll, *The Annotated Alice: Alice's Adventures in Wonderland & Through the Looking-Glass*, Martin Gardner, ed. (New York: Clarkson N. Potter, 1960), p. 287. Future references to this edition will be incorporated into the text.

ing-Glass and What Alice Found There in a snug, semi-fetal position, encircled by a protective armchair and encircling a plump kitten and a ball of yarn. She seems to be a beautiful child, but the position of her head makes her look as though she had no face. She muses dreamily on the snowstorm raging outside, part of a series of circles within circles, enclosures within enclosures, suggesting the self-containment of innocence and eternity.

Behind the purity of this design lie two Victorian domestic myths: Wordsworth's "seer Blessed," the child fresh from the Imperial Palace and still washed by his continuing contact with "that immortal sea," and the pure woman Alice will become, preserving an oasis for God and order in a dim and tangled world. Even Victorians who did not share Lewis Carroll's phobia about the ugliness and uncleanliness of little boys saw little girls as the purest members of a species of questionable origin, combining as they did the inherent spirituality of child and woman. Carroll's Alice seems sister to such famous figures as Dickens' Little Nell and George Eliot's Eppie, who embody the poise of original innocence in a fallen, sooty world.

Long after he transported Alice Liddell to Wonderland, Carroll himself deified his dream child's innocence in these terms:

What wert thou, dream-Alice, in thy foster-father's eyes? How shall he picture thee? Loving, first, loving and gentle: loving as a dog (forgive the prosaic simile, but I know of no earthly love so pure and perfect), and gentle as a fawn: . . . and lastly, curious—wildly curious, and with the eager enjoyment of Life that comes only in the happy hours of childhood, when all is new and fair, and when Sin and Sorrow are but names—empty words, signifying nothing![1]

From this Alice, it is only a step to Walter de la Mare's mystic icon, defined in the following almost Shelleyan image: "She wends serenely on like a quiet moon in a chequered sky. Apart, too, from an occasional Carrollian comment, the sole medium of the stories is *her* pellucid consciousness."[2]

But when Dodgson wrote in 1887 of his gentle dream child, the real Alice had receded into the distance of memory, where she had drowned in a pool of tears along with Lewis Carroll, her interpreter and creator. The paean quoted above stands at the end of a long series of progressive falsifications of Carroll's first conception, beginning with Alice's pale, attenuated presence in *Through the Looking-Glass*. For Lewis Carroll remembered what Charles Dodgson and many later commentators did not, that while *Looking-Glass* may have been the dream of the Red King, *Wonderland* is Alice's dream. Despite critical attempts to psychoanalyze Charles Dodgson through the writings of Lewis Carroll, the author of *Alice's Adventures in Wonderland* was too precise a logician and too controlled an artist to confuse his own dream with that of his character. The question "Who dreamed it?" underlies all Carroll's dream tales, part of a pervasive Victorian quest for the origins of the self that culminates in the controlled regression of Freudian analysis. There is no equivocation in Carroll's first *Alice* book: the dainty child carries the threatening kingdom of Wonderland within her. A closer look at the character of Alice may reveal new complexities in the sentimentalized and attenuated Wordsworthianism many critics have assumed she represents, and may deepen through examination of a single example our vision of that "fabulous monster," the Victorian child.

Lewis Carroll once wrote to a child that while he forgot the story of *Alice*, "I think it was about 'malice.' "[3] Some Freudian critics would have us believe it was about phallus.[4] Alice herself seems aware of the implications of her shifting name when at the beginning of her adventures she asks herself the question that will weave through her story: "I wonder if I've been changed in the night? Let me think: *was* I the same when I got up this morning? I almost think I can remember feeling a little different. But if I'm not the same, the next question is, 'Who in the world am I?' Ah, *that's* the great puzzle!" (p.37). Other little girls traveling through fantastic countries, such as George Macdonald's Princess Irene and L. Frank Baum's Dorothy Gale, ask repeatedly *"Where* am I?" rather than *"Who* am I?" Only Alice turns her eyes inward from the beginning, sensing that the mystery of her surroundings is the mystery of her identity.

Even the above-ground Alice speaks in two voices, like many Victorians other than Dodgson-Carroll:

She generally gave herself very good advice, (though she very seldom followed it), and sometimes she scolded herself so severely as to bring tears into her eyes; and once she remembered trying to box her own ears for having cheated herself in a game of croquet she was playing against herself, for this curious child was very fond of pretending to be two people. (pp. 32–33)

The pun on "curious" defines Alice's fluctuating personality. Her eagerness to know and to be right, her compulsive reciting of her lessons ("I'm sure I can't be Mabel, for I know all sorts of things") turn inside out into the bizarre anarchy of her dream country, as the lessons themselves turn inside out into strange and savage tales of animals eating each other. In both senses of the word, Alice becomes "curiouser and curiouser" as she moves more deeply into Wonderland; she is both the croquet game without rules and its violent arbiter, the Queen of Hearts. The sea that almost drowns her is composed of her own tears, and the dream that nearly obliterates her is composed of fragments of her own personality.[5]

As Alice dissolves into her component parts to become Wonderland, so, if we examine the actual genesis of Carroll's dream child, the bold outlines of Tenniel's famous drawing dissolve into four separate figures. First, there was the real Alice Liddell, a baby belle dame, it seems, who bewitched Ruskin as well as Dodgson.[6] A small photograph of her concludes Carroll's manuscript of *Alice's Adventures Under Ground*, the first draft of *Wonderland* (figure 8.1). She is strikingly sensuous and otherworldly; her dark hair, bangs, and large inward-turned eyes give her face a haunting and haunted quality which is missing from Tenniel's famous illustrations. Carroll's own illustrations for *Alice's Adventures Under Ground* reproduce her eeriness perfectly (figure 8.2). This Alice has a pre-Raphaelite langour and ambiguity about her which is reflected in the shifting colors of her hair.[7] In some illustrations, she is indisputably brunette like Alice Liddell; in others, she is decidedly blonde like Tenniel's model Mary Hilton Badcock; and in still others, light from an unknown source hits her hair so that she seems to be both at once.[8]

Mary Hilton Badcock has little of the dream child about her.[9] She is blonde and pudgy, with squinting eyes, folded arms, and an intimidating frown (figure 8.3). In Carroll's photograph of her, the famous starched pinafore and pumps appear for the first time (Alice Liddell seems to have been photographed in some sort of nightdress) and Mary moves easily into the clean, no-nonsense child of the Tenniel drawings (figure 8.4). Austin Dodson wrote,

> Enchanting Alice! Black-and-white
> Has made your charm perenniel;
> And nought save "Chaos and old Night"
> Can part you now from Tenniel.

But a bit of research can dissolve what has been in some ways a mis-leading identification of Tenniel's Alice with Carroll's, obscuring some of the darker shadings of the latter.[10] Carroll himself initiated the shift from the subtly disturbing Alice Liddell to the blonde and stolid Mary Badcock, as "under ground" became the jollier-sounding "Wonder-land," and the undiscovered country in his dream child became a nursery classic.

The demure propriety of Tenniel's Alice may have led readers to see her role in *Alice's Adventures in Wonderland* as more passive than it is. Although her size changes seem arbitrary and terri-fying, she in fact directs them; only in the final courtroom scene does she change size without first wishing to, and there, her sudden growth gives her the power to break out of a dream that has become too dangerous. Most of Wonderland's savage songs come from Alice: the Caterpillar, Gryphon, and Mock Turtle know that her cruel parodies of contemporary moralistic doggerel are "wrong from beginning to end."[11] She is almost always threatening to the animals of Wonder-land. As the mouse and birds almost drown in her pool of tears, she eyes them with a strange hunger which suggests that of the *Looking-Glass* Walrus who weeps at the Oysters while devouring them behind

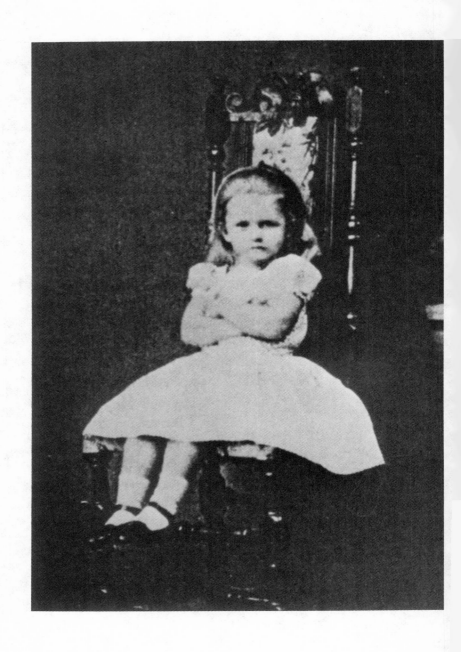

his handkerchief. Her persistent allusions to her predatory cat Dinah and to a "nice little dog, near our house," who "kills all the rats" finally drive the animals away, leaving Alice to wonder forlornly—and disingenuously—why nobody in Wonderland likes Dinah.

　　　Dinah is a strange figure. She is the only above-ground character whom Alice mentions repeatedly, almost always in terms of her eating some smaller animal. She seems finally to function as a personification of Alice's own subtly cannibalistic hunger, as Fury in the Mouse's tale is personified as a dog. At one point, Alice fantasizes her own identity actually blending into Dinah's:

'How queer it seems," Alice said to herself, "to be going messages for a rabbit! I suppose Dinah'll be sending me on messages next!" And she began fancying the sort of thing that would happen: " 'Miss Alice! Come here directly, and get ready for your walk!' 'Coming in a minute, nurse! But I've got to watch this mousehole till Dinah comes back, and see that the mouse doesn't get out.' "

(p. 56)

While Dinah is always in a predatory attitude, most of the Wonderland animals are lugubrious victims; together, they encompass the two sides of animal nature that are in Alice as well. But as she falls down the rabbit hole, Alice senses the complicity between eater and eaten, looking-glass versions of each other:

"Dinah, my dear! I wish you were down here with me! There are no mice in the air, I'm afraid, but you might catch a bat, and that's very like a mouse, you know. But do cats eat bats, I wonder?" And here Alice began to get rather sleepy, and went on saying to herself, in a dreamy sort of way, "Do cats eat bats? Do cats eat bats?" and sometimes, "Do bats eat cats?" for, you see, as she couldn't answer either question, it didn't matter which way she put it.

(p. 28)

We are already halfway to the final banquet of *Looking-Glass*, in which the food comes alive and begins to eat the guests.

Even when Dinah is not mentioned, Alice's attitude toward the animals she encounters is often one of casual cruelty. It is a measure of Dodgson's ability to flatten out Carroll's material that the prefatory poem could describe Alice "in friendly chat with bird or beast," or that he would later see Alice as "loving as a dog . . . gentle as a fawn." She pities Bill the Lizard and kicks him up the chimney, a state of mind that again looks forward to that of the Pecksniffian Walrus in *Looking-Glass*. When she meets the Mock Turtle, the weeping embodiment of a good Victorian dinner, she restrains herself twice when he mentions lobsters, but then distorts Isaac Watt's *Sluggard* into a song about a *baked* lobster surrounded by hungry sharks. In its second stanza, a Panther shares a pie with an Owl who then becomes dessert, as Dodgson's good table manners pass into typical Carrollian cannibalism. The more sinister and Darwinian aspects of animal nature are introduced into Wonderland by the gentle Alice, in part through projections of her hunger onto Dinah and the "nice little dog" (she meets a "dear little puppy" after she has grown small and is afraid he will eat her up) and in part through the semi-cannibalistic appetite her songs express. With the exception of the powerful Cheshire Cat, whom I shall discuss below, most of the Wonderland animals stand in some danger of being exploited or eaten. The Dormouse is their prototype: he is fussy and cantankerous, with the nastiness of a self-aware victim, and he is stuffed into a teapot as the Mock Turtle, sobbing out his own elegy, will be stuffed into a tureen.

Alice's courteously menacing relationship to these animals

is more clearly brought out in *Alice's Adventures Under Ground*, in which she encounters only animals until she meets the playing cards, who are lightly sketched-in versions of their later counterparts. When expanding the manuscript for publication, Carroll added the Frog Footman, Cook, Duchess, Pig-Baby, Cheshire Cat, Mad Hatter, March Hare, and Dormouse, as well as making the Queen of Hearts a more fully developed character than she was in the manuscript.[12] In other words, all human or quasi-human characters were added in revision, and all develop aspects of Alice that exist only under the surface of her dialogue. The Duchess's household also turns inside out the domesticated Wordsworthian ideal: with baby and pepper flung about indiscriminately, pastoral tranquillity is inverted into a whirlwind of savage sexuality. The furious Cook embodies the equation between eating and killing that underlies Alice's apparently innocent remarks about Dinah. The violent Duchess's unctuous search for "the moral" of things echoes Alice's own violence and search for "the rules."[13] At the Mad Tea Party, the Hatter extends Alice's "great interest in questions of eating and drinking" into an insane modus vivendi; like Alice, the Hatter and the Duchess sing savage songs about eating that embody the underside of Victorian literary treacle. The Queen's croquet game magnifies Alice's own desire to cheat at croquet and to punish herself violently for doing so. Its use of live animals may be a subtler extension of Alice's own desire to twist the animal kingdom to the absurd rules of civilization, which seem to revolve largely around eating and being eaten. Alice is able to appreciate the Queen's savagery so quickly because her size changes have made her increasingly aware of who she, herself, is from the point of view of a Caterpillar, a Mouse, a Pigeon, and, especially, a Cheshire Cat.

The Cheshire Cat, also a late addition to the book, is the only figure other than Alice who encompasses all the others. William Empson discusses at length the spiritual kinship between Alice and the Cat, the only creature in Wonderland whom she calls her "friend."[14] Forence Becker Lennon refers to the Cheshire Cat as "Dinah's dream-self" (p. 146), and we have noticed the subtle shift of identities between Alice and Dinah throughout the story. The Cat shares Alice's equivocal placidity: "The Cat only grinned when it saw Alice. It looked good-natured, she thought: still it had *very* long claws and a great many teeth, so she felt it ought to be treated with respect" (pp. 87–

88). The Cat is the only creature to make explicit the identification between Alice and the madness of Wonderland: " 'We're all mad here. I'm mad. You're mad.' 'How do you know I'm mad?' said Alice. 'You must be,' said the Cat, 'or you wouldn't have come here.' Alice didn't think that proved it at all" (p. 89). Although Alice cannot accept it and closes into silence, the Cat's remark may be the answer she has been groping toward in her incessant question, "Who am I?"[15] As an alter ego, the Cat is wiser than Alice—and safer—because he is the only character in the book who is aware of his own madness. In his serene acceptance of the fury within and without, his total control over his appearance and disappearance, he almost suggests a post-analytic version of the puzzled Alice.

As Alice dissolves increasingly into Wonderland, so the Cat dissolves into his own head, and finally into his own grinning mouth. The core of Alice's nature, too, seems to lie in her mouth: the eating and drinking that direct her size changes and motivate much of her behavior, the songs and verses that pop out of her inadvertently, are all involved with things entering and leaving her mouth.[16] Alice's first song introduces a sinister image of a grinning mouth. Our memory of the Crocodile's grin hovers over the later description of the Cat's "grin without a Cat," and colors our sense of Alice's infallible good manners:

> How cheerfully he seems to grin,
> How neatly spreads his claws,
> And welcomes little fishes in,
> With gently smiling jaws!
> (p. 38)

Walter de la Mare associates Alice with "a quiet moon" which is by implication a full moon. I think it is more appropriate to associate her with the grinning crescent that seems to follow her throughout her adventures, choosing to become visible only at particular moments, and teaching her the one lesson she must learn in order to arrive at a definition of who she is.

Martin Gardner pooh-poohs the "oral aggressions" psychoanalysts have found in Carroll's incessant focus on eating and drinking by reminding us of the simple fact that "small children are obsessed by eating, and like to read about it in their books" (*The*

Annotated Alice, p. 9). Maybe his commonsense approach is correct, but Lewis Carroll was concerned with nonsense, and throughout his life, he seems to have regarded eating with some horror. An early cartoon in *The Rectory Umbrella* depicts an emaciated family partaking raptly of a "homeopathic meal" consisting of an ounce of bread, half a particle of beer, etc.; young Sophy, who is making a pig of herself, asks for another molecule. Throughout his life, Carroll was abstemious at meals, according to his nephew and first biographer, Stuart Dodgson Collingwood: "The healthy appetites of his young friends filled him with wonder, and even with alarm." When he took one of his child friends to another's house for a meal, he told the host: "Please *be careful,* because she eats a good deal too much." [17] William Empson defines his attitude succinctly: "Dodgson was well-informed about foods, kept his old menus and was winetaster to the College; but ate very little, suspected the High Table of overeating, and would see no reason to deny that he connected overeating with other forms of sensuality." [18] To the man who in *Sylvie and Bruno* would define EVIL as a looking-glass version of LIVE, "gently smiling jaws" held teeth which were to be regarded with alarm; they seemed to represent to him a private emblem of original sin, for which Alice as well as the Knave of Hearts is finally placed on trial.

When the Duchess' Cook abruptly barks out "Pig!" Alice thinks the word is meant for her, though it is the baby, another fragment of Alice's own nature, who dissolves into a pig. The Mock Turtle's lament for his future soupy self later blends tellingly into the summons for the trial: the lament of the eaten and the call to judgment melt together. When she arrives at the trial, the unregenerate Alice instantly eyes the tarts: "In the very middle of the court was a table, with a large dish of tarts upon it: they looked so good, that it made Alice quite hungry to look at them—'I wish they'd get the trial done,' she thought, 'and hand round the refreshments!' " (p. 143). Her hunger links her to the hungry Knave who is being sentenced: in typically ambiguous portmanteau fashion, Carroll makes the trial both a pre-Orwellian travesty of justice and an objective correlative of a real sense of sin. Like the dog Fury in the Mouse's tale, [19] Alice takes all the parts. But unlike Fury, she is accused as well as accuser, melting into judge, jury, witness, and defendant; the person who boxes on the ears as well as the person who "cheats." Perhaps the final verdict would tell Alice who she is at last, but if it did, Wonderland would threaten to overwhelm her. Before it comes, she "grows"; the parts of her nature rush back together; combining the voices of victim and accuser, she gives "a little scream, half of fright and half of anger," and wakes up.

Presented from the point of view of her older sister's sentimental pietism, the world to which Alice awakens seems far more dreamlike and hazy than the sharp contours of Wonderland. Alice's lesson about her own identity has never been stated explicitly, for the stammerer Dodgson was able to talk freely only in his private language of puns and nonsense, but a Wonderland pigeon points us toward it:

> "You're a serpent; and there's no use denying it. I suppose you'll be telling me next that you never tasted an egg!"
> "I have tasted eggs, certainly," said Alice, who was a very truthful child; "but little girls eat eggs quite as much as serpents do, you know."
> "I don't believe it," said the Pigeon; "but if they do, why, then they're a kind of serpent: that's all I can say."
> This was such a new idea to Alice, that she was quite silent for a minute or two.
>
> (p 76)[20]

Like so many of her silences throughout the book, Alice's silence here is charged with significance, reminding us again that an important technique in learning to read Carroll is our ability to interpret his private system of symbols and signals and to appreciate the many meanings of silence. In this scene, the golden child herself becomes the serpent in childhood's Eden. The eggs she eats suggest the woman she will become, the unconscious cannibalism involved in the very fact of eating and desire to eat, and finally, the charmed circle of childhood itself. Only in *Alice's Adventures in Wonderland* was Carroll able to fall all the way through the rabbit hole to the point where top and bottom become one, bats and cats melt into each other, and the vessel of innocence and purity is also the source of inescapable corruption.

Alice's adventures in Wonderland foreshadow Lewis Carroll's subsequent literary career, which was a progressive dissolution into his component parts. Florence Becker Lennon defines well the schism that came with the later books: "Nothing in *Wonderland* par-

els the complete severance of the Reds and Whites in *Through the
Looking-Glass*. In *Sylvie and Bruno*, author and story have begun to
sintegrate. The archness and sweetness of parts, the utter cruelty and
athsomeness of others, predict literal decomposition into his ele-
ents" (p. 156). The Alice of *Through the Looking-Glass*, which was
blished six years after *Wonderland*, represents still another Alice, Al-
e Raikes; the character is so thinned out that the vapid, passive Ten-
el drawing is an adequate illustration of her. *Wonderland* ends with
lice playing all the parts in an ambiguous trial which concludes with-
t a verdict. *Looking-Glass* begins with an unequivocal verdict: "One
ing was certain, that the *white* kitten had nothing to do with it—it
as the black kitten's fault entirely" (p. 175). Poor Dinah, relegated
the role of face-washer-in-the-background, has also dissolved into
r component parts.

Throughout the books, the schism between Blacks (later
eds) and Whites is developed. Alice's greater innocence and passivity
e stressed by her identification with Lily, the white pawn. The dom-
ant metaphor of a chess game whose movements are determined by
visible players spreads her sense of helplessness and predestination
er the book. The nursery rhymes of which most of the characters
rm a part also make their movements seem predestined; the char-
ters in *Wonderland* tend more to create their own nursery rhymes.
he question that weaves through the book is no longer "Who am I?"
t "Which dreamed it?" If the story is the dream of the Red King
he sleeping embodiment of passion and masculinity), then Alice, the
hite Pawn (or pure female child), is exonerated from its violence,
though in another sense, as she herself perceives, she is also in greater
nger of extinction. Her increasing sweetness and innocence in the
cond book make her more ghostlike as well, and it is appropriate
at more death jokes surround her in the second *Alice* book than in
e first.

As Carroll's dream children became sweeter, his attitude
ward animals became increasingly tormented and obsessive, as we
n see in the hysterical antivivisection crusade of his later years. In
e of his pamphlets, "Vivisection as a Sign of the Times," cruelty to
imals, which in the first Alice was a casual instinct, becomes a sy-
cdoche for the comprehensive sin of civilization:

"But the thing cannot be!" cries some amiable reader, fresh from an interview with that most charming of men, a London physician. "What! Is it possible that one so gentle in manner, so full of noble sentiments, can be hardhearted? The very idea is an outrage to common sense!" And thus we are duped every day of our lives. Is it possible that that bank director, with his broad honest face, can be meditating a fraud? That the chairman of that meeting of shareholders, whose every tone has the ring of truth in it, can hold in his hand a "cooked" schedule of accounts? That my wine merchant, so outspoken, so confiding, can be supplying me with an adulterated article? That my schoolmaster, to whom I have entrusted my little boy, can starve or neglect him? How well I remember his words to the dear child when last we parted. "You are leaving your friends," he said, "but you will have a father in me, my dear, and a mother in Mrs. Squeers!" For all such rose-coloured dreams of the necessary immunity from human vices of educated men the facts in last week's *Spectator* have a terrible significance. "Trust no man further than you can see him," they seem to say. "Qui vult decipi, decipiatur."

(Quoted in Collingwood, p. 162

"Gently smiling jaws" have spread themselves over England. The sweeping intensity of this jeremiad shares the vision, if not the eloquence, of Ruskin's later despairing works.

As the world becomes more comprehensively cruel, the Carrollian little girl evolves into the impossibly innocent Sylvie in *Sylvie and Bruno* and *Sylvie and Bruno Concluded*, who is more fairy or guardian angel than she is actual child. Here, the dream belongs not to Sylvie but to the strangely maimed narrator. Any hint of wildness in Sylvie is siphoned off onto her mischievous little brother Bruno, whom she is always trying to tame as the first Alice boxed her own ears for cheating at croquet; and any real badness is further placed at one remove in the figure of the villainous Uggug, an obscenely fat child who finally turns into a porcupine. Uggug's metamorphosis recalls that of the Pig-baby in *Wonderland*, but in the earlier book, the Cook let us know that Alice was also encompassed by the epithet—terrible one in Carroll's private language—"Pig!"

Like Alice's, Sylvie's essential nature is revealed by her attitude toward animals. But while Alice's crocodile tears implicate her in original sin, Sylvie's tears prove her original innocence. In a key scene, the narrator tries to explain to her "innocent mind" the meaning of a hare killed in a hunt:

"They hunt *foxes,*" Sylvie said, thoughtfully. "And I think they *ill* them, too. Foxes are very fierce. I daresay men don't love them. Are hares ierce?"

"No," I said. "A hare is a sweet, gentle, timid animal—almost s gentle as a lamb." [Apparently no vision of the snappish March Hare eturned to haunt Lewis Carroll at this point.]

"But, if men *love* hares, why—why—" her voice quivered, and er sweet eyes were brimming with tears.

"I'm afraid they *don't* love them, dear child."

"All *children* love them," Sylvie said. "All *ladies* love them."

"I'm afraid even *ladies* go to hunt them, sometimes."

Sylvie shuddered. "Oh, no, not *ladies!*" she earnestly pleaded. . . In a hushed, solemn tone, with bowed head and clasped hands, she put er final question. "Does GOD love hares?"

"Yes!" I said. "I'm *sure* He does. He loves every living thing. ven sinful *men.* How much more the animals, that cannot sin!" [Here the vhole *Wonderland* gallery should have risen up in chorus against their creator!]

"I don't know what 'sin' means," said Sylvie. And I didn't try o explain it.

"Come, my child," I said, trying to lead her away. "Wish good- ye to the poor hare, and come and look for blackberries."

"Good-bye, poor hare!" Sylvie obediently repeated, looking over er shoulder at it as we turned away. And then, all in a moment, her self- ommand gave way. Pulling her hand out of mine, she ran back to where the ead hare was lying, and flung herself down at its side in such an agony of rief I could hardly have believed possible in so young a child.[21]

Sylvie's weeping over a dead hare is an unfortunate conclusion to Al- ce's initial underground leap after a live rabbit. Dodgson has been riven full circle here to embrace the pure little girl of Victorian con- ention, though he is ambivalent in this passage about "ladies." But is deterioration should be used as a yardstick to measure his achieve- nent in the first of the *Alice* books, which a brief survey of some ypical portraits of children in nineteenth-century literature may help s to appreciate.

Victorian concepts of the child tended to swing back and orth between extremes of original innocence and original sin; Rous- eau and Calvin stood side by side in the nursery. Since actual children vere the focus of such an extreme conflict of attitudes, they tended to be a source of pain and embarrassment to adults, and were therefore told they should be "seen and not heard." Literature dealt more freely with children than life did, so adult conflicts about them were allowed to emerge more openly in books. As Jan Gordon puts it:

> The most amazing feature of, say, Dickens' treatment of children, is how quickly they are transformed into monsters. Even Oliver Twist's surname forces the reader to appreciate the twisting condition normally associated with creatures more closely akin to the devil! One effect of this identification with evil adults . . . is that the only way of approaching childhood is by way of the opposite of satanic monstrosities—namely, the golden world of an edenic wonderland whose pastoral dimension gives it the status of a primal scene.[22]

In its continual quest for origins and sources of being, Victorian literature repeatedly explores the ambiguous figure of the child, in whom it attempts to resolve the contradictions it perceives much as *Sylvie and Bruno* does: by an extreme sexual division.

Little boys in Victorian literature tend to be allied to the animal, the Satanic, and the insane. For this reason, novels in which a boy is the central focus are usually novels of development, in which the boy evolves out of his inherent violence, "working out the brute" in an ascent to a higher spiritual plane. This tradition seems foreshadowed by the boy in Wordsworth's *Prelude,* whose complexity undercuts the many Victorian sentimentalizations about Wordsworth's children. The predatory child in the first two books, traveling through a dark landscape that seems composed largely of his own projected fears and desires, has in fact a great deal in common with Carroll's Alice.[23] Carroll is truer than many of his contemporaries to the ambiguities of Wordsworth's children, but he goes beyond Wordsworth in making a little girl the focus of his vision. Wordsworth's little girls tend to be angelic, corrective figures who exist largely to soothe the turbulence of the male protagonists; his persona in *The Prelude* is finally led to his "spiritual eye" through the ministrations of an idealized, hovering Dorothy.

David Copperfield must also develop out of an uncontrolled animality that is close to madness—early in the novel, we learn of him that "he bites"—and he can do so only through the guidance of the ghostly Agnes, pointing ever upward. Dr. Arnold's Rugby, which eflected and conditioned many of the century's attitudes toward boys, was run on a similar evolutionary premise: the students were to develop out of the inherent wickedness of "boy nature" into the state of "Christian gentleman," a semidivine warrior for the good. In the all-male society of Rugby, Dr. Arnold was forced to assume the tradition-lly female role of spiritual beacon, as the image of the Carlylean hero supplanted that of the ministering angel. Thomas Hughes' famous tale of Rugby, *Tom Brown's School Days,* solves this problem by making Tom's spiritual development spring from the influence of the femin-zed, debilitated young Arthur and his radiantly ethereal mother: only after their elaborate ministrations is the young man able to kneel by he doctor's casket and worship the transfigured image of the-Doctor-s-God. Women and girls are necessary catalysts for the development of the hero out of his dangerously animal state to contact with the God within and without him.

Cast as they were in the role of emotional and spiritual atalysts, it is not surprising that girls who function as protagonists of Victorian literature are rarely allowed to develop: in its refusal to sub-ect females to the evolutionary process, the Victorian novel takes a ignificant step backward from one of its principal sources, the novels of Jane Austen. Even when they are interesting and "wicked," Vic-orian heroines tend to be static figures like Becky Sharp; when they are "good," their lack of development is an important factor in the Victorian reversal of Pope's sweeping denunciation—"Most women have no characters at all"—into a cardinal virtue. Little girls in Victorian iterature are rarely children, nor are they allowed to grow up. Instead, hey exist largely as a diffusion of emotional and religious grace, rep-esenting "nothing but love," as Dodgson's Sylvie warbles. Florence Dombey in Dickens' *Dombey and Son* may stand as their paradigm. Representing as she does the saving grace of the daughter in a world dominated by the hard greed and acquisitiveness of men—the world that kills her tender brother Paul—Florence drifts through Mr. Dom-bey's house in a limbo of love throughout the book, waiting for her father to come to her. She ages, but never changes, existing less as a character than as a "spiritual repository into which Mr. Dombey must slip if he is to be saved."[24] Dickens' Little Nell and Little Dorrit are equally timeless and faceless. Though both are in fact post-pubes-cent—Little Nell is fourteen, Little Dorrit, twenty-two—they combine the mythic purity and innocence of the little girl with the theoretical marriageability of the woman, diffusing an aura from a sphere separate from that of the other characters, a sphere of nonpersonal love without change.

Charlotte Brontë's Jane Eyre and George Eliot's Maggie Tulliver are two more sharply-etched little girls who grow into women, but even they represent, in an angrier and more impassioned way, "nothing but love." Neither develops in the course of her book, because neither needs to change: all both need is acceptance of love they have to offer, which in Jane Eyre's case is fervently erotic and ethical, and in Maggie Tulliver's is passionately filial and engulfing. Both triumph at the end of their novels because they are allowed to redeem through their love the men they have chosen, who, as Victorian convention dictated, have undergone a process of development up to *them*. This reminds us once more that in Victorian literature, little boys were allowed, even encouraged, to partake of original sin; but little girls rarely were.

We return once more to the anomaly of Carroll's Alice, who explodes out of Wonderland hungry and unregenerate. By a subtle dramatization of Alice's attitude toward animals and toward the animal in herself, by his final resting on the symbol of her mouth, Carroll probed in all its complexity the underground world within the little girl's pinafore. The ambiguity of the concluding trial finally, and wisely, waives questions of original guilt or innocence. The ultimate effect of Alice's adventures implicates her, female child though she is, in the troubled human condition; most Victorians refused to grant women and children this respect. The sympathetic delicacy and precision with which Carroll traced the chaos of a little girl's psyche seems equaled and surpassed only later in such explorations as D. H. Lawrence's of the young Ursula Brangwen in *The Rainbow,* the chaos of whose growth encompasses her hunger for violence, sexuality, liberty, and beatitude. In the imaginative literature of its century, *Alice's Adventures in Wonderland* stands alone.

9.

Falling Alice, Fallen Women, and Victorian Dream Children

The prosaic but strangely haunting Alice we think we know was many Alices from her inception. Alice Liddell first coaxed her into existence, but that enchanting, unattainable child was flanked by two sisters and overborne by a formidable mother and an eminent father; our Alice is serenely unanchored even by a family name. Alice Raikes, who grew up to become an author herself, inspired the Looking-Glass world because she had the mental agility to imagine herself on the other side of the mirror, a leap of imagination which seems to have been beyond that enticing muse, Alice Liddell.[1] The clean, blonde, primly pinafored Alice whom Tenniel introduced to the world is not the dark, sensuous brooder of Carroll's initial illustrations.[2] None of these girls is the eerie dream child of Carroll's prefatory and concluding poems, which inflate our brisk traveling companion into an abstract and awful divinity:

> Still she haunts me, phantomwise,
> Alice moving under skies
> Never seen by waking eyes.[3]

The child of the text, imperturbably civilized yet uncannily adaptable, is still another being from the inspirations and exegeses that surround her. Her aplomb makes her unrecognizable as a child, but her cool response to flamboyant violence makes her the ideal hostess for dreams and nightmares: effortlessly and instinctively, she turns madness to etiquette.

Since the original Alice was a mutable, composite creature, it is not surprising that in the twentieth century, she continues to have many selves. In the 1930s, when the horrors of Freudian analysts were infused into Lewis Carroll's gardens, Alice became in compensation impossibly pure.[4] Immunized by being a girl child from the body's unacknowledged lusts, Alice also seemed impervious of the horrors of war: the golden child about whom Mrs. Miniver read to her family during a bombing was an eternal talisman against destruction. More recently, though, this impassive innocent has been seen as herself a bomb, bringing "death, predation, and egoism" into the comic harmony of Wonderland.[5] Like actual women in the 1970s, the disruptive, incipiently violent Alice refuses to function as remote redeemer. Her polite rapacity insists with the Wonderland pigeon that a little girl is "a kind of serpent" (p. 76). Rather than remaining an immunizing visitation, our contemporary Alice is herself an agent of fear.

Do Alice's many manifestations cohere into a single vision? Is it possible to unify the pure child with the predator, the blonde with the dark model, the guarded, inscrutable muse of Alice Liddell with the avid, questing child Alice Raikes evokes? A unified vision of Alice may lie only in the complex mobility of Lewis Carroll's visual genius.

He saw and collected pictures as avidly as he invented them, hovering enthusiastically around the pre-Raphaelites and their circle.[6] The mutable Alice who obsessed him thus took much of her contradictory life from the visual iconography of her age. As an amalgam of purity and subversive power, of propriety and holy exile, Alice is a nursery avatar of a grand pre-Raphaelite icon: the fallen woman, scandalous and blessed.[7]

"Down, down, down. Would the fall *never* come to an end?" Alice wonders dreamily at the beginning of her pilgrimage (p. 27). For many Victorian women, as for this golden child, it seems that the fall never did. Actual, unglamorous prostitutes abounded in urban England, living vulnerable, precarious lives as scapegoats of family respectability and the Victorian bad conscience, yet majestic fallen

women cut operatic figures in fiction, art, and the stage. Dante Gabriel
Rossetti's *Found,* which was Carroll's favorite among his paintings,
depicts a crouched prostitute as a figure of garish, irresistible grandeur,
her monumentality dwarfing surrounding ordinariness (see figure 9.1).[8]
In similar fashion, Alice dwarfs and overturns the worlds she invades.
By convention, the fallen woman must writhe in tortured postures of
remorse until she dies penitent at the end of her story. Alice is equally
alienated, equally tortured by the writhing and disruptive activities of
her own body; throughout her journeys she is the object of veiled murderous threats; in both books, she can save herself from devastation

by her dream only by awakening into a vaporous normality. But like the fallen woman, Alice is a titanic outcast, dooming as well as doomed, whose fall endows her with the power to smash and transcend all rooms she enters and all countries to which she travels.

The hidden power of the seemingly inviolate Alice aligns her with this popular Victorian descendant of Pandora and Eve. Like that of the fallen woman in Rossetti's *Found*, who draws irresistible strength from the wall which shelters her, Alice's fall is both a punishment for her inveterate curiosity and an alliance with mysterious underground laws that empower her. Like Milton's Eve, the ever-ravenous Alice is a creature of curiosity and appetite. Eve fell through eating to become a god, and Alice, who is always hungry, becomes the creator of worlds through falling. As her curiosity causes her fall, so her hunger impels her rise: eating and drinking produce the size changes that at times place her at the mercy of Wonderland but ultimately allow her to rule it. In this loving parody of Genesis and of contemporary fallen women, Alice is simultaneously Wonderland's slave and its queen, its creator and destroyer as well as its victim. Carroll's pure little girl, so painfully careful of her etiquette, takes much of her paradoxical power from an army of women whose activities she would not have been allowed to know.

Carroll's peculiarly Victorian triumph lay in his amalgamation of the fallen woman with the unfallen child. His Alice is most insistently herself when she is placed among other, more untroublingly adorable Victorian children. It suits her to reveal herself in pictures as well as conversations, for since she is well brought up, she is generally seen rather than heard. Like the stammering artist who created her, she is more comfortable looking than she is speaking. Like many women and womanly children, she greets shock with a mask of vapidity, responding to hysterical assaults with speaking silence.

Alice's verbal decorum, her apparent translucency, may seem at first to align her with another dear Victorian child: the placid subject of John Everett Millais' famous *Bubbles*. The conceit that underlies this popular painting equates the little boy with the pastel transparency of his own bubbles, beautiful, characterless ephemera that break when touched. The characterlessness of ideal Victorian children is enshrined in Ford Madox Brown's delicate portrait of Madeline Scott, who could be watching a pastoral picnic, a rudely prying viewer, or a wolf eating her grandmother with equal placidity. She seems worlds away from the sharp, unwomanly slash of pre-Raphaelite fallen women, living as a series of circles, repetitively restful to the eye, suggestive of eternity or of nullity according to the viewer's perspective. While the Victorian fallen woman proclaims her existence by destroying whatever community she is part of, Brown's little girl is obediently plastic, the receptacle of any identity the viewer likes. Superficially, her demure malleability and dreamy circularity belong to the same golden vision of a purified childhood that Carroll's books immortalize.

But even as Tenniel draws her, Alice offers only a troubling repose (see figure 9.2). Here she is at last, at her most sublimely, determinedly vacant. If Carroll had written a conduct book for girls instead of a dark, amoral dream, he might have called this illustration A Young Lady Transcending Circumstances. Like Millais' bubble blower or Brown's Madeline Scott, Alice is composed in a series of restful circles, forming an island of purity around the pig she is forced to cradle. But these circles enclose rather than exclude the pig, whose own bloated circularity parodies the little girl's purity. Like those of the witch and her familiar, these shapes hint at buried metamorphic possibilities whereby each might become the other; Irving Massey's fascinating The Gaping Pig locates the pig as the central metamorphic image in Western iconography, suggesting that Alice may be embracing her own hidden potential for insidious changes.[9] Though Tenniel's Alice is sometimes jarringly mannequin-like, his composition here captures perfectly the suggestiveness of Carroll's text: a little girl is simultaneously "a kind of serpent," the epithet "Pig!" applies to all available auditors (p. 83), and a child's impassive purity is large enough to include the wriggles of indeterminate matter.

Unlike that of Millais' bubble blower, Alice's purity does not align her with the ephemeral; like her hunger, it gives her power over size and scale. Like the grandly metamorphic fallen woman, she can make daily reality "softly and suddenly vanish away" as she unexpectedly, and threateningly, grows.

Lewis Carroll's own drawings for Alice's Adventures Under Ground insist upon Alice's bigness as Tenniel and his successors, whose Alice is generally more dainty than mighty, do not (see figure 9.3). Coiled in the White Rabbit's house, as imperturbable as ever, Alice seems poised to spring as she curls into her own monumentality. Her

cumbersome majesty links her less with the reassuringly vacant child of Victorian stereotype than with such awkwardly outsize pre-Raphaelite deities as the fallen Madonna who looms toward us in Ford Madox Brown's *Take Your Son, Sir,* or Dante Gabriel Rossetti's Astarte Syriaca, an invading ancient divinity who seems about to swell out of her frame. The surprising friendship between Carroll and Rossetti may have been cemented by their shared, horrified fascination with female growth. For though Carroll often lost his child friends once they had grown up, he was riveted by the streaks of adulthood in their youth. His photographs of Alice Liddell as a streetwise "Beggar Girl," or of tiny Alice Donkin (his brother's future wife) coolly enacting "The Elopement," expose the incipient woman secreted within the child. His culture idealized the child-woman, hymning the overgrown child who made the perfect wife, but Carroll found his main inspiration in the woman who revealed herself within the child's mask. Similarly, as his career develops, Rossetti's demigoddesses grow increasingly enormous.[10] A chronological examination of the many versions of his *Found* discloses a wispy, starved-looking model swelling into the operatic dimensions of Fanny Comforth.[11] In the course of her evolution, Rossetti's demidivine fallen woman grows as Carroll's Alice does in the course of her story. The growth of each endows her with a menacing fascination.

Though as verbal and visual artist Carroll's one true subject was the little girl, his fascination stems not from her littleness but from her potential to grow big. His photographs of his child friends

caress their subjects not in condescension to their pathos, but in respect for their latent power. The force of growth compressed within
his little women is one manifestation of the pre-Raphaelite obsession
with the latent powers of impassive womanhood. For the pre-Raphaelites, Tennyson's Lady of Shalott swells into the central emblem of
power confined; Carroll locates his central explosive force in the polite
little girl who possesses the vital secret of her own adult potential. It
may be that this anomalous creature arose out of pained Victorian
doubts as to where the boundaries of childhood lay, doubts which intensified the insulation of childhood purity in sentimental Victorian
art.[12] I suspect, though, that Carroll's Alice grew out of a more poi-
gnant insight: his awareness of the fragility of female adulthood in an
infantilizing life. In the ideology of Victorian womanhood, marriage
signaled not maturity but death into a perpetual nursery. Thus, paradoxically, the intact child is in securest possession of the mobility and
power of her potential adult future. This irony that underlay the actual
lives of girls, rather than a peculiarly pathological terror of adult sexuality, animates the morbid prefatory poem to *Through the Looking-
Glass.*

> Come, harken then, ere voice of dread,
>   With bitter tidings laden,
> Shall summon to unwelcome bed
>   A melancholy maiden!
> We are but older children, dear,
> Who fret to find our bedtime near.
> (p. 173)

This conflation of the marriage with the deathbed, noted by Empson,
suggests a double death: that of the innocent child and of her mighty
adult future. The integrity of this vision of the female child lies in
seeing in her not a rarefied and fragile shelter from adult experience,
but a force of growth complete in herself, for whom adult life will
constitute a violation of power.

    Carroll's photographs of children differ from grand pre-
Raphaelite female icons in that the latter tend to be marmoreal still-
lives, while the former are remarkable for their mobility, their promise
of perpetual activity and change. To elicit the essence of his sitters,
Carroll seems to have encouraged them to act, thus releasing the metamorphic potential he saw coiled within little girls: the hallmark of his
photographs is his use of costumes, props, and the imaginative inten-

sity of an improvised scene caught at midpoint. Carroll's love for the theater was one of the sirens that lured him from the seemingly inevitable but "unwelcome bed" of full ordination. His passionate affection for the young Ellen Terry, which seems to have been a more profound devotion than George Bernard Shaw's would be in the actress's middle age, his intensifying obsession with child actresses in general in his later years, his infusion of theatricality even into his photographs of nonactresses—all suggest that the mobile self-definition of acting crystallized the potential power he found in the little girl. His photographic allegiance to the performing self suggested a commitment to the metamorphic mystery of personality which few artists, then and now, are brave enough to pledge. His July 16, 1887, letter to the *St. James Gazette,* defending the good health and high spirits of stage children, evokes the vitalism acting epitomized. After describing "the vigor of *life*" in three stage children who accompanied him to Brighton, he concludes: "A taste for *acting* is one of the strongest passions of human nature. . . . Stage children show it almost from infancy . . . they simply rejoiced in their work 'even as a giant to run his course.' "[13]

The inexhaustible gusto and intensity of these three young actresses embody the lure of the Carrollian little girl. The poignance of her fleeting performance is a protest against an adulthood that robs her not of innocence or chastity, but of vitality. In *Literary Women,* Ellen Moers finds a similar protest in the poems of Christina Rossetti and in Emily Brontë's *Wuthering Heights* against an adulthood that censors the intense erotic violence permitted to little girls.[14] The erotic excitement one can hardly deny in Carroll's love for his girl children may find one source in the eroticism female childhood sanctioned. Some such emotion seems to underlie his admission to Gertrude Thomson: "I confess I do *not* admire naked *boys,* in pictures. They always seem to me to need *clothes:* whereas one hardly sees why the lovely forms of girls should *ever* be covered up!"[15] Could Carroll have sensed that to "cover up" a girl in the panoply of womanhood is to smother a wealth of erotic energy, while to "cover up" a boy in the uniforms of manhood is to sanction and to symbolize childhood's aggressive vitalism?

Carroll's faith in performing little girls was a virtually unique tribute, a denial of the shrouded langour so many Victorians wanted

women and children to embody. His use of props to define and set off
the sitters in his photographs is a familiar device in Victorian visual
art, particularly in its representations of women and girls, but Carroll
uses props in bold and striking fashion. Perhaps nineteenth-century
artists sensed that the power of women was so overwhelming, but of-
ficially so undefined, that they relied on properties less as pure deco-
ration than as foils, defining obliquely what woman was and was not;
the foils claim to explain the mystery of womanhood, but more often
than not they intensify it. We remember Alice's subtle relation to the
pig in Tenniel's illustration, where the pig functions as the navel both
of the composition and of Alice's body: at the same time as it completes the circle she makes, her imperious purity both eschews and
acknowledges its implication of her. In the same way, Victorian art
uses foils and contrasts both to intensify the suggestive potential of
women and girls and to exorcise the unnamed disturbances they arouse.

So, in later, sentimental illustrations, Alice is kept chastely
remote from the creatures of Wonderland (see figure 9.4). Though her
incessant question in the novel—her recurrent, plaintive "Who am
I?"—suggests the fluid boundaries between Alice and the creatures of
her dream, these illustrations exorcise Carroll's disturbing suggestions:
his dynamic fallen child, taking to herself the monsters and monstros-
ities of Wonderland, becomes a coolly immunized traveler. Unlike
Tenniel's pig drawing, Rackham's charming illustration acts in this
reassuringly sentimental way: its contrasts dispel our fears for the pres-
ervation of Alice's identity. The mushroom's forbidding head, and her
own inquisitive distance, push her back from the Caterpillar; the straight
light line of her body aligns her compositionally with the neutrality of
the mushrooms' stems, not with the Caterpillar's sinuous dark grotesquerie. The monster as foil reassures us of the little girl's purity.

These various ways of juxtaposing Alice with the monsters
she dreams exemplify the tensions Victorian artists perceived between
Beauty and the Beast, two perennial types in their art. Generally, the
artist wants to shield Beauty against contamination by her hybrid interlocutor, but in some representations, his alienation from humanity
mirrors her own. Walter Crane's elegant illustration of the fairy tale,
where Beauty and Beast sit facing each other on a drawing-room sofa,
holds these dual possibilities in suspension (see figure 9.5). The monster is defined by compositional aggression, leaning toward the wom-

an's self-enclosed sphere while she shrinks delicately away. Nevertheless, there are witty subterranean hints of an alliance between Beauty
and Beast, or at least of a certain droll bestiality in the woman that
makes this picture more subtle and sophisticated than most Victorian
foil paintings. In a visual symphony of pink and red, Beauty and the
Beast wear complementary colors, the red slashes in Beauty's dress,
her hair, and her fan seeming to beckon toward the Beast's blatant red
waistcoat and hooves. Moreover, though her diminutive red feet are
tucked demurely under her dress, her skirt extends out to meet the
Beast's cloven hooves and to echo their shape. The Beast does not
exorcise, but arouses, his counterpart within Beauty; Crane's foil whispers to us the happy hint that a lady can survive in a drawing room
with gently cloven feet. The hint of kinship in Crane's illustration
reminds us of *Alice* in its covert, affectionate complicity between the
female's politeness and the monster's assault, a complicity that still
arouses us in the charged confrontations of woman and monster in
such popular films as *King Kong* and *Alien,* whose women and monsters converge within a male-controlled and maddened world.

      In some of the most interestingly savage Victorian chil-
dren's books, this interchangeability of Beauty and Beast is a central
theme (see figure 9.6). In Christina Rossetti's *Speaking Likenesses,*

illustrated here by Arthur Hughes, an angry little girl dreams of
birthday party invaded by monstrous, anarchic creatures, over which
she herself presides in the guise of a furious Queen. In Hughes' illus
tration, Lewis Carroll's symbolism becomes explosively explicit: though
the helpless little girl at the center of the composition is as boneless
pure, and inexpressive as we would expect, monsters form themselve
from the planes and contours of her body, her very malleability givin
shape to weird personifications of misrule. Like the mad Queens i
the *Alices*, Hughes' doppelgänger Queen is a dream of suppressed fe
male fury whose monstrosity is the foundation of her power. The com
position of this mad birthday party allows no doubt that the energy o
monsters inheres in a little girl's graceful attitudes, monsters who (i
a dream at least) become the agents of rule. The foils no longer insu
late the female from contamination, but fuel a nightmare of her laten
power.

Hughes' illustration of Christina Rossetti's vision is safel
tucked away within the framework of a moralistic children's book i
which, upon the little girl's awakening, her dream of power reduce
itself to a dream of terror. Similarly, in Lewis Carroll's dream books
an acknowledged influence on Christina Rossetti's, the complexities o
the little girl's dream decompose into idyllic wonderment when sh
awakes. But within the confines of fantasy or dream, the pure femal
reveals latent and powerful incarnations. When these dreams are illus
trated, their sharply contoured symbolism does not dispel itself int
golden memories or cautionary morals; a richly conceived foil like Al
ice's pig expands the reader's easy formulations about the purity o
women and girls, eliciting the boundless potential within polite femal
respectability, defining not what the little girl is exempt from, but wha
she might become. The popularity of fairy photographs in late Victo
rian England, in which a bourgeois, beribboned little girl is often pose
with a supposedly authentic flying fairy, epitomizes the child's poten
tial for transformation and flight. The subversive import of *Beauty an
the Beast* galvanizes the sharp contrasts of Victorian melodrama: Dickens
manic, misshapen Quilp, for example, lends forbidden energy to hi
stern Little Nell, while Christina Rossetti's Laura and Lizzie in *Goblin
Market* must amputate their own irresistible potential toward becomin
goblins themselves. Gothic literature, too, whispers of these forbidde
transformations. In "The Lifted Veil," George Eliot's Gothic tale,

proper heroine becomes a lamia when seen truly, and a female corpse is suddenly galvanized into enraged life; the vampirized women in Bram Stoker's *Dracula* outdo their diabolical master in virtuoso self-transformations, peregrinations, and flights of perception. Even Tenniel's well-known illustration of Carroll's "Jabberwocky" presents a long-haired youth, who shown from behind looks suspiciously like Alice, facing a horrible swooping monster that suggests a looking-glass self. The best-known interchange between Beauty and Beast in Victorian literature may come from *Wuthering Heights,* when the pure, sheltered heroine plaintively evokes her goblin self with the cry "I *am* Heathcliff." The very emphasis in Victorian iconography on female placidity and passivity, on exemption from mobile and passionate energy, expands into dreams of metamorphosis, transcendence, and redemptive monstrosity.

It is in this context of iconographic examination of female nature that the fascination of Lewis Carroll's Alice becomes clear. The little girl alone is free to dream, to grow, to metamorphose; she is a pristine but safely guarded vehicle of female power. In Carroll's own illustrations and photographs, though, the affinity between Beauty and Beast lacks intimacy; monsters do not form themselves from the contours of her body; the secret interchange between child and creature generates not so much mutuality as vertigo. Alice's relation to the Victorian type of the fallen woman extends beyond the simple fact of her fall and the powers it bestows on her to create and destroy worlds: like her adult counterparts in literature and art, Alice is a "fabulous monster" of solitude, nibbling at the identities of the creatures she encounters without disappearing into them. Alice shares with her dream creatures their mobility, their obsessions, but like the fallen woman, that aloof and outcast pariah, she refrains from embracing them.

Part of the intensity of the *Alice* books comes from this perpetual tension between intimacy and estrangement (see figure 9.7). Lewis Carroll's own drawing of Alice and the Rabbit exemplifies the simultaneous power of relationship and revulsion. The mesmeric intensity of Alice's gaze, and the Rabbit's taut awareness of it, is far more suggestive than the ceremonial indifference Rackham depicts between Alice and the Caterpillar. Alice and the Rabbit are welded to each other by the power of their gaze, though there remains an electric distance between looker and object.

More disturbing still, unlike his subsequent illustrators,
Carroll divides the focus of the drawing so that Alice is not central to
it: we initially see neither Alice nor the Rabbit, but the significant no-
man's-land between them. This is not an illustration of a remote child
spectator, but of the complex relationship between Alice and her creature. Carroll compounds this emphasis on interrelationship by drawing
the picture to the scale of the Rabbit, rather than using Alice as scale,
so that we see with him Alice looming toward him, a curious prophecy
of the "fabulous monster" the *Looking-Glass* Unicorn will discover
when he sees her, or even of the looming Jabberwocky itself. A rabbit
in a frock coat becomes our norm of size, a demure little girl our
looming monster: identities here are so bewildered between Beauty and
Beast that the viewer can do nothing but circle back and forth between
them. No later illustrator dared let a figure other than Alice provide
the scale of an illustration. Only the author himself deprives us of our

orms by providing this final turn of the screw, stripping his beloved
ᶜhild of her last human immunity from the world she both dreams
ᶰd becomes.

The dream license with which Carroll allowed Alice to as-
ᵤme the perversities of the fallen woman and the distortions of the
ᵐonster represents either a mad assault on or a profound appreciation
ᶠ the integrity of female childhood; our perspective depends upon who
ᵉe are. By now, we have all had to learn that within the "golden
ᶠternoon" of Wonderland lie dark books indeed, rife with anxiety and
ᵃggression, the agony of forgetting countered only by the agony of
ᵐemory.[16] Freudian critics have bequeathed to us the specter of Lewis
ᶜarroll as himself the perverse monster, brandishing pen and camera
ᵃ he looms over the pure little girl to violate her: the main impact of
ᵗe Freudian vogue of the 1930s was a feeling that innocent children
ᵐould be saved from the *Alice* books. A demonic *Alice* has lurked in
ᵗe wings for a long time, shadowing and titillating our appreciation
ᶠ this paean to the purity of little girlhood.

Now that Morton N. Cohen has published replicas of some
ᶠ Carroll's notorious nude photographs, the idea of which has shocked
ᵤr own century far more than it did the Victorians, the possibly de-
ᵐonic and perverse Carroll surfaces in our minds once more.[17] Ques-
ᵗons tease us about the ultimate direction of his verbal and visual
ᵉlebrations of little girls: are they a violation of childhood, however
ᵛoyeuristic and oblique, or is Carroll the purest Arnoldian critic of
ᶠmale children, appreciating the object as in itself it really is, adopting
ᵗe camera's loving detachment in order to define its subject's value
ᵗ the world? Feminist viewers might find themselves particularly per-
ᵈlexed by Carroll's obsessive celebration of girlhood, uncertain whether
ᵗis worship violates his subject or comprehends it.

Answers to these oracular questions suggest themselves only
ᵗ pictures. Consider a particularly innocent one of still another Alice,
ᵃlice Price (see figure 9.8). As opposed to the monstrous Alice who
ᵃzed somewhat hungrily at a white rabbit, Alice Price is the center of
ᵃ pristinely sentimental Victorian tableau, a little girl with her doll,
ᵃdiating exemplary femininity, contented domesticity, and future
ᵐotherhood. But the more we look at this apparent emblem of femi-
ᶰine virtue, the more we see it grow into suggestions of monstrosity.

The pensive sensuality of the child's pose, the erotic hunger of her expression, become more apparent to us as we look, until the doll becomes less a thing to nourish than a thing to eat. This suggestive gem of a photo subtly mocks proper little motherhood by supplying a mobile child with a foil as rich in contradictory implications as Tenniel's pig. The discreetly carnivorous rapture with which Alice eyes her doll will suffuse the expression of a later Victorian child gazing at a different sort of doll: Aubrey Beardsley's elegantly ravenous Salomé as she leans forward to kiss the dead lips of John the Baptist. In Beardsley's fin-de-siècle variant of a familiar Victorian motif, the foil appropriates all the picture's purity, the little girl all its monstrous lust. Carroll's photograph is content to whisper the possibility of this inversion, hinting at an uneasy rapport between the domestic and the demonic as they threaten to merge altogether. Softly loving Alice Price grows into another manifestation of the hungry Alice we know, an uncontained pioneer whose "deepest impulses [involve] power and aggression."[18]

Carroll's extraordinary tact as an artist infuses acceptable little girls with an energy that was in itself unacceptable. Despite his safe life, his career tiptoes along the dangerous line that separates coziness from unease. The explosive potential he sensed in his dream children is a pervasive but unspoken awareness in Victorian iconography, where the line between sentimentality and perversity stretches so thin as to be at times invisible. Redemptive love itself becomes a dangerous issue, though love was the only emotional activity most readers found acceptable in women. Its holy influence was supposed to defuse the self, its hungers, its ambitions, its energy, its drive for power. Yet, in fin-de-siècle literature particularly, love threatens to become a new, and dangerous, source of power in itself. Hardy's Tess falls in love and finds gratification through murder; Wilde's Salomé falls in love and creates a murder that is a triumph of perverse aestheticism. Throughout the century, the popular icon of the fallen woman fuels with forbidden love a drive for power Victorian society taboos in women. The blessed emotion that was supposed to obliterate women becomes an illicit source of female strength. This tortured perception of the mixed potential of women in love finds one culmination in D. H. Lawrence's great novel of that name, whose Ursula and Gudrun seem to promise the solace of repose, but whose love is underlain by their lethal, and irrepressible, energy.

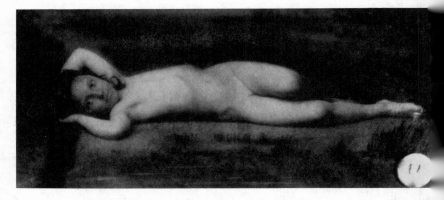

The power and erotic energy within a dream of purity all inhere in the mutable little girls Carroll immortalized (see figure 9.9). His photographs of nude children need no metaphorical foils to define their powers: they are simply the objects themselves. Some embarrassed viewers have tried to see no sexuality in these photographs, but it seems to me needlessly apologetic to deny the eroticism of this beautiful little odalisque. Since her sexuality is not imaged forth in foils, emblems, or metaphors, Carroll's Evelyn Hatch seems to me a far more healthily realized figure than Beardsley's Salomé, who needs the Baptist's purity to define her lust, or even than Nabokov's sadomasochistic dream of Lolita, for Evelyn Hatch is allowed to be at one with her own implied powers. Thus, the achievement of this photograph lies in its pure acceptance of what Carroll's Victorian contemporaries perceived as demonic and dangerous. Unlike Alice, Evelyn Hatch needs no creatures to inform us that she is both animal and dreamer, pig and pure little girl. Carroll as camera eye does perfect justice to the self-transforming mobility of his model. The eroticism, along with the passionate and seditious powers this had come to imply, belongs to the child; the artist merely understands it. Though he spoke a halting, cryptic language, Lewis Carroll recognized the fallen woman's metamorphic complexity within an unfallen child on a golden afternoon. As an infallibly courteous Victorian gentleman, he granted Alice and the rest of his child friends the powers that were theirs.

III.

Female Traditions

10.

Artists and Mothers:
A False Alliance

o our wombs silently dictate when we write? Are women's books poor replicas of unborn babies? In the popular image of the creative process, creativity and childbirth are often entangled, so that a childless woman writer seems wistfully to turn herself into a mother by some poignantly incomplete process of parthenogenesis. Virginia Woolf shyly touches on this assumption in *A Room of One's Own* as she forms an imaginary community of four great nineteenth-century women novelists: "Save for the possibly relevant fact that not one of them had a child, four more incongruous characters could not have met together in a room."[1]

But Woolf evades defining the "possibly relevant" conjunction between childlessness and art. Did the Brontës, Jane Austen, and George Eliot write out of a thwarted need to give birth, sadly making substitute dream children out of their novels? Or did they produce art that allowed them a freer, finer, more expansive world than the suppressions of nineteenth-century motherhood allowed? Perhaps out of a defensive awareness of her own childlessness, Woolf allows us to hover between both suggestions, just as our picture of the childless woman writer has typically hovered on the borderline between deprivation and defiance.

Our perceptions about women are still so infused with biological mythology that even contemporary feminist critics may see the creation of a world in books as a token of a destiny missed rather than of one triumphantly forged. Thus Cynthia Griffin Wolff's feminist biography *A Feast of Words: The Triumph of Edith Wharton* uncritically echoes Wharton's sad self-doubt in her old age: "So rich in the offspring of her creative intelligence—'my children,' she used to call her fictions as she scolded them into compliance and dressed them and spanked them into shape (these were *her* terms in letters to her friends)— she was barren of biological progeny."[2] "Barren" and "biological" end the sentence with an alliterative, authoritative thud, negating the "feast of words" that made Wharton worthy of a biography in the first place. Even in feminist reevaluations of notable women, it is difficult to escape a retreat to the womb.

Well-known female psychiatrists have endorsed the idea that childbirth is the only significant reality in a woman's life, reducing every other need and impetus to the shadowy status of metaphor. Helene Deutsch's influential *The Psychology of Women: A Psychoanalytic Interpretation* (1945) defines its vision by the titles of its two volumes: *Girlhood* and *Motherhood*. The two stand as inescapable poles of the "normal," a monolithic destiny in which maturity means only maternity: all other goals are an evasion. Even in the early work of Karen Horney, whose feminism led her to break with Freud, the womb replaces God's word as the only true creator, of which civilization itself is but a poor, proud replica. "The Flight from Womanhood" (1926) forces even men into complicity with the universal urge to define one's humanity in motherhood: "Is not the tremendous strength in men of the impulse to creative work in every field precisely due to their feeling of playing a relatively small part in the creation of living beings, which constantly impels them to an overcompensation in achievement?"[3] In all three of the above statements, motherhood is not one manifestation of our multifaceted creative gift, but a means of belittling the variety of human achievement. Horney reduces all men to the pathos of the aging Edith Wharton, trying in vain to spank a book that has no bottom.

This traditional view of motherhood as the "onlie begetter," by which all art is ultimately explicable and to which it is reducible, has cast a long pall over women's lives. Only recently have women egun to fight free of this shackling of their thoughts to their wombs, often with the help of sympathetic men such as the psychoanalyst Robert Seidenberg in his sensible "Is Anatomy Destiny?" (1970): "Without in the least knocking the value and delights of having babies, writing books would seem to be another thing again" (in Miller, p. 309). This sane understatement is long overdue. To me, at least, it is a relief to find a male analyst appreciating rather than diagnosing the clearheaded distinctions of such women writers as Mary Ellmann— "This idealization of childbirth obscures the distinction between involuntary and voluntary achievement which we depend upon in describing any achievement as *creative*"—or Cynthia Ozick: "To call a child a poem may be a pretty metaphor, but it is a slur on the labor of art. Literature cannot be equated with physiology, and woman through her reproductive system alone is no more a creative artist than was Joyce by virtue of his kidneys alone, or James by virtue of his teeth. . . . A poem emerges from a mind, and mind is, so far as our present knowledge takes us, an unknowable abstraction."[4] In this decomposition of a sentimental equation, the artist's identity makes its own definition. It no longer needs to justify its existence by a pious metaphorical association with motherhood.

The very existence of this conflict between psychiatrists suggests their underlying difficulty in perceiving an adult woman without reference to children. As Helene Deutsch's categories suggest, a woman passes only from being a child to bearing one. Attempting to bring a new flexibility to these rigid imperatives, Jean Baker Miller deplores the absence of psychiatric paradigms for adult womanhood: "The attributes toward which women are still expected to aim are those that are linked with childish or infantile qualities, e.g., helplessness, dependency, and the like. Women are not expected to grow toward those attributes associated with men; to do so would be unfeminine. In fact, we seem to have no model for women's growth at all" (Miller, p. 387). This vacuum where the adult female should be, the paradox whereby her existence is defined only in reference to children, explains much of our difficulty not only in creating our own lives, but in assessing the lives of women in the past. This difficulty is compounded when we look at the lives of childless women in the nineteenth century, struggling against universal approval of large families and paeans to the holiness of motherhood. For the nineteenth-century popular imagination, motherhood was not merely a biological fact, but a spiritual essence inseparable from pure womanhood; thus, whatever their marital status, the large, anomalous band of "lady novelists" were most charitably regarded as a peculiar species of mother. Whether actual or metaphorical, maternity alone was the seal of respectable female maturity. The honorary motherhood bestowed on woman artists, in the nineteenth century as today, seems to have created a nagging confusion in the self-perception of two of the century's greatest and most determinedly childless novelists: Jane Austen and George Eliot.

Jane Austen's letters define a world where, after marriage, incessant confinements constitute the business of a woman's life, and often, as in the case of her sister-in-law Fanny who died bearing her fourth child, its premature termination as well. Children were inescapable and often welcome invaders of Austen's cottage at Chawton, though she never confused them with the manuscripts that could be slipped quietly under a blotter when nieces and nephews burst into the rooms; but confinement was more pernicious. The very word has undertones of enforced incarceration, even of burial alive, that echo in Austen's perceptions of motherhood. Her seemingly callous, unapologetic distaste for childbearing has shocked generations of critics,[5] perhaps because their stereotypes become dislodged when a woman novelist lashes out against parturition. Her most widely quoted description of motherhood is a Gothic comedy of marriage's abortion and biology's grotesque invasion: "Mrs. Hall, of Sherbourne, was brought to bed yesterday of a dead child, some weeks before she expected, owing to a fright. I suppose she happened unawares to look at her husband."[6] Considering this ruthless vision of misadventure, it seems unlikely that Jane Austen's novels represent sighs over lost fulfillment.

Later in her life, she enthusiastically supported her niece Anna's attempt to write a novel, reading her manuscript with gusto and criticizing it with professional scrupulousness; but she lost all interest in Anna when she married and had a child. In her passage from writer to mother, Anna sinks into a lower order of being, forfeiting her humanity, her youth, and perhaps life itself: "Poor Animal, she will be worn out before she is thirty.—I am very sorry for her" (March 23, 1817, 2:488). Austen's dismissal suggests an unpassable abyss between writer and mother, human and animal, the dancing creativity of the mind and the monotonous attrition of the womb. In motherhood, Anna has relinquished life rather than created it.

Jane Austen's anger at childbirth suggests less a squeamish shrinking from biology than a deep awareness of its potential to betray the aspiring consciousness. Yet when *Sense and Sensibility,* her first published novel, was in proof, she wrote exultantly to Cassandra: "No indeed, I am never too busy to think of S & S. I can no more forget it, than a mother can forget her sucking child" (April 25, 1811, 2:272). This triumphant letter contains one of the very few conventionally maternal images in all of Jane Austen's writings, and it is also one of her sparse employments of formal figurative language. The unaccountable conventionality of this metaphor, compared with the indelible portrait of Mrs. Hall of Sherbourne, is underlined by its appropriation from Isaiah 49:15: "Can a woman forget her sucking child, That she should not have compassion on the son of her womb?" In casting about for a form for the unprecedented elation of success, Jane Austen seems to have turned to the Bible rather than life. Perhaps she might later have dismissed this sentence, along with its self-consciously biblical simile, as "thorough novel slang." Though a Freudian might suggest that her unconscious broke through her defenses just this once, the secondhand language and metaphor make their emotional validity dubious: in Austen's letters as in her novels, true feeling cannot express itself in clichés. Though the tangible accomplishment of her first set of proofs made art and motherhood leap together in her language, the borrowed equation seems less a vehicle of spontaneous joy than an index of the paucity of language defining women's achievements. Jane Austen did not give us a new language, but in her later letters, she uses the old easy metaphors as a vehicle of cutting irony.

For as she gained confidence in her own achievement, she came to value art precisely for its separation from childhood, creating her books as preservatives of a precious space for the free, mercurial adult—a brief consciousness of mobile womanhood between the twin oppressions of girlhood and marriage. When Anna was still her colleague in fiction rather than an alien mother, Austen's suggestion that Anna delete her heroine's childhood contained her own mature credo: "One does not care for girls till they are grown up" (September 9, 1814, 2:402). But "grown up" does not mean ground down into a

"Poor Animal." Writing to her niece Fanny, to whom she turne
tenderly after Anna's defection, Austen defined the incompatibilit
between the spiritual freedom her novels celebrate and the subsidenc
of motherhood: "Oh! what a loss it will be when you are married. Yo
are too agreeable in your single state, too agreeable as a Niece. I sha
hate you when your delicious play of Mind is all settled down int
conjugal & maternal affections" (February 20, 1817, 2:478–79). Wa
she thinking of Anna when she used the word "hate"?

The equation between childbearing and creativity arises agai
in a letter to Anna, in simple language this time and with a dangerou
edge. Juxtaposing her own creation with that of her newly delivere
niece, Austen writes: "As I wish very much to see *your* Jemima, I ar
sure you will like to see *my* Emma, & have therefore great pleasure i
sending it for your perusal. Keep it as long as you chuse, it has bee
read by all here" (December ?, 1815, 2:449). In the earlier letter, th
maternal image insisted on the identity of the writer's with the moth
er's ecstasy; here, no metaphor insists on unity, and the simple clause
are kept delicately and deliberately apart. Moreover, both writer an
recipient must have been aware that in the past, it was Anna who ha
sent her novels to her aunt, and that Jemima was not dedicated to th
Prince Regent at his own royal request. The simple parallelism of th
syntax juxtaposing the two possessive pronouns makes the gulf be
tween them, and between the clauses that contain them, glaringly clea
Separateness is now the essence of the metaphor. Jemima and Emm
are a different order of child entirely, and in that difference lies bot
the wit and the irony of their conjunction.

Jane Austen's dream children, "my Elinor" and "m
Elizabeth" of whom she is so proud, are precious precisely becaus
they are not children: their adulthood is a brief reprieve from an in
fantilizing life. The sight of real children brought Austen no Words
worthian sense of continuity and renewal; rather, she distrusted th
confinement of the flashing adult self they represented. During her la
illness, she wrote wearily, "I am quite tired of so many Children
(March 23, 1817, 2:488), as if they were a symptom of the illne
that was wearing down her life. The tone of this letter is echoed in h
last and most romantic novel: in *Persuasion*, Captain Wentworth sig
nals his continuing love for Anne Elliot by removing a burdensom
child from her back; most nineteenth-century heroes would depos

he child in the heroine's arms. Adult love becomes the ally of art in redeeming the dutifully maternal woman by an alternative world.

Jane Austen's fiction subtly reinforces her allegiance to childless adulthood. Though the novels avoid autobiography and give us no portrait of the complete artist, Austen's strongest, if most undisciplined, heroine defines the life she is not equipped to live. The "imaginist" Emma Woodhouse aspires to shape art out of life, to turn her neighbors into characters for her plot, and among Austen's heroines, Emma is the most remote from motherhood. Not only is she motherless herself—which for Mr. Knightley explains her dangerous will to control—but she alone coolly rejects motherhood for herself in favor of an aunt's artistic distance. The future she wrongly predicts for herself is the life her creator actually lived: "There will be enough for every hope and every fear; and though my attachment to none can equal that of a parent, it suits my ideas of comfort better than what is warmer and blinder. My nephews and nieces—I shall often have a niece with me."[7] Like Jane Austen, Emma preserves the fine distinction between the artist as aunt and the "Poor Animal" as parent. Though her own capacity for artistic distance is questionable, her sensitivity to hierarchical nuances could never blur two such radically unlike relationships.

Emma is unequipped to live her own prediction, but we never learn whether she will follow Anna's pattern, turning to maternity when she gives up her art under the glare of Mr. Knightley and the normal; as far as we see, the marriages that conclude Jane Austen's novels have no progeny. When the last chapter surveys the future, the heroines are never seen surrounded by a dimpled brood, as Victorian heroines infallibly are. In Austen's novels, the consummately adult art of life may fulfill itself in marriage, but motherhood seems antithetical to it. Like Charlotte Brontë's Jane Eyre, Austen, too, might have been troubled by a menacing nightmare of carrying a child as a portent of peril and loss. Far from endowing Austen with secondhand motherhood, her identity as an artist represented an escape from confinement into a child-free world with space for mind and spirit, time for change, and privacy for growth.

George Eliot was born as a literary sibyl in an age when it was less easy for mind to laugh away the "Poor Animal." Though individual mothers could still be paragons of idiocy, as are many of

Eliot's own creations, Victorian motherhood came to incarnate humanity's holiest state, in which alone divinity returned to blend with
flesh. Perhaps as a result, Eliot hymned maternity in theory as powerfully as she avoided it in practice. Her early essay "Silly Novels by
Lady Novelists" endorses the "precious specialty" women bring to fiction, "lying quite apart from masculine aptitudes and experiences."⁸
In a later letter, Eliot develops this hint that maternity is the hidden
generator of both womanliness and woman's art: "We can no more
afford to part with that exquisite type of gentleness, tenderness, possible maternity suffusing a woman's being with affectionateness, which
makes what we mean by the feminine character, than we can afford to
part with the human love, the mutual subjection of soul between a
man and a woman—which is also a growth and revelation beginning
before all history."⁹

These genuflections to motherhood may account for the
insufferably cute toddlers who tug at the reader in the early novels
Tottie, Eppie, and their ilk may be Eliot's unconvincing attempt to
demonstrate that she, too, is in possession of woman's "precious specialty." Though her one plausible child, Maggie Tulliver, is a "wild
thing" whose estrangement repudiates all nurturing, Eliot's self-conscious
protestations about the holiness of motherhood strike an uncomfortably
false note in her work. They may also have inspired one of her most
astute twentieth-century critics to this simplistic diagnosis of her genius: "What compelled this woman to create so compulsively, ever
after she had amassed a more than modest fortune by her writings?
What was it that drove her to read scores of dry volumes on topogra-
phy, art, history, prosody, mythology, law, religion, medicine, in order
to sustain her occasionally flagging 'inspiration'? Was there a link between this obsession to give birth to fictional offspring and the sterility
enforced by social convention on the loving 'Mutter' of Lewes' three
legitimate sons?"¹⁰

If offered both dry volumes and wet diapers, I suspect this
writer would choose the former under no "compulsion" beyond a sense
of vocation, just as George Eliot did before him. Unfortunately, in
accordance with the pieties of her age and her own desire for inclusion
and veneration, Eliot herself provided some fuel for vulgar misreadings
of her career, for until the end of her life she repeatedly defined her
own sense of moral mission in the imagery of motherhood. But if we

ook more closely at her own descriptions of the creative process, it
seems that like her own characters in *Middlemarch,* she allowed her
thoughts to "entangle themselves in metaphors." For if her books
evoked any aspect of motherhood to her, it was not the possession of
tender fulfillment, but the unending frustration of parental estrangement: "My own books scourge me," she wrote to Sara Hennell (August 23, 1863, 4:104), suggesting implicitly that a dream child like a
real one is the future's revenge on the hopes that created it.

   But books alleviate the pain of parenthood in that unlike
children, their presence evaporates with time. Requesting that her
publisher bring out *Silas Marner* before *Romola,* she wrote: "My chief
reason for wishing to publish the story now, is, that I like my writings
to appear in the order in which they are written, because they belong
to successive mental phases, and when they are a year behind me, I
can no longer feel that thorough identification with them which gives
zest to the sense of authorship" (February 24, 1861, 3:382–83). Unlike
the unalterable future a real child creates, one's future with one's book
allows the renewal of forgetfulness. Ten years later, Eliot defines this
healing departure more clearly to Sara Hennell: "But do not write to
me about [*Middlemarch*], because until a book has quite gone away
from me and become entirely of the non-ego—gone thoroughly from
the winepress into the casks—I would rather not hear or see anything
that is said about it" (November 21, 1871, 5:214–15). Unlike that
of motherhood, the essence of literary creation is the promise of inevitable detachment. As Jane Austen regained perspective on her works
by shutting the manuscripts in a drawer for months at a time, so
George Eliot exorcises the pain of her novels by forgetting them. The
inconstancy of art bestows a completeness distinct from the perpetuity
of motherhood. Eliot's awareness of the centrality of partings makes
one suspect that it was character rather than "the sterility enforced by
social convention" that made her one of a small band of Victorian
women who we know practiced birth control;[11] nor does it seem an
accident that her first literary triumph was the lachrymose set piece of
the worn-down mother Milly Barton's death, as if the birth of the
author into "the honours of print and pay"[12] was simultaneously the
death of the mother and of motherhood itself.

   For as her most recent biographer points out,[13] Mary Ann
Evans' one authentic child was not a novel, but her own transfigured

self: like Milton's Satan, she gave birth to a persona who would reign rather than serve. But ironically, in an age whose language of womanhood was inseparable from the language of family, her very imperiousness associated her with motherhood. Thus when Mary Ann Evans was eight, the gravity with which she shunned other children led them to dub her "little Mamma," not perceiving that a dislike of children might disqualify one for that title: habitual association links female authority only to motherhood. Later, when she had evolved into George Eliot, her Victorian acolytes made of her a massively philosophic earth mother. Lewes gave the tone and the vocabulary to this collective adoration: he made her anomalous role in his household more conventionally palatable by bestowing on her the Germanic title of "Mutter," adding a lofty touch of Goethe to her relationship with his grown sons, who, however, were beyond the age of tending. As with "little Mamma," the title was more suggestive of role-playing than of reality. Eliot's testy response to a feminist who addressed her as "Miss Evans" shows her clinging to the name as an index of social acceptance: "When I tell you that we have a great boy of eighteen at home who calls me 'mother,' as well as two other boys, almost as tall, who write to me under the same name, you will understand that the point is not one of mere egoism or personal dignity, when I request that any one who has a regard for me will cease to speak of me by my maiden name" (April 1, 1861, 3:396).

Names here carry their own autonomous life; Eliot never examines the relationships they are intended to define. Later on, Lewes' "Mutter" became his "Madonna," under which affectionate title she presided over solemn Sundays at the Priory, but this Victorian Madonna is upstaged by no divine child: she gives birth only to her own regality. Indeed, George Eliot seems to have shied away from worshippers who presumed to call themselves the children of her cosmic motherhood. At the height of her eminence, a cult of adoring women adopted her as their "spiritual mother," begging to be called (as one of them put it) "by the sweet name of 'Daughter.' "[14] Eliot regarded this cult ambivalently perhaps not entirely because of its lesbian and separatist undercurrents. In confronting this swarm of clamorous, adoring progeny rather than in her distant fondness for Lewes' highly independent sons, Eliot seems to have found herself too close to the reality behind the matriarchal title; she was in danger of strangling in her Madonna's obes. The emotional demands of Edith Simcox, her most persistent nd fervid "daughter," led her finally to repudiate both the name and he thing: "She did not like for me to call her 'Mother'. . . . she new it was her fault, she had begun, she was apt to be rash and ommit herself in one mood to what was irksome to her in another. Not with her own mother, but her associations otherwise with the ame were as of a task, and it was a fact that her feeling for me was ot at all a mother's—any other name she didn't mind." [15]

Only in the last year of her life, when her persona threatned to take on literal reality, was she able to work free of the charade hat had at first dignified, then oppressed her. Paradoxically, her abanlonment of this persona might explain her late, and brief, marriage to ohn Cross, for she evolved with him a new set of fantasy relationships hat avoided the name, and the game, of motherhood. Though he was wenty years her junior, and turned to Eliot just after the death of his eloved mother, he never perceived himself as one of her progeny. nstead, they addressed each other teasingly during Lewes' lifetime as 'Nephew" and "Aunt," in a manner recalling Jane Austen's allegiance o the aesthetic distance an aunt could claim. Moreover, she signed er first love letter to Cross by a private name remote from Lewes' 'Mutter": "Thy tender Beatrice" (October 16, 1879, 7:211–12). Stimulated by their joint reading of Dante, her image of herself has rogressed from cosmic, if childless, motherhood to that of an absolute piritual essence purified of maternal qualities. Doubtless this role, too, eft out essential elements in their relationship. Still, Eliot's late rejecion of the posture of "mother" may be one reason why she selected ohnny, who asked of her no noble maternal poses, rather than the lependent "daughter" Edith as her chief worshipping comforter after he death of Lewes.

For in rejecting the image of motherhood, Eliot was coming to terms with the reality of her past. Though Lewes bestowed the lorifying title on her, this indefatigably nurturing man was the sole nother in their relationship, restoring to her as best he could the comorting identities of "daughter" and "little sister" from which she was xiled.[16] For she had left her family, first emotionally and then in fact, vhen she was still in the position of dependent child to her imperious ather and brother, and her life beyond them played out the cycle of amilial roles only in wary, fitful charade. Her central self, and the

apparent source of her art, was not the all-nourishing mother of her
grandiose aspirations, but the more humble and dependent creature
she had been in the family she left, whom she recalled in her autobiographical sonnet sequence "Brother and Sister":

> But were another childhood-world my share,
> I would be born a little sister there.[17]

Lewes' mothering was sufficiently sensitive to enable its object to play
at maternity, to gain the glory with which Victorian society endowed
it without submitting to the sacrifice at its essence. The creator and
persona George Eliot is the happiest offspring of Lewes' sense of play.

Though in her ambiguous role as "Mrs. Lewes" George
Eliot took the name of "mother" solemnly, her novels do not. Infanticide is a persistent, and sometimes tempting, activity, and like Jane
Austen's, Eliot's most artistically inclined heroines are the least motherly. The powerfully built Dorothea Brooke does not become the robust matriarch she might have, but surprises us by almost dying in
childbirth; in the somber conclusion to *Middlemarch,* a description of
Dorothea's maternity modulates into an image of a grim and solitary
death. Maggie Tulliver, compact of passion and the need for love, violently mutilates her dolls in a manner that does not augur well for her
nurturing future.[18] In George Eliot's novels, as in Jane Austen's letters, there is an implicit equation between motherhood and the igno-
miny of death, rather than creation and renewal.

But only in Eliot's last novel, *Daniel Deronda,* does a fully
fledged woman artist eloquently assert the distinction between motherhood and art; she is the Princess Leonora Halm Eberstein, whose
essence (like George Eliot's) has gone into her stage name, Alcharisi.
Though the novel's action condemns her abandonment of her son, it
condemns more radically the uniformity forced on women: the real
crime is that, like Gwendolen Harleth, Alcharisi can gain a modicum
of adult freedom only by marrying. Alcharisi is the only female artist
in Eliot's novels, and she stands strikingly aloof from woman's "precious specialty" as "Silly Novels by Lady Novelists" defined it: "Every
woman is supposed to have the same set of motives, or else be a monster. I am not a monster, but I have not felt exactly what other women
feel—or say they feel, for fear of being thought unlike others. When
you reproach me in your heart for sending you away from me, you

mean that I ought to say I felt about you as other women say they feel about their children. I did *not* feel that. I was glad to be freed from you." [19]

The artist does not embody the vague invocation in the prelude to *Middlemarch* of "the common yearning of womanhood"; this artist, at least, is bravely exempt from it. Alcharisi's defiant apologia seems to spring from the same new self-acceptance that led George Eliot to deny herself as "spiritual mother" to Edith Simcox. She gives Alcharisi two ringing sentences that might stand as the definitive epitaph of her own identity as artist and "Mutter": "I was living a myriad lives in one. I did not want a child" (p. 689). This simple statement seems a truer record of her creative life than the mantle of the Madonna with which she decorated it. After a career of entanglement and role-playing, Eliot, like Austen, frees her art from the metaphor of maternity and allows it to stand alone, as its own justification and its own treasure.

George Eliot's liberation of art from the trappings of motherhood was a belated and difficult assertion, and it is for us as well. Even today, almost a hundred years after her death, it is a difficult insight for those who accept traditional psychiatric paradigms of women, which postulate, as George Eliot did in *Middlemarch*, a "common yearning of womanhood" that denies the many possible goals and shapes female adulthood can choose. It is tempting but misleading to yoke artistic and biological creativity. In the lives of Jane Austen and George Eliot, two woman artists made inescapably aware of the social assumptions equating womanhood with motherhood, art is a liberation from that demand, not a metaphoric submission to it. It is the bounty of "a myriad lives in one," bringing release from limitation to a common destiny. Austen and Eliot both turned away from motherhood and embraced a creativity they defined as more spacious, more adult, more inclusive. Our study of women artists, and of women, has still much to learn from their fine attunement to differences that are not monstrous, but part of our inherited wealth. [20]

11.

Dorothy L. Sayers and the Amazons

A community of women without men is a defiance of God, a sin against nature, and a linguistic impossibility: left solitary and tailless, the poor prefix can wail only "wo-." Nevertheless, despite the fact that language makes them wail, women without men have always existed, and like other things that exist, they have been written about with fear and with love. Dorothy L. Sayers writes about them very often, but never with as much fear and as much love as she bestows on them in *Gaudy Night,* in which she celebrates female self-sufficiency and abandons it with Harriet Vane. But although the women of Shrewsbury exist firmly alone, *Gaudy Night* as a whole gains strength from its conjunction with other works, for in celebrating the mythical purity and purpose of Shrewsbury College, which she plumps with "monstrous impertinence" in the middle of the Balliol cricket ground, Dorothy L. Sayers gives a dry twist to the tail of a tradition that extends back to the beginning of our literature.

The Amazons of Greek mythology give us our first picture of a community of manless women, and predictably, their name denotes their loss: in Greek folk etymology, "Amazon" means "without breast," reminding us that these legendary warriors sliced off their right breasts in order to shoot more effectively. The operation apparently worked, because the Amazons successfully arrogated to themselves the male prerogative of violence, while managing with the help of a mating season to bear and nurture enough females to keep their community replenished; male children were destroyed at birth, presumably going the way of the superfluous breast. Their patron goddess, Artemis, the virgin of the hunt, is an Amazon raised to Olympian stature. Clear, pure, and savage, Artemis embodies both the integrity and the potential for disease in a woman who emulates men and discards them: she coolly has Actaeon rent to pieces when he invades the privacy of her bath, and we learn in *Gaudy Night* that those arrows she shoots so cleanly "are plagues and death."[1] Even in ancient Greece, a world of manless women seems a contradiction in terms, being simultaneously stronger and weaker, purer and more violent, cleaner and more fetid, than a world with men in it as well.

In Shakespeare's *Antony and Cleopatra*, the fetidness of such a world is pronounced. Inhabited primarily by women, eunuchs, and "pretty dimpled boys," Cleopatra's Egypt is redolent of mud and perfume. But in *Antony and Cleopatra*, the women ooze with breasts, no longer standing erect and shooting their arrows with the speed and accuracy of men. Violence, now called "honor," has become the exclusive privilege of the masculine Roman sphere; it is threatened, not emulated, by female sensuality and duplicity. The men who try to confront this empire are menaced less by slaughter in battle than they are by dissolution into feminine ooze. "Transform us not to women," the blustering soldier Enobarbus begs the weeping, feminized Antony; and later on, Antony realizes the enormity of his loss when he bellows at the eunuch Mardian: "O, thy vile lady! She has robb'd me of my sword." Swords are only stage props in Cleopatra's Egypt; the queen herself is a signally incompetent warrior; "the beds i'the east are soft," and in them, the straightforward allegiances of masculine honor sink in a slough of lies, love, and decay. "Let's have one other gaudy night," cries Antony at the hour of his defeat in Egypt. "Fill our bowls once more; Let's mock the midnight bell." The overflowing femininity of Egypt floods the regular march of time's measurements. But not so in Dorothy L. Sayers' stately Oxford. Overlooking its straight and eternal spires, Lord Peter Wimsey salutes and bypasses the mud of a woman's world in his direction to Harriet Vane: "We'll have one other gaudy night, and comfort our souls with the Bach concerto for two violins (p. 381). After wrapping himself in the "motionless austerity" of the "great, striding fugue," Wimsey proposes to Vane and is accepted in succinct, measured Latin. The potentially grotesque disorder of a "gaudy night" presided over by women is lifted by art and ritual to an impersonal sublimity that transcends Egyptian witchery to become religion.

But before Dorothy L. Sayers can scrub an Amazonian community clean and yoke its aspirations to the branchy towers of Oxford, it undergoes a further attenuation in English literature. Elizabeth Gaskell's *Cranford* is "in possession of the Amazons,"[2] but in Victorian England, the word has dwindled into tender irony: the impoverished old maids who inhabit the tucked-away little village, living on kindness and charity and memories of their parents' gentility, seem all maimed pathos, with little of their original strength. Their arrows have become the tingling barbs of gossip that orbit through their genteel card parties and sentiment, the faded goodwill of which provides a soft and subtle antagonist to the outside world of men, money, and commerce into which Roman "honor" has deteriorated.

But even the sweetly incompetent ladies of Cranford carry a faint whiff of Artemis' witchery: the men who enter Cranford mysteriously die, fall ill, or disappear. Only to preserve itself does Cranford open its doors to a man who survives. The presiding spirit of the village is the fluttery and loving Miss Matty, and the slight plot that knits together the various episodes turns on Miss Matty's bankruptcy in a bank failure and her fumbling attempt to support herself by running a tea shop, though she persists in running her business like a hostess and giving its contents away to all who enter. At this point her brother Peter is allowed to enter the community and save it at the end by restoring her fallen fortunes; and Peter has disgraced himself as a boy by assuming woman's dress, a shame that seems to insure his safe entrance into Cranford later on. Though Cranford ladies might have hidden reserves of destruction tucked away, a womanized man is permitted to save the community. In his providential appearance and inexhaustible largesse, Peter might be a direct ancestor of the altruistic and somewhat epicene Lord Peter Wimsey, who enters Shrewsbury at the critical moment and saves it from the stigma of sexual abnormality, which presented as great a threat to the Freudianized generation of the 1930s as the bankruptcy which prostrated Miss Matty did to the Victorians.

In most American delineations, the Amazonian world is as remote from the values and activities of men as Cleopatra's Egypt and Miss Matty's Cranford are; but their cleansing and their fetid possibilities tend to divide off from each other. In Louisa May Alcott's *Little Women*, the all-female March household is a taproot of nurturance; from that first Christmas day when they troop out to deposit their breakfast at the destitute Hummels, to their gift of a blancmange to the ailing Laurie, to the love and fun they spread when they diffuse into the world, the March girls exist to bring wholesomeness to the less fortunate; even the debilitated Beth spends her last conscious days dropping little knitted gifts of warmth to the poor children who shiver beneath her window. Any hostility that the March girls may harbor rises to the surface in the wives' ghetto of Clare Boothe Luce's *The Women*, which presents a woman's world as a jungle of bitchery, as emotionally fetid and claustrophobic as the neurotic Vassar of Mary McCarthy's *The Group*. Appropriated into an all-female sphere, love and rage split apart to create the emotional atmospheres that make of a woman's world a "little" haven, in which feelings are yoked to no larger missions that will give them shape and scope.

For in later literature, the Amazons retain their name, with all the negation and mutilation it implies, without retaining their purpose. Whether they are healing or diseased, well-scrubbed havens or swamps of perfume, the women's worlds that descend from Cleopatra's Egypt have one thing in common with it: all are bound to, and by, the individual, the personal. In these communities, Cleopatra's pointed questions to her messenger skewer the individual from the crowd: "Is she as tall as me?" "Is she shrill-tongued or low?" "What majesty is in her gait?" "Guess at her years, I prithee." "Is [her face] long or round?" "Her hair, what colour?" Whether it is planted in ancient Egypt, a village in England or New England, or a modern city, a woman's world—in literature, at any rate—is crowded with subtle differentiations between faces, ages, voices, colors. It redeems the detached detail and thrives on it. Othello is insane when he stamps into the private haven of his wife's boudoir intoning, "It is the cause, it is the cause, my soul"; grand battlefield honor cannot be transplanted in a woman's world that thrives, nurtures, and kills from its very cause-lessness.

This brief sketch of a tradition may help us to appreciate the anomaly of Dorothy L. Sayers' Shrewsbury, a vision of a world that lives on impersonality. In its freedom from "personal contacts, personal spites, personal jealousies," its avoidance of "the hand-to-hand struggle with the insistent personalities of other people, all pushing for a place in the limelight," of "the accidents of one's own personal adventure" (p. 20), Shrewsbury is surely like no academic community that ever existed. The academic world chafes with personalities, but Shrewsbury is miraculously free from them, a *hortus conclusus* of detachment governed by women. Othello's "cause" is translated into Shrewsbury's grand governing principle: "To be true to one's calling, whatever follies one might commit in one's emotional life, that was the way to spiritual peace" (p. 28). The cause thrives in the hands of these women, while the larger world without—from the careerism of Annie's Arthur to the literary feuds Harriet flees and the irascible diplomats Peter tries to mollify in Rome—is seen as rancid with personalities and crowded with selves: the outer world, in short, becomes the personal, and thus, the "little," inner world that women have traditionally lived in. The women of Shrewsbury are unique because they provide a haven from the self, not for it. In endowing them only with objectivity and honor and relegating personality to the lesser world outside the garden, Dorothy L. Sayers restores to the Amazons their arrows and stops worrying about their breasts.[3]

In concept at least, the women of Shrewsbury—unlike many manless women in literature, including the Amazons themselves—are not defined by negation; they are seen vigorously, in terms of what they have, not of what they lack. Not only are they committed to their cause, but Sayers reveals with enormous shrewdness the fact that this commitment demands no sacrifice whatever: rarely and winningly, she perceives how much they *enjoy* their cause, and that alone. No other academic novel that I know of captures so well the fun that peers out from the methodological rigor and high seriousness of academic life, and the exhilarating privilege of belonging to it. The "pretty feet" of Shrewsbury's beaming Dean do not suffer because they have chosen to walk through gardens where no man can fall at them; they are alive with purpose, because they are where they want to and must be. When Miss de Vine finally arrives at Oxford, she forgets to miss the man she left behind. Recalling him, she can murmur only: "Fundamental mistakes arise out of lack of genuine interest. In my opinion, that is" (p. 149). Her misty, far-reaching eyes pierce through the many literary wails emitting from women who have lost their love, and light on the fact that for some women, love is boring, and fidelity to the fact is completion. Women like the Dean and Miss de Vine embody not the involuntary mystery of passion, but the greater, because the fully human, mystery of conscious choice.

But if Shrewsbury were a paradise, it would tell us nothing; like life, it has its share of thwarted women. Sayers takes care of the familiar stereotypes of the bitter spinster and the frustrated mother by embodying them in Miss Hillyard and Miss Shaw and defining them as aberrated *within* the Amazonian community; a truer use of them, I think, than we find in Muriel Spark's Jean Brodie, who infuses both stereotypes with a wild visionary energy that may cloak their familiarity from the dazzled reader as it does from her dazzled students. The stereotype of the "crazy spinster" is both the serpent in the garden and the pivot of the mystery, and Sayers depends on her readers' complicity in it to befog the clues that are even more transparently laid out than the clues in the other Wimsey books are; in this case, unraveling the very easy mystery requires not so much chess-game ingenuity as it does a freedom from sexual myths that few novelists can expect to find in their readers. Jean Brodie, dominant and dangerous, seems to embody all the romantic energy of an Amazonian world; but amid the real fervor of Shrewsbury, female frustration is an interloper and an anomaly. "It's the pottiness, you know, that's so awful," murmurs the Dean (p. 80), and that wonderful pun recurs through the novel, defining the female world of madness, excreta, and babies that is incomprehensible and finally boring when seen by the clear light of "masculine" abstractions like truth and honor. The gaudy muddy nights of Cleopatra's Egypt are not the only empire women can command. Given brains and a cause, they can erect and preside over an intellectual Camelot.

This is the strong and challenging vision of Shrewsbury with which the novel opens; but its subsequent dramatic realization is a bit of a falling-off. For one thing, stereotypes like Miss Hillyard and Miss Shaw serve an important tactical function in defining the positive fervor and achievement of Shrewsbury; but stereotypes like Miss de Vine and Miss Lydgate undermine it. Why is it impossible for Miss de Vine to keep her hair in order, and Miss Lydgate her proof sheets? It seems unlikely that women with their capacity to organize and regulate their careers, their lives, and their community should be so girlishly helpless and incompetent. We can accept an incompetence that arises from indifference—the academic world abounds in women who equate brilliance with defiant sloppiness—but Miss de Vine and Miss Lydgate are always fretting about hair and galley proofs, respectively. It seems rather that Sayers is succumbing here to the old vision of women as carriers of disorder: the Amazons embody all the barbaric savagery that threatens civilization, Cleopatra's kingdom overflows with mud and slime, Miss Matty's tea shop spills over with tea and sweets and the books are never in order, Freud's prototypical Dora is entangled in her own snarl of complexes and desires, a wife's pocketbook is always a mess. But I simply do not believe that Shrewsbury women would be so messy, unless they wanted to be or didn't care whether they were or not.

Moreover, like the Wimsey series as a whole, *Gaudy Night* suffers from a confusion of genres: opposites are yoked by violence together. Peter Wimsey himself is a battlefield of opposites, whom we are asked to respond to as simultaneously the God-like, imperturbable detective of convention, and a human being bristling with emotional complexes and hidden wounds. But *Gaudy Night* suffers from a particular, and deeper, schism of its own: the setting fights the action, and a community we are asked to see as happily and productively celibate is forced to do double duty as the breeding ground of a love story. Sayers seems to have in mind the dynamic counterpoint of metaphysical poetry, in which art is generated from the tension between passionate chastity and passionate love; but she achieves only the popular author's trick of having her cake and eating it as well. Fruitful tension is replaced by a bland and cozy confusion in which one kind of emotion does duty for the other because in the end, neither one is terribly important. It is a kind of artistic Anglican compromise as Sayers herself describes it in *Gaudy Night*, "soothing and ceremonial," "very exquisitely robed, very cheerful in a serious kind of way, a little mannered, a little conscious of [its] fine courtesy" (p. 231); finally, it is a little sickening in its insistence that the vigorous women of Shrewsbury fall into their places as Harriet's jolly bridesmaids, like those frisky nuns in *The Sound of Music* decking up Mary Martin for her wedding to the magnanimous Baron. In effect, Sayers kills off her Amazons by bestowing on them the Freudian kiss of being "normal after all." As she herself might have said with clear-minded reverence in another mood, God forbid that they should be so.

For the real soft spot in Sayers' Anglican compromise—the flaw that divests her Amazons of more than a breast—is not so much the marriage between Peter and Harriet that concludes *Gaudy Night* as it is the impossible marriage between Freudianism and Christianity that destroys its foundations. In the person of Harriet Vane, Sayers glimpses a higher, more remote Catholicism than her own: "It was entertaining to imagine a Freudian University indissolubly wedded to a Roman Establishment: they certainly would not live so harmoniously together as the Anglican Church and the School of Litterae Humaniores" (p. 232). But being an Englishwoman to the core, Sayers cannot take the uncompromising road to Rome. Instead, she tries very hard to make the blindly imperious Freudian processes *look* harmoniously bound to the staunch Christian soul, until they petrify into a frozen blissful smile and the series ends.

Odd as this may seem, Sayers' Anglo-Catholicism walks hand in hand with her feminism, for, like the detective novel itself, both presuppose the sanctity and inviolability of individual will and choice. In her introduction to her translation of the *Inferno*, Sayers writes illuminatingly of the "Christian and Catholic view of ourselves as responsible rational beings. We must abandon any idea that we are the slave of chance, or environment, or our subconscious; any vague notion that good and evil are merely relative terms, or that conduct and opinion do not really matter; any comfortable persuasion that, however shiftlessly we muddle through life, it will somehow or other all come right on the night. We must try to believe that man's will is free, that he can consciously exercise choice, and that his choice can be decisive to all eternity."[4] Her essays on women in *Unpopular Opinions* ("Are Women Human?" and "The Human-Not-Quite-Human") are equally insistent that each woman be taken as a free and conscious self, not as a representative member of a sexual class; in these days of solidarity, she brings to feminists a refreshing reminder of the sanctity of differences. Both her Catholicism and her feminism insist upon the solitary choice and the many roads available.

But Freudianism, with its knowingly coercive categorizing, keeps popping up in the Wimsey novels. In *Gaudy Night*, it takes the form of Miss Edwards the biologist, who joins the Senior Common Room in the middle of the book and assumes an archly choric role there. The first demonstration of her scientific brilliance is her cheery axiom that "women are messier by nature" than men. She has a habit of sending waves of biological approval across the High Table to the "imperious" Peter, and, when Harriet seems oblivious to his sexiness, says insinuatingly, "Ah! . . . In your novels, you deal more in material facts than in psychology, don't you?" (p. 311); a simple-minded equation between biology and psychology that seems incredible even at humanities-oriented Oxford in the benighted 1930s. Further, Miss Edwards' scientific moralizing is reinforced by the increasing prominence of the love-starved Miss Hillyard in the second half of the novel. The fact that the other women recede into the background makes her pathetic mooning after Peter seem perforce typical of Shrewsbury women, rather than her own idiosyncrasy. Revealing once again her confident grasp of scientific principles, Miss Edwards labels it for Harriet and for us: "If people will bring dynamite into a powder factory, they must expect explosions" (p. 313). This bit of wisdom erodes the novel's ostensible premise that Shrewsbury is not a sexual and emotional powder factory, but a cool refuge from the blast.

Sayers' flirtation with Freudian definitions is evident throughout the Wimsey series, reinforcing her own unfortunate tendency to stereotype people rather than see them. At her worst, her Freudianism feeds into her tendency to snobbishly label her characters and put them through stock paces; at its best, her Catholicism enhances her respect for the integrity and completeness of their individual souls. The contradictions in this alliance are most evident in her treatment of the single women who flock around Peter throughout the series. Miss Climpson, a brighter cousin of Agatha Christie's Miss Marple, is such a wittily self-effacing investigator that she almost steals Peter's thunder; the séance she conducts in *Strong Poison* out-Peters Peter in the brilliance of its showmanship and audience manipulation. But by *Busman's Honeymoon*, Miss Climpson seems to have metamorphosed into the thoroughly pathetic Miss Twitterton, who has "no husband to cling to" and so exists primarily as a wailing counterpoint to Peter and Harriet's quotation-studded abandon in marriage. By the idyllic end of the series, the Amazons have fulfilled their name and cast off their function by existing as sheer negation. In "Talboys," its embarrassingly beatific coda, the spinster (significantly labeled "Miss Quirk") exists only to be cast out of the very married and traditional *hortus conclusus:* her Freudian ragings are answered in kind by Peter's insertion of a Freudian serpent in her bed, which sends her the way of all quirks in a garden of ladies'-magazine fulfillment. Perhaps her expulsion was forecast earlier, in *Unnatural Death,* where a brisk and sturdy lesbian horse dealer was murdered by her serpentine lesbian niece, the most cosmically evil character in the Wimsey series: the poisonous and negative aspect of the Amazon, or manless woman, murders her healthy and affirmative aspect, just as the Wimsey series itself will do. Sic transit the Amazons in the garden.[5]

This gradual metamorphosis of the Amazon into a gargoyle whose grotesque "quirks" counterpoint the sublimity of the marriage-cathedral is at one with the gradual petrification of Harriet Vane. Harriet's gain of love is a loss of life and power: the "trauma" of the Philip episode increases in intensity throughout the series, as do the solicitous murmurings from Duke's Denver, the storybook Wimsey estate, about her "inferiority complex." The resilient spring of the opening of *Have His Carcase,* with its bold aphoristic echo of Jane Austen—"The best remedy for a bruised heart is not, as so many people seem to think, repose upon a manly bosom. Much more efficacious are honest work, physical activity, and the sudden acquisition of wealth"[6]—sinks depressingly into Harriet's retrospective self-pity in *Busman's Honeymoon:* "Well, it *seems* like a miracle to be able to look forward—to—to see all the minutes in front of one come hopping along with something marvellous in them, instead of just saying, Well that one didn't actually hurt and the next may be quite bearable if only something beastly doesn't come pouncing out—."[7] The world beyond "repose upon a manly bosom" has shrunk from a moral and emotional gymnasium to a threatening menagerie of beastly pouncing things; and the "smudged" and honest prisoner of *Strong Poison,* who mutters gruffly that no man can give her a "square deal," has become a weak and wily dependent who "manages" her temperamental husband and dubs him "my Lord" on their wedding night. In the course of *Busman's Honeymoon,* the contours of Harriet's world shrink to the dimensions of Peter's needs. She obliterates herself systematically in order to fill his needs, disappearing finally into the placid sewing sphinx of the "Talboys" idyll. Biological determinism joins hands with the rightness of the class structure and the divinely endowed predominance of the husband-Lord to subdue Harriet's courage and soften her will. Abdicating from her role as feminist, Christian, and detective, she no longer chooses to be: she becomes. Peter's identity also softens and submerges itself under love, but he has at least married a writer who can compose his epitaph in the face of Miss Quirk's idiosyncratic fulminations: "My dear Miss Quirk! Peter's fifty-two, and he's reverting to type." One can no longer write novels when one's characters so sink away from their ability to choose. The death of the detective is the disappearance of the man and the end of the series.

Dorothy L. Sayers' Anglican compromise with Freud is death, at least, to the Wimseys. Under its aegis, her characters devolve back into the types whence they sprang, shedding their own whimsical variations and shedding their lives in the process. Lord Peter dies as a character weeping in the arms of his good wife, who seems to have become all bosom enfolding him away from the march of time and consequences and death. The war came and went; Harriet learned to sew and provided Peter with three manly boys; and Dorothy L. Sayers turned her mind to higher things, as the world settled in the nursery.

12.

Charlotte Brontë:
The Two Countries

Charlotte Brontë is out of critical fashion at the moment. Despite the recent appearance of two careful studies of her artistic technique,[1] her novels are still often considered extravagant and inchoate, lacking the ironic distance and formal control of her sister Emily's *Wuthering Heights*.

There is some justice in this charge. We cannot find in Charlotte the almost allegorical precision of design we find in *Wuthering Heights*, and some of the most interesting criticism of her novels has eschewed analysis of pattern and design in order to locate an image at the center of her work that defines her sense of subterranean influences working within the self and possibly the cosmos.[2] It seems appropriate to search for a language of images in a novelist who plunges so far below conventional definitions of action and character, and who lived, perhaps fortunately for her art, before modern psychiatry attempted to evolve a new language of the psyche; but a single image does not seem sufficient to define Charlotte Brontë's world of constant conflict. The self is born in her novels out of a clash of extreme and opposing forces, and is rarely able to rest in the stability of a final synthesis. This essay will examine Charlotte Brontë's war within the self as it evolves in her two first-person narratives, *Jane Eyre* and *Villette*.

Until she was at least twenty-three years old, Charlotte Brontë lived in two countries at once: the cold northern climate of Yorkshire was balanced by the tropical zone of Angria, the southern continent she created with Branwell, where her most significant emotional life seems to have been spent. Apparently fearing for her sanity she struggled out of Angria in 1839, and it is not surprising that her first important image of the self should be based on this geography: "I long to quit for awhile that burning clime where we have sojourned too long—its skies flame—the glow of sunset is always upon it—the mind would cease from excitement and turn now to a cooler region where the dawn breaks grey and sober, and the coming day for a time at least is subdued by clouds."[3]

Her mind moves always through an unresolved dialectic which she will continue to translate into the image of a divided country: she passes from a land with a sun that burns and flames dangerously to a land with no sun or color at all. It is a critical cliché that Charlotte Brontë is concerned with the conflict between reason and passion or imagination, but her use of these abstractions is defined by her peculiar imagery: the "cooler region" of reason or reality that follows the "burning clime" of impulse and imagination is not a temperate zone between two extremes, but is itself an extreme of deprivation. In *Jane Eyre* and *Villette*, it is equated with the polar regions.

The struggle between the worlds represented by fire and ice underlies both novels, and their vitality comes from the energy of the battle, not from the fulfillment of resolution. Like many Victorians, Charlotte Brontë was a Manichean—a continual clash of opposed forces gives birth to her world—and the world of ice is an active force in her novels, not a mere negation of energy. Indulging in the sexual sparring which is perhaps the major characteristic of Charlotte Brontë's love scenes, St. John Rivers says to Jane Eyre: "I am cold: no fervour infects me.' [Jane answers:] 'Whereas I am hot, and fire dissolves ice. The blaze there has thawed all the snow from your cloak.' "[4] But in the total structure of Charlotte Brontë's world, snow is not so easily thawed. Lucy Snowe, the narrator-heroine of *Villette*, gives us only single description of her "present" self: "My hair which till a late period withstood the frosts of time, lies now, at last white, under white cap, like snow beneath snow."[5] If either element finally triumphs in the perpetual warfare that constitutes these novels, it may be that "la flamme à l'âme" Paul Emmanuel perceives in the young Lucy is put out at last.

But there is a more striking transition in the movement from *Jane Eyre* to *Villette*. In *Jane Eyre*, the narrator's conflict is externalized and embodied in the entire universe, while in *Villette*, the narrator is alone in a foreign country whose culture is always alien to her, subjected to the divisions within her own mind. Jane Eyre is reflected by her world; Lucy Snowe is denied by hers. The movement from *Jane Eyre* to *Villette* seems almost the movement of the nineteenth century, which begins with Wordsworth's comforting sense of immanence linking man to the universe, and ends with Hardy's vision of man homeless in an alien landscape, creature of nature's mistake. The battle between fire and ice remains constant, but the mode of presentation shifts from mythopoeic romance to abnormal psychology, as the outside world recedes from the speaker.

Jane Eyre: The Divided Landscape.

It was not a bright or splendid summer evening, though fair and soft: the hay-makers were at work all along the road; and the sky, though far from cloudless, was such as promised well for the future: its blue—where blue was visible—was mild and settled, and its cloud strata high and thin. The west, too, was warm: no watery gleam chilled it—it seemed as if there was a fire lit, an altar burning behind its screen of marbled vapor, and out of apertures shone a golden redness.

(*JE*, 2:4)

The strange sky Jane sees seems to reflect what she is. Apparently temperate, its "mild and settled" exterior moves into the more ambiguously suggestive connotations of *"marbled* vapor" whose apertures open to reveal a sudden fire.[6] As she heads toward Thornfield to be proposed to by Mr. Rochester, the fire moves closer to the surface of the marble, though without consuming it. The dialectic that constitutes her nature seems momentarily at rest.

For Jane Eyre is a double character, although she is not paralyzed by the divisions in her nature as Lucy Snowe will be. On the one hand, she is "plain," the perfect governess: she demurely tidies up the unruly passions of Thornfield, preserving her master from the "bathos of sentiment" with her British common sense and from the sin of hubris with her Protestant piety; she subjugates her own passions with an iron hand to the rules of principle and duty.

On the other hand, she is close to the figure of "la belle dame sans merci" who fascinated Swinburne and was the muse of fin -de-siècle literature: she has felt from her childhood a weird pull toward a magic landscape, she paints erotic, surrealistic pictures, she seems to Rochester an elf or a witch and to the innkeeper in the town to have "bewitched" her master. She often talks oddly about her "powers," which, in the call-and-answer scene at the end, are potent enough to triumph over St. John's Christian mission and over the laws of space and time: 'It was *my* time to assume ascendancy. *My* powers were in play, and in force" (2:240–41).

Her two aspects are defined in relation to the amount of emotion she allows herself to spend, and in relation to heat and cold. When she first arrives at Thornfield, she defines in "cool language" her "conscientious solicitude" for her charge Adèle, refusing to "echo cant" by coloring a pedestrian reality with strong feeling. Then, after a transitional paragraph of description, she describes "a tale my imagination created, and narrated continuously; quickened with all of the incident, life, *fire,* feeling, that I desired and had not in my actual existence" (1:138, my italics). Charlotte and Branwell referred to Angria as "the world below," and like Angria, Jane's world below has nothing to do with the one above. It is also a mental world, requiring a meager expenditure of feeling in the name of truth and duty.

We are not aware of Jane being a divided character as we read *Jane Eyre,* in part because the oppositions in her nature do not paralyze her power of action, for, although some of the most memorable passages in the book describe states of feeling, *Jane Eyre* is a novel of action rather than of character: the people in the book have little significant existence apart from what they say and do. But more important, we are not aware of Jane's duality because her conflicts are externalized into myth, becoming the environment through which she travels; the world of the book becomes a metaphor of Jane Eyre's psy-the. The cold, starving worlds of Lowood and Moor House (insofar as Moor House is presided over by St. John Rivers) are pitted against the flammable abundance of Thornfield, and they come together uneasily at the end in the "insalubrious site" of Ferndean.

The opening chapters at Gateshead function as a prelude, defining the interaction of the two countries in miniature. Despite the fairy-tale wickedness of Mrs. Reed and her brood, Jane—unlike Dickens' children and even George Eliot's Maggie Tulliver—is not sentimentalized into being a vessel of feeling in a world without love. She shares the emotional tone of her surroundings: "If they did not love me, in fact, as little did I love them" (1:13). "I never saw a girl of her age with so much cover," says the servant Miss Abbot (1:9). A frozen child, she longs to enter the "death-white realms" illustrated in Bewick's *History of British Birds,* "that reservoir of frost and snow, where firm fields of ice, the accumulation of centuries of winter, glazed in Alpine heights above heights, surround the pole, and concentrate the multiplied rigors of extreme cold" (1:3).

Nature and God are extensions of the hostile atmosphere of Gateshead Hall. It is impossible to go outdoors in the bleak winter weather, and God is a Calvinist monster associated with death, defined to Jane by his appropriately named minister, Miss Abbot: "God will punish her: he might strike her dead in the midst of her tantrums, and then where would she go?" (1:9).

After the rage she has been suppressing flares up in her sudden attack on John Reed, Jane is locked in the red room, where "the world below" rises up and terrifies her: she sees herself in the mirror as "one of the tiny phantoms, half fairy, half imp," and imagines that she is locked in the room with a ghost. The red room terrifies her because in it she meets her doppelgänger, the undiscovered country in herself that had been frozen over. Her sudden initiation into the world of emotion is expressed characteristically in the language of fire: " 'Come, Miss Jane, don't cry,' said Bessie, as she finished. She might as well have said to the fire 'don't burn!' " (1:22). The regions through which she will travel in adulthood are defined at Gateshead: a frozen inner and outer "reality" forces her into the red room of "the world below."

Lowood School is an extension of Gateshead, but it contains no red room. It is so cold that the water in Helen Burns' basin freezes; food is scarce and inedible; and these physical conditions reflect an emotional cold and starvation which equate repression of feeling with virtue. Lowood's God is defined by Mr. Brocklehurst's sadistic Calvinism, an anti-life force whose main function is to send wicked children to hell. Nature is still man's enemy. Winter is bitter, and when spring finally comes, it breathes disease and death, not renewal: "That forest-dell, where Lowood lay, was the cradle of fog and fog-bred pestilence; which, quickening with the quickening spring, crept into the Orphan Asylum, breathed typhus through its crowded school-room and dormitory, and, ere May arrived, transformed the seminary into an hospital" (1:94).

Jane is guided through Lowood by Miss Temple and Helen Burns, who are not a contrast to this world, but its best ministers. Helen's goodness is an anti-life force; she embraces death in as exemplary a fashion as the children do in the pious tracts written by William Carus Wilson, on whom the character of Mr. Brocklehurst was based. Her name, hell in-burns, points forward to St. John Rivers' gigantic struggle to repress his feelings in the name of God. Jane pictures herself married to him and choosing the identity he projects on her, "forced to keep the *fire* of my nature continually low, to compel it to *burn inwardly* and never utter a cry, though the imprisoned flame consumed vital after vital" (2:223–24, my italics).

Miss Temple is also a restraining and tempering influence rather than a kindling one. At one point, she is described as a marble statue, looking forward to the frozen St. John's "marble immobility of feature": "Miss Temple had looked down when [Mr. Brocklehurst] first began to speak to her; but she now gazed straight before her, and her face, naturally pale as marble, appeared to be assuming also the coldness and fixity of that material; especially her mouth closed as if it would have required a sculptor's chisel to open it, and her brow settled gradually into petrified severity" (1:77).

This passage defines the almost expressionistic quality of Charlotte Brontë's "real world," which is no more real than the horse described by Bitzer at the beginning of Dickens' *Hard Times*. It is a world without warmth or roundness, as haunted and terrifying as the more conventional Gothic motifs of her "infernal world." [7]

Lowood is defined by "coldness and fixity," its emblem being the ice in Helen Burns' water basin. Jane's eventual passage to

Thornfield repeats her journey from the "death-white" polar regions illustrated in Bewick's *History* to the red room and its attendant specters. Lowood's pinched little girls in brown uniforms become Adèle Varens, spoiled, sensual, clothes conscious, and—worst of all—half-French. Lowood's ice becomes Rochester's "flaming and flashing" eyes, recurrent imagery suggesting his kinship to his pyromaniac wife: "He seemed to devour me with his flaming glance: physically, I felt, at the moment, powerless as stubble exposed to the draught and glow of a furnace" (2:103).

The monolithic Calvinist God of Lowood abdicates in favor of nature and the nature sprites Jane and Rochester are always evoking; their "natural sympathies" are defined by a common interest in fairy tales, and we are reminded that English fairies are the old pagan nature deities gone underground at the birth of Christ. Mr. Brocklehurst's dogma was: "We are not to conform to nature." Rochester, Jane's new master, says hopefully: "I think you will learn to be natural with me." Warm weather at Thornfield is not the tainted thaw that came to Lowood. It is "splendid Midsummer" when Rochester proposes in his "Eden-like" garden, though behind this *hortus conclusus* lies the "fiery west-Indian night," the burning sky, under which Rochester married Bertha Mason. Instead of shutting Jane out, nature is solicitous of her, bursting into storm when Rochester proposes bigamous marriage. Only at Thornfield does Jane display her strange, surreal paintings—we heard elsewhere about conventional landscapes and portraits—and dream premonitory dreams, which she feels "may be but the sympathies of Nature with man." Only at Thornfield does nature nurture Jane's buried life.

Thornfield and Rochester are from the beginning a reflection of Jane's inner world. She applies for the position only after Miss Temple has left Lowood, when she feels in herself "the stirring of old emotions" which had, presumably, been frozen over by Lowood and subdued by Miss Temple. At Thornfield, the fairy tales of her childhood, associated especially with the red room, seem to come to life: the drawing room seems "a fairy place," she approaches Bertha's quarters and thinks prophetically of "a corridor in some Bluebeard's castle," she hears Rochester's horse and thinks of "Bessie's Gytrash." Jane alone can speak French to Adèle, a language which had ambiguous underground connotations for Charlotte Brontë: she may have associated it with the sudden conflagration of emotion brought about in Brussels by M. Heger, to whom she spoke and wrote only in French. Bertha puts on Jane's wedding veil and looks in her mirror: in the red room, Jane had seen herself in the mirror as "half fairy, half imp," and now Bertha's reflection reminds her of "the foul German spectre— the Vampyre." Adèle, the sensual child, and Bertha, whose uncontrolled passion has run into insanity, come from Jane's own fire, just as Helen Burns and Miss Temple came from her ice. Thornfield embodies the attraction and the danger of the desires that arise when Miss Temple's restraint is withdrawn; just before Jane flees Rochester's anarchic love for her, she dreams that she is lying once again in the red room at Gateshead.

Away from Thornfield, the world is again obdurate and hostile. Jane arrives in a town that is "no town . . . but a stone pillar." The "sympathies of Nature with man" are withdrawn, though at first she expects still to be cherished by the "universal mother, Nature":

I touched the heath: it was dry, and yet warm with the heat of the summer-day. I looked at the sky; it was pure: a kindly star twinkled just above the chasm ridge. The dew fell, but with propitious softness; no breeze whispered. Nature *seemed to me* benign and good; *I thought* she loved me, outcast as I was; and I, who from man could anticipate only mistrust, rejection, insult, clung to her with filial fondness. Tonight, at least, I would be her guest—as I was her child: my mother would lodge me without money and without price.
(2:111–12, my italics)

But on the next night, the sentimental hope that lingers from Thornfield is dispelled by the return of the hostile nature of Lowood and Gateshead: "My night was wretched, my rest broken: the ground was damp, the air cold; besides, intruders had passed near me more than once, and I had again and again to change my quarters: no sense of safety or tranquillity befriended me. Toward morning it rained; the whole of the following day was wet" (2:119). At Moor House, she will refer to nature as a "stinted stepmother."

St. John Rivers is the emotional alternative to Rochester in a world that seems to generate only extremes of fire and ice. The snow-ice-stone imagery that surrounds him, and his severe Christianity, recall the world of Lowood, Mr. Brocklehurst, and hell in-burns.

The parallel family structure, two sisters and a brother, even looks back to the unyielding Reeds at Gateshead and their "death-white" landscape. Improbably as Charlotte Brontë handles the incident, it is important to the novel that St. John is Jane's cousin, and that Moor House is as close as she comes to arriving at her origins, the home she has inherited. His ice is in Jane as well. When her buried emotions began to stir, Thornfield rose up embodying them; when she forces down her passion in the name of Christian principle, she meets her icy cousin, who is forcing down *his* passion for Rosamond Oliver in order to fulfill his spiritual mission. Even his name, St. John, suggests Jane's own potential sanctification. If nature was aroused by Rochester's proposal, heaven is aroused by St. John's: "All was changing utterly, with a sudden sweep. Religion called—Angels beckoned—God commanded—life rolled together like a scroll—death's gates opening, showed eternity beyond: it seemed, that for safety and bliss there, all here might be sacrificed in a second" (2:239). The apocalyptic imagery underlines the fact that the governess Jane always had the potential of becoming a Blakean angel.

Jane's marriage to Rochester at Ferndean and her final home there seem less a synthesis of the two worlds than a partial conquest of one world by the other. The fire of Thornfield is extinguished with Rochester's "flaming and flashing" eyes, and replaced by motifs from the Lowood—Moor House world: Rochester is "stone blind," a "sightless block," and Bertha, the source of the fire, is now "dead as the stones on which her brains and blood were scattered." Like Lowood, Ferndean is built on an "ineligible and insalubrious site": nature no longer nurtures the self, but is somewhat threatening and tainted. Rochester's unlikely conversion to orthodox Christianity suggests the triumph of the Calvinist God, who has been an anti-life force throughout the novel, over the pagan pantheon of Thornfield: there are "no flowers, no garden-beds" at Ferndean; it is "as still as a church on a weekday." The book does not end with Rochester's love lyrics, but with St. John's self-immolating cry to this implacable and unnatural divinity. Despite the apparent victory of Jane's fire over St. John's ice, of her "powers" over his God, his country and Mr. Brocklehurst's seem to have triumphed after all. Everything that Rochester represented was crushed with Thornfield, and our final sense of the book is that "reality" is "imagination," broken and blind.[8] Jane, who would not be

Rochester's mistress, becomes his governess, and the triumph of this side of her character sends us forward to Lucy Snowe, in whose nature "the world below" is a more imperious force, requiring an even greater distortion of nature to suppress it.

VILLETTE: THE DIVIDED SELF

"Who *are* you, Miss Snowe?" (*Vil.*, 2:72).

With its odd structure, unappealing heroine, and obscurity of purpose, *Villette* seems in many ways inaccessible. But it is an extraordinary achievement. If its setting and conflicts are less clearly delineated than those of *Jane Eyre*, in its obscurity it tells us more about ourselves. Charlotte Brontë has gone down to the roots of the romantic warring universe she depicted in *Jane Eyre*, and located the part of the mind where they are found.

The first paragraph of *Villette* defines a norm which its heroine, Lucy Snowe, is never able to achieve: "My godmother lived in a handsome house in the clean and ancient town of Bretton. Her husband's family had been residents there for generations, and bore, indeed, the name of their birthplace—Bretton of Bretton: whether by coincidence, or because some remote ancestor had been a personage of sufficient importance to leave his name to the neighborhood, I know not" (1:1).

"Bretton of Bretton": the concord between person and place is so firm that the names are interchangeable. Polly *Home*, whose sunny existence is unobtainable by the stormy Lucy, also defines by her name a certain oneness with the world. Jane Eyre was in similar concord with a universe whose dominant elements of frost and fire were her own. But Lucy is always homeless. Descriptions of her childhood contain a noncommittal reference to "kinfolk with whom was at that time fixed my permanent residence," but after a mysterious shipwreck destroys them and divides her from Bretton, she spends a brief period in "two hot, close rooms" tending the invalid Miss Marchmont, and then passes to Villette for the rest of the book, where she is always a stranger in a strange land.

The conventual atmosphere of Madame Beck's *pension-nat,* where Lucy becomes an English teacher, is composed of intrigue, espionage, and secrets she can never fully penetrate; she can finally define her taciturn employer only as the leader of a "secret junta" in league against her happiness. Language isolates her further: she gradually becomes able to read French, but unlike Jane, she never speaks it well. Even the God of Brussels is a stranger: Lucy's honest Protestantism is bewildered by Catholic craft, theatricality, and intrigue, making her an outsider in a way that Jane Eyre never was. The shadowy, nocturnal life of the Rue Fossette, and Lucy's especial seclusion there, define the mystery of her world: her favorite spot is *l'allée défendue,* where no one else walks but the ghost of the mysterious nun, and which in its dark secrecy seems an inverted link to the pagan opulence of the *hortus conclusus* at Thornfield. Lucy is superstitious and a fatalist, she feels that her destiny may be guided by certain portentous events, but the omens and strange coincidences never lead to anything definite: unlike the linear progression of *Jane Eyre,* the plot of *Villette* is cyclical, and Lucy ends as she began, estranged by shipwreck from her one possible home.

The mystery of her surroundings spreads over the action of the novel, which is never clearly defined. We never learn the nature of the storm that devastates Lucy's youth, nor do we know anything of her origins. The motives of the characters who mean most to her, such as Dr. John Bretton, Madame Beck, and Paul Emmanuel, are similarly murky. Lucy is an unreliable narrator because her world is unreliable. Madame Beck's *pensionnat* is not knowable as the injustices of Lowood and the excesses of Thornfield were knowable; we see only Lucy's uncertain attempts to shape events into symbols, to bestow meaning on ambiguous circumstances.

Because *Villette* is set in a city, the setting takes on an unrelenting impersonality that adds to Lucy's estrangement. On the one hand, Villette is an emblem of desolation, a city of the dreadful night: the book's most famous episodes are Lucy's half-delirious nocturnal walks through the nightmare of the city. This image looks forward to such films as Ingmar Bergman's *The Silence,* which is also dominated by a woman walking aimlessly in a foreign city, whose inhabitants speak a strange language and worship strange gods.

With this desolation goes a sense of suffocation and claustrophobia. During a theatrical performance, there is a fire, and both heroines are almost trampled during the ensuing panic: "Our pioneer proved strong and adroit; he opened the dense mass like a wedge; with patience and toil he at last bored through the flesh-and-blood rock— so solid, hot, and suffocating—and brought us to the fresh, freezing night" (2:12). Jane Eyre faces the threat of starvation in an emotionally starved world, but never the possibility of being abandoned or trampled by crowds of people who don't see her. A fundamental kinship has been broken in the movement from a mythopoeic landscape to a modern city.

The most dramatic landscape in *Villette* is an inner landscape. The outside world is always half-shrouded:

The sky . . . was monotonously gray; the atmosphere was stagnant and humid; yet amidst all these deadening influences, my fancy budded fresh and my heart basked in sunshine. These feelings, however, were well kept in check by the secret consciousness of anxiety lying in wait on enjoyment, like a tiger crouched in a jungle. The breathing of that beast of prey was in my ear always; his fierce heart panted close against mine; he never stirred in his lair but I felt him: I knew he waited only for sundown to bound ravenous from his ambush.

(1:71)

The sunny nook with a secret jungle behind it reminds us of Rochester's Edenic garden at Thornfield, lurking behind whose midsummer splendor was Bertha's madness and the flaming tropical sky she brought with her. But here, this landscape has moved inward, and there is nothing in the sunless sky of reality to reflect it. The "principles" that were so dear to Jane Eyre have also evaporated in *Villette*. Jane described her conflict between frost and fire in ethical abstractions: "Conscience, turned tyrant, held passion by the throat" (*JE*, 2:76). In the world of *Villette*, which seems to contain no firm values but only layers of secrecy, morality becomes psychology, and Lucy replaces "conscience" with our modern word "anxiety."

Lucy Snowe, who originally was to have been named Lucy Frost, is prey to far more extreme and explicit clashes between frost and fire than Jane Eyre was. Lucy's "underlife" also thaws as the book progresses, but the shrouded world of Villette contains little objective correlative for her desires: the worlds of Lowood and Thornfield are

locked inside her. Her split nature is defined in images of extraordinary
violence: "This longing, and all of a similar kind, it was necessary to
knock on the head; which I did, figuratively, after the manner of Jael
to Sisera, driving a nail through their temples. Unlike Sisera, they did
not die" (*Vil.*, 1:135). The wounded pagan, Rochester, in the form of
the Canaanite, Sisera, also moves inside the mind.

Reason, whose values had objective sanction in *Jane Eyre*,
also becomes a figure of pathology: "Reason still whispered me, laying
on my shoulder a withered hand, and frostily touching my ear with
the chill blue lips of eld" (*Vil.*, 1:289). " 'But if I feel, may I *never
express*?' '*Never!*' declared Reason. . . . This hag, this Reason, would
not let me look up, or smile, or hope: she could not rest unless I were
altogether crushed, cowed, broken-in, and broken-down. . . . Reason
is vindictive as a devil. . . . Often has [she] turned me out by night,
in mid-winter, on cold snow, flinging for sustenance the gnawed bones
dogs had forsaken" (1:290).

The fire of emotion, personified in part by the ravaged
actress Vashti, is equally violent and demonic. Vashti is "wasted like
wax in flame," shaken by "the passions of the pit," "torn by seven
evils." Her fire becomes briefly externalized when the theater actually
begins to burn, but this leads only to the stampede of frightened spectators described above. It has none of the cathartic and final effects of
the fire at Thornfield in *Jane Eyre*.

Since Lucy usually holds herself in ferocious check, and
since her world contains no equivalent of her desires, these desires are
always struggling to break out of control and create their own objects:
Imagination was roused from her rest, and she came forth impetuous
and venturous. With scorn she looked on Matter, her mate—'Rise!'
she said. 'Sluggard! this night I will have *my* will; nor shalt thou pre-
vail' " (2:255). The violence of this contest is at the heart of *Villette,*
and it seems strangely disconnected from the love story. Victorian critics were disturbed by a heroine who could love two men at once, and
it does seem odd when Lucy describes her feeling for Dr. John in the
following terms while she is half-distracted with love for the absent
Paul Emmanuel: "All my life long I carried it folded in the hollow of
my hand—yet, released from that hold and constriction, I know not
but its innate capacity for expanse might have magnified it into a
tabernacle for a host" (2:265). In fact, Lucy's hallucinatory struggles

seem almost independent of both men: her feelings ebb and swell with only a slight connection to external events. This strange dislocation of the heroine's strongest emotions from what little plot the novel has contributes to our sense of its difficulty, its shrouded obscurity, and also to its modernity. The plot of *Jane Eyre* expresses Jane's central conflict, but the plot of *Villette* obscures and stifles Lucy Snowe's. Lucy Snowe seems cut off even from the action of the story she herself is narrating, as Charlotte Brontë dives below circumstances to explore the sources and the workings of a deeply divided mind.

In a setting and narrative that, to such a great extent, shut the heroine out, isolating her within her violently divided self, the division in her nature rebounds on the outside world, as she takes revenge on the characters who exclude her by splitting them in two. Characterization in *Jane Eyre* was monolithic: pairs of contrasting simple characters were used to define two poles of emotional possibility, as Helen Burns was opposed by Adèle Varens, Miss Temple by Bertha Mason, Rochester by St. John, and so on. But characterization in *Villette* is refracted by Lucy Snowe in a manner she herself defines: "Reader, if, in the course of this work, you find that my opinion of Dr. John, undergoes modification, excuse the seeming inconsistency. I give the feeling as at the time I felt it; I describe the view of character as it appeared when discovered" (1:242).

Characterization in *Jane Eyre* is unified and shaped by the stable perspective of a matronly Jane writing ten years later. Characterization in *Villette* has as little perspective as a cubist painting. Lucy does not reflect the stable essence of character; she presents "the *view* of character" as it fluctuates from moment to moment, refracted by the split in Lucy herself. This method of characterization is appropriate to a world whose absolute definition is problematical, where the only reality available is inward battle.

The fragmentation of Graham Bretton—Isodore—Dr. John is defined by his three names. As a child, Lucy senses something "faithless" and "subtle" about him, something that will entice out strong emotion only to play with it: Polly's open devotion "struck me as strangely rash; exciting the feeling one might experience on seeing an animal dangerous by nature, and but half-tamed by art, too heedlessly fondled" (1:31). At Villette, Graham becomes Dr. John, who radiates warmth and health and becomes the object of Lucy's own

ormented feelings, and Isidore, upright, hopeless suitor of the coquette Ginevra Fanshawe. The fractured nature of the characterization
s emphasized by Lucy's concealment from the reader of her knowledge
that Graham, Dr. John, and Isidore are the same person. When Polly
appears, metamorphosed in Villette into the Countess Paulina Mary
Home de Bassompierre, Isidore vanishes and Graham's streak of perversity is never integrated into the character of the golden Dr. John.
Finally, it disappears altogether: "His faults decayed, his virtues rip-
ned . . . all dregs filtered away, the clear wine settled bright and
tranquil" (2:238). The double focus of the portrait is dissolved but
never resolved, as Dr. John fades out of the action.

    Polly-Paulina, whom Lucy sees as her "double," is split
up in a similar way. As a child, she is the shivering and deprived waif
who appears throughout Charlotte Brontë's fiction. Lucy, whose own
emotions are safely frozen over, sees Polly as one who will always be
the victim of feeling: "These sudden, dangerous natures—*sensitive* as
they are called—offer many a curious spectacle to those whom a *cooler*
temperament has secured from participation in their angular vagaries.
The fixed and heavy gaze swum, trembled, then *glittered in fire*" (1:11,
last two italics mine). "During an ensuing space of some minutes, I
perceived she endured agony. She went through, in that brief interval
of her infant life, emotions such as some never feel; it was in her
constitution; she would have more of such instants if she lived. . . .
I, Lucy Snowe, was calm" (1:22).

    In Villette, when Lucy is in the grip of her own loneliness
and frustration, Polly returns, transformed. She is now the beautiful
and cherished Countess Paulina, sheltered from life's storms, sensitive
and docile as a pet spaniel. According to Lucy's odd, inverse identification with Polly-Paulina, when her own emotions are suppressed, they
overwhelm Polly; when the extremes of frost and fire in her own nature are tearing her apart, Paulina achieves a delicate integration Lucy
can never reach: "Paulina, that gentle hoar-frost of yours, surrounding
so much pure, fine flame, is a priceless privilege of nature" (2:159).

    When Polly-Paulina marries Graham—Dr. John, the im-
age of the golden couple eclipses the strain of pathology Lucy had
defined in their relationship earlier. As children, they were moved by
somewhat unwholesome emotions; as adults, they are "Nature's elect,
harmonious and benign." As Lucy depicts them, both characters lack

a stable ego, and their love story has no fixed essence which would enable us to perceive it in itself. Their marriage is described in a chapter called "Sunshine," which exists only to balance Lucy's chapter, "Cloud," describing her own painful and problematical relationship with Paul Emmanuel.

All the characters who exclude Lucy are split up in this way: lacking a fixed essence, they become unknowable. Madame Beck also has two faces: "Madame's face of stone (for of stone in its present night-aspect it looked: it had been human and, as I said before, motherly, in the salon) betrayed no response" (1:83). Even Ginevra Fanshawe, the blonde belle of Madame Beck's *pensionnat,* is a comic variation on this theme of a character compounded of two opposite qualities. When Lucy first meets her, she is an insubstantial, aristocratic butterfly, whose future Lucy prophesies as she had Polly's, in her characteristic Cassandra voice: "Many a time since have I noticed, in persons of Ginevra Fanshawe's light, careless temperament, and fair, fragile style of beauty, an entire incapacity to endure: they seem to sour in adversity, like small beer in thunder" (1:67).

But the fragile Ginevra gets fatter throughout the book and develops an unfortunate tendency to lean on Lucy's arm, so that her bulk and weight are increasingly stressed. By the end, she is quite palpable: " 'I have got my portion!' she cried at once; (Ginevra ever stuck to the substantial; I always thought there was a good trading element in her composition, much as she scorned the 'bourgeoisie;')" (2:289–90). The butterfly's powers of endurance turn out to be unlimited, adept as she is at finding other people to pay her bills. Like the fragile Polly, she is able to find shelter from the storms that devastate Lucy, but even Ginevra Fanshawe is broken in two by the conflicts of the woman who perceives her.

Throughout most of the book, Paul Emmanuel, too, is perceived in warring extremes of tyranny and soft benevolence. In chapter 30, he is Napoleon Bonaparte, and in chapter 35, he is a Christian knight; his masculine and feminine components split into extremes that can't join. But when he presents Lucy with the house in the Faubourg Clotilde, symbol of love, home, and professional independence in one, her vision achieves a moment of wholeness in which the opposites in his character come briefly together: "Magnificent-minded, grand-hearted, dear, faulty little man! You deserved candor, and from me always had it" (2:304).

The double ending which seems to have irritated many readers grows out of the nature of the novel's world: Paul's ship is both destroyed and preserved, as the reader likes it. Lucy's history begins and ends with this image of a double sea voyage, in which triumphant return and wreck are juxtaposed without resolution. The cyclical and ambiguous structure of *Villette*, unlike the firm linear path of *Jane Eyre*, reflects a change in Charlotte Brontë's perception of reality. She has moved into a darker and larger world, whose reality is ambiguous and internal; her development is the development from romance to psychology, from myth into modernism. A relatively neglected Victorian novel, *Villette* locates Charlotte Brontë's key "myth," the perpetual war between fire and ice, within the isolated and estranged self, reaching toward a reality that can coalesce into nothing beyond projection.

13.

"This Changeful Life"
Emily Brontë's Anti-Romance

Gondal was the secret room in Emily Brontë's imagination. In transcribing poems she wanted no one but herself to see, she segregated the notebook headed "Gondal poems" from a second notebook which critics have optimistically labeled "personal poems." Despite the Victorian predilection for undiscovered countries, Brontë excised all references to Gondal from the poems she included in her sisters' ill-fated collection in 1846, changing what had begun as fluid dramatic utterances into grand general statements. Her ambition sprang from Gondal but could not include it.

Gondal is similarly sealed off from *Wuthering Heights,* Brontë's most direct attempt at literary success: the novel is embedded indelibly in Yorkshire. Moreover, it adheres to the fictional conventions of the day in that it is both a love story and a domestic drama while Gondal is neither. Love in the novel assumes eternal status by the combined fiat of Catherine and Heathcliff, while its domestic rituals endure longer than do the humans who perform them. "Time will change it, I'm well aware": thus its heroine scornfully dismisses her love for Edgar Linton. But she is dismissing the hidden country of Gondal as well, whose imperious queen embodies time and feeds on change.

In her *Gondal's Queen: A Novel in Verse,* Fannie E.
Ratchford has reconstructed the world Emily Brontë set so carefully
apart.[1] In doing so, she has decompartmentalized Gondal from Brontë's
other poems, creating her own version of a golden notebook which is
the unity of Brontë's imagination: "The majority, perhaps all of [the
poems], pertain to . . . Gondal."[2] Ratchford's "arrangement" of
Brontë's "novel in verse" embraces the fluctuating world both *Wuth-*
ring Heights and Brontë's own poetic tradition struggled to transcend.

Brontë's poetry has been dismissed too easily as a late-
blooming attempt at Victorian Romanticism, ignoring the "drear" integrity of its self-created world. Apparent echoes of Wordsworth, Byron, and Blake (though she is not known to have read Blake) often
ask scathing, subtle questions which recast inherited material into a
wry new shape.[3] Childhood in Gondal, for instance, is quietly but
firmly demystified of its Romantic aura.

Typically, Romantic children are eternity's promise to time.
Radiating pure Being, they deny the mutability in which they are trapped by their births. In *Songs of Innocence* (1789), the birth of Blake's
"Infant Joy" is an act of glad and perpetual self-discovery. The "I"
characteristically finds delight only in his own being as a radiantly eternal abstraction:

> I have no name
> I am but two days old.—
> What shall I call thee?
> I happy am
> Joy is my name,—
> Sweet joy befall thee![4]

Infant Joy clings exclusively to his own eternal essence amid the con-
tingencies of life in time, while his counterpart in *Songs of Experience*
(1793), "Infant Sorrow," has only his own rage to shield him against
the "dangerous world" of his new prison:

> My mother groand! my father wept.
> Into the dangerous world I lept:
> Helpless, naked, piping loud;
> Like a fiend hid in a cloud.
>
> Struggling in my fathers hands:
> Striving against my swaddling bands:

> Bound and weary I thought best
> To sulk upon my mothers breast.
>
> (p. 28)

In joy and sorrow, Blake's infants are particles wrenched out of eternity to violation by time. But in Wordsworth's vision, the peerless childhood self is a less reliable object of worship than its alluringly immutable source, "that imperial palace whence he came." The little girl in "We Are Seven" imbibes permanence from the security of her setting. Eternal life is located only "Twelve steps or more from my mother's door" (l. 39), in the graveyard where time and loss are recovered. Eternity is available in acts of obsessive return:

> "My stockings there I often knit
> My kerchief there I hem;
> And there upon the ground I sit,
> And sing a song to them.
>
> "And often after sun-set, Sir,
> When it is light and fair,
> I take my little porringer,
> And eat my supper there."
>
> (ll. 41–48)

The Wordsworthian child clings to unity of setting as tenaciously as Blake's "Infant Joy" clings to unity of self. But Emily Brontë's Augusta Geraldine Almeda, who will grow up to rule all the Gondals, clings to nothing. A. G. A. joyfully begins her "changeful life" with a song that embraces fluctuation of scene, time, and being itself:

> Tell me, tell me, smiling child,
> What the past is like to thee?
> "An Autumn evening soft and mild
> With a wind that sighs mournfully."
>
> Tell me, what is the present hour?
> "A green and flowery spray
> Where a young bird sits gathering its power
> To mount and fly away."
>
> And what is the future, happy one?
> "A sea beneath a cloudless sun;

A mighty, glorious, dazzling sea
Stretching into infinity."

(#3)

The lilting cadences of A. G. A.'s greeting to time and nature are less Blake-like than their joy and innocence suggest. For the young A. G. A., selfhood expresses itself not in insistent reiterations of "I" and "my," but in self-forgetfulness within a joyfully shifting landscape. Ironically, her temporal pageant lacks the culminating snowscape that will become the motif of her maturity and of the Gondal saga as a whole; but given its bare imminence, the little girl's "mighty, glorious, dazzling sea" has none of the celestial finality of "that immortal sea" whose sight crowns Wordsworth's majestic "Ode: Intimations of Immortality from Recollections of Early Childhood" (1802–1804). It provides as mortal and momentary a blessing as does the "cloudless sun" which gives it its glory.

Unlike that of the Wordsworthian child, who finds continual restoration through permanence of setting, the young A. G. A.'s vision of the mournful autumnal past expresses her early assurance that the past is lost, while the vernal present of the second stanza is ever about to vanish with its bird. Were Wordsworth her tender questioner, he would find it ominous that the little girl is so blithely at home in time: the cycle of past-present-future evokes for her a string of delicious idylls, in which temporality is not a "prison-house," but loss and gaiety in one. Though her culminating cloudless sea is "stretching into infinity," the present participle suggests the tension of a process that is never consummated. Emily Brontë's child celebrates mutability as wholeheartedly as Blake's and Wordsworth's children struggled against it. She seems to have no eternal home to miss, having popped, like the child in the nursery rhyme, "out of the nowhere into the here."

Under A. G. A.'s adult reign, children are less a Wordsworthian "eye among the blind" than inert objects to be dispatched: banishment or infanticide is the most common emotion they evoke in their raging parents, whose point of view we share. In sending the worshipful Amedeus, the "dark boy of sorrow," into exile, A. G. A. herself becomes the devouring time threatening the Romantic "holy child":

> And what shall change that angel brow
> And quench that spirit's glorious glow?
> Relentless laws that disallow
> True virtue and true joy below.
> ("A. A. A.," #112, 15–18)

In dealing with her own child, A. G. A. identifies herself
even less obliquely with time's "relentless laws." After the assassination of the great love of her life, the usurping emperor Julius Brenzaida, A. G. A. flees with their baby daughter to the snow-buried
mountains, where she inexplicably abandons the child in a storm. This
murder of the seal of her marriage to Julius, and perhaps of their empire as well, has no discernible motive in the text: infanticide seems as
simple and compulsive an instinct to A. G. A. as it will be to George
Eliot's Hetty Sorrel, replacing motherhood as the great overriding impulse that need ask no questions about itself. But to provide herself
with philosophical justification, A. G. A. once again evokes the Romantic pieties her own childhood denied. She finds that the true home
of the child is not earth, but the eternity in her eyes:

> "Methought the heaven, whence thou has come,
> Was lingering there awhile;
> And Earth seemed such an alien home
> They did not dare to smile.
>
> "Methought, each moment something strange
> Within their circles shone,
> And yet, through every magic change,
> They were Brenzaida's own."
> ("Geraldine," #150, 25–32)

The child's existence as a remnant of eternity, both in itself and as
the immortality of beloved Brenzaida, is twisted with Grand Guignol
relish into the reason for its destruction. With dark wit, Emily Brontë
takes Romantic child worship as a motive for the annihilation of
childhood itself:

> "Say, sin shall never blanch that cheek,
> Nor suffering charge [change?] that brow;
> Speak, in thy mercy, Maker, speak,
> And seal it safe from woe!"
>
> "Why did I doubt? In God's control
> Our mutual fates remain;

And pure as now my angel's soul
Must go to Heaven again."
(#150, 41–48)

No shades of the prison house will darken little Princess Alexandrina. Romanticism has provided the epic with a motive for death, if not a guide to life. By Emily Brontë's sardonic use of its definitions, the child becomes most sacrosanct when the snow that is Gondal takes to itself her "frozen limbs and freezing breast" (#108, 32).

In her dance through time and her denial of the children that are eternity, A. G. A. is the anti-Wordsworthian spirit of Gondal, whose saga begins at birth and ends with assassination by her vengeful stepdaughter. Her reigning murderousness may suggest the "swaddling bands" of Blake's Female Will, who in *Europe: A Prophecy* (1794) manacles a continent in the gloating form of "mother Enitharmon"; but A. G. A. is "mother" only long enough to be killer. She enslaves the men and women who cluster about her, not by the murderous possessiveness Blake associated with "womans triumph," but by her commitment to mutability which repeatedly drives them away. She does not bind time, but sets it free.

Her unyielding self-assertion never collapses into the self-luxuriance of Byronism. Taking to herself the mantle of time's "relentless laws," A. G. A. never erects her ruined self against the process of love's erosion, as Childe Harold had done so frequently. *Don Juan,* an epic of potential endlessness, chooses to laugh at time's ocean in order not to weep at it. But Emily Brontë sails on it matter-of-factly, electing neither laughter, tears, nor Childe Harold's challenge. Love in Gondal is at one with parting, and its emotional essence lies in the laconic acceptance of "Song":

Let us part, the time is over
When I thought and felt like thee;
I will be an Ocean rover,
I will sail the desert sea
Day by day some dreary token
Will forsake my memory
Till at last all old links broken
I shall be a dream to thee.
(#118, 9–12, 21–24)

Unlike that of Blake's Female Will, or of Brontë's own Heathcliff, Gondal's love does not enforce eternity, but ruthlessly refuses it. The change A. G. A. embraces on her release from prison is the change she offers in return for love:

> But this is past, and why return
> O'er such a past to brood and mourn?
> Shake off the fetters, break the chain,
> And live and love and smile again.
>
> (#15, 69–72)

A. G. A.'s sin against relationship, and her gift to it as well, lie in her precise inability to play the mothering, generating, and possessive role of Blake's Enitharmon. Like that of Blake's own Oothoon, A. G. A.'s longing to "break the chain" of possessive love is a cry for freedom from limiting nature.

For Gondal's queen is less a worshipper of nature than its furious victim. Her identification of herself with time seems at one with her denial of the Wordsworthian assurances of eternity through "nature and the language of the sense." Wordsworth's gateways become A. G. A.'s prison. Thus, in some of Brontë's most remarkable lines, A. G. A. wails against dawn's joyful awakening with an intensity of phallic and murderous imagery that makes Wordsworth's exhortation in "To My Sister" to "come forth and feel the sun" seem a bland invitation to execution:

> Blood-red he rose, and arrow-straight
> His fierce beams struck my brow:
> The soul of Nature sprang elate,
> But mine sank sad and low!
>
> (#184, 21–24)

The rhythms of A. G. A.'s own soul are in total opposition to nature's, as she defies its unified "soul" in favor of the calm multitudinousness of night's heavenly bodies presiding over the vicissitudes of her own consciousness:

> I was at peace, and drank your beams
> As they were life to me
> And revelled in my changeful dreams
> Like petrel on the sea.
>
> (#184, 9–12)

A. G. A.'s life and her rule lie in fidelity to her "changeful dreams"; restorative nature is her brand of Cain. Her antagonism to nature, and to all the Romantic pieties that accompany it, is more comprehensible if we believe with Fannie Ratchford that the sun in this poem is the birth of "Julius as the sun of her life, paling into invisibility all other loves and loyalties" (*Gondal's Queen*, p. 87). Thus, A. G. A.'s revolt is at one with Catherine Earnshaw's cry in her dream against the consummation of heaven and the unification of love: "I was only going to say that heaven did not seem to be my home; and I broke my heart with weeping to come back to earth; and the angels were so angry that they flung me out, into the middle of the heath on the top of Wuthering Heights; where I woke sobbing for joy. . . . I've no more business to marry Edgar Linton than I have to be in heaven; . . . It would degrade me to marry Heathcliff now."[5]

Here at least, Catherine equates Heathcliff as well as Edgar with the alien reductiveness of heaven. Love and beatitude are threats to the living self and the integrity of its "changeful dreams." As Catherine asserts her dreams against love, marriage, and heaven, the monumental pillars of novelistic bliss, so A. G. A. asserts hers against a standard moment of blessing in nineteenth-century poetry: the aubade that consecrates the imagination, as the rising dawn blesses Wordsworth's coming prophetic poems in book IV of *The Prelude*. But A. G. A.'s sexual and cosmic loyalty to the manifold and changing seems fruitless against the tyranny of unity and union:

> It would not do—the pillow glowed
> And glowed both roof and floor,
> And birds sang loudly in the wood,
> And fresh winds shook the door.
>   (#184, 33–36)

A. G. A.'s senses have no power against this choric dominion. Wordsworth's embrace of "all the mighty world of eye, and ear" is here a mighty betrayal. In Gondal, the senses collaborate with "the hostile light" of that coercive, vampiristic nature "that does not warm, but burn— / That drains the blood of suffering men" (#184, 44–45). A. G. A. accepts but inverts Wordsworth's contention that the senses are bulwarks against time and change. For her, they are thereby in league with the soul's enemy, instead of being potential organs of the soul as they are in Blake's *Marriage of Heaven and Hell:* "If the doors of perception were cleansed every thing would appear to man as it is, infinite" (p. 39).

Defining Brontë's quest for visionary freedom in terms of Blake's subordinates Brontë's uniqueness and her quietly biting wit. Standing alone, Blake's nature reduces itself to the weary cycle of generation grinding down the aspiring spirit, which our visionary capacity alone can surmount: properly "cleansed," our "vegetable" can meet our "visionary" eye. But in Gondal's spying, suspicious world, there is little hope that eyes and ears are our friends in our quest for liberty. Despite her supposed "Blakean" affinities, Brontë would only smile at the claim in *For the Sexes: The Gates of Paradise* that our mighty eye can determine the shape of the ravaging sun itself: "The Suns Light when he unfolds it / Depends on the Organ that beholds it" (p. 257). A. G. A.'s eye allows traitorous passage to the sun which violates the soul, while finally, in *A Vision of the Last Judgment,* Blake's eye simply becomes indistinguishable from soul and sun: " 'What,' it will be Question'd, 'When the Sun rises, do you not see a round Disk of fire somewhat like a Guinea?' O no, no, I see an Innumerable company of the Heavenly host crying, 'Holy, Holy, Holy is the Lord God Almighty' " (p. 555). This ultimate collusion of self, nature, and vision is eternally possible to the Blakean "I," but Brontë is comforted by no such crowning epithalamium. If there is an "Innumerable company" in her sun, it is in league with nature and the eye to insult the straining power of the bound-down self:

> Oh, dreadful is the check—intense the agony
> When the ear begins to hear and the eye begins to see;
> When the pulse begins to throb, the brain to think again,
> The soul to feel the flesh and the flesh to feel the chain!
> ("Julian M. and A. G. Rochelle," #190, 85–88)

These lines were not written for A. G. A., whom little checks or chains, but for a feebler victim of the civil war between the Republicans and the Royalists. In the poem's dramatic context, the prisoner's recoil from her own senses is a symptom of her well-motivated death wish, which the robust A. G. A. scarcely shares. But queen and captive speak with the voice of a common rage against two great engines of eternity transmitted by Wordsworth and his acolytes: "nature and the language of the sense." Like his eternal "Child of Joy," these mighty gifts from the great patriarch of Rydal become in the hands of Emily Brontë's embattled women a poisoned fruit that strangles the soul it is supposed to feed, threatening with immutability the "changeful dreams" of the multitudinous self.

Equally blighting is the faculty which enriches and makes holy Wordsworth's trinity of child, nature, and sense: the baptismal visitation of memory. If A. G. A., daughter of time and anticipation, could become absolute monarch of her universe, she would decree a world without memory; but in the life she must inhabit, memory comes like blood-red dawn as a deadening invader. The Wordsworthian vocabulary of "awful," "roll," "flood," "sterner power," portends here the interfusion of an enemy:

> Listen, 'tis just the hour,
> The awful time for thee;
> Dost thou not feel upon thy soul
> A flood of strange sensations roll,
> Forerunners of a sterner power,
> Heralds of me?
> (#37, 11–16)

In Gondal, memory is invariably the blighting conduit of guilt and sorrow, contaminating the joy it touches like the "spectre ring" A. G. A. finds in the sodden grass:

> A mute remembrancer of crime,
> Long lost, concealed, forgot for years,
> It comes at last to cancel time,
> And waken unavailing tears.
> ("A. G. A.," #96, 5–8)

The "time" memory "cancel[s]" is the only saving power in Gondal's world. Neither love nor nature, memory nor sense, can provide the sustenance of the cycle of change, or of A. G. A.'s futile prayer to "forget them—O forget them all" (#15, 76). Even the two famous elegies to Julius, "Cold in the Earth" and "Death, that struck when I was most confiding" (#182, #183), are paeans to forgetting and elegies to memory. The Julius evoked in "Cold in the Earth" is not the living, powerful man memory can reanimate—which is not surprising, as it was his coronation rather than his assassination that prostrated

A. G. A. with brain fever. Instead of reanimating her lover, as Heathcliff does Catherine, she replaces the man with his grave, and the poem's
sensuous excitement comes from the evocation of the changing face of
that grave with time:

> Cold in the earth, and fifteen wild Decembers
> From those brown hills have melted into spring—
> Faithful indeed is the spirit that remembers
> After such years of change and suffering!
>   ("R. Alcona to J. Brenzaida," #182, 13–16)

Young love is not eternalized in memory, as was the bond of family in
"We Are Seven," but embodied and hymned as mutable earth. A. G.
A., here called Rosina, closes the poem with her tender promise to
forget her dead husband: "Sweet Love of youth, forgive if I forget thee
/ While the World's tide is bearing me along: . . . And even yet, I
dare not let it languish, / Dare not indulge in Memory's rapturous
pain" (#182, 13–14, 29–30). Memory here is not the source of growth,
but a dark call like suicide, denying fullness of being and promise.
       Similarly, in the lament which immediately follows Julius'
death, A. G. A./Rosina prays to die, not because she cannot live without her love, but because she knows she will forget to mourn him.
Despairingly, she recalls her quick recovery from an earlier despair:

> Little mourned I for the parted Gladness,
> For the vacant nest and silent song;
> Hope was there and laughed me out of sadness,
> Whispering, "Winter will not linger long."
>   (#183, 17–20)

"Time for me must never blossom more!" (#183, 32), she cries loy-
ally (and disingenuously) at the end, not because time compounds her
loss, but because she knows time cannot fail to restore it. In the rhythm
of her life, memory is the blight and time is the blossom. Adherence
to memory alters Wordsworth's source of renewed and deepened life
to flagrantly melodramatic self-destruction: there can be no connective
principle unifying the self against its life in time.
       Savage, cold, but endlessly receptive to the endless changes
of her world, A. G. A. was the character with whom Emily Brontë

spent the longest and most intense period of her creative life. Catherine and Heathcliff seem to have been mere bubbles on its surface,
while the Gondal saga spanned her career; and their incessant clinging
to a fixed childhood image of union may be subtly criticized by A. G.
A.'s calm assurance that love and eternity are incompatible. The storm
that presides portentously over her birth is as lurid in its fury as the
storm that is the lovers' motif in the novel, but it bestows on her an
adaptability they lack—that of a perpetual present tense:

> Shining and lowering and swelling and dying,
> Changing for ever from midnight to noon;
> Roaring like thunder, like soft music sighing,
> Shadows on shadows advancing and flying,
> Lightning-bright flashes the deep gloom defying,
> Coming as swiftly and fading as soon.
>   (#5, 13–18)

If this storm, like those of *Wuthering Heights*, portends the heroine's
violent life and destiny, its repeated contrasts also endow her with the
ambiguous gift of "changing for ever." Her ruling mutability bestows
on her the royal ability both to kill and to let die. Born under the aegis
of perpetual flashes of change, she fears most of all the traditional
happy ending—the resolution into unity that banishes contrast:

> "I well may mourn that only one
> Can light my future sky
> Even though by such a radiant sun
> My moon of life must die."
>   ("To A. G. A." #110, 34–37)

As prelude to the great hymn of hate against the scorching, draining
sun, this poem is a cosmic lament that the gentle, manifold signs of
night and its "changeful dreams" must succumb to the monolithic
tyranny of consciousness and day; while in the romance plot of Gondal, the poem is A. G. A.'s complaint that she cannot have two men
at once, but must abandon her marriage to the gentle Lord Alfred to
consummate her passion for imperial Julius Brenzaida. But above all,
the first line of the quatrain—"I well may mourn that only one"—
laments to the death Wordsworth's relieved discrimination among the
richness of apparent chaos: "Fair as a star, when only one / Is shining

in the sky" ("She Dwelt Among the Untrodden Ways," ll. 7–8)
"But there's a Tree, of many, one, / A single Field which I hav
looked upon" ("Intimations Ode," ll. 51–52).

The Wordsworthian choice "of many, one" is truly A. G
A.'s death knell. "The Death of A. G. A.," Gondal's longest narrativ
in which her assassination is starkly presented, locates her death in th
disappearance of the change and contrast that were her identity:

> You might have seen the dear, dear sign of life
> In her uncovered eye,
> And her cheek changing in the mortal strife
> Betwixt the pain to live and agony to die.
>
> But nothing mutable was there.
>   (#143, 270–75)

From birth to death, change confirms her cherished life in time. Th
mutability affirmed in this equivocal, epic queen, and in the empii
that takes her shape, seems a unique virtue in the poetry of an ag
that yearned increasingly for fixity.

Gondal's land finds its being in its storm: changes—psychic
seasonal, and political—appear to rock its world forever. Such fluctua
tions fight against the unity Wordsworth sought in a nature whei
change threatened a betrayal so radical that his only defense was res
olution into "of many, one." Despite the determined reaction of latei
"High" Victorian poetry against many of its own perceptions of Ro
manticism, Wordsworth's will to draw the one out of the many grow
into near-obsessive dominance. Tennyson's authoritative elegy *In Me
moriam A. H. H.* (1850) typically concludes its record of emotiona
and natural fluctuations with their resolution into "one God, one law
one element, / And one far-off divine event, / To which the whol
creation moves" ("Epilogue," ll. 142–44).

This insistently reiterated "one . . . one . . . one" wa
death rather than consolation to A. G. A., whose healing power spran
only from the interminable rhythms Tennyson's speaker mourns an
fears:

> The hills are shadows, and they flow
> From form to form, and nothing stands;

They melt like mist, the solid lands,
Like clouds they shape themselves and go.
                    (*In Mem.*, CXXIII, 5–8)

'hough from Tennyson's own day to ours there has been little doubt
1at this woeful vision of mutability spoke for the cosmic anguish of
the Victorians," at least one contemporary poetic vision took from
1is same flow its only certainty that life remained.

For Robert Browning this vision of incessant change seems
1ore vigorously compelling, but it, too, finally exists to be repudiated.
1 *Dramatic Romances,* published in 1845 when Emily Brontë was
eep in Gondal, his "Englishman in Italy" eyes ambivalently the vio-
nt combat of a landscape about to be devastated by Scirocco:

In the vat, halfway up on our house-side,
    Like blood the juice spins,
While your brother all bare-legged is dancing
    Till breathless he grins
Dead-beaten in effort on effort
    To keep the grapes under,
Since still when he seems all but master,
    In pours the fresh plunder
From girls who keep coming and going
    With basket on shoulder,
And eyes shut against the rain's driving;
    Your girls that are older,—
                    (ll. 74–85)

Dead-beaten" but grinning bravely in his dance to outface the om-
ivorous proliferation of "plunder," Browning's harvester seems to be
ghting a losing battle against the perpetual motion that foments into
1e warning cry: "Scirocco is loose!" Unlike Gondal's, this storm does
ot define the poem's heroic virtues, but submerges them: "No refuge,
it creep / Back again to my side and my shoulder, / And listen or
eep" (ll. 126–28). The threat to humanity underlying this sensuous
ance may affect Browning's turn away from mutability and multitu-
inousness in the long poem he considered his great epic statement,
he Ring and the Book (1868–69), whose introductory admonition
ates the theme and shape of the work to come:

Rather learn and love
Each facet-flash of the revolving year!—
Red, green, and blue that whirl into a white,
The variance now, the eventual unity,
Which make the miracle.[6]

The heart of Browning's epic follows the Wordsworthian and Tenny-
sonian resolutions: "of many, one"; "of variance, unity." Though thi
attempt to resolve diversity in unity, to make the dance of chang
"whirl into a white," is central to the nineteenth-century ideal of epic
the perpetual explorations of Gondal have no room for it. "The Gondals are discovering the interior of Gaaldine," Emily Brontë wrot
provocatively in her notebook, eschewing both "have discovered" an
"will discover." In this initiation to her world, as in that world itself
the present participle dominates as discovery perpetually takes place ii
a perpetual present. To "whirl" such a process "into a white" woul
destroy the very miracle these poems reveal.

To say that Emily Brontë alone wrote an epic about mutability in which mutability was not shunned is not to say that sh
embraced the anarchy that seems constantly seething up against th
desperately grinning culture of Browning's grape harvester. As Fanni
Ratchford has taught us, the excesses of Gondal generate their ow
retribution.[7] Though "changing for ever" seems the insignia for A. G
A. and the world that expresses her, one thinks back to the Gonda
epic as a checkerboard of dungeons. Ever-changing nature is mos
often a tantalizing flutter seen through the window of prison. In Gondal, dungeons are ruthlessly punitive, amenable to none of the Romantic transformations available in Wordsworth's "Nuns Fret Not a
Their Convent's Narrow Room": "In truth the prison, into which w
doom / Ourselves, no prison is" (ll. 8–9). The cultural survey of Child
Harold's pilgrimage similarly observes that, at least in exotic Albania
enclosure becomes a hermitage of self-sufficient space for a lovin
woman:

Here woman's voice is never heard: apart,
And scarce permitted, guarded, veil'd, to move,
She yields to one her person and her heart,
Tamed to her cage, nor feels a wish to rove:
For, not unhappy in her master's love,
And joyful in a mother's gentlest cares,

Blest cares! All other feelings far above!
Herself more sweetly rears the babe she bears,
Who never quits the breast, no meaner passion shares.
(CHP, canto II, st. LXI)

Female devotion reveals that the fixity of prison can become one with
eternity. But in Gondal, both male and female prisoners are agoniz-
ingly possessed by the "wish to rove." Romantic transfiguration of a
static protective spot is reduced to a sophistical denial of wholeness
and joy:

In dungeons dark I cannot sing,
In sorrow's thrall 'tis hard to smile:
What bird can soar with broken wing,
What heart can bleed and joy the while?
(#77)

For Emily Brontë prison is always prison, because like the fixity of
eternity it locks its inhabitant away from change. Briefly incarcerated
after the death of Elbe, A. G. A. grasps from her cell at mutability's
very essence in "To a Wreath of Snow": "O transient voyager of
heaven!" (#39, 1). In this transience is all the life the prisoner is denied. Although a wreath of snow will "melt like mist," as Tennyson
was to write, denial of its properties is an excruciating denial of voy-
aging life itself.

But A. G. A. is not Brontë's only prisoner to yearn out
of permanence for the shifting and changing. While Byron's Prisoner
of Chillon involuntarily and tragically "grew friends" with the self-
complete space of his dungeon, the captive in "Gleneden's Dream" is
haunted only by a nature that is, like Browning's Italy, a country of
verbs, a perpetual process:

Tell me, watcher, is it winter?
Say how long my sleep has been?
Have the woods I left so lovely
Lost their robes of tender green?

Is the morning slow in coming?
Is the night-time loath to go?
Tell me, are the dreary mountains
Drearier still with drifted snow?
(#63, 1–8)

Nature is time, change, the cycle of seasons, and imprisonment from
it is no hermitage, but simply the end of life. Next to the daily reality
of incarceration, Byron's cries in the "Sonnet on Chillon" seem grandiose slogans: "Brightest in dungeons, Liberty! thou art"; "Chillon
thy prison is a holy place" (ll. 2,9). Ideally this heroism of the imagination should be possible for the Byronic "I," though Byron's prisone
himself manages to become a survivor only by shrinking into an inmate; but Gondal's characters can conceive no victory of consciousnes
in thriving away from time and space. When Julius betrays and im-
prisons Gerald Exina to lock all the islands under his empire, Gerald'
incarceration embodies only the finality of immutability and death:

> Set is his sun of liberty;
> Fixed is his earthly destiny;
> A few years of captivity,
> And then a captive's tomb.
>   (#125, 21–24)

Transfiguration of enclosure dwindles into the fantasy with which
prisoner flatters himself. The epic's many dungeon poems assure u
that if change is sustenance, fixity is not liberty but despair, and Gon
dal needs no other hell than the self-created heavens of many of it
contemporaries. Cause of countless deaths, A. G. A can be no mor
damned in any world than she is by her faithful servant's epitaph
"But nothing mutable was there" (#143, 274).

    Yet Gondal's queen is not obliterated by eternity. If he
body's ironic doom is immutability, the survival of her essence is as
sured; not because she is remembered, but because she is forgotten a
in "Cold in the Earth" she pledged herself to forget. Only her servan
mourns the lack of mourners that insure the survival of her vision
"How few, of all the hearts that loved, / Are grieving for thee now!"
("E. W. to A. G. A.," #171, 1–2).

    In a century that enshrined memory and recovered th
elegy, Emily Brontë alone fled the prison suggested by the words "i
memoriam." In releasing her queen from the dungeon of memory an
permanence, she allows her to live, not as Wordsworth's Lucy did a
an immortal thing among things—"No motion has she now, no force
/ She neither hears nor sees" ("A Slumber Did My Spirit Seal," l

5–6)—but as a consciousness of motion and a pledge to "changeful dreams":

> Blow west wind, by the lonely mound,
> And murmur, summer streams,
> There is no need of other sound
> To soothe my Lady's dreams.
>
> (#173, 25–28)

In death as in life, A. G. A. is queen of a perpetual present. In this continued empire of mutability and departure, Emily Brontë remains true to the vision of an epic that quietly relinquished her century's hope of transcendence and saw no reason to mourn its loss. Seen as a whole, Gondal shows us the power and the exhilaration of a world that refuses to end in a cosmic epithalamium. The saga of its queen and the silence of its creator suggest that this gaunt woman who wanted never to leave her father's parsonage was a braver navigator into the straits of time and change than the sterner, more sonorous bards whose poetry constituted her age's official voice.[8]

14.

The Power of Hunger: Demonism and Maggie Tulliver

Hunger was more powerful than sorrow*

W
e do not expect to meet vampires and demons on the fla*
plains of George Eliot's St. Ogg's, or to find witches spyin*
on the regular rotations of the mill on the Floss. Georg*
Eliot's insistence on a moral apprehension of the real seems to banis*
all such strange shapes from her landscape.

But the stolid world of *The Mill on the Floss* is more re*
ceptive to the uncanny than its surface appears to be. The novel i*
often condemned for a loss of moral balance arising from George Eliot'*
overidentification with her heroine, Maggie Tulliver.[1] It is true tha*
Maggie's pull on the novel causes George Eliot to relinquish her sharpl*
defined moral perspective in favor of a sense of immediate immersio*
in "the depths in life"—a loss of perspective that is in many ways *

"Poscia, più che 'l dolor, potè 'l digiuno," Dante Alighieri, *Inferno,* canto 33, l. 75. I shoul*
like to thank Victoria Kirkham for her crisp translation of the line, which John D. Sinclair'*
edition of *Dante's Inferno* translates as "Then fasting had more power than grief" (New York*
Oxford University Press, 1974), p. 409.

gain, as the author herself seems to realize, for she begins the novel by abandoning herself to her material in a refusal to be our sage. The first voice we hear is the narrator's cry for submergence in a half-drowned landscape, a defiance of the perspective of the normal: "I am in love with moistness, and envy the white ducks that are dipping their heads far into the water here among the withes, unmindful of the awkward appearance they make in the drier world above."[2]

In chapter 4, Maggie mimics the ducks' defiance of dryness and perspective by suddenly plunging her head into a basin of water, "in the vindictive determination that there should be no more chance of curls that day" (p. 25). The repetition of this gesture suggests an important area of experience in the novel, one that the narrator leans toward herself: plunging one's head underwater entails the exchange of a clear vision for a swimming vision, a submergence in experience at the cost of objectivity and judgment. Maggie Tulliver lives in such a swimming perspective, and *The Mill on the Floss* is her story.

Though many critics find loss of perspective to be the besetting artistic sin of *The Mill on the Floss*, the experience of perspectivelessness is in part what the novel is about. In one of its many nostalgic evocations, it defines childhood vision as "the strangely perspectiveless conception of life that gave the bitterness its intensity," admonishing us that if we could recapture this intense vision, "we should not pooh-pooh the griefs of our children" (p. 60). But it is part of Maggie's nature that, like Peter Pan, she never grows away from her capacity to plunge into the moment, to submerge herself exclusively in what is near. In her first intense awareness of Stephen Guest, she is "absorbed in the direct, immediate experience, without any energy left for taking account of it and reasoning about it" (p. 352). When she drifts down the river with him, her sensations are described as unique in their passionately immediate perspective, which gives to objects usually seen at a distance the fractured intensity of an impressionist painting: "Such things, uttered in low broken tones by the one voice that has first stirred the fibre of young passion, have only a feeble effect—on experienced minds *at a distance* from them. To poor Maggie *they were very near:* . . . and the vision for the time excluded all realities—all except the returning sun-gleams which broke out on the waters as the evening approached, and mingled with the visionary sunlight of promised happiness—all except the hand that pressed hers, and the voice that spoke to her, and the eyes that looked at her with grave, unspeakable love" (p. 411, my italics). Here as so often in Maggie's life, reality is what the senses swallow undigested.[3]

Maggie's—and George Eliot's—capacity to dissolve experience into its constituent vivid moments and sensations looks forward to Pater as much as her fostering of memory looks forward to Proust.[4] In its emotional vividness, Maggie's renunciation seems as gratifying as her abandonment to passion, for in it she achieves not the "stupefaction" Philip envisions, but a state George Eliot defines more equivocally as "that mysterious wondrous happiness that is one with pain" (p. 456). What post-Freudian critics might be tempted to dismiss as Maggie's "masochism," a neurosis that should be beneath George Eliot's noble gaze, becomes for George Eliot herself part of the virtuosity in suffering that makes a heroine: "But if Maggie had been that [wealthy and contented] young lady, you would probably have known nothing about her: her life would have had so few vicissitudes that it could hardly have been written; for the happiest women, like the happiest nations, have no history" (p. 335). In such passages as this, George Eliot seems to be abandoning moral placement entirely and applying a Paterian criterion of intensity to Maggie's history: the well-lived life is the vividly felt life that feeds into art. Seen in this light, the flood that justifies Maggie's life and destroys it is her only adequate consummation, because only through an upheaval of this magnitude can she attain, not merely her brother's love, but the intensity she craves from existence and cannot find there.

The fervor with which Maggie sees and is seen is thrown into relief by the emotional deadness of the medium she lives in. It is true that as a moral commentator, George Eliot gave scrupulous due to the tenacity and respectability of Tom and the Dodsons, as she herself asserted in response to Eneas Sweetland Dallas' review of the novel:

I have certainly fulfilled my intention very badly if I have made the Dodson honesty appear "mean and uninteresting," or made the payment of one's debts appear a contemptible virtue in comparison with any sort of "Bohemian" qualities. So far as my own feelings and intentions are concerned, no one class of persons or form of character is held up to reprobation or to exclusive admiration. Tom is painted with as much love and pity as Maggie, and I am so far from hating the Dodsons myself, that I am rather aghast to find them ticketed with such very ugly adjectives.[5]

But no matter how tolerant and broad-minded a moralist George Eliot may be, she is disingenuous here about herself as an artist. Tom's self-denying struggle to pay his father's debts and restore the mill to the family is simply subordinated to the high drama of Maggie's love affairs with Philip and Stephen. Though we are told about his honor and ability, we are rarely allowed to see Tom at his disciplined, determined best, but only as Maggie's vindictive prosecuting angel. As for the Dodsons, occasional pious commentary about their honest virtues does not obscure the narrator's glee at the overwhelming ridiculousness of Aunt Pullet and Aunt Glegg and their muttering husbands. Nor does it counterbalance such authorial outbursts as: "A vigorous superstition, that lashes its gods or lashes its own back, seems to be more congruous with the mystery of the human lot, than the mental condition of these emmet-like Dodsons and Tullivers" (p. 238). This sudden endorsement of sheer intensity seems to overwhelm the novel's carefully constructed moral antitheses.

The narrator's outburst in favor of a "vigorous," even a violent, superstition is at one with her impulse to follow the ducks and Maggie in plunging her head underwater in revolt against a drier world's perspective. This tendency in *The Mill on the Floss* to oppose provincial respectability with an ambiguous emotional explosiveness that culminates in pain allies the novel with a Victorian subgenre of dubious respectability: the novel of sensation and, more particularly, the Gothic romance.

Of course, Gothic romance is in many ways alien to the George Eliot that most of us know. Her rootedness in the near mitigates against it, for Gothicism is a call of the wild, the remote in time and space. As Jane Austen's Catherine Morland puts it after Henry Tilney has led her into the sunlight of British common sense: "Among the Alps and the Pyrenees, perhaps, there were no mixed characters. There, such as were not as spotless as an angel, might have the dispositions of a fiend. But in England it was not so; among the English, she believed, in their hearts and habits, there was a general though unequal mixture of good and bad."[6] To be Gothic is to be unadulterated and therefore un-English; and George Eliot's native tolerance seems to eschew the violent moral extremes of foreign landscapes.

Gothicism, too, is a summons from a remoter past than George Eliot wants to know; *Romola,* her one excursion into the Italian Renaissance, endows even the wild-eyed Savonarola with the secular bias and ideological complexity of an enlightened Victorian sage. Ann Radcliffe's Emily St. Aubert, on the other hand, must journey from the sunlight of home and the enlightenment of the Renaissance to a medieval Catholic setting before she can palpitate to the terrors of obscurity and night. Coleridge's Ancient Mariner sails from the Christian Middle Ages into a pagan and primitive seascape. Bram Stoker's Jonathan Harker and Joseph Conrad's Marlow also journey from secular contemporaneity into a haunted past, the realm of "a vigorous superstition, that lashes its gods . . . [and] lashes its own back": the world that George Eliot invokes but does not inhabit in *The Mill on the Floss.* Even Victor Frankenstein, whose researches suggest the Promethean aspirations of the "modern" scientist, travels into the past in the course of his narrative, going from the relatively stable community of an English ship to increasingly wild Alpine landscapes until he touches the primitive solitudes of Coleridge's "land of mist and snow"; moreover, his research is inspired in the first place by the medieval pseudoscience of alchemy. All Gothic journeys seem to take place in time machines.

St. Ogg's, too, "carries the traces of its long growth and history like a millennial tree" (p. 104), and "the Catholics," those traditional conduits of Gothic terror, are a vague threat in the novel due to the rumblings of Catholic emancipation. But St. Ogg's is prosaically immune to its haunted past: "The mind of St. Ogg's did not look extensively before or after. . . . the present time was like the level plain where men lose their beliefs in volcanoes and earthquakes, thinking to-morrow will be as yesterday, and the giant forces that used to shake the earth are for ever laid to sleep" (p. 106). The sensibly level vision of St. Ogg's is as perspectiveless as Maggie's intensely momentary one, denying the wide swings through time and space that constitute the rhythms of Gothic fiction.

George Eliot's sympathetic naturalism and her tendency to make the boundaries of the community the boundaries of reality are in some ways like the vision of St. Ogg's. Her humanistic bias is suspicious of solitary aberration, emphasizing always the "threads of connection" rather than the potentially grotesque disjunctions between people. In a famous passage from *Romola*, which is often taken as George Eliot's central statement of belief, Romola banishes the shadows of the self:

What reasonable warrant could she have had for believing in . . . [Dino's mystical and solitary] vision and acting on it? None. True as the voice of foreboding had proved, Romola saw with unshaken conviction that to have renounced Tito in obedience to a warning like that, would have been meagre-hearted folly. Her trust had been delusive, but she would have chosen over again to have acted on it rather than be a creature led by phantoms and disjointed whispers in a world where there was the large music of reasonable speech, and the warm grasp of living hands.[7]

Yet even within *Romola*, this declaration is ambivalent, for the solitary and irrational whisper of foreboding has proved true; and throughout the novels, George Eliot's characters turn with longing to the "disjointed whispers" of uncertain origin that come only in solitude. At the end of her career, the visionary Mordecai in *Daniel Deronda* is apotheosized as an inspired descendant of the Hebrew prophets.[8] George Eliot's reason and trust did indeed shun solitary Gothic shadows, but her imagination did not: just before beginning *The Mill on the Floss*, she turned from the rather overinsistent naturalism of *Scenes of Clerical Life* and *Adam Bede* to write "The Lifted Veil," a short story in which Gothic fantasies run wild.[9] Latimer, the story's misanthropic, clairvoyant hero, comes together rather uneasily with the story's *Frankenstein*-like Alpine setting at the beginning and its reanimated corpse at the end, and George Eliot was probably right to deny her authorship of the story until 1877; but it gives us a telling glimpse of the shadows that were moving through her mind when she envisioned the dark and dreaming figure of Maggie Tulliver, standing rapt on a bridge under "the deepening grey of the sky," "like a wild thing" refusing to take her place around the family fire.

The intonations of Gothicism that run through the language of *The Mill on the Floss* converge in the "loving, large-souled" figure of Maggie, who broods over its landscape. The turbulent hair that is her bane as a child is an emblem of destructive powers she is only half-aware of and unable to control; its roots reach back to the serpent tresses of the Greek Medusa, peer through the "wanton ringlets" of Milton's Eve, and stretch down from mythology into Gothicism when the female narrator of a late Victorian vampire story— Eric, Count Stenbock's "The True Story of a Vampire" (1894)— describes her "long tangled hair [which] was always all over the place, and never would be combed straight." The traditionally demonic connotations of unruly hair are reinforced by Maggie's life. The intensity with which she flings herself at the moment contains a certain murderousness, even when she is nursing a doll "towards which she [has] an occasional fit of fondness in Tom's absence, neglecting its toilette, but lavishing so many warm kisses on it that the waxen cheeks [have] a wasted unhealthy appearance" (p. 18). From the beginning, Maggie's kisses take life rather than bestow it.

In her worm-eaten attic, she keeps another doll as a fetish, whose head she mauls and pounds into unrecognizability during outbursts of sheer violence which do not take the shape of love. Pounding her fetish, Maggie embodies "the vigorous superstition, that lashes its gods or lashes its own back" for which the narrator will pine in the desert of Dodson modernity. She turns from these two "love-dismembered" dolls to Tom, on whose neck she hangs "in rather a strangling fashion" throughout the novel, though adulthood brings her greater awareness of the draining tendency in her love: "I think I am quite wicked with roses—I like to gather them and smell them till they have no scent left" (p. 387). Maggie's rapacity has something in common with that of Tennyson's Ulysses, who sails away from commonality proclaiming "I will drink life to the lees"; and something else in common with that of Sheridan Le Fanu's Carmilla, a demure vampire who literally does so.

Maggie's recurrent pattern of action is to enter worlds and explode them. Her destructive aura takes shape in the associations of demonism, witchery, and vampirism that surround her, which will be examined more closely below, and which, despite the narrator's insistence on the prosaic narrowness of Lincolnshire village life, are in part an outgrowth of the environment defined by the "emmet-like Dodsons and Tullivers."

"Emmet-like" is actually an unfair dismissal of the intricacies of Dodson and Tulliver perceptions. Part, at least, of the elaborate Dodson metaphysic can be summed up in a single penetrating sentence: "It was necessary to be baptised, else one could not be buried in the churchyard" (p. 239). Given their tendency to embalm life's great crises in layers of ritual, it does not seem unfair to the spirit of the Dodsons to translate this sentence as "It was necessary to be born, else one could not die." Life for the Dodsons is a tedious rehearsal for the triumphant performance of death. Aunt Glegg secretes her best hairpieces and linen, Aunt Pullet her treasured medicine bottles, Mrs. Tulliver (before the bankruptcy) her best china, so that they will be intact and pristine when that great day arrives. The aunts admire pink-and-white little Lucy, primarily because she is able to simulate the deathlike immobility of an icon: "And there's Lucy Deane's such a good child—you may set her on a stool, and there she'll sit for an hour together, and never offer to get off" (p. 39). It is one of the novel's muted ironies that only Aunt Deane, the most shadowy because the least Dodsonian of the sisters, achieves death in the course of the narrative. The other aunts are forced to survive beyond the end, presumably still quoting their wills and rehearsing their funerals. In a moment of uncharacteristic self-transcendence, Aunt Glegg places her husband's death before her own in this wistful reverie about the consummation of her widowhood:

It would be affecting to think of him, poor man, when he was gone; and even his foolish fuss about the flowers and garden-stuff, and his insistence on the subject of snails, would be touching when it was once fairly at an end. To survive Mr. Glegg, and talk eulogistically of him as a man who might have his weaknesses, but who had done the right thing by her . . . all this made a flattering and conciliatory view of the future.

(pp. 113–14)

The bristlingly proper Aunt Glegg takes the romantic Liebestod a step beyond itself: death is not merely love's climax, but its birth. Like Poe's protagonists or the converts of vampire literature, she venerates death not as a gateway to the hereafter, but as a state complete in itself; for her its trappings and machinery are objects of fascination and delight. We need think only of such embalmed Victorian icons as Little Nell in her tomb, Tennyson's Elaine in her coffin, Millais' lavishly drowned Ophelia, to recall the loving fascination with which high Victorian art embraces and embellishes its corpses.

This reverence for and simulation of death is a pall that winds through Maggie's childhood and survives in the strikingly un-nurturing quality of her love, which eats rather than nourishes its objects. When Tom comes home from school for the first time, her suggestively sterile love token is a hutch of dead rabbits for him—a symbol that Lawrence may have borrowed for *Women in Love*, in which a paralyzed rabbit becomes a token of the deathly kinship between Gerald and Gudrun. The defaced dolls, shattered cardhouses, and spoiled hopes with which Maggie's life is littered suggest that in her own messy, overheated Tulliver fashion, she inherits the Dodson penchant for death and its trappings, carrying it from respectability down toward Gothicism. The cake she crushes and the wine she spills at Aunt Pullet's have a touch of black mass in them, for example; and her love-dis-membered dolls anticipate the children from whose blood all the female vampires in *Dracula* take life instead of giving it. The unwom-anly, because unnurturing, woman of whom Maggie Tulliver is a small type will come into her own in vampire literature, to be hymned most erotically in the ecstatically infertile lesbianism of *Carmilla*.

Maggie's faint taste of demonism is also shot through with Tulliver blood, in an inheritance more complex than mere impulsive-ness. In fact, despite her father's proud claims for his sister, Maggie's love is sufficiently nongenerative to align her with the Dodson sisters rather than with the wearily prolific Aunt Gritty, whom we can never envision defacing a doll rather than nourishing it. Maggie is closer to her father in her capacity to destroy things with the most loving of intentions, and her demonic leanings reveal an affinity with him that is intellectual as well as temperamental:

Mr. Tulliver was, on the whole, a man of safe traditional opinions; but on one or two points he had trusted to his unassisted intellect, and had arrived at several questionable conclusions; among the rest, that rats, weevils, and lawyers were created by Old Harry. Unhappily he had no one to tell him that this was rampant Manichaeism, else he might have seen his error.

(p. 14)

The Manichaean heresy, which defines evil as an active, autonomous, and potent force rather than as the mere absence of good, expresses perfectly a world Mr. Tulliver sees madly twisting in the grip of Old Harry and his progeny. In granting to evil its own independent and powerful existence, Manichaeism is the necessary premise of Gothic sensationism, and, like the Dodson worship of death and the death-like, it has a powerful effect on young Maggie's sense of who she is and where she will find her life.

For Maggie's philosophical isolation, the fact that she has access to no ideology other than that of her family, is stressed again and again. Nor is the narrator able to provide one, for Maggie or for us. Her assertion of Maggie's tragic ignorance of "the irreversible laws within and without her, which, governing the habits, becomes moral-ity, and, developing the feelings of submission and dependence, be-comes religion" (pp. 252–53), seems, like so much Victorian affir-mation, a sonorous hedge: these "laws" are a vague postulate, unrealized in the explosive course of a novel, the mystery of whose workings may after all be most appropriately productive of a primitive and pain-rid-den superstition. Lacking an overall rational structure to define our experience while reading, we are thrown back with Maggie on an ethos of sensationalism, even of demonism.[10] To unravel her world, Maggie turns naturally to books; but they cannot provide for her the key "that would link together the wonderful impressions of this mysterious life, and give her soul a sense of home in it" (p. 208). Instead of opening a window into spaciousness and coherence, Maggie's books become a mirror reflecting her own dark impulses. In fact, an examination of the world she sees in books provides us with a striking portrait of Maggie herself.

As a child, Maggie invokes her demonic self out of her books. On our first extended view of her, she is poring over a picture of a witch: "O, I'll tell you what that means. It's a dreadful picture, isn't it? But I can't help looking at it. That old woman in the water's a witch—they've put her in to find out whether she's a witch or no, and if she swims she's a witch, and if she's drowned—and killed, you know—she's innocent, and not a witch, but only a poor silly old woman. But what good would it do her then, you know, when she was drowned? Only, I suppose, she'd go to heaven, and God would make it up to her" (pp. 16–17).

In a passage that recalls Latimer in its near clairvoyance, Maggie projects the ambiguity of her own nature and destiny. Her interpretation of the picture is a miniature reflection of the narrator's attitude toward her: a mélange of demonism, rationalism, and a wistful faith that, after all, God will apologize in the end and redeem her innocence. But Maggie's first intuition springs out in a searing declarative statement: the woman in the water's a witch. Is Maggie? Witchery is entangled in her pull toward the smoky, nocturnal underworld of the gypsies, in "the night of her massy hair" (p. 382) with its suggestion of a somewhat smothering sexuality, and, most interestingly, in her charged relationship both to animals and to the natural world.

Traditional accounts of witchcraft place the witch in an intense and equivocal relationship to the animal kingdom.[11] Animal masks are worn at the witches' Sabbath, where Satan frequently presides in the costume of a bull; animals are worshipped and used as conduits for spells, the witch's nature seeming at times interchangeable with that of her familiar. But one of the commonest manifestations of witchery is the power to blight and cause disease in the animal kingdom. Here we can see the affinity between the legends of the witch and those of the vampire. The vampire, too, has a magical sympathetic kinship with animals, being able to assume the shape of dog and wolf as well as bat. But in some legends, animals shun him: he is a scourge of cattle and sheep, and dogs howl and even die in terror at his approach. Both witch and vampire simultaneously spring from animals and are fatal to them.

Maggie, too, both blights animals and becomes them. The hutch of starved rabbits is presented as the first symbol of her love for Tom, suggesting a silent murderousness of which the animals are conduit and fetish. Yet much of the animal imagery in the novel clusters around Maggie. Her affinities with animals range from simple descriptive similes—she shakes the water from her hair "like a Skye terrier escaped from his bath" (p. 25)—to intimations of metamorphosis that carry magical suggestions, such as this image of Philip's: "What was it, he wondered, that made Maggie's dark eyes remind him of the stories about princesses being turned into animals? . . . I think it was that her eyes were full of unsatisfied intelligence, and unsatisfied, beseeching affection" (p. 158). Philip's vocabulary and the narrator's reassuring explication soften the power of the picture, which is sinister. Witches in folklore are more likely to turn into animals than princesses are; and as well as expressing the rootedness of the witch in her familiar, the image evokes a string of pagan goddesses with the bodies of animals and the heads of women, of whom the lamia, the vampire's pagan ancestor, is one of the darkest.

Maggie's alliance with trees also connotes witchcraft, which is traditionally linked to tree worship: the dance around the fairy tree and invocation to it are perennial features of witches' Sabbath rituals in England. The tree appears first when little Maggie is possessed by "small demons": "a small Medusa with her snakes cropped," she pushes Lucy into the mud and retreats impenitently to the roots of a tree, to glower at Tom and Lucy "with her small Medusa face" (p. 91). In the sequence with Philip in the Red Deeps, the association recurs, amplified and beautified: "With her dark colouring and jet crown surmounting her tall figure, she seems to have a sort of kinship with the grand Scotch firs, at which she is looking up as if she loved them well" (p. 261). Philip, who seems possessed by the association of Maggie with metamorphosis, insists upon this kinship, finally painting Maggie as "a tall Hamadryad, dark and strong and noble, just issued from one of the fir-trees" (p. 285).[12] Philip's artist's eye continually captures Maggie in the process of equivocal transformation, which his less true language muffles by such adjectives as "noble." To one familiar with English witchcraft legends and rituals, these images of Maggie carry their own undercurrents, which hardly need Lucy's more explicit reinforcement later on: "I can't think what witchery it is in you, Maggie, that makes you look best in shabby clothes" (p. 324). Another of Lucy's innocent remarks, about the secret liaison with Philip, carries more complex ironies: "Ah, now I see how it is you know Shakespeare and everything, and have learned so much since you left school; which always seemed to me witchcraft before—part of your general uncanniness" (p. 338). Lucy's initial intuition is correct, for Maggie learned about Shakespeare in the Red Deeps, which, as Philip senses, is the proper setting for and a powerful projection of her "general uncanniness."

But in the prophetic doppelgänger that arrests the young Maggie from the pages of Defoe, the witch is not lodged in an animal or a tree; she is bobbing in water, an element that follows Maggie and shapes her life. The origin of the English ducking ritual places the witch in a typically ambiguous relationship to water. In theory, a witch will not drown because the pure baptismal element must cast out the evil thing. But there is an obverse explanation of the witch's ability to float: perhaps her magical kinship with a more darkly defined water allies her with the element and prevents it from destroying her. The witch's dual relationship to nature is evident in the ducking ritual as it is in her power over animals: do they feed on or repel each other? Is the witch a growth from or an enemy of the natural world?

The vampire's relationship to water is as ambiguous as the witch's. In many versions of the legend, he is unable to cross running water on his own power. This abrupt paralysis is a suggestive dark gloss on the figure of the Virgin of the Flood, Maggie's holy analogue in *The Mill on the Floss,* whom local legends depict wailing by the river bank to be ferried across, unable to work her magical transformation until Beorl has allowed her to enter his boat. But Maggie's "almost miraculous" flight across the river to Tom shows her powers gushing out on the water, and so, in some stories, do the vampire's. Count Dracula feasts triumphantly on the ship's crew during an ocean voyage; he is able to control storms and tides; and Mina Harker's unholy "marriage" to him is revealed under hypnosis through a shared sense of "the lapping of water . . . gurgling by." The implicit question that runs through the legends of witches and vampires also runs through Maggie's voyages in *The Mill on the Floss:* is the pure baptismal element itself a conduit blending what is unholy with what is potentially divine?

Like the crises in the lives of Romola, Gwendolen Harleth, and Daniel Deronda, the great crises in Maggie's life come when she abandons herself to the movement of the tides. We first see her staring intently over the gloomy water; before we hear her speak, her mother prophesies darkly about her proclivity for "wanderin' up an' down by the water, like a wild thing" (p. 12);[13] her father's mad fear that irrigation will drain the mill of its water deprives her of her childhood home; the flight with Stephen that uproots so many lives takes place by water; and so, of course, do Maggie's much-criticized apotheosis and death in the final flood, which raise more questions than they resolve.

These questions are the same as those raised by the childish Maggie about the witch in Defoe who is her psychic mirror: is the woman in the water a witch or not? Does she float or sink? Is water her friend or foe, condemning her to spiritual exile forever or sweeping her to final vindication and "home"? " 'O God, where am I? Which is the way home?' she crie[s] out, in the dim loneliness" of a flooded world (p. 453), and the book's conclusion only echoes this cry. Everything has plunged its head underwater with the ducks, as the narrator had yearned to do at the beginning. The difficult ending will always be unsatisfactory for those seeking a drier world's perspective, but it is at one with the ethos of Gothic romance as Robert Kiely defines it: "We have seen over and over again that romantic novels have troubled and unsatisfactory endings. One may say that a resistance to conclusion is one of the distinguishing characteristics of [Gothic] romantic fiction." Kiely gives a darker and more detailed account of these concluding visions in his discussion of *The Monk*, which can be translated illuminatingly into the world of *The Mill on the Floss*: "Lewis's final vision is of a chaos which neither man nor art has the capacity to control or avoid. Indeed, uncontrollable energy would seem to be the only energy there is in the world of *The Monk*. The artist, like the monk who seeks liberation from lifeless conventions, is apt to find himself unexpectedly on the side of the flood."[14]

Certainly, Maggie seems to be on the side of the flood, since it seeps into the house as an efficacious, though indirect, answer to her despairing prayer. Does she "cause" it, as the vampire evokes storms and controls the tides? Are the waves on which she magically rides her final destructive ally against the commonality that expels and entices her? To some extent, at least, the flood is Maggie's last and strongest familiar, and it is not described through a soothing haze of death and rebirth imagery, but as a fury that crashes through houses, destroys livestock, and drowns crops. "Nature repairs her ravages—but not all" (p. 457) is the narrator's final quiet statement about a phenomenon that uproots and scars more life than it restores.

But it preserves Maggie until she has obtained Tom. Floating toward him, she is envisioned ambiguously with "her wet clothes [clinging] round her, and her streaming hair . . . dashed about by the wind" (p. 453). Like the witch's watery cousin, the Lorelei or mermaid, she lures Tom out of the house where he has found temporary protection—for the waters have stopped rising—into the dangerous tides. The loosely sacramental language of the ending tells us that preternatural forces have been evoked and revealed without disclosing their source. Tom is possessed by the "revelation to his spirit, of the depths in life, that had lain beyond his vision," leaving him "pale with a certain awe and humiliation" (p. 455). At last, "a mist gather[s] over the blue-grey eyes," he falls under Maggie's spell, rows the boat into the dangerous current, clings to her, and sinks, a devotee at last.

The mist that gathers over Tom's eyes at the end concludes the pattern of imagery that centers around what I have called the "swimming vision," a vision of eyes that project upon rather than reflect the world, associated in the novel with explosions of undirected energy reminiscent of sensationalism. Like the witch that leaps at Maggie from the pages of Defoe, the shining eyes the child sees in Bunyan reflect her own in the mask of the devil: " 'Here he is,' she said, running back to Mr. Riley, 'and Tom coloured him for me with his paints when he was at home last holidays—the body all black, you know, and the eyes red, like fire, because he's all fire inside, and it shines out at his eyes' " (p. 18).

Throughout the novel, Maggie's potent power shines out at her eyes as the devil's does. Shortly after the above speech, we learn that the powdery white of the mill makes "her dark eyes flash out with new fire" (p. 26). When "small demons" impel her to push Lucy into the mud, the Medusa-like power of her eyes is referred to twice and is demonstrated later in her bewitching effect on Philip and Stephen. Her eyes evoke Philip's vision of her as a woman metamorphosed into an animal, with its suggestions of witch, vampire, and lamia; and Stephen, after remarking prophetically "an alarming amount of devil there" (p. 328), falls under Maggie's spell and thirsts obsessively for her *look*. Burning or swimming, Maggie's eyes invoke or transmit more than they see, suggesting an infernal dimension to "the depths in life," that new realm which the intensity of her gaze reveals to Tom in the boat.

If Maggie uses books primarily to invoke mirror images of her own demonic tendencies, the reflections they show her may not always be malign. Bob Jakin's present of Thomas à Kempis' *Imitation of Christ* reveals to her a doctrine of renunciation and self-suppression which some critics, at least, interpret as Maggie's true path to whatever salvation the novel has to offer.[15] At the very least, Thomas à Kempis presents Maggie with a new, celestial image of herself which prompts her to reject the books Philip offers to entice her out of isolation: Madame de Staël and Walter Scott, with their familiar, banished reflections of the "dark, unhappy ones."

But whatever Thomas à Kempis' doctrine may be in itself, it becomes in Maggie's hands another "fetish" that explodes communities and blights lives. The "law of consequences," that ethical variant of utilitarianism which operated so stringently against Arthur and Hetty in *Adam Bede*, judges actions according to their detonations on others, not the high-minded hopes that accompany them; and by its criteria at least, Maggie's applications of Kempis' strictures are disastrous. In her first liaison with Philip, renunciation erupts into hunger for love and talk and books, and clouds over Tom's triumphant restoration of the family honor—an effect which is dwelt on with greater immediacy than the checkered fulfillment of her meetings with Philip in the Red Deeps. When she falls in love with Stephen's strong arm, she renounces renunciation and momentarily abandons herself to the tides of her feeling for him; but when morning comes, the "law" she had found in Thomas à Kempis returns, somewhat transmuted in form, but even more disastrous in effect.

Maggie's second dedication to renunciation takes the form not of mystical quietism, but of a humanistic reverence for ties sanctioned by the past and kept alive by memory: "If the past is not to bind us, where can duty lie? We should have no law but the inclination of the moment" (p. 417). Through this new application of Kempis, Maggie attempts to free herself from the momentariness bordering on sensationalism that has possessed her throughout her life. The "memory" she invokes is actually a myth-making faculty that makes of the past a sanctuary against the present rather than its seeding ground; and the narrator has reminded us earlier that such memories sculpted into myths can be a saving anchor against the chaos of space: "But heaven knows where that striving might lead us, if our affections had not a trick of twining round those old inferior things—if the loves and sanctities of our life had no deep immovable roots in memory" (p. 135).

But while adherence to memory can be a ballast, the retreat from Stephen which it results in can at that point produce only chaos. The ties to Philip and Lucy to which Maggie declares allegiance have already been snapped by her flight; Tom, the protective deity of her earliest memory, must repudiate her; memory casts her out into a present which denies her as well, containing only a shamed family, an irate community, and a devastated lover. The novel's heavy irony against "the world's wife" does not mean the wife is wrong in seeing that Maggie's wild swerve toward renunciation and her solitary return after the fact are the most destructive choices she can make. Marriage to Stephen would have hurt fewer people than a renunciation whose consequences fling Maggie and all the characters attached to her into a morass where, as the well-meaning Dr. Kenn perceives, each immediate step is "clogged with evil." In terms of its effect on other lives, even a potentially celestial book like Thomas à Kempis' can be a source of evil in Maggie's hands because, once it finds its way into her life, it does evil things.

Though in several forms the world inside books is a demonic mirror for Maggie, turning away from it to the world outside seems demonic as well. If one motif shows her avidly devouring books, another shows her obliterating them in dreams or flinging them aside. When we first meet her, she is "dreaming over her book" instead of reading it, and upon hearing Tom's name, she jumps "up from her stool, forgetting all about her heavy book, which [falls] with a bang within the fender" (p. 16). This sound reverberates through her first visit to Tom at school, when her abandon at seeing him again sends a fat dictionary crashing to the floor. Later on, caught in her family's dreary poverty, she dreams intermittently of using her learning to invade the world of men and so escape from home; but "somehow, when she sat at the window with her book, her eyes *would* fix themselves blankly on the out-door sunshine; then they would fill with tears, and sometimes, if her mother was not in the room, the studies would all end in sobbing." The swimming vision which is her motif in the novel leads her eyes from book to window, and thence to "fits even of anger and hatred" which "flow out over her affections and conscience like a lava stream, and frighten her with a sense that it [is] not difficult for her to become a demon" (p. 252). The path outward from book to nature makes of the window a demonic mirror as well, and at Lucy's house later on, her eyes move from book to window for the last time: "Lucy hurried out of the room, but Maggie did not take the opportunity of opening her book: she let it fall on her knees, while her eyes wandered to the window" (p. 326). Soon afterward, Maggie and Stephen will pass through this same window toward the river, in a voyage whose destructive effects we have already looked at.[16] Both the world in books and the world beyond them are for Maggie reflections of "the depths in life" whose emissary she is forced to be in "the drier world above."

For whether they are devouring books or thirsting toward the world beyond the window, Maggie's eyes have the demonic power of transfixing and transforming what they illuminate into their own images. The power of transformation has always been central in witchcraft legends; the witch's ability to impress herself on others by fixing on them the evil eye or making of them a waxen effigy strikes at the heart of our fear that we will disappear into the image of ourselves that others see. In the two most famous nineteenth-century novels of terror, *Frankenstein* and *Dracula,* the demon's power of transformation takes on sweeping racial overtones: both the monster and Dracula threaten the human species with extinction by their hunger to propagate their own corpselike kind. If, as was said above, such female demons as Carmilla absorb some of their power from their perverse infertility, a demon with reproductive organs is more demonic still. In such a vision, evolutionary fears join with the fertility of death and the weariness of rebirth in a concluding cycle of life evolving forever into death, death into life again. The prolific destructiveness of Maggie Tulliver, the mode in which she spills into her environment by breaking and overturning things, has some of this aura. But the blight she is able to spread crystallizes in the figure of the thoroughly demonic Bertha in "The Lifted Veil," as she sits eyeing a corpse: "But I asked myself how that face of hers could ever have seemed to me the face of a woman born of woman, with memories of childhood, capable of pain, needing to be fondled? The features at that moment seemed so preternaturally sharp, the eyes were so hard and eager—she looked like a cruel immortal, finding her spiritual feast in the agonies of a dying race."[17]

In the ensuing action of the story, the corpse Bertha eyes hungrily is actually restored to "life." Though in terms of the plot's rather awkward and incoherent machinery the reanimated corpse is Bertha's nemesis, the conjunction between female demon with feasting eyes and the renewal of life in death is suggestive, if not causal. It reminds us that because of her fertility, the female monster in *Frankenstein* is more deadly than the male, and must be ripped savagely apart before she has been born. Apparently the nineteenth-century fear that evolution will lead to an Armageddon of demons subsuming life into death eternally is still with us, on the evidence of two contemporary American Gothic novels, Ira Levin's *Rosemary's Baby* and Thomas Tryon's *Harvest Home*. Both are pristine antifertility myths, in which the women's hunger to reproduce threatens all the norms we are supposed to cherish. Once she has been supernaturally infected, the "natural" woman casts the most dangerous shadow of all, for she is able to breed within her the germ of a new death.

George Eliot seems aware of this deeper note in her passage from the unnatural Bertha Latimer to Maggie Tulliver, who is unmistakably a woman as the author defines the species above: she is flooded by memories of childhood, an awareness of pain, and the need to be fondled. The intensity with which her womanliness is realized may obscure the extent to which Maggie, like Bertha, is spiritually feasting on the world she lives in. The language of hunger and thirst is used to define her as frequently as the nearly ubiquitous water imagery is, and its implications crystallize in an attempt to explain Philip's pull toward Maggie: "The temptations of beauty are much dwelt upon, but I fancy they only bear the same relation to those of ugliness as the temptation to excess at a feast, where the delights are varied for eye and ear as well as palate, bears to the temptations that assail the desperation of hunger. Does not the Hunger Tower stand as the type of the utmost trial to what is human to us?" (p. 289).

The allusion is to the Hunger Tower where Ugolino is imprisoned in canto 33 of Dante's *Inferno*. The emotional complexity of *The Mill on the Foss* finds a precise illustration in Ugolino's life and his afterlife. In the *Inferno*, the scent of cannibalism hovers even over the love between parent and child, and its final implicit suggestion that the pain of the man who must eat is far more excruciating than that of the man who is eaten is an instructive gloss on the intimations of vampirism we have found in Maggie's avid love. Unlike that of the vampire, the horror of whose being lies in the fact that he is a body without a soul, Maggie's hunger is never denied its spirituality. Its essence is captured in a beautifully resonant line from Richard Wilbur's poem "The Undead," an elegy for a creature who is abandoned "to pray on life forever and not possess it." The power of hunger is at one with the wish of a loving prayer. The final flood that sweeps over the novel and ravages its landscape is the last yearning efflorescence of a young woman who prays from her soul.

The suggestions of demonism we have found in Maggie Tulliver are by no means unique in George Eliot's female characters. We have already looked at the preternaturally evil Bertha in "The Lifted Veil," who in Latimer's first vision of her swims in the water imagery that always engulfs Maggie: "The pale-green dress, and the green leaves that seemed to form a border about her pale blond hair, made me think of a Water-Nixie,—for my mind was full of German lyrics, and this pale, fatal-eyed woman, with the green weeds, looked like a birth from some cold sedgy stream, the daughter of an aged river" (Writings 2:266–67). Some of this "Water-Nixie" imagery also surrounds the more convincingly murderous Rosamond in *Middlemarch,* and it swarms over Gwendolen Harleth in *Daniel Deronda,* with her "lamia beauty," her green-and-white colors, her blonde pallor, her sinister associations with drowning and the sea.

But George Eliot allows us to doubt whether the loveless Bertha, Rosamond, and Gwendolen are "woman born of woman." Bertha is "sarcastic," "without a grain of romance in her"; Rosamond is coldly ambitious, the riding accident that causes her to miscarry bringing with it faint memories of Hetty Sorrel's infanticide; and the involutions of Gwendolen's psychic frigidity and hatred of love are brilliantly traced. But in *The Mill on The Floss,* "if life had no love in it, what else was there for Maggie?" (p. 208). Although Maggie does say at one point, "I wish I could make myself a world outside [loving], as men do" (p. 361), George Eliot's sharp delineation of her fitful, solipsistic reading reveals that her efforts in this direction are not great. The demonism of Maggie Tulliver is planted in her very womanliness—as George Eliot defines it—and adds another dimension to the author's attitude toward a character whom many critics have accused her of overfondling. Her overt moral statements about Maggie are not always clear, but her feelings seem to have been: in Maggie Tulliver, she reveals a woman whose primordially feminine hunger for love is at one with her instinct to kill and to die. And she expresses her intertwined sense of Maggie, not in the explicit idiom of the "masculine intellect" critics have praised her for, but in the conventionally "feminine," subterranean language of the George Eliot that many deplore: the language of Gothic romance.

IV.

Women Acting

15.

Secret Performances: George Eliot and the Art of Acting

It seems right that the real George Eliot, if there ever was such a person, still lies in an unconsecrated corner of Highgate Cemetery next to George Henry Lewes, while the self she created with her novels has just been resurrected into the immodestly pompous eternity of Westminster Abbey. These dual graves are one dramatization of a divided life, whose painful care for its own privacy and artistic attentiveness to the private consciousness of others fought a hunger for self-dramatization and an irrepressible instinct for self-display.

Perhaps because we have been told so dampeningly often that she was ugly, we do not commonly think of George Eliot as a performer. Compared with Dickens' staginess, in his novels and his life, the artist and woman George Eliot emerges too exclusively as she wanted us to see her: as an austere truth teller who mistrusted any heightening of the naturally felt and commonly perceived solidity of "the real." Yet she was a discriminating theatergoer from the beginning of her association with Lewes; she considered writing a play for Helen Faucit and originally conceived *Daniel Deronda* as a play as well as a novel. Moreover, though she did not crown her success by ascend-

ing a stage as Dickens did, hers was a subtler theatrical triumph: with
the help of Lewes, she arranged her life as a continual public presentation, eliciting in its majesty a devotional awe that Dickens never
received. Moreover, Dickens performed only his books; his life beyond
the footlights was a mesh of secrets that only our modern weapons of
infrared photography have made public. George Eliot's life may still
have missing links, but even while it was lived it had no major secrets.
Unlike Dickens' affair with Ellen Ternan, George Eliot's "marriage"
to George Henry Lewes was consecrated entirely by her insistence on
public acknowledgment. In the same way, in the final lionized stages
of her career, George Eliot needed no footlights to display her own
self as her greatest creation and most powerful property.

Descriptions of the artist and sibyl receiving audiences at
the Priory exude theatricality. Matilda Betham-Edwards, for example
can respond to her only as spectator: "Even her best friend could not
introduce anyone without permission. So I waited inside the gate til
my hostess [Barbara Bodichon] beckoned me, and there I was in the
presence of a tall, prematurely old lady wearing black, with a majestic
but appealing and wholly unforgettable face. A subdued yet penetrating
light—I am tempted to say luminosity—shone from large dark eyes
that looked all the darker on account of the white, marble-like complexion. She might have sat for a Santa Teresa."[1] This air of immac-
ulate presentation is intensified when George Eliot receives Betham-
Edwards at home: "There in the centre of the room, as if enthroned
sat the Diva; at her feet in a semicircle gathered philosophers, scien-
tists, men of letters, poets, artists—in fine, the leading spirits of the
great Victorian age" (p. 42). Like her magnetic contemporary Eller
Terry, "the Diva" triumphs over her age almost as much, it seems, by
artful self-placement as by the painstaking and essentially solitary perfection of her art.

Dickens performed his own characters, but George Eliot
wins applause by transcending her characters to transform herself in
her own person, as Henry James perceived when he visited the Priory
to worship and to scrutinize: "To begin with she is magnificently ugly—
deliciously hideous. She has a low forehead, and jaw-bone *qui n'en
finissent pas.* . . . Now in this vast ugliness resides a most powerful
beauty which, in a very few minutes steals forth and charms the mind

so that you end as I ended, in falling in love with her. Yes, behold me literally in love with this great horse-faced blue-stocking. I don't know in what the charm lies, but it is thoroughly potent."[2] For James and for many less articulate worshippers, the charm of the self-creating presence exists independently of the books. Celebrating "the Diva," James achieves the same blend of iconoclasm, facetiousness, and reverence that in twenty years was to distinguish George Bernard Shaw's criticism of the actresses he insulted and adored. As sibyl and cynosure at the end of her life, George Eliot eclipses her solitary triumphs of creation by the wonder of her public self-creation.

To imagine George Eliot as an actress for whom the role of Great Author is merely the culmination of a life of continual self-creation and self-display should not tarnish our awareness of her as mighty truth teller, though it would have been sure to do so in her own day. At that time the theater still hovered uneasily between the seaminess of the bordello and the reverent stiffness of church; moreover, though acting was one of the few professions in which a woman could win money and glory, the phrase "public woman" applied equally well to performer and to prostitute.[3] Redolent of unwomanly assertion as well as sexual experience, the public woman is a threatening invader into a sphere that is by definition masculine.

But George Eliot might have been more troubled by the assumption that she was by definition a liar as well. Wilkie Collins' popular thriller *No Name* (1862–63) embodies this equation of the public woman with the false woman, dismissing the actor as a dangerous simulator of human qualities. Collins' heroine, Magdalen Vanstone, is "a born actress"; when her parents abruptly die, she learns that she and her sister are illegitimate and thus stripped of legal existence. She embarks on a quest to recover the family name and fortune by assuming an alarming series of false names and brilliant disguises whereby she will uncover and marry the true heir. Magdalen's acting has no dimension beyond a dazzling skill at disguise that will lead her to perdition. Like her name, her gift brands her as fallen before the intrigue begins, while the novel's title provides a deeper indictment still. For Magdalen the fallen woman, orphan, bastard, and actress must lack an essential self; her dangerous psychic void creates the fascination of the novel which denounces her. In Magdalen Vanstone, the decade's dark image of the actress, the disguised orphan and fallen woman Mary Ann Evans might have seen a shadow of her most deeply feared self.

In an early essay, "Acting by One Who Does Not Believe in It" (1889), George Bernard Shaw would attack such facile disjunctions between acting and sincerity; Shaw asserts grandly that though "acting, in the common use of the word, is self-falsification, forgery, and fraud . . . the true goal of the stage-player is self-realization, expression, and exhibition."[4] But George Eliot had already brilliantly anticipated the Shavian defense of the actor's honesty in *Daniel Deronda*. Though she sees herself as a damned woman, the great diva Alcharisi is the one woman George Eliot created who is as gifted as her author. The complex truth of her theatricality illuminates George Eliot's life as well as her fiction:

The speech was in fact a piece of what might be called sincere acting: this woman's nature was one in which all feeling—and all the more when it was tragic as well as real—immediately became matter of conscious representation: experience immediately passed into drama, and she acted her own emotions. In a minor degree this is nothing uncommon, but in the Princess the acting had a rare perfection of physiognomy, voice, and gesture. It would not be true to say that she felt less because of this double consciousness: she felt—that is, her mind went through—all the more, but with a difference: each nucleus of pain or pleasure had a deep atmosphere of excitement or spiritual intoxication which at once exalts and deadens.[5]

This magnificent anatomy of "sincere acting" anticipates Shaw's defense and transcends it in dramatic passion. George Eliot's last, most contrived and difficult novel is her most profoundly honest act of self-expression.[6] In *Daniel Deronda,* the saved as well as the damned characters present themselves as public personae, through various stagy gestures and theatrical flourishes. Grandcourt, the one character who refuses to act, is a pathological feeder on life, not, as was the equally taciturn Adam Bede, a noble and stern exemplum whose sincerity reproached dangerous posturers. Having become a diva herself, George Eliot need no longer cling to the dogma of homely and commonplace realism as the sole repository of truth. Her new understanding of the intricate honesty of the performing self is a new acceptance of the multiple woman she, like her heroines, always was.

For with her many shifting names and flamboyant reli-

gious allegiances, George Eliot was an actress long before she became
a writer and a diva. She retained an early memory of herself as a shy
child who, however, " 'in order to impress the servant with a proper
notion of her acquirements and generally distinguished position' . . .
had played on the piano, of which she did not know a note."[7] In this
infant artist, aggrandizing public display is a stronger impulse than
sanctified Wordsworthian solitude. Her first piece of writing to survive
is a sanctimonious homily on the suggestive topic "Affectation and
Conceit"; according to Gordon Haight, it is signed "in large, ornate
script" with the Frenchified pen name "Marianne Evans." The young
woman's later skill at languages and her initial career as a translator
extend her early genius at mimicry, the tendency of her mind to become creatively multiple. A letter written immediately after her father's
death reveals her fears of this potential in herself: "What shall I be
without my Father? It will seem as if a part of my moral nature were
gone. I had a horrid vision of myself last night becoming earthly sensual and devilish for want of that purifying restraining influence."[8]

Significantly, she asks not "What shall I do without my
father?" which was the real question she confronted when deprived of
his invalidism as her ostensible reason for living, but the more fundamental, what shall I *be* without fatherly definition? Like Wilkie Collins' Magdalen, who disappears without family into an uncontrolled
repertoire of disguises, George Eliot confronts the diabolical possibility
of mutation into unprecedented selves. She fears death less than she
does her own aptitude at self-transformation, though once she is re-
cuperating in Geneva, she can boast of this gift to the Brays: "You
know, or you do not know, that my nature is so chameleon I shall lose
all my identity until you keep nourishing the old self with letters"
(*GEL*, 1:302).

The compulsive mobility that shaped the rest of her life
was countered by her novels' hymns to the saving power of roots, just
as her fear of performance as devilish disguise was countered by her
proud generosity of self-presentation. Her liaison with George Henry
Lewes endorsed the mobile public woman. Grandson of a great
eighteenth-century comedian, Lewes added to his almost uncanny versatility careers as drama critic, playwright, and actor. His presence was
inseparable from her meteoric rise as a novelist; in fact, like that of
George du Maurier's preternaturally gifted Trilby whose genius lives

only in Svengali's mesmeric powers, George Eliot's career in fiction began only with their union and died when Lewes did. From its inception their relationship has some suggestion of an impresario eliciting and controlling the potential of a newly discovered star. Their intimacy began with visits to the theater, with Lewes the drama critic squiring her backstage and introducing her to actors and managers. As Gordon Haight puts it, "It was a glimpse of a new world" (p. 128). Their shared life begins with an initiation into a theatricality from which it will never separate itself.

Shortly thereafter, Lewes initiated her into the exalted seclusion of fallen woman and of artist; like the great Victorian actor-managers, he indefatigably created a setting appropriate to her new, splendid but fragile incarnation. Initially, he feared her work might "want the highest quality of fiction—dramatic representation" (*GEL*, 2:407), but her performance of "Amos Barton" reassured him: reading it aloud to him, as she was always to do, she had the star's gift of transforming the critic into the ideal audience. These dramatic exchanges between performer and manager/audience were the foundation of George Eliot's literary career. Having heard her novels first as performances, Lewes never dropped the idiom of theatricality when speaking of them, as when he argues to Blackwood that the Jews in *Deronda* will "make a Rembrandtish background to her dramatic presentation" (*GEL*, 6: 196). Lewes stage-managed not only the appearances of the public woman in their stately receptions at the Priory, but the very nature and form of the novels themselves as they live within George Eliot's growing confidence in her own capacity for performance.

Lewes' own respect for actors must have strengthened his protégée's aptitude at acting her own life. His collection *On Actors and the Art of Acting* (1875) is an early tribute to the need for an organized criticism adequate to the actor's difficult and unappreciated art. The first half of the collection borrows the form of Carlyle's *On Heroes and Hero-Worship*, with each small essay devoted to a larger-than-life evocation of a particular actor's qualities. It moves into anatomies of acting styles as they embody national characteristics, ending with a discerning appreciation of the opulent Italian tragedian Salvini, a man large enough to encompass and embody his nation. Lewes' fascination with varieties of performance, both as a complex art in itself and as an exemplification of time, place, and nation, ignited the talents of the

awkward, experimenting woman who transformed herself into Magdalen, artist, and diva. Even her best biographer, Gordon Haight, becomes somewhat defensive about her final virtuosity: "Like the rest,
Mrs Posonby] felt some charismatic force that no acting, no stage
management could possibly explain. Deep sincerity underlay it, and
genuine human interest" (p. 454). But like Alcharisi's, the deep underlying sincerity is less the antidote to acting than the actor's strongest ally. Madame Ignaz Monscheles, a contemporary observer, was
shrewder if less secure in her definitions: "There is something a little
like affectation sometimes, but I don't expect it's it" (quoted in Haight,
p. 510). As with Alcharisi's "sincere acting," the imperceptible boundary
between sincerity and dissimulation is the eternal distinction of the
true performer.

Another essay by Shaw provides the most trenchant Victorian definition we have of the dual vision of acting as disguise and
acting as, not truth, but the hairline fracture between sincerity and
affectation. In 1895, Shaw contrasted the competing performances of
Bernhardt and Duse as Magda in Sudermann's *Heimat*. As she woos
the audience with all the childish glee of her cajolery, Bernhardt is
described by makeup and mannerisms alone. In contrast, though a
modern disciple of Stanislavsky might expect an ecomium to the emotional truth of Duse's Magda, Shaw lauds the completeness of her
disguise: "Every part is a separate creation." Duse's apparent realism
springs from a perfection of versatility and controlled self-manipula-
tion that eclipses Bernhardt's primping. Her Magda is described not
by the composition of its rouge, but by the blush that seems spontaneously to overwhelm her during a crucial scene. What intoxicates Shaw
as a student of actors is not the sincerity of the blush, but the extraordinary virtuosity it represents: "After that feat of acting I did not need
to be told why Duse does not paint an inch thick. I could detect no
trick in it; it seemed to me a perfectly genuine effect of the dramatic
imagination. . . . and I must confess to an intense professional curiosity as to whether it always comes spontaneously."[9]

Duse's blush embodies the sort of consummate theatricality that underlies George Eliot's sincerity in life and her realism in
fiction: it marries disguise so perfectly to self-display that one cannot
find the trick in it. At first glance, George Eliot's novels seem sternly
to condemn their performing heroines in favor of the subdued auster-

ity of idealism, but in fact, the mirror-bound egoistic posing of a Hett
Sorrel, Rosamond Vincy, or Gwendolen Harleth resembles that of Shaw'
Bernhardt: these anti-heroines do not stand for the morally repellen
deceit of acting, but simply for acting that is bad. For Shaw, Duse'
blush provides a more powerful performance than Bernhardt's rouge
George Eliot anticipates the controlled mobility of this sort of perfor
mance in the many names and nicknames, the continually startlin
new incarnations, in which she allows her absorbent selfhood to tak
definition. She allows her strong women the same theatrical triump
of sincerity controlled and magnified. Dinah Morris and Dorothe
Brooke, those seemingly self-suppressing heroines of epic inclination
strive in their performances beyond woman's traditional world of self
display before a private mirror toward power in "that mighty drama"
which in *Daniel Deronda* becomes equated with personified Histor
itself.

I believe that Ellen Moers was the first critic to spot th
essential theatricality of those paragons Dinah Morris and Dorothe
Brooke. Previous critics had taken them at their own inhumanly al
truistic valuation, while Moers' shrewd and witty chapter "Performin
Heroinism" lays bare their florid exhibitionism as it emanates fron
Madame de Staël's self-dramatizing myth of Corinne.[10] Though Moer
does not consider the almost boundless repertoire of roles that consti
tuted George Eliot's life, she places the noblest heroines in a femal
literary tradition she seems at heart to deplore. Moers' mistrustful ex
posure of acting partakes of Shaw's "common view" of it as affecta
tion and sham. But if we associate these performing heroines wit
those ardent Victorian defenders of the art of acting, George Henr
Lewes, Oscar Wilde, and George Bernard Shaw, we see that their at
titudinizing represents an aggrandizement of self, a breadth of capacit
like their author's own rebirth as artist, fallen woman, and sibyl. Fo
George Eliot, the capacity to perform is a mark of the true heroine
since there is nothing grand they are allowed to do, through actin
alone her women transcend incarceration in the private, domestic spher
as well as the constricting mediocrity her own realistic aesthetic threat
ens to make inescapable.

From our first sight of her picturesque presence on th

Green to her final retirement into domestic obscurity, Dinah Morris in *Adam Bede* is incontrovertibly an actress. George Eliot plays characteristically with a vulgar version of this idea, only to leave its deeper truth inexplicit. Our perniciously sentimental, "normative" observer sees her and thinks: "A sweet woman . . . but surely nature never meant her for a preacher." The sardonic narrator replies: "Perhaps he was one of those who think that nature has theatrical properties, and, with the considerate view of facilitating art and psychology, 'makes up' her characters, so that there may be no mistake about them."[11]

In fact, *Adam Bede*'s nature is not far from theater: it is simply subtler in its "making up." Just before the stranger's rumination, the narrator had concluded a touch-by-touch description of Dinah's winsome face, hovering over her as delicately as a makeup man to insure that her sweet spirituality will harmonize with the pastoral scene. Aided by the designing author, nature does not conform to social stereotypes, but she is nevertheless consummately, if ineffably, theatrical.

Dinah's sermon rivets its audience almost exclusively through the inflections of her miraculous voice, "which had a variety of modulation like that of a fine instrument touched with the unconscious skill of musical instinct" (p. 24). The spiritual triumph in this scene is clearly the performer's rather than God's. As with Dorothea's resonant "voice of deep-souled womanhood," a moving counterpoint to Rosamond's silvery, neutral tones, Dinah's speech moves auditors independently of its words. The voices of both Dinah and Dorothea mark them as magnificent, specially chosen beings, distinguished less for their moral grandeur than for their irresistible power as personified works of art.

The Victorian age was elocutionary. The great actor exuded his personality into the musical, miraculous range of his voice: the century that adored the theatrical excitement of opera translated its properties to straight dramatic performances. The great actor defined his presence by his voice, and like her heroines, George Eliot moved those who met her by the compelling music of her low-toned speech. According to Haight, her " 'chameleon-like nature,' as Cross calls it, impelled her to adopt as a child the musical modulations of her first teacher, Miss Rebecca Franklin" (p. 11). When she grew into a public woman, her voice became her blazon of distinction, so that

there might have been a Svengali-like touch of possessive pride in
Lewes' dismissal of a first night at the Lyceum: "Play horribly acted
throughout—not one of them able to *speak* (quoted in Haight, p
484).

Dinah's voice, then, expresses less her spiritual message
than the art of her own nature. Her sermon ends with the narrator's
ambivalent reminder of its drama: "Dinah had been speaking at least
an hour, and the reddening light of the parting day seemed to give a
solemn emphasis to her closing words. The stranger, who had been
interested in the course of her sermon, as if it had been the development of a drama—for there is this sort of fascination in all sincere
unpremeditated eloquence, which opens to one the inward drama of
the speaker's emotions—now turned his horse aside, and pursued his
way, while Dinah said, 'Let us sing a little, dear friends' " (p. 29). Is
Dinah's sermon a drama, or an unpremeditated outpouring? The assertion of Dinah's "sincerity" leads finally not to the denial of drama
but to a deeper drama in which sincerity is at one with compelling
display. Though George Eliot's language equivocates, its essence will
become *Daniel Deronda*'s piercing apologia for Alcharisi's, and perhaps
her author's, "sincere acting": "Experience immediately passed into
drama, and she acted her own emotions."

Though it does undermine her self-sacrificial sanctity, Dinah's acting is more than the affectation the young George Eliot feared
and Ellen Moers disapprovingly exposed. Like George Eliot's, Dinah's
transcendence of the commonplace lies in her ability to move an audience. Thus, her superiority to her cousin and foil Hetty Sorrel lies
not in the fact that she is humble while Hetty is ambitious, sincere
while Hetty is vain, or in any way good while Hetty is bad: Dinah is a
successful performer and Hetty, a conceited amateur. Some such en-
vious awareness seems to motivate Hetty when she convulses the family by appearing in Dinah's Methodist costume, recognizing it as the
garb less of self-mortification than of stardom. Similarly, Hetty's secret self-worshipping rituals before the mirror are condemned in contrast to the public drama of Dinah's sermon. Readers have seen in this
little more than a symptom of George Eliot's vindictiveness against
pretty women, but since Dinah is also pretty, we might consider a
more radical defect of Hetty's mirror: like woman's traditional sphere,
it is self-defeating in its privacy, its lack of an audience. George Eliot

repeatedly contrasts the mirror-fixated woman (Hetty, Rosamond Vincy, Gwendolen Harleth) with the noble woman standing before a window (Dinah, Dorothea Brooke, Romola di'Bardi). These are more than face emblems of egoism and altruism. The woman kissing her own reflection is swallowed in privacy, while the woman looking out of the window may also be looked at. Hetty's solitary affectations are self-defeating by nature, while Dinah's public performances show the self enlarged beyond domesticity, taking possession of public life.

Supreme as a public presence, Dinah upstages pretty little Hetty throughout the novel, until she marries Hetty's fiancé, comes full circle, and disappears into private life. Despite her hidden dreams of supremacy, Hetty's story reveals her crippling incapacity at public performance. Even on trial for infanticide, she is helplessly, self-destructively mute, and she allows Dinah to steal center stage from her even in her dramatic journey to be hanged:

It was a sight that some people remembered better even than their own sorrows—the sight in that grey clear morning, when the fatal cart with the two young women in it was descried by the waiting watching multitude, cleaving its way toward the hideous symbol of a deliberately-inflicted sudden death. . . . Dinah did not know that the crowd was silent, gazing at her with a sort of awe—she did not even know how near they were to the fatal spot, when the cart stopped, and she shrank appalled at a loud shout hideous to her ear, like a vast yell of demons. (p. 386).

The staginess of the language is an appropriate tribute to Dinah's superior theatricality. The essence of the contrast between the two women is not so much moral as dramatic, emphasizing in Dinah's displacement of Hetty the saving art of the performer who is not swallowed by crowds because she has the capacity to move them.

In *Middlemarch*, the performer's magic similarly upstages the artful private woman in the encounter between Dorothea and Rosamond. Disenchanted with her husband Lydgate, Rosamond hopes to entice Will Ladislaw into an affair, but the electric entrance of Dorothea captivates Rosamond's husband, her potential lover, and finally Rosamond herself, who is helpless under the magnetism of Dorothea's powerful presence. Though Dorothea is neither preacher nor actress, she is the novel's star, her entrances striking spectators with awe though her impulses toward goodness are ineffectual. As Dinah's effective simplicity overwhelmed Hetty's finery, so the Quaker-like Dorothea draws all attention from lovely vain Rosamond, who is at home with no audience but her mirror. In the nineties, that similarly flamboyant Puritan Bernard Shaw would show the winning artifice of Bernhardt similarly upstaged by the commanding art of Duse, who triumphs, as George Eliot's heroines do, not by abandoning the art of acting but by making it the consummate expression of her mobile being.

We think of *Middlemarch* as a triumph of austere realism, not as a theatrical novel. Yet even beyond the magnetic star presence of Dorothea, its atmosphere is suffused with suggestions of the stage. The novel abounds in sudden metaphorical changes of light which are more suggestive of deft stage design than of the monotonous sun. At a key moment, for instance, the "dim lights" of the initial setting become a cruel spotlight: "A very searching light had fallen on [Bulstrode's] character, and she could not judge him leniently."[12] These dramatic lighting shifts are often instantaneous: "Whatever else remained the same, the light had changed, and you cannot find the pearly dawn at noonday" (p. 145); "The lights were all changed for him both within and without" (p. 347). Nature's gradually lengthening shadows become dramatic discords, more appropriate to modernistic stage design than to naturalistic pastoral. At a key moment, Dorothea herself moves from star to lighting designer: "The presence of a noble nature, generous in its wishes, ardent in its charity, changes the lights for us: we begin to see things again in their larger, quieter masses, and to believe that we too can be seen and judged in the wholeness of our character" (p. 558). Dorothea's tricky manipulation of lighting and perspective reprises more subtly Dinah's opening sermon: in both, the star collaborates with a personified Nature who is an ingenious and omnipotent theatrical manager. At times, one feels, they merge into the awesome stage-managing divinity of *Middlemarch*: "Destiny stands by sarcastic with our *dramatis personae* folded in her hand" (p. 70).

This subtle theatricality in the book's ambience is more delicate than but not radically different from Dickens' grandiose orchestration of fog and sunshine effects in *Bleak House*. But unlike Dickens in his most ambitious novels, George Eliot employs in *Middlemarch* an actress, Laure, as a paradigm of her epic anatomies of provincial marriage. An actress seems an anomaly in somber Middle-

narch, whose large cast is distinguished by its common inability to act
at all; at first glance, the book seems a study of paralysis, not performance. Yet Laure belongs in this novel whose apparent sincerity is its
greatest art. Her onstage murder of her husband touches that fine
point between honesty and dissimulation with which George Eliot is
most concerned. Since he dies as part of the performance, the question
is, "Was it murder?" (p. 112). In a superbly equivocal answer, Laure
defines the boundaryless art of acting: "I did not plan: it came to me
in the play—*I meant to do it*" (p. 114). The onstage "I" appropriates
capacities beyond the calculations of common law or of Lydgate's romantic science.

Laure's brief turn in the novel associates acting with marriage and marriage with murder.[13] These associations recur in four key
marriage/murders: those of the Bulstrodes, the Lydgates, the Casau-
bons, and, as far as we can see, the Ladislaws. In the first and simplest,
the stolid Mrs. Bulstrode learns to perform at the revelation of her
husband's disgrace: her sincerity suddenly flowers in an inspired costume change. As Hetty Sorrel had done, "She took off all her orna-
ments and put on a plain black gown, and instead of wearing her
much-adorned cap and large bow of hair, she brushed her hair down
and put on a plain bonnet-cap, which made her look suddenly like an
early Methodist" (p. 550). Her allegiance to a marriage whose deceit
has murdered "all the gladness and pride of her life" can be defined
only by a performance as consummate, and as equivocal, as Laure's.

Rosamond is an inept ingenue, with her incessant posturing and her metallic voice, but her finishing school amateurism is as
lethally effective as Laure's finished art: "[Lydgate] once called her his
basil plant; and when she asked for an explanation, said that basil was
a plant which had flourished wonderfully on a murdered man's brains"
(p. 610). Like her aunt Bulstrode, Rosamond is also murdered by a
marriage that has robbed her of "all the gladness and pride of her life";
like Dorothea's with Casaubon, her own ambitions are suffocated in
an enforced charade of wifely obedience.[14] The mutual performance of
their marriage duties allows no absolute moral diagnosis, finally throw-
ing us back on the question society put to the mocking Laure: "Was
it murder?"

As the star of the novel, Dorothea does less and suggests
more than any of the other actors. The novel's first sentence intro-

duces us, not to her, but to her effect: "Miss Brooke had that sort of beauty which seems to be thrown into relief by poor dress" (p. 5). Throughout the novel, Dorothea glorifies herself by the clothes she pretends not to care about. Ellen Moers points out that her smashing series of entrances are triumphs of exotic costuming, thus associating herself with Mrs. Cadwallader as a jaundiced spectator of a heroine "always playing tragedy queen and taking things sublimely" (p. 391). Dorothea is indeed unable to sit without posing for a heroic painting, unable to move except in stage directions: "Then in her ardent way, wanting to plead with him, she moved from her chair and went in front of him to her old place in the window, saying, 'Do you suppose I ever disbelieved in you?' " (p. 462). As the novel's consummate diva, Dorothea is best qualified to restate Laure's equivocal entanglement of marriage with murder: "I mean, marriage drinks up all our power of giving or getting any blessedness in that sort of [adulterous] love. I know it may be very dear—but it murders our marriage—and then the marriage stays with us like a murder—and everything else is gone" (p 584). The performance of marriage becomes one with a confession of guilt.

The mutual murder of her marriage to Edward Casaubon is obvious and chilling. His intellectual and psychic "damp" murders her energy; in revenge, she exposes to him the futility of his book and the pettiness of his actions, and he dies of the upset. But perhaps her most lethal act is her desire to put Casaubon on a stage. Her contempt for Celia's harping on his "two white moles with hairs on them" does not suggest a concern for his "great soul," to which she has no access. Rather, it indicates that the shortsighted Dorothea envisions a remote, onstage husband whose imperfections fade away under the lights. In trying to wrench him from his batlike solitude to publish his book, she tries to force him into being the "ardent public man" Will Ladislaw will in fact become. The intense if undefined theatrical ambition that creates her murderous demand for an actor-husband may explain her attraction to that stagy juvenile Ladislaw, the only man in the novel who poses as instinctively as she does.

But the novel's elegiac epilogue reminds us that marriage to an "ardent public man" murders Dorothea the public woman. Her destiny is seen as tragic not because she does nothing; she has done nothing throughout the novel but hector littler people. We are to mourn not inactivity but obscurity, the knowledge that this dynamic, spontaneously artful woman is "not widely visible." Mr. Brooke is not far from his creator when he laments Dorothea's future "amongst people who don't know who you are" (p. 597): the narrator's outbreak of sorrow at the end comes from just this murder of her heroine's public nature. Her destiny and the novel end with a sad consignment to "unvisited tombs," but this doom seems inappropriate to a loved woman: won't her worshipful family bother to visit her tomb? Yet for the public, theatrical George Eliot, the merely personal is allowed no consecrating value: only a tomb in Westminster Abbey would provide enough visitors to state this heroine. The star's offstage life-in-death at the end of the novel is dignified only by the accents of tragedy pronouncing the implacable equation between "a hidden life" and "unvisited tombs." The invisible is the doubly dead.

Though she is directly acknowledged only in passing, the actress is central to George Eliot's achievement as woman and artist. Like the prostitute, this public woman is shunned and emulated. She brings forbidden private ambitions into the light and legitimizes them with the power of public performance; she provides an image of the commanding public woman which need not constitute an overt feminist statement; she provides a conduit for the hidden, and often the dark, richness of the self; she is a talisman against anonymity. The performances that George Eliot lived and wrote offer a tacit apprehension of the nature of acting whose sophistication surpassed even that of George Henry Lewes. For in the 1860s, when George Eliot became famous, artists were warned not to "bring a blush to the cheek of the young (and inevitably female) person"; it was not until the 1890s that Shaw celebrated the theatrical artistry of Duse's blush. Long before Shaw's analysis, George Eliot experienced and wrote about the ways in which prescribed modes of female self-concealment could be transfigured into irresistible vehicles of self-revelation.

16.

Ellen Terry's Victorian Marriage

In one of her many scripts of *Hamlet*, Ellen Terry recorded next to Ophelia's name the most important decision of her life: "Monday. 30 December 1878 = My first appearance at Lyceum." Joining the role and the theater that were to bless and shackle her was a tender inscription from Henry Irving:

> My fairest—sweetest
> Loveliest Ophelia
> Only this
> *Your* Hamlet.

"Only this," and what more could there be? When her gorgeously witty Portia led Henry Irving to invite the new young star to become the leading lady of his company at the Lyceum, Ellen Terry moved into a happy ending glowing with the promises of Victorian fiction. Shortly, her best biographer assures us, she was receiving "the highest salary earned by a woman in Britain during the late nineteenth century—£200 a working week, together with the lump sums acquired from benefit performances."[1] Moreover, in a vagabond profession, she

All quotations from Ellen Terry's annotations, notebooks, and journals, are taken from material at the Ellen Terry Museum at Smallhythe Place, and are quoted by permission of the Trustees of the Museum.

had found a home, one whose social prestige soared under Irving's magnetism and shrewd command.

Irving's Lyceum radiated a respectability new for theater people and especially helpful to Ellen Terry, for the "hoydenish" actress (as Irving called her) had already abandoned the stage twice. At sixteen, she married the painter G. F. Watts, posed for him indefatigably for a year, and then was mysteriously expelled from his eccentric household. Shortly thereafter, in 1867, she ran off with the architect and stage designer Edward Godwin, the father of her two children and her lifelong personification of romance. Only when their love and money were wearing out did she return, almost accidentally, to the stage. The fey, towheaded girl with the startling face of a pre-Raphaelite saint had defied not only Victorian sexual morality, but the sterner code of the theater: she had twice abandoned her art to become the lover of artists. The graciousness of Irving's Lyceum seemed infinitely redemptive, though Ellen Terry had never asked for redemption.

The myths of Victorian culture could promise no tenderer consummation than the Lyceum. In its crucible, the laughing, wayward girl was forged into lady and divinity; the actress Oscar Wilde apotheosized as "Our Lady of the Lyceum" was dubbed at her Jubilee in 1906 "this uncrowned queen of England." And at its height, the Lyceum did seem to be Tennyson's Camelot as well as his palace of art. As its success grew, it took on the aegis of a great and just society: its opulent productions were generally followed by still more opulent dinners in the Beefsteak Room, bringing monarchs together with stars of politics and the arts. Under Irving's reign and Terry's charm, barriers between the classes dissolved in a new aristocracy forged for the space of a banquet. If the Lyceum had the limitations of all the solid homes that have redeemed and encircled heroines, its unhomely lure allowed the world to pass through it.

Moreover, the Lyceum brought Ellen Terry two new artist/lover/divinities in place of Watts and Godwin; this time love and performance were one. The patriarchal hand that led her to respectability was Henry Irving's; it may have been the most interesting hand in England. The Svengali-like Irving was mannered to the point of grotesquerie; his intensely self-obsessed performances, onstage and off, moved his adoring assistant Bram Stoker to create the lordly vampire

Dracula. Like Napoleon, with whom he was obsessed, Irving was torn between the lure of respectability and that of the outcast. He played electrifying villains—Shylock, Mephistopheles, Eugene Aram, the murderer Mathias in *The Bells*—but in 1895, he became the first actor to receive a knighthood, his penchant for the diabolical erecting him into a saint of the British theater's crusade for irreproachability. The commemorative statue beside the National Portrait Gallery is indistinguishable from surrounding lofty monuments to political dignitaries; it is purged of the Mephistophelean glow, the dynamic oddities, that won Irving his fame. It was this contradictory man, this simultaneous demon and philosopher king, who became Ellen Terry's Hamlet, partner, and (in the Lyceum family) stage husband in 1878. As with many Victorian husbands, his rule was absolute, but unlike most of them, he justified the extravagant worship he demanded.

With Irving as her Hamlet and professional husband, Ellen Terry had gained what many women desired, but with him, in life and in art, she was forbidden to be important. In the mid-nineties, when she was growing too old for the dewy ingenue roles to which she was relegated, she was ruthlessly forced out of his life and his company. She had always known that "he [did] not care for anybody much," that he was "crafty," but he had the magnitude which many actual wives failed to find in their husbands. Few Victorian women were important, but, more tragically for them perhaps, neither were the men who determined their lives. Ellen Terry gloried in a praise whose grounds were true, inscribing on a pamphlet about Irving the vicarious boast: "There is none like him—none." At his death, Ellen Terry's lament in her journal was a more authentic cry of hero worship than those that decorated the florid widowhood of Queen Victoria: "13 Friday 1905—Henry died today—'and now "there is nothing left remarkable beneath the visiting moon"—'." The death of Irving is so absolute an occasion that it allows Ellen Terry to make her own the great wail of Shakespeare's Cleopatra—one of the many great parts she was never assigned at the Lyceum, though Bernhardt and Duse, the continental "queens" with whom Ellen Terry was often grouped, both played memorable Cleopatras. As the God of her stage life, Irving withheld the role; the grandeur of his death justified a grand trespass. In death as in life, the immensity of Henry Irving's claims gave meaning to the self-subjection that was demanded of all obedient Victorian women.

Not only does his death exalt her into becoming Cleopatra, but it is an occasion fit to marry Shakespeare's words; as she once said to Irving, Shakespeare was the only man she had ever really loved. Ellen Terry's symbolic marriage at the Lyceum transcended her alliance to the preterhuman monarch Irving; her performances as Beatrice, Portia, Imogen, and the rest were her union with the invisible magic of Shakespeare himself, who for many Victorians embodied the sacramental principle in his own mystic person. Her fidelity to a company that granted Shakespeare a place of honor, even if he came trimmed and tailored to Irving's dimensions, was as self-glorifying as it was ultimately self-defeating. Sounding more reactionary than she was, Ellen Terry wrote in 1891: "I . . . love Portia and Beatrice better than Hedda, Nora, or any of [Ibsen's] silly ladies." "I prefer presenting to an audience, and living familiarly with, Queen Katherine and Imogen rather than with Dr. Ibsen's foolish women."[2] In the same issue of *The New Review*, Henry James praised Ibsen lavishly for the glorious new opportunities he offered actresses, but Ellen Terry stayed with the avenues of consecration she had known. For her as for Coleridge, "In Shakespeare all the elements of womanhood are holy."[3] She held back from modernity until it was too late to change in order to save her grandeur, not to sacrifice it. In its transfiguration of history and its glorification of character, Lyceum Shakespeare appropriated some of the promise of a waning religion. Bram Stoker celebrates it: "I often say to myself that the Faith which still exists is to be found more often in a theatre than in a church."[4] Within this new-old faith, the benediction shed by Shakespeare's familiar characters, with their seemingly endless fund of self-renewing life, promised bounteous incarnations of a holy past made flesh. Ellen Terry's unorthodox division of Shakespeare's heroines into "triumphant" and "pathetic" women epitomizes the sort of power she drew from his plays. The perpetuity of Shakespeare was a glimpse of eternity on earth. In marrying the bard through his heroines, she took possession of his glorifying divinity, writing to him as husband, as hero, as God, and as omnipotent self: "My friend, my sorrow's cure, my teacher, my companion, the very eyes of me."

As symbolic bride of the Lyceum, Ellen Terry made a truer marriage than she had to Watts or than she would do with her two later ephemeral husbands; even to her beloved and unforgotten

Godwin, she was less intricately pledged. As woman, as artist, and as soul hungering for salvation and exaltation, she embraced a host of nineteenth-century promises in marrying the Lyceum. This marriage bestowed money and power as marriage was supposed to do, translating a hoydenish girl to a lady, simultaneous idol and servant of great men. In the Satanic godhead of his role as performing husband, Henry Irving provided an authentic correlative for Ellen Terry's fund of celebratory awe; even when the roles he assigned her oppressed her, there was "none like him." Real husbands came and went, but Irving was blazoned with eternity. His reign was sanctioned by the magic of Shakespeare, Ellen Terry's invisible bridegroom and holy ghost, a more reliably loved agent of self-transforming immortality than any of the nineteenth century's official priests and divinities. "Reader, I married them all," Ellen Terry seems to say, with a more widely radiating triumph than Jane Eyre's. Having given herself in a marriage that both fulfilled her culture's precepts and transcended them, the charming ingenue should allow us to close our books with a smiling sense of consummation.

  Yet Ellen Terry makes us uneasy, as she made her contemporaries uneasy. For her most discerning acolytes, she was not a woman glorified in union, but a reminder of perishability and waste. They agreed that the Lyceum had failed her, lamenting her as an emanation of hauntingly unfulfilled promise. If the Lyceum symbolized everything Victorian culture promised its loveliest and most gifted women, it also—like that culture itself—stood for promises gone awry, for bounty gloriously wasted. The radiant bride became an emblem of her own betrayal. The subtle uses Ellen Terry made of that betrayal illuminate the fine line she and other talented women walked between their self-glorifying joy in their art and their sympathy with the resentful compliance of the women in the audience. Ellen Terry's mystic marriage in becoming Irving's loveliest Ophelia exemplifies the eerie similarity between Victorian rewards and punishments, as the triumphant woman touches hands with her pathetic double.

  The seductive letters of a brash young Bernard Shaw create a countermyth in which Ellen Terry's holy bridegroom Irving/Shakespeare metamorphoses into a Bluebeard, assassinating in her person the rich theatrical life Shaw's modernist drama would let flourish: "(Oh G O D: do you remember that tent scene in King Lear, when he kept you waiting in an impossible pose for five minutes between 'I will not swear' and 'these are my hands'?) He has no idea of the play, no idea of the other people: he is hypnotised with his own effect, and sacrifices everything and everybody else to it. . . . [If] you once realize that the sacrifice of the other parts is not a conscious, malicious, direct act of his, but an inevitable condition of his methods and effects, you will see that you, too, must be sacrificed."[5]

In Shaw's persuasive myth, the devouring demon Irving becomes associated with a ghoulish Shakespeare who "is as dead *dramatically* as a doornail." Their pernicious collusion makes of the Lyceum an "ogre's den in which your talent has been thrown and eaten"[6]—a den from which only the combined heroics of modernism, Ibsenism, and Shavianism can save the captive maiden. Victorian novels, and the fairy tales at their heart, suffused Shaw's imagination of Ellen Terry as she aged bravely at the Lyceum. Exploiting the grim domestic prisons of *Middlemarch,* he casts himself as a sunny young Will Ladislaw, rescuing his performing Dorothea from the Casaubon-like strangulation of a dead past. Exploiting the rarefied comedy of Meredith's *The Egoist,* he thrusts on Irving the insane conceit of Sir Willoughby Patterne, smothering his vibrant Ellen Terry–like fiancée until the dashing Vernon Whitfield—Shaw, of course—saves her for the artful nature of the modern world. The redemption from Victorianism Shaw held out rests on an eminently Victorian dream.

But there were to be no more male rescuers for Ellen Terry. As an epistolary Vernon Whitfield, Shaw promised more redemption than he performed. Once she did stand free of the Lyceum, Shaw decided shrewdly but cruelly that "she had waited too long." In her valiant if fumbling attempts to meet the twentieth century in the new drama he had prescribed for her, she played to dubious if charitable reviews Hjordia in Ibsen's *Vikings* and Lady Cecily in Shaw's own *Captain Brassbound's Conversion.* Thereafter, though she brought herself to plead, Shaw had no more parts for her. The triumphant heroines of his maturity were surely inspired by his dream of an Ellen Terry released into her own powers, but he forbade Ellen Terry to embody them. The new world her imprisonment helped conceive was closed to her.

Most animating when she was least free, "Our Lady of the Lyceum" fed the conflicting dreams of an audience hungry for salvation. Believers saw her as a holy vessel consecrating the combined wizardry of Irving and Shakespeare; iconoclasts saw an enthrallment that bred myths of a liberating new St. George of a theater, one which would rescue their heroine from the dragon of the bad old ways. But if Ellen Terry's symbolic marriage evoked the comic redemptions of Victorian novels, her actual departure from the Lyceum was truer to the ironic structure of Tennyson's "Lady of Shalott": her release from enthrallment was the death of her imperial artistry. Holman Hunt's famous painting reminds us that the Lady of Shalott, like the mad-woman in the attic, celebrates the power imprisonment fosters (figure 16.1); so did the myth of Ellen Terry. She performed gamely throughout the three decades of her life beyond the Lyceum, but almost at once she lost her immediate influence to become a beloved memento mori. The applause she drew in her freedom, like the Lady of Shalott's, was a nostalgic benediction tinged with condescension: "She has a lovely face." In what ways did the impediments of her Lyceum years turn themselves into a strange indirect power that dissipated in freer, post-Victorian air?

At the Lyceum, Ellen Terry exuded lovely grief in ancil-lary roles. As Marguerite in W. G. Wills' *Faust,* as Guinevere in J. Comyns-Carr's *King Arthur,* as Rosamund in Tennyson's *Becket,* as Shakespeare's Lady Anne, Cordelia, Juliet, Imogen, Desdemona, Lady Macbeth (in a strangely frail and dreamlike incarnation), and above all as Ophelia—the part that began her Lyceum career, clinging to her even before she acted it—she sighed and suffered. Even her Portia and Beatrice, the comic successes that brought her to the Lyceum, were subdued to Irving's single-minded intensity; so, in 1884, was the Vi-ola she played briefly to his Malvolio. Her first Portia, at the Prince of Wales', had scintillated with comic panache; her Lyceum Portia's joy was thrown awry by Irving's unremittingly tragic Shylock, forcing her to become a still sterner justicer than her antagonist. The Ellen Terry Museum at Smallhythe displays a heavy bust of this grim lawgiver; Millais painted her as a columnar figure among columns, gazing sadly at the sins of a world she is not part of, more spectator than star (figure 16.2). The mercy speech modulates from witty ploy to pious incantation, "a noble kinsman to the Lord's Prayer, on which indeed it is modelled," as Ellen Terry explained in *Four Lectures on Shake-*

speare (p. 121). The glittering chatelaine of Belmont subdued herself
to sadder, if better, womanhood.

The triumphant Beatrice she brought to the Lyceum was
similarly reduced by Irving's Benedick. As Ellen Terry's *Memoir* describes it: "It was not the same Beatrice at all. A great actor can do
nothing badly, and there was very much to admire in Henry Irving's

Benedick. But he gave me little help. Beatrice must be swift, swift, swift! Owing to Henry's rather finicking, deliberate method as Benedick, I could never put the right pace into my part."[7] Moreover, she continues, his insistence on a traditional "gag" in the climactic church scene quenched the blazing anger animating Beatrice's wit; Beatrice's sudden "kill him—kill him if you can" was swallowed in buffoonery.

Moreover, since *As You Like It* had no part for Irving, Ellen Terry was barred from the mobile, managing Rosalind she seemed born to play; in compensation, she was miscast as Juliet to Irving's equally miscast Romeo. For the tears she elicited, she was forced to relinquish the laughter that was the essence of her personality. William Archer was one of the few critics who abandoned sentiment to mourn the loss: "To those who, in tragic parts, demand more than graceful attitudes and a sing-song recitation, it must seem a pity that this most charming of all actresses of comedy should have been translated into a sphere in which she is so far from home."[8] This disjunction from her parts did indeed wound her as an actress, but it galvanized the cult of her personality. In the words of the Ophelia she never wanted to play, Ellen Terry fascinated because she was fundamentally out of tune.

There was indeed something dangerous in the comic spirit Irving amputated. Clement Scott's appreciation, which celebrates Ellen Terry with Beatrice's motif "a star danced," evokes the manic, anarchic potential of her laughter: "Of her it may indeed be said, she was born to speak 'all mirth and no matter.' I have seen her sit on the stage in a serious play and literally cry with laughing, the audience mistaking her fun for deep emotion; and actors have told me that in the most pathetic scenes she had suddenly been attracted by the humorous side of the situation and almost made them 'dry up,' as the saying goes."[9]

From the beginning of her career, Ellen Terry's impulse was to drown her plays in laughter. Between her marriage to Watts and her flight with Godwin, she had released her anger and displacement by committing the cardinal sin of laughing onstage. The queenly lady as well as the young hoyden used laughter to fight and transcend the roles she was given. Like a true Meredithian patriarch, Irving crowned her by submerging her comic spirit; but if Ellen Terry's laughter had not been multilated into pathos, she would probably never have become a triumphant heroine.

Despite her famous boast, Queen Victoria *was* amused, but only by men: comedy was more radically tabooed in Victorian women than sexuality was. Matthew Arnold, Dickens, Disraeli, Gilbert and Sullivan, Lewis Carroll, Edward Lear, Oscar Wilde, won love and blessings for their antic comedy; even Carlyle's Teufelsdrockh emits his prophetic afflatus in a gargantuan laugh. But the age's revered women—Florence Nightingale, George Eliot, Charlotte Brontë, Harriet Martineau, the queen herself—looked sternly serious. Their martyred, militant heroines were Antigone, Cassandra, Joan of Arc; they cared no more for Shakespeare's Beatrice than Irving did. In 1813, Jane Austen's Elizabeth Bennet had mused about the powerful man who loved her: "He had yet to learn to be laught at, and it was rather too early to begin."[10] Throughout the century it remained "too early" to laugh at powerful men. They accepted abuse from angry women demanding their rights; they would even be mangled and chastened with Rochester, or drowned with Tom Tulliver or Grandcourt in a symbolic flood of female ire; but a woman who laughed was a woman who went too far.

As writers and audience, women were equally uneasy about comedy. Light-minded characters like Hetty Sorrel or Ginevra Fanshawe are generally expelled from women's fiction; it may be that the essential funniness such characters find around them threatens to trivialize—or worse, to transcend—the pain and anxiety women endure. For both patriarchs and their most eloquent victims, oppression was more comfortable than comedy. It was not Henry Irving alone who muffled Ellen Terry. A funny woman who cries with secret laughter at her supposedly serious roles was as alien to female struggles as she was to male prejudices. The comedienne Ellen Terry might have been, instead of the beloved woman she was, is one of those Victorian specters who take allure from their very impossibility.

Like less famous women, Ellen Terry lived with her regrets. Her father and first actor-manager Ben never let her forget that the public's darling Desdemona or Ophelia should have been playing Rosalind. She admitted he was right in impassioned marginal conversations with her library. In 1898, she carefully embellished with clippings, pictures, contradictions, and commentary a book about herself by Charles Hiatt. On one margin she writes in bold pen: "I wish H. I. had not been always so fond of *'horrors'!*" Underneath she adds in smudged and timid pencil: "Then we might have played 'As You Like It.'" When Rosalind is mentioned, she notes: "Alas! the part I shall never have the happiness of acting = "; she adds to the index of her roles, "Never Rosalind. Alas!" As if to subdue this yearning for forbidden fruit, she sharply corrects Hiatt's discussion of her ambition: "Never had 'ambition'." "Not at all. I was a paid servant and had to, at least *try* to do it—." The *"useful* actress" Ellen Terry tried to make herself confronts her lost laughter more starkly than she does in the elegant self-presentation of her *Memoir.*

The parts Ellen Terry never had the happiness of acting became more real to her, and eventually to us, than the parts she did play. But though Rosalind came to stand for these lost parts, more was lost than she. Ellen Terry never played Shakespeare's comic, subversive, imperial Cleopatra, whose "infinite variety" seems perfectly suited to Ellen Terry's mobile irreverence. Though she disclaimed any affinity with so wanton and insincere a queen, the most famous portrait we have of her is steeped in Egyptian associations. The famous beetle-winged costume she wore as Lady Macbeth, in which Sargent painted her, evokes in its sinuous amalgam of serpent and Amazon other climates than Scotland's; as Wilde put it, "Judging from the banquet, Lady Macbeth seems an economical housekeeper, and evidently patronises local industries for her husband's clothes and the servants' liveries; but she takes care to do all her own shopping in Byzantium" (figure 16.3).[11] Sargent's unforgettable portrait apotheosizes her in this costume, taking frenzied possession of a crown Shakespeare's character covets only for her husband; the perfect wife claims her own empire in a dress that summons the serpent of old Nile, crowning an assertion the stage could not contain.

The margins of Ellen Terry's scripts claim other parts she never performed: those of Shakespeare's men. She boasted often that as apprentice actresses, she and her sister Kate *"studied* all the female parts of all the plays we were in," but she leaves the male parts unmentioned. One script of *The Merchant* begins with her shrewd note on Antonio: "Laughing *at himself*—gently & sadly." A *Macbeth* script spills over with notes on the all-male I, iii, ending with: "Ross and Angus are most important parts to make the play *alive.*" In V, i, when

he male rebels meet the exiled Macduff, she translates his eager ques-
ons about Scotland thus: "Is my sweetheart as lovely as she was? _love_
1 saying the word 'Scotland' shows _here"_; there follows detailed cho-
eography of Macduff's physical actions in his agony. Claudio's open-
1g oration in _Hamlet_ II, i, carries the witty paraphrase: "Britons never
ever never will be _slaves._" In _Cymbeline,_ she gives her own Imogen
uch perfunctory directions as "smile" and "be sweet," together with
 series of hieroglyphic suns to mark emphases; while the villain Ia-
himo (Irving, of course) receives the vivid suggestion when he steals
p to the sleeping Imogen: _"Try_ and remove something from a sleep-
1g person and you'll find your heart beating and hear the noise[—]
ou'll feel faint and have to sit down. Good business." The intense
mpathy these notes reveal for male characters, even villains, resurrect
he passion with which our Lady of the Lyceum lived in imagination
er unacted parts.

   Like the women in her audience, Ellen Terry dreamed
erself into forbidden roles. Her quality onstage of distraction, of barely
uppressed laughter simmering in loveliness—what Shaw called "an
mpression of waywardness: of not quite fitting into her part and not
/anting to"—explain the spell this obediently useful actress cast over
he most dynamic women of her day. Like George Eliot's Dorothea
3rooke, Ellen Terry evoked more than she could be; the inadequacies
f her Lyceum roles were redolent of suppressed possibilities and stronger
ves. Virginia Woolf's _Between the Acts_ defines the sorts of promises
Ellen Terry held out to women by sharing their thwarted condition
nd at the same time transcending it. Here is Mrs. Swithin's tribute
o Miss La Trobe: "What a small part I've had to play! But you've
nade me feel I could have played . . . 'Cleopatra!' . . . 'You've stirred
n me my unacted part,' she meant." [12]

   Miss La Trobe is in fact a portrait of Ellen Terry's daugh-
er Edith Craig, who created a woman-centered theater beyond her
nother's conception: from 1914 to 1925, she managed the Pioneer
Players, an experimental company specializing in female pageants of a
ransfigured history. But Edy's feminist reclamations of the English
ast only translate her mother's legacy into a more overtly defiant id-
om. Ellen Terry's compelling presence in secondary roles stirred women
o imagine their own unacted parts, the laughter it was still too early
o indulge, the triumph betrayed into pathos. Her determined useful-

ness to Irving spoke more painfully to women of their own condition
than the most regal Cleopatra would have done.

For better or worse, Ellen Terry became Ophelia—a role
she did not like, in which she did not like herself. Today, theater
historians hint delicately that her Ophelia was bland and even dull.
For Christopher St. John, her feminist chronicler, it represents her
crucial abdication; with Ophelia she "abandoned . . . all chances of
empire."[13] But its pathos allowed a kind of triumph as well, if only a
wry one. In her *Memoir,* Ellen Terry describes a mad scene in Chicago
which showed her what Ophelia could do: "This frail wraith, this poor
demented thing, could hold them in the hollow of her hand. . . . It
was splendid! 'How long can I hold them?' I thought: 'for ever!' Then
I laughed. That was the best Ophelia laugh of my life."[14]

The "frail wraith" is a permissible conduit for her urge to
laughter and power. Rosalind's sane laugh would tell the audience too
much, but Ophelia's mad one—like Bertha Mason's—is licensed to
command. Such devious displays of strength allowed Victorian audiences to be delighted connoisseurs of mad scenes, but Ophelia's generally got the crown. As William Ernest Henley exclaims in his introduction to *The Graphic Gallery of Shakespeare's Heroines,* "Her mad
scene is the most famous in literature; in the hands of Miss Ellen
Terry, it is one of the most moving and withal the most beautiful in
acting." At the Lyceum, the reign of madness alone allowed Ellen
Terry to emulate Henry Irving's Napoleonic command of the stage.

Pallid though she appears, Ophelia herself breathed power
into Ellen Terry's unwilling and possibly tepid performance—a power
whose irony the actress was thoroughly aware of. For the Victorian
Ophelia had secret and seditious French connections. In the 1820s,
French Romantics made of her a cult figure embodying their own
turbulent hopes; for Berlioz, Hugo, and Delacroix, Ophelia swelled
into a magic symbol of an erotic and aesthetic awakening that soared
far beyond her ancillary role in Shakespeare's play. In his moving book
Fair Ophelia, Peter Raby tells the story of Harriet Smithson Berlioz, a
vapid Drury Lane actress who in 1827 inflamed French audiences as
Ophelia; she married the volatile Berlioz and fell victim to her own
cult. But her Ophelia lived beyond her (figures 16.4, 16.5). Delacroix
and his followers snatched upon her madness for their own purposes,
painting her bare breasted like the spirit of liberty, a harbinger of rev-

olutions in nature and art, a Dionysian transformer with a magic beyond her small part and pathetic death.

Ellen Terry never bared her breasts, nor was her mad scene steeped in metamorphoses, but the power of a performance in which she herself did little was in part an echo of continental Romanticism. So was Ophelia's omnipresence in English literature and art. Alive and betrayed, she was a cipher, but her drowning—which in *Hamlet* receives only a sketchy, secondhand description—assumed a mystic ritual's sacred power when it was realized by such pre-Raphaelites as Millais and Arthur Hughes. Ophelia's "mermaidlike" suspension between natural growth and living death, the details of botany and the incantations of art, the pathos of sanity and the florid triumph of madness, aligned her with other compelling hybrid women—the water nixies, Undines, mermaids, lamias, and serpent women who haunted Victorian dreams of a new dispensation. Accordingly, Mary Cowden Clarke's popular *Girlhood of Shakespeare's Heroines* endows this frailest of maidens with prophetic afflatus. As she is about to meet Hamlet, "the rose of Elsinore" is stricken with a vision of the King's murder and all the ensuing anguish; the tragedy is refracted not in the noble mind of the sweet prince, but in the magic glass of an Ophelia divinely mad from

the beginning of her story. As the nineteenth century recast her, Ophelia was less character than preternatural visitation, glorified beyond Shakespeare's play into weird pageants of triumphant misrule.

Ellen Terry looking thoughtful with a lily seems aloof from this visionary cult (figure 16.6); she was adept at tapping the religious fantasies of her culture while remaining healthily immune from their implications. Yet if she inaugurated no reign of terror, she evoked terror; nowhere can we see this more vividly than in her impact on the paintings of G. F. Watts. Long before she played the part in 1878, she possessed her husband with a phantasmagoria of Ophelias. Even the radiant ingenue in the early *Choosing* (figure 16.7) is, like Ophelia,

inextricably—and poignantly—identified with the fate of her flowers. Already, dead flowers predominate; already, constraints and loss compose the girl's allure, as her lovely face tries vainly to surge out of the painting's enclosures. A slightly later portrait (figure 16.8) features a beseeching Ellen Terry in a more overtly Gothic setting, shrouded by heavy dark curtains, an iconography adopted by Ellen Terry's son, Gordon Craig, in his tribute to his mother as an Ophelia beset by black and menacing forms and ruthlessly blocked space (figure 16.9).

Watts' later "Ophelia" is less concerned with her ominous surroundings and more aware of her ominous self (figure 16.10). This painting exploits the actual, witchlike qualities of Ellen Terry's profile. Most Victorian artists and photographers masked the eerie

proximity of her nose to her chin; Watts turns her into a witch whose
madness is her face. She gazes with a sibylline calm into the water that
will drown her, as if it were a crystal ball making her death one with
her magic. In "Ophelia's Madness" (figure 16.11), a haunting oil painted
around 1880 from a photograph of Ellen Terry, her bloated face seems
to look up at us from the bottom of that water. That lovely face is
purged here of recognizable contour; Ellen Terry's identity is submerged in an expressionistic mask of horror and estrangement. But its

very purity of horror gives it Medusa-like power over the viewer. The swollen face that claims the canvas has lost its humanity to become a personification of madness, transfixing the viewer to its compelling state.

Watts' evolving dream of Ellen Terry as Ophelia is a sinister but urgent tribute to her power. The mournful, floral maiden in her enclosure becomes the watery witch and submerged Medusa, luring us into dangerous states of consciousness. Ophelia is a crucible wherein the actress is destroyed as a woman while she takes on the occult might of an abstraction. This savage cycle of paintings traces the dark power bestowed on Ellen Terry by a role that betrayed her. The con-

traints of Watts' marriage to her in art were those of Irving's Lyceum
marriage. In both, Ophelia's lost face evokes a wealth of unwritten
tragedies and bitter comedies.

Ellen Terry's laughter was her secret from her mythmak-
ing audiences, but she allowed it to harmonize with the mad laugh of
Ophelia. Her triumph was her ability to evoke the complex mythog-
raphy of her age; her pathos was the pliability that tempted her to do
this. She was relegated to pathetic parts, but their very inadequacy
galvanized her cult and made her part of her age's iconography. She
never played, or played in mutilating conditions, the parts she seemed
born for; but the banished Rosalind that haunted her admirers brought
her a peculiarly Victorian sort of victory that was a subtler and more
enduring creation of Ellen Terry's unquenchably comic spirit than purer
comedy would have been.

Notes

INTRODUCTION

1. Carolyn Heilbrun, *Reinventing Womanhood* (New York: Norton, 1979).
2. Kate Millett, *Sexual Politics* (New York: Doubleday, 1970); Ellen Moers, *Literary Women: The Great Writers* (New York: Doubleday, 1976).
3. Adrienne Rich, "Jane Eyre: The Temptations of a Motherless Woman" (1973), printed in *On Lies, Secrets, and Silence: Selected Prose, 1966–1978* (New York: Norton, 1979), . 89–106, and Sandra M. Gilbert and Susan Gubar, *The Madwoman in the Attic: The Woman riter and the Nineteenth-Century Literary Imagination* (New Haven, Conn.: Yale University Press, 979), have been particularly influential in the canonization of Charlotte Brontë.

1. JANE AUSTEN AND ROMANTIC IMPRISONMENT

1. George Henry Lewes, "The Lady Novelists," *Westminster Review* (July 1852), printed in B. C. Southam, ed., *Jane Austen: The Critical Heritage* (London: Routledge & Kegan aul, 1968), p. 140.
2. Stuart M. Tave, *Some Words of Jane Austen* (Chicago: University of Chicago ress, 1973), p. 1.
3. A lively and flourishing critical school insists that Jane Austen's greatness springs ot from her repose, but from the dynamic and unresolved tensions in her mind and her art. mong recent critics, see especially Tony Tanner's brilliant introductions to *Sense and Sensibility* d *Mansfield Park* (Middlesex, Eng: Penguin, 1969, 1966), pp. 7–34, 7–36; Bernard J. Paris, *haracter and Conflict in Jane Austen's Novels* (Detroit: Wayne State University Press, 1978); d Alison G. Sulloway, "Emma Woodhouse and *A Vindication of the Rights of Woman*," *The ordsworth Circle* (1976), 7:320–32.
4. See Karl Kroeber, "Jane Austen, Romantic," *The Wordsworth Circle* (1976), 7:291– 5. This fascinating issue of *The Wordsworth Circle*, devoted to an exploration of Jane Austen as Romantic writer, was the first inspiration for my own essay.
5. Page references to the works of Jane Austen are to the Oxford University Press lition, R. W. Chapman, ed.
6. L. J. Swingle's rich study of the Romantic love of enclosures, "The Perfect Happ-ness of the Union: Jane Austen's *Emma* and English Romanticism," *The Wordsworth Circle* 976), 7:312–19, does not consider their imprisoning possibilities. Swingle's "The Romantic mergence: Multiplication of Alternatives and the Problem of Systematic Entrapment," *Modern*

Language Quarterly (1978), 39:264–83, defines elegantly a spacious and flexible Romanticism that admits Jane Austen and other apparent dissenters.

7. "I have read the Corsair, mended my petticoat, & have nothing else to do." Jane Austen, *Jane Austen's Letters to Her Sister Cassandra and Others*, R. W. Chapman, ed., 2 vols (Oxford: Clarendon Press, 1932), 2:379.

8. To George Henry Lewes, January 12, 1848, reprinted in Southam, *Jane Austen*, p. 126.

9. As, for example, Joseph Kestner does in "Jane Austen: The Tradition of the English Romantic Novel, 1800–1832," *The Wordsworth Circle* (1976), 7:297–311.

10. M. H. Abrams, *Natural Supernaturalism: Tradition and Revolution in Romantic Literature* (New York: Norton, 1971), p. 193. Abrams' book has been a useful source in crystallizing Romantic paradigms, though it ignores some dark twists that are equally Romantic.

11. William Godwin, *Caleb Williams* (1974; reprint, New York: Norton, 1977), p 107. Future references to this edition will appear in the text.

12. "The Tale of Guzman's Family" provides the final turn of the screw.

13. See Ellen Moers, *Literary Women: The Great Writers* (New York: Doubleday 1976), pp. 91–99, for her influential discussion of Frankenstein as a female myth of childbirth. On p. 135, Moers mentions the divided image of the father in *The Mysteries of Udolpho*, o which I elaborate below.

14. Austen, *Letters*, 1:24. For a more detailed discussion of Austen's dislike children, see my "Artists and Mothers: A False Alliance," *Women and Literature* (1978), 6:3 15.

15. Ann Radcliffe, *The Mysteries of Udolpho* (1794; reprint, London: Oxford University Press, 1970), p. 305. Future references to this edition will appear in the text.

16. In *Melmoth the Wanderer*, bells are used to remind Monçada and the reader the chillingly dehumanizing nonhumanity of the objects of religious ritual. Horrified by a dyin monk's revelation of his hypocrisy, Monçada pleads, "But your regularity in religious exercise . . ." only to be stopped by the bitter reminder: *"Did you never hear a bell toll?"* (p. 86, Matu rin's italics).

17. For a fuller discussion of Darcy's irreconcilable double nature, see my *Commu nities of Women: An Idea in Fiction* (Cambridge, Mass.: Harvard University Press, 1978), p 52–55.

18. See, most recently, my "O Brave New World: Evolution and Revolution i *Persuasion*," *ELH* (1972), 39:212–28; William A. Walling, "The Glorious Anxiety of Motio Jane Austen's *Persuasion*"; and Gene W. Ruoff, "Anne Elliot's Dowry: Reflections on the End ing of *Persuasion*." The latter two essays are both in *The Wordsworth Circle* (1976), 7:333–4 342–51.

19. Profound thanks to my contagiously lively graduate students at the Universit of Pennsylvania in the spring 1978 semester. The vigorous Romantic fictions of English 75 honed and inspired my own efforts.

2. JANE AUSTEN'S DANGEROUS CHARM
FEELING AS ONE OUGHT ABOUT FANNY PRICE

1. Jane Austen, *Minor Works*, R. W. Chapman, ed. (1954; reprint, London: Ox ford University Press, 1969), p. 432.

2. Lionel Trilling, "*Mansfield Park*," reprinted in Ian Watt, ed., *Jane Austen: Collection of Critical Essays* (Englewood Cliffs, N.J.: Prentice-Hall, 1963), p. 128.

3. Avrom Fleishman, *A Reading of "Mansfield Park"* (1967; reprinted, Baltimor Johns Hopkins University Press, 1970), pp. 57–69.

4. Kingsley Amis, "Whatever Became of Jane Austen?" (1957), reprinted in Watt, *Critical Essays*, p. 142.

5. "Keeping the monster at bay is one part of the realist enterprise. The other is to keep him, or her, alive." George Levine, *The Realistic Imagination: English Fiction from Frankenstein to Lady Chatterley* (Chicago: University of Chicago Press, 1981), p. 80. Judith Wilt, in *Ghosts of the Gothic: Austen, Eliot, and Lawrence* (Princeton, N.J.: Princeton University Press, 1980), pp. 121–72, provides an eerily suggestive discussion of the terror that infuses Jane Austen's vision of commonality.

6. Wayne Booth, *A Rhetoric of Fiction* (Chicago: University of Chicago Press, 1961), p. 245.

7. Jane Austen, *Mansfield Park* (1814; reprint, Middlesex, Eng: Penguin, 1966), p. 127. Future references to this edition will appear in the text.

8. George Levine speculates about the monstrous potential of Jane Austen's more inquisitive heroines, though he assumes, overhastily in my opinion, that Fanny's passivity exempts her from monstrosity (*The Realistic Imagination*, p. 41). Sandra M. Gilbert and Susan Gubar are more catholic in their definition: "[Austen's] heroines, it seems, are not born like people, but manufactured like monsters, and also like monsters they seem fated to self-destruct." Gilbert and Gubar, *The Madwoman in the Attic: The Woman Writer and the Nineteenth-Century Literary Imagination* (New Haven, Conn.: Yale University Press, 1979), p. 129. For more capacious examinations of Jane Austen's dark Romanticism, see Wilt, *Austen, Eliot, and Lawrence,* pp. 121–72, and my "Jane Austen and Romantic Imprisonment," in David Monaghan, ed., *Jane Austen in a Social Context* (London: Macmillan, 1981), pp. 9–27.

9. See Maurianne Adams, "*Jane Eyre:* Woman's Estate," in Arlyn Diamond and Lee R. Edwards, eds., *The Authority of Experience: Essays in Feminist Criticism* (Amherst: University of Massachusetts Press, 1977), pp. 137–59, and Fleishman, *A Reading of "Mansfield Park,"* p. 72, for more discussion of Fanny as orphan. For a broader discussion of the subversive implications of fictional orphanhood, see my "Incarnations of the Orphan," *ELH* (Fall 1975), 42:395–419.

10. See Janet Todd, *Women's Friendship in Literature* (New York: Columbia University Press, 1980), pp. 246–74, for a provocative analysis of Fanny's, and Jane Austen's, rejection of female friendship and the radical autonomy it provides.

11. See, for instance, Donald Greene, "Jane Austen's Monsters," in John Halperin, ed., *Jane Austen: Bicentenary Essays* (Cambridge: Cambridge University Press, 1975), pp. 262–78. Amis, in Watt, *Critical Essays*, p. 144, and Julia Prewitt Brown, in *Jane Austen's Novels: Social Change and Literary Form* (Cambridge, Mass.: Harvard University Press, 1979), p. 100, do in passing call Fanny Price a monster, but this appellation seems more a cry of horror than an expression of sustained literary interest.

12. See Fleishman, *A Reading of "Mansfield Park,"* pp. 36–42.

13. A somewhat shorter version of this paper was presented as the keynote address of the 1980 meeting of the Jane Austen Society. Their kind invitation to speak made me wonder for the first time how I ought to feel about Fanny Price.

3. O BRAVE NEW WORLD:
EVOLUTION AND REVOLUTION IN PERSUASION

1. Jane Austen, *Northanger Abbey* and *Persuasion*, 3d ed., R. W. Chapman, ed. (London: Oxford University Press, 1933), p. 182. All subsequent references will be to this edition.

2. See, for example, Robert Liddell, *The Novels of Jane Austen* (London: Longmans, Green, 1963), p. 134.

3. Jane Austen, *Sense and Sensibility,* 3d ed., R. W. Chapman, ed. (London: Oxford University Press, 1933), pp. 48–49, my italics.

4. Paul Zeitlow, "Luck and Fortuitous Circumstance in *Persuasion:* Two Interpretations," *ELH* (1965), 32:179–95.

5. Jane Austen, *Pride and Prejudice,* 3d ed., R. W. Chapman, ed. (London: Oxford University Press, 1933), p. 109, my emphasis.

6. Mary Wollstonecraft, *Vindication of the Rights of Woman,* Everyman's Library (London: J. M. Dent, 1929), p. 5, Mary Wollstonecraft's emphasis.

7. See D. W. Harding, "Regulated Hatred: An Aspect of the Work of Jane Austen," *Scrutiny* (1940), 8:346–62, for an early discussion of Jane Austen's use of this technique.

8. "I have turned over various books written on the subject of education, and patiently observed the conduct of parents and the management of schools; but what has been the result?—a profound conviction that the neglected education of my fellow-creatures is the grand source of the misery I deplore, and that women, in particular, are rendered weak and wretched by a variety of concurring causes, originating from one hasty conclusion." Wollstonecraft, *Vindication,* p. 3.

4. INCARNATIONS OF THE ORPHAN

1. See, for instance, R. W. B. Lewis, *The Picaresque Saint* (Philadelphia and New York: Lippincott, 1959).

2. Ian Watt notably refuses to own it as one in *The Rise of the Novel* (Berkeley and Los Angeles: University of California Press, 1965). But Denis Donoghue, in "The Values of *Moll Flanders," Sewanee Review* (1963), 71:287–303, feels that Defoe's vision is sufficiently coherent for him to be called the first English novelist.

3. Robert Alter, in "A Bourgeois Picaroon," *Rogue's Progress: Studies in the Picaresque Novel* (Cambridge, Mass.: Harvard University Press, 1964), pp. 35–57, argues subtly that Moll's tone is too grim for the novel to be truly picaresque. But most studies of the picaresque genre include the novel as a matter of course. See, for instance, Claudio Guillén, "Toward a Definition of the Picaresque," *Literature as System: Essays Toward the Theory of Literary History* (Princeton, N.J.: Princeton University Press, 1971), pp. 71–106; and Stuart Miller, *The Picaresque Novel* (Cleveland: Press of Case Western Reserve University, 1967).

4. "Well, at last I found this amphibious creature, this land-water-thing call'd a gentleman-tradesman, and as a just plague on my folly I was catch'd in the very snare which, as I might say, I laid for myself." Daniel Defoe, *Moll Flanders,* James Sutherland, ed. (Boston: Houghton Mifflin, 1959). Further references to this edition will appear in the text.

5. "Moll cannot be said to have a character at all": Donoghue, *"Moll Flanders,"* p. 298. But David Goldknopf, in *The Life of the Novel* (Chicago: University of Chicago Press, 1972), follows such critics as Virginia Woolf in *The Common Reader* (London and New York: Harcourt Brace, 1948), who write eloquently about the Moll they perceive.

6. Guillén, "Definition of the Picaresque," p. 137.

7. Jane Austen's Emma sees Jane Fairfax as "wrapt up in a cloak of politeness." Both Jane Fairfax and Frank Churchill seem to be semi-picaresque orphans playing manipulative games with a fixed social medium. Harriet Smith seems to be Jane Austen's version of the Romantic orphan-waif. Her passive pliability is deceptively enticing; by the end of the novel, she has almost become Emma's Frankenstein monster.

8. Samuel Richardson, *Pamela,* William M. Sale, Jr., ed. (New York: Norton 1958), p. 142. Future references to this edition will be included in the text.

9. "What connexion can there be, between the place in Lincolnshire, the house in

town, the Mercury in powder, and the whereabout of Jo the outlaw with the broom who had that distant ray of light upon him when he swept the churchyard-step? What connexion can there have been between many people in the innumerable histories of the world, who, from opposite ends of great gulfs, have, nevertheless, been very curiously brought together?" Charles Dickens, *Bleak House*, Morton Zabel, ed. (Boston: Houghton Mifflin, 1956), p. 167. In this tableau, Jo stands as a diminutive and faintly glowing symbol of the Victorian orphan in his equivocal beatitude, isolated from the community he mystically purges and unifies, the secret soul of the social body.

10. Guillén, "Definition of the Picaresque," p. 105. Guillén's essay includes a suggestive analysis of the role of orphanhood, an invariable attribute of the picaroon's character. For this reason, I find it odd that he does not link the picaroon to the orphan heroes who flourish in the nineteenth-century English novel.

11. Charlotte Brontë, *Jane Eyre*, Richard J. Dunn, ed. (New York: Norton, 1971), p. 1. Future references to this edition will appear in the text.

12. Emily Brontë, *Wuthering Heights*, William M. Sale, Jr., ed. (New York: Norton, 1963), p. 38.

13. I believe J. Hillis Miller, in *The Disappearance of God* (Cambridge, Mass.: Harvard University Press, 1963), was the first critic to discuss Heathcliff's function as a catalyst of his society's purification. According to Miller, Heathcliff and Cathy must pass through and beyond their world to save it.

14. John Henry Newman, *Apologia Pro Vita Sua*, David DeLaura, ed. (New York: Norton, 1968), p. 187.

15. Charles Dickens, *Great Expectations*, Angus Calder, ed. (Middlesex: Penguin, 1965), p. 247. Future references to this edition will appear in the text.

16. An analysis of Dickens' many uses and variations of this paradigm would constitute a long article in itself.

17. Dorothy Van Ghent, *The English Novel: Form and Function* (New York, Rinehart, 1933), pp. 125–38.

18. Eppie in *Silas Marner* is of course a benign crystallization of the orphan myth, and I think Dorothea in *Middlemarch* a saddened rejection of it; but George Eliot treats orphanhood in too idiosyncratic a fashion to explore fully here.

19. W. M. Frohock, "The Failing Center: Recent Fiction and the Picaresque Tradition," *Novel: A Forum on Fiction* (Fall 1969), 3:62–70.

20. Joyce Cary, *The Horse's Mouth* (reprint; New York: Grosset & Dunlap 1957), p. 278. Future references to this edition will appear in the text.

21. I should like to thank Avrom Fleishman, Roger Sale, and Jan Van Meter, for the invaluable suggestions they made while I was writing this essay.

5. WOMEN ON WOMEN'S DESTINY: MATURITY AS PENANCE

1. Patricia Meyer Spacks, *The Female Imagination* (New York: Knopf, 1975); Ellen Moers, *Literary Women: The Great Writers* (New York: Doubleday, 1976); Elaine Showalter, *A Literature of Their Own: British Women Novelists from Brontë to Lessing* (Princeton, N.J.: Princeton University Press, 1977).

2. Kate Millett, *Sexual Politics* (New York: Doubleday, 1970).

3. Joanna Russ, "Why Women Can't Write," in Susan Koppleman Cornillon, ed., *Images of Women in Fiction: Feminist Perspectives*, rev. ed. (Bowling Green, Ohio: Bowling Green University Popular Press, 1973), p. 5. See also Cynthia Griffin Wolff, "A Mirror for Men:

Stereotypes of Women in Literature," *The Massachusetts Review* (1972), 13:207: "The stereotypes of women vary, but they vary in response to different masculine needs. . . . [Women] appear not as they are, certainly not as they would define themselves, but as conveniences to the resolution of masculine dilemmas." Wolff's article implicates women writers only in their collusion with masculine stereotypes; but five years later, I have come to the reluctant conclusion that women frequently "define themselves" in even more insidiously limited a fashion.

4. Robie Macauley in the *New York Times Book Review*, March 27, 1977, p. 7. See also Elin Schoen, "Kiss, Kiss, Kvetch, Kvetch: What's Ailing the New Belles of Letters?" *New York Magazine*, May 23, 1977, pp. 59–69, which excoriates the insult to female readers expected to identify with trapped and miserable heroines.

5. George Eliot, *Middlemarch* (1871–72; reprint, Cambridge, Mass.: Riverside Press, 1956), p. 202. Future references to this edition will appear in the text.

6. See Jerome Beaty, "Text of the Novel: A Study of the Proof," in Barbara Hardy, ed., *Middlemarch: Critical Approaches to the Novel* (New York: Oxford University Press, 1967), pp. 61–62.

7. Thomas Hardy, *Jude the Obscure* (1894–95; reprint, Boston: Houghton Mifflin, 1965), pp. 277–78.

8. Henry James, *The Portrait of a Lady* (1881; reprint, New York: New American Library, 1963), p. 318.

9. Spacks, in *The Female Imagination*, makes this point, p. 100.

10. For a fuller discussion of Jo's role throughout the March trilogy, see my *Communities of Women: An Idea in Fiction* (Cambridge, Mass.: Harvard University Press, 1978), pp. 55–73.

11. See Northrop Frye, "The Mythos of Spring: Comedy" in *Anatomy of Criticism: Four Essays* (1957; reprint, New York: Atheneum, 1968), pp. 163–86.

12. Gail Godwin, *The Odd Woman* (1974; reprint, New York: Berkley Medallion Books, 1976), p. 246.

6. ROBERT BROWNING'S LAST WORD

1. William Irvine and Park Honan, *The Book, the Ring, & the Poet: A Biography of Robert Browning* (New York: McGraw Hill, 1974), and Clyde de L. Ryals, *Becoming Browning: The Poems and the Plays of Robert Browning, 1833–1846* (Columbus: Ohio State University Press, 1983), pp. 254–55.

2. Helen Cooper, "Working Into Light: Elizabeth Barrett Browning," in Sandra M. Gilbert and Susan Gubar, eds., *Shakespeare's Sisters: Feminist Essays on Women Poets* (Bloomington: Indiana University Press, 1979), pp. 65–81; Dorothy Mermin, "The Female Poet and the Embarrassed Reader: Elizabeth Barrett Browning's *Sonnets from the Portuguese*," *ELH* (1981), 48:351–67; Dolores Rosenblum, "Face to Face: Elizabeth Barrett Browning's *Aurora Leigh* and Nineteenth-Century Poetry," *Victorian Studies* (1983), 26:321–38; Sandra M. Gilbert, "From *Patria* to *Matria*: Elizabeth Barrett Browning's Risorgimento," *PMLA* (1984), 99:194–211.

3. Flavia Alaya, "The Ring, the Rescue, & the Risorgimento: Reunifying the Brownings' Italy," *BIS* (1978), 6:1–41.

4. Phyllis Rose, *Parallel Lives: Five Victorian Marriages* (New York: Knopf, 1983), p. 7.

5. Elizabeth Barrett Browning, *Aurora Leigh and Other Poems* (1853–56; reprint, London: The Woman's Press, 1978), book III, ll. 90–91. Future references to this edition will appear in the text.

6. Robert Browning, *The Ring and the Book,* Richard D. Altick, ed. (New Haven, Conn.: Yale University Press, 1971), "The Ring and the Book," ll. 35–36. Future references to this edition will appear in the text.

7. As is true in Lawrence Lipking, *The Life of the Poet: Beginning and Ending Poetic Careers* (Chicago: University of Chicago Press, 1981).

8. Elvan Kinter, ed., *The Letters of Robert Browning and Elizabeth Barrett Barrett, 1845–1846* (Cambridge, Mass.: Harvard University Press, 1969), 1:7.

9. Robert Browning, "Old Pictures in Florence," from *Men and Women 1855,* Paul Turner, ed. (Oxford: Oxford University Press, 1972), st. 24. Future references to *Men and Women* are from this edition and will be cited in the text.

10. Robert Langbaum, *The Poetry of Experience: The Dramatic Monologue in Modern Literary Tradition* (1957; reprint, New York: Norton, 1963). For a view of Browning's shaping auditor that is closer to my own, see Dorothy Mermin, *The Audience in the Poem: Five Victorian Poets* (New Brunswick, N.J.: Rutgers University Press, 1983), pp. 47–82.

11. Quoted in William Benzie, *Dr. F. J. Furnivall: Victorian Scholar-Adventurer* (Norman, Okla. 1983), p. 139.

12. Nina Auerbach, *Woman and the Demon: The Life of a Victorian Myth* (Cambridge, Mass.: Harvard University Press, 1982), pp. 7–62.

13. See J. E. Shaw, "The 'Donna Angelicata' in *The Ring and the Book,*" *PMLA* (1926), 41:58–63.

14. For a discussion of the essential soliloquy within Pompilia's apparent dramatic monologue, see Roy E. Gridley, "Browning's Pompilia," *JEGP* (1968), 67:64–83.

15. U. C. Knoepflmacher, "Projection and the Female Other: Romanticism, Browning, and the Victorian Dramatic Monologue," *Victorian Poetry* (1984), 22:139–59.

7. DICKENS AND DOMBEY: A DAUGHTER AFTER ALL

1. Quoted in Gladys Storey, *Dickens and Daughter* (London: Müller, 1939), p. 100.

2. Angus Wilson, in *The World of Charles Dickens* (New York: Viking Press, 1970), p. 59, regrets Dickens' attenuated treatment of sexual relationships, but he does not deplore it, while Kate Millett, in *Sexual Politics* (New York: Doubleday, 1970), and Carolyn Heilbrun, in *Toward a Recognition of Androgyny* (New York: Knopf, 1973), treat this lack as the central fact about Dickens' novels. Despite Heilbrun's relative dismissal of Dickens, her ideal of a dehumanizing sexual polarity giving way to a healthily reconciling androgyny is, I think, an apt concept to apply to him.

3. Patricia Thomson, *The Victorian Heroine: A Changing Ideal, 1837–1873* (London: Oxford University Press, 1956), p. 93.

4. Andrew Sinclair, *The Better Half: The Emancipation of the American Woman* (New York: Harper & Row, 1965), p. 164. But recently Dickens has had ample defenders to make his women more palatable to a self-consciously liberated age. Sylvia Manning, in *Dickens as Satirist* (New Haven, Conn.: Yale University Press, 1971), traces the development in his heroines away from debility to physical strength and muscular activity; Ellen Moers, in *"Bleak House:* The Agitating Women," *The Dickensian* (January 1973), 69:13–24, discusses the plenitude of active, bustling, mobile women in that novel; and Alex Zwerdling, in "Esther Summerson Rehabilitated," *PMLA* (May 1973), 88:429–39, subtly exposes to us Esther's neurotic patterns, a "rehabilitation" that would have been desecration in any century but our own.

5. Elizabeth C. Wolstenholme, "The Education of Girls, Its Present and Its Fu-

ture," in Josephine Butler, ed., *Woman's Work and Woman's Culture* (London: Macmillan, 1869), pp. 290–330.

6. Dickens' "Violated Letter," published in the *New York Tribune*, August 16, 1858, and reproduced by Ada Nisbet, *Dickens and Ellen Ternan* (Berkeley and Los Angeles: University of California Press, 1952), p. 67. In one of those telling distortions gossip can produce, the English actress Blanche Galton referred to Ellen Ternan in 1928 as "Dickens's god-daughter." Nisbet, *Dickens and Ellen Ternan*, p. 24.

7. Pearl Chesler Solomon, *Dickens and Melville in Their Time* (New York: Columbia University Press, 1975), p. 80.

8. Page references to *Dombey and Son* are to the New Oxford Illustrated Dickens.

9. Manning, *Dickens as Satirist*, pp. 46–47. See also Michael Steig, "Iconography of Sexual Conflict in *Dombey and Son*," in Robert B. Partlow, Jr., ed., *Dickens Studies Annual* (Carbondale and Edwardsville: Southern Illinois University Press, 1970), 1:161–67. Steig traces the pervasive motif of the battle of the sexes in *Dombey*, showing how it surfaces in the smallest details of the text and illustrations.

10. Sarah Lewis, *Woman's Mission* (Boston: J. W. Parker, 1840, "from the English edition"), p. 13.

11. Leonore Davidoff discusses the transition from rural to railroad time units in *The Best Circles: Society Etiquette and the Season* (Totowa, N.J.: Rowman & Littlefield, 1973), pp. 34–35.

12. John Ruskin, *Sesame and Lilies* (London: Smith, Elder, 1865), p. 146.

13. See Julian Moynahan, "Dealings with the Firm of Dombey and Son: Firmness vs. Wetness," in John Gross and Gabriel Pearson, eds., *Dickens and the Twentieth Century* (London: Routledge, 1962), pp. 121–31. This essay is one long and witty shudder at the death Florence carries about with her; Moynahan's insights are brilliant, but his assumption that Dickens is not responsible for his own effects seems needlessly patronizing. Alexander Welsh, in *The City of Dickens* (London: Oxford University Press, 1971), subtly defines the love and death which Dickens' heroines offer his heroes as a manifestation of "Victorian angelology"; he has a particularly good definition of Florence Dombey.

14. Florence's familiarity with the dying is a perfect education, according to Sarah Ellis, *The Women of England: Their Social Duties and Domestic Habits* (New York: Fisher, 1843). According to Mrs. Ellis, female education is bad for the health if it strains the intellect and bad for the soul if it teaches accomplishments: a young girl should acquire only those duties she will need in marriage, of which the foremost is the gentle skill of behavior in a sickroom. Dombey conveniently ignores the cultivation of her mind—she teaches herself enough to teach Paul—and she has no mother to instill in her those accomplishments which "a world of mothers" were inflicting on their marriageable daughters; as far as her education goes, it seems that her family's dexterity in dying or almost dying is the best possible training she could have. Abandoned by a corrupting world, orphans make the purest of women.

15. Moynahan, "Firmness vs. Wetness," p. 126.

16. Lewis, *Woman's Mission*, p. 95.

17. Obviously, I disagree with accounts of the novel such as Grahame Smith's *Dickens, Money, and Society* (Berkeley and Los Angeles: University of California Press, 1968), pp. 103–20. According to Smith, *Dombey and Son* is too purely personal to rank with Dickens' greatest works: the firm of Dombey and Son lacks the overwhelming symbolic magnitude of Chancery in *Bleak House* or the Circumlocution Office in *Little Dorrit*. To me, the firm is deliberately intangible, Dombey's dream rather than Dickens' reality; the symbolic poles of the novel are the railroad and the sea, both of them very much alive. *Dombey* is not, in my opinion, a failed social anatomy, but an achieved embodiment of a world divided into sexual antinomies.

t is not, in other words, a sketch for what Dickens was to do more successfully later, but a work
conceived and executed in terms unique in the canon.

18. Welsh aligns the train with Florence, as a vision of her rises before Dombey on
his death-charged journey to Leamington in chapter 20. But, though *to Dombey* his daughter
blends with the train in a vision of death, in the novel's scheme the nature of the train is that
of the man.

19. John R. Reed, in *Victorian Conventions* (Athens: Ohio University Press, 1975),
pp. 45–46, analyzes at length Hablot K. Browne's illustration of the Edith-Carker confrontation
in Dijon, showing the wealth of "masculine, almost heroic" associations surrounding Edith, in
contrast to Carker's lax vulnerability.

20. Eliza Lynn Linton, "The Girl of the Period," *Saturday Review* (March 14,
1868), 25:339–40.

21. Quoted in John Forster, *The Life of Charles Dickens* (London: Everyman's Library, 1966), 2:197.

22. Quoted in Edgar Johnson, *Charles Dickens: His Tragedy and Triumph* (New
York: Simon & Schuster, 1952), 2:1008.

23. Mamie Dickens, *My Father as I Recall Him* (Westminster, Eng.: Roxburghe
Press, 1896), p. 8.

24. Quoted in Storey, *Dickens and Daughter*, p. 219.

8. ALICE AND WONDERLAND: A CURIOUS CHILD

1. Lewis Carroll, "Alice on the Stage," *The Theatre* (April 1, 1887), 9:181.

2. Walter de la Mare, *Lewis Carroll* (London: Faber & Faber, 1932), p. 55.

3. Letter to Dolly Argles, November 28, 1867. Quoted in Evelyn Hatch, ed., *A
Selection from the Letters of Lewis Carroll (The Reverend Charles Lutwidge Dodgson) to His Child-
Friends* (London: Macmillan, 1933), pp. 48–49.

4. See Martin Grotjahn, "About the Symbolization of *Alice's Adventures in Wonderland,"* *American Imago* (1947), 4:34, for a discussion of Freud's "girl = phallus equation" in
relation to Alice.

5. Edmund Wilson's penetrating essay "C. L. Dodgson: The Poet Logician" is the
only criticism of *Alice* to touch on the relationship between dream and dreamer in relation to
Alice's covert brutality: "But the creatures that she meets, the whole dream, *are* Alice's personality and her waking life. . . . she . . . has a child's primitive cruelty. . . . But though Alice
is sometimes brutal, she is always well-bred." Wilson cites as examples of brutality her innuendos
about Dinah to the mouse and birds. *The Shores of Light*, 2d ed. (1952; reprint, New York:
Noonday Press, 1967), pp. 543–44.

6. See Florence Becker Lennon, *The Life of Lewis Carroll*, rev. ed. (New York: Col-
lier Books, 1962), p. 151, for Ruskin's beatific description of a secret nocturnal tea party presided over by Alice Liddell.

7. Lewis Carroll knew the Rossetti family and photographed them several times.
Dante Grabriel Rossetti later claimed that Carroll's Dormouse was inspired by his own pet wom-
bat. Perhaps his elongated, subtly threatening heroines had a deeper, if more indirect, impact on
Carroll.

8. Lewis Carroll, *Alice's Adventures Under Ground: A Facsimile of the 1864 Manuscript*, Martin Gardner, ed. (New York: Dover, 1965).

9. There is some debate as to whether Tenniel actually used the photograph of Mary
Badcock as a model for his illustrations. Carroll, who was never fully satisfied with Tenniel's
work, claimed he did not and so the head and feet of his drawing were sometimes out of pro-

portion. But the resemblance between drawing and photograph is so great that I think we must assume he did.

10. George Shelton Hubbell, in "Triple Alice," *Sewanee Review* (April 1940), 48:174–96, discusses some of the differences between Tenniel's Alice and Carroll's.

11. It is significant that the Alice of *Looking-Glass,* a truly passive figure, is sung at more than she sings; the reverse is true in *Wonderland.* Tweedledum and Tweedledee sing the most savage song in *Looking-Glass,* "The Walrus and the Carpenter," which seems to bore Alice.

12. In *Alice's Adventures Under Ground,* Queen and Duchess are a single figure, the Queen of Hearts and Marchioness of Mock Turtles.

13. Donald Rackin makes the same point in "Alice's Journey to the End of the Night," *PMLA* (October 1966), 81:323.

14. In *Looking-Glass,* the pathetic White Knight replaces the Cheshire Cat as Alice's only friend, another indication of the increasing softness of the later Alice. William Empson, *Some Versions of Pastoral,* 2d ed. (London: Chatto & Windus, 1950).

15. Jan B. Gordon, in "The *Alice* Books and the Metaphors of Victorian Childhood," relates the *Alice* books to Michel Foucault's argument that in the nineteenth century, madness came to be regarded as allied to childhood rather than to animality, as it had been in the eighteenth century. Robert Phillips, ed., *Aspects of Alice: Lewis Carroll's Dreamchild as Seen through the Critics' Looking-Glasses, 1865–1971* (New York: Vanguard Press, 1971), p. 101.

16. Does it go too far to connect the mouth that presides over Alice's story to a looking-glass vagina? Carroll's focus on the organ of the mouth seems to have been consistent throughout his life: it is allied to both his interest in eating and the prodigious number of kisses that run through his letters to his child friends. Kissing and cats seem often to have been linked together in his mind.

17. Stuart Dodgson Collingwood, *The Life and Letters of Lewis Carroll* (London: T. Fisher Unwin, 1898), p. 134, italics mine.

18. Empson, *Some Versions of Pastoral,* pp. 263–64.

19. " 'I'll be judge, I'll be jury,' said cunning old Fury; 'I'll try the whole cause, and condemn you to death' " (p. 51). Fury, of course, is also plaintiff.

20. Empson, in *Some Versions of Pastoral,* p. 270, refers to this passage as the Pigeon of the Annunciation denouncing the serpent of the knowledge of good and evil.

21. Lewis Carroll, *Sylvie and Bruno* (London and New York: Macmillan, 1890) 1:319–20.

22. Gordon, "The *Alice* Books," p. 109. Peter Coveney's *The Image of Childhood,* rev. ed. (Baltimore: Penguin Books, 1967), is the most famous and comprehensive survey of Victorian attitudes to childhood. See especially pp. 291–92 for a discussion of these two conflicting currents.

23. I am indebted to Edward Dramin for suggesting this similarity to me.

24. I am indebted for this fine phrase to an unpublished undergraduate honors thesis by Harry Baldwin, of California State College, Los Angeles.

9. FALLING ALICE, FALLEN WOMEN, AND VICTORIAN DREAM CHILDREN

1. See John Pudney, *Lewis Carroll and His World* (New York: Scribner's, 1976), pp. 80–81.

2. See George Sheldon Hubbell, "Triple Alice," *Sewanee Review* (April 1940), 48:174–96.

3. Lewis Carroll, *The Annotated Alice*, Martin Gardner, ed. (1960; reprint, New York: World Publishing, 1971), p. 345. Future references to this edition will appear in the text.

4. Paul Schilder is dire on the "cruelty, destruction, and annihilation" of Wonderland, but his Alice is no more than its anxious victim; see Paul Schilder, "Psychoanalytic Remarks on *Alice in Wonderland* and Lewis Carroll" (1938), reprinted in Robert Phillips, ed., *Aspects of Alice: Lewis Carroll's Dreamchild as Seen Through the Critics' Looking-Glasses, 1865– 1971* (New York: Vanguard Press, 1971), pp. 283–92. William Empson's classic celebration of the cerebral, sexless Alice is by far the richest tribute to her immunity from Wonderland's aggression; see William Empson, *"Alice in Wonderland: The Child as Swain"* (1935), reprinted in Phillips, *Aspects of Alice*, pp. 344–73.

5. James R. Kincaid, "Alice's Invasion of Wonderland," *PMLA* (January 1973), 88:94. Nina Auerbach, in "Alice and Wonderland: A Curious Child," *Victorian Studies* (September 1973), 77:31–47, unearths a similarly aggressive Alice with more emphasis on her femaleness.

6. Jeffrey Stern's "Lewis Carroll the Pre-Raphaelite: 'Fainting in Coils,' " in Edward Guiliano, ed., *Lewis Carroll Observed: A Collection of Unpublished Photographs, Drawings, Poetry, and New Essays* (New York: Clarkson N. Potter, 1976), pp. 161–80, is an illuminating account of Carroll's pre-Raphaelite connections.

7. For the fallen woman in Victorian iconography, see especially Susan P. Casteras, "Down the Garden Path: Courtship Culture and Its Imagery in Victorian Painting," PR.D. dissertation, Yale University, 1977; Linda Nochlin, "Lost and *Found:* Once More the Fallen Woman," *Art Bulletin* (1978), 60:139–53; and Nina Auerbach, "The Rise of the Fallen Woman," *Nineteenth-Century Fiction* (June 1980), 35:29–52.

8. For Carroll and *Found,* see Florence Becker Lennon, *The Life of Lewis Carroll*, 3d rev. ed. (New York: Dover, 1972), p. 162.

9. Irving Massey, *The Gaping Pig: Literature and Metamorphosis* (Berkeley and Los Angeles: University of California Press, 1976).

10. David Sonstroem's *Rossetti and the Fair Lady* (Middletown, Conn.: Wesleyan University Press, 1970) is a compelling account of the iconographic history of Rossetti's woman worship.

11. Nochlin, "Lost and *Found,* " pp. 143, 147–48.

12. Excellent discussions of the ambiguity of Victorian childhood can be found in in Jan B. Gordon, "The *Alice* Books and the Metaphors of Victorian Childhood," Phillips, *Aspects of Alice*, pp. 93–113, and Deborah Gorham, "The 'Maiden Tribute of Modern Babylon' Re-examined: Child Prostitution and the Idea of Childhood in Late-Victorian England," *Victorian Studies* (Spring 1978), 21:353–79.

13. Quoted in Lennon, *Lewis Carroll*, pp. 245–46.

14. Ellen Moers, *Literary Women: The Great Writers* (New York: Doubleday, 1976), pp. 99–107.

15. February 27, 1893. Lewis Carroll, *The Letters of Lewis Carroll*, Morton N. Cohen, ed., 2 vols. (New York: Oxford University Press, 1979), 2:947.

16. *Aspects of Alice* is a symphony of dark Alices. For a moving account of their dependence on memory, see Lionel Morton, "Memory in the *Alice* Books," *Nineteenth-Century Fiction* (December 1978), 33:285–308.

17. See Morton N. Cohen, *Lewis Carroll, Photographer of Children: Four Nude Studies* (New York: Clarkson N. Potter, 1979).

18. Kincaid, "Alice's Invasion," p. 95.

10. ARTISTS AND MOTHERS: A FALSE ALLIANCE

1. Virginia Woolf, *A Room of One's Own* (1919; reprint, New York: Harcourt, Brace & World, 1957), p. 69.

2. Cynthia Griffin Wolff, *A Feast of Words: The Triumph of Edith Wharton* (New York: Oxford University Press, 1977), p. 342.

3. Karen Horney, "The Flight from Womanhood: The Masculinity Complex in Women as Viewed by Men and by Women," reprinted in Jean Baker Miller, ed., *Psychoanalysis and Women* (Baltimore: Penguin Books, 1973), p. 11.

4. Mary Ellmann, *Thinking About Women* (New York: Harcourt Brace Jovanovich, 1968), p. 63; Cynthia Ozick, "Women and Creativity: The Demise of the Dancing Dog" (1969), reprinted in Vivian Gornick and Barbara K. Moran, eds., *Women in Sexist Society: Studies in Power and Powerlessness* (New York: New American Library, 1972), p. 439.

5. The most recent critic to disapprove is the iconoclastic Patricia Beer in *Reader, I Married Him: A Study of the Women Characters of Jane Austen, Charlotte Brontë, Elizabeth Gaskell, and George Eliot* (New York: Barnes & Noble, 1974), pp. 4–5.

6. October 27, 1798. In Jane Austen, *Jane Austen's Letters to Her Sister Cassandra and Others*, R. W. Chapman, ed., 2 vols. (Oxford: Clarendon Press, 1932), 1:24. Hereafter cited in the text by date, volume, and page.

7. Jane Austen, *Emma*, R. W. Chapman, ed. (London: Oxford University Press, 1952), p. 86.

8. George Eliot, "Silly Novels by Lady Novelists," *Westminster Review* (October 1856), 66:461.

9. To Emily Davies, August 8, 1868. In George Eliot, *The George Eliot Letters*, Gordon S. Haight, ed., 7 vols. (New Haven, Conn.: Yale University Press, 1954–55), 4:468. Hereafter cited in the text by date, volume, and page.

10. U. C. Knoepflmacher, "Mr. Haight's George Eliot: 'Wahrheit und Dichtung,' " *Victorian Studies* (June 1969), 12:430.

11. See Gordon S. Haight, *George Eliot: A Biography* (New York and Oxford: Oxford University Press, 1968), p. 205.

12. The ceremonial phrase belongs to her publisher, John Blackwood, as quoted in Haight, *George Eliot*, p. 214.

13. See Ruby V. Redinger, *George Eliot: The Emergent Self* (New York: Knopf, 1975).

14. Quoted in Haight, *George Eliot*, p. 452.

15. Simcox autobiography, December 26, 1879. Quoted in Haight, *George Eliot*, p. 533.

16. Redinger, in *The Emergent Self*, makes this point, pp. 286–88.

17. George Eliot, *Poems* (London: Hawarden Press, 1899), p. 170.

18. For further discussion of Maggie as an anti-maternal principle, see my "The Power of Hunger: Demonism and Maggie Tulliver," *Nineteenth-Century Fiction* (September 1975), 30:150–71.

19. George Eliot, *Daniel Deronda* (1876; reprint, Middlesex, Eng.: Penguin English Library, 1967), p. 691. Future references to this edition will appear in the text.

20. This paper was originally presented, in somewhat altered form, at a special session at the 1977 MLA Convention, "Psychiatric Paradigms of Woman Artists," chairperson, Kathleen Fishbun.

11. DOROTHY L. SAYERS AND THE AMAZONS

1. Dorothy L. Sayers, *Gaudy Night* (1935; reprint, New York: Avon Books, 1968), p. 220. Future references will be to this edition and will be incorporated into the text.

2. Elizabeth Gaskell, *Cranford* (1851; reprint, London: J.M. Dent, 1969).

3. The most apt literary antecedents of *Gaudy Night* can probably be found in the Amazonian communities of George Gissing's *The Odd Women* and Henry James' *The Bostonians*. But an important generation separates them from the vitality of Shrewsbury. These feminist *horti conclusi* are largely negative and proscriptive; personal relationships are abandoned only for a vague militant fervor; the breast has been cut off with only the faintest hint of the arrow—the Cause—that the future will grant.

4. Dante Alighieri, *Hell*, Dorothy L. Sayers, trans. (1949; reprint, Middlesex, Eng.: Penguin, 1973), pp. 10–11.

5. Dorothy L. Sayers, *Strong Poison* (1937; reprint, London: New English Library Times Mirror, 1968); "Talboys," written in 1942, was published posthumously in James Sandoe, ed., *Lord Peter* (New York: Avon Books, 1972), pp. 431–53; *Unnatural Death* (1927; reprint, New York: Avon Books, 1964); *Busman's Honeymooon* (1937; reprint, New York: Avon Books, 1968).

6. Dorothy L. Sayers, *Have His Carcase* (1932; reprint, New York: Avon Books, 1968), p. 9.

7. Sayers, *Busman's Honeymoon*, pp. 210–11.

12. CHARLOTTE BRONTE: THE TWO COUNTRIES

1. Robert Martin, *The Accents of Persuasion: Charlotte Brontë's Novels* (New York: Norton, 1966); and Earl Knies, *The Art of Charlotte Brontë* (Athens: Ohio University Press, 1969).

2. Robert Heilman, in "Charlotte Brontë, Reason, and the Moon," *Nineteenth-Century Fiction* (March 1960), 14:283–302, defines the moon as Charlotte Brontë's key symbol for irrational and quasi-sacramental forces within and without the self. David Lodge, in "Fire and Eyre: Charlotte Brontë's War of Earthly Elements," *Language of Fiction*, 3d ed. (New York: Columbia Paperback Edition, 1967), pp. 114–43, emphasizes the role of fire in her elemental imagery, though he does not explore in detail the relation of fire to the other elements.

3. Journal entry quoted in Fannie E. Ratchford, *The Brontës' Web of Childhood* (New York: Columbia University Press, 1941), p. 149. There is a similar image at the beginning of *Shirley* of the flaming sky of romance juxtaposed against the "real, cool, and solid," which is by implication a world without a sun.

4. Charlotte Brontë, *Jane Eyre*, Shakespeare Head Brontë, 2 vols. (Oxford: Shakespeare Head Press, 1931), 2:192. Subsequent references will be to this edition and will be incorporated into the text.

5. Charlotte Brontë, *Villette*, Shakespeare Head Brontë, 2 vols. (Oxford: Shakespeare Head Press, 1931), 1:52. Subsequent references will be to this edition and will be incorporated into the text.

6. Lodge, in "Fire and Eyre," p. 121, discusses the association of rock and stone with ice—and thus of earth and water—in his analysis of Charlotte Brontë's elemental imagery.

7. "The infernal world" was another of Charlotte and Branwell's names for Angria.

8. Richard Chase, in "The Brontës: A Centennial Observance," *Kenyon Review* (Autumn 1947), 9:487–596, has a famous definition of the triumph of the anti-life forces at the end of *Jane Eyre*, with the masculine energy of the universe crushed and castrated by the eternal feminine. I agree with his idea that life and energy are crushed at the end, not tamed and

incorporated into a larger synthesis, but the central conflict in the novel seems to be more encompassing and in a sense more important than Chase's battle of the sexes.

13. "THIS CHANGEFUL LIFE" EMILY BRONTE'S ANTI-ROMANCE

1. Fannie E. Ratchford, *Gondal's Queen: A Novel in Verse* (1955; reprint, Austin: University of Texas Press, 1977).
2. In Emily Brontë, *The Complete Poems of Emily Jane Brontë*, C. W. Hatfield, ed. (New York: Columbia University Press, 1941), p. 14. Future references to Brontë's poems in the text will be to the headings, numbers, and lines in Hatfield's edition.
3. See Keith Sagar, "The Originality of *Wuthering Heights*," in Anne Smith, ed., *The Art of Emily Brontë* (New York: Barnes & Noble, 1976), p. 159: "Emily Brontë was a great romantic rebel and a great religious mystic, and at the same time an unsparing critic of romantic rebellion and religious mysticism. Her stage spans, like a cosmic rack, the space between the necessary and the possible."
4. William Blake, *The Poetry and Prose of William Blake*, David V. Erdman, ed. (New York: Doubleday, 1965), p. 16. Future references to this edition will appear in the text.
5. Emily Brontë, *Wuthering Heights* (1846; reprint, New York: Norton, 1963), p. 72.
6. Robert Browning, *The Ring and the Book* (1868–69; reprint, New York: Norton, 1961), p. 31.
7. See Fannie E. Ratchford, *The Brontës' Web of Childhood* (1941; reprint, New York: Russell & Russell, 1964), p. 102.
8. I should like to thank Stuart Curran for his patient readings of successive versions of this essay and for our invaluable discussions of Blake and Byron. His ideas were important illuminations to me as I wrote, though all prejudices and misconceptions remain my own. I should also like to thank the Gyral Foundation for its most generous support during the writing of the essay.

14. THE POWER OF HUNGER: DEMONISM AND MAGGIE TULLIVER

1. This conception of a central flaw in George Eliot's perspective originates in F. R. Leavis' *The Great Tradition* (London: Chatto Windus, 1948), but it has been adhered to in such widely divergent treatments of *The Mill on the Floss* as Lawrence Lerner's *The Truthtellers* (New York: Schocken Books, 1967); U. C. Knoepflmacher's *George Eliot's Early Novels: The Limits of Realism* (Berkeley and Los Angeles: University of California Press, 1968); and Henry Auster's *Local Habitations: Regionalism in the Early Novels of George Eliot* (Cambridge, Mass.: Harvard University Press, 1970). Leavis is so vehement in his denunciation of the "emotional," "immature," "feminine" side of George Eliot that one sometimes feels she would be an even greater representative of his tradition if she were a man. Critics have been diffident about finding virtues in this "flawed" George Eliot he would like to cut away.
2. George Eliot, *The Mill on the Floss*, Gordon S. Haight, ed., Riverside Editions (Boston: Houghton Mifflin, 1961), p. 8. All page references in the text are to this edition.
3. W. J. Harvey finds the last volume of the novel plausible in conception but sketchy and unrealized in execution, particularly in its treatment of Stephen; see *The Art of George Eliot* (London: Chatto & Windus, 1963), pp. 123–24. The fractured rush of events seems quite real to me, because the action is presented as Maggie lives and perceives it; Stephen's

sketchiness reflects her perception of him as less a whole man than a smell, a hand, a soothing voice, and the promise of ease in an unhappy life.

4. For studies of George Eliot's relation to Pater, see U. C. Knoepflmacher, *Religious Humanism and the Victorian Novel: George Eliot, Walter Pater, and Samuel Butler* (Princeton, N.J.: Princeton University Press, 1965); and David J. DeLaura, "*Romola* and the Origin of the Paterian View of Life," *Nineteenth-Century Fiction* (1966), 21:225–33. Both Knoepflmacher and DeLaura treat George Eliot's impact on *Marius the Epicurean*, but the sensationalist strain in *The Mill on the Floss* might have made its way into *Studies in the History of the Renaissance* and its notorious conclusion. For treatments of George Eliot's influence on Proust, see Franklin Gary, "In Search of George Eliot: An Approach Through Marcel Proust," *Symposium* (1933), 4:182–206; and L. A. Bisson, "Proust, Bergson, and George Eliot," *Modern Language Review* (1945), 40:104–14.

5. George Eliot, *The George Eliot Letters*, Gordon S. Haight, ed., 7 vols. (New Haven, Conn.: Yale University Press, 1954–55), 3:299.

6. Jane Austen, *Northanger Abbey* (with *Persuasion*), R. W. Chapman, ed. (London: Oxford University Press, 1954), p. 200.

7. George Eliot, *Romola*, Everyman's Library (London, Dent, 1968), p. 317.

8. For an excellent analysis of the visionary and occult strain running through *Daniel Deronda*, see Robert Preyer, "Beyond the Liberal Imagination: Vision and Unreality in *Daniel Deronda*," *Victorian Studies* (1960), 4:33–54. But while Preyer treats this late supernaturalism as a solitary departure, I see it as an inherent and important element in all her fiction.

9. George Eliot's reiteration of her intention to limit her novels to the boring and unadorned lives her readers supposedly live is reminiscent of Charlotte Brontë's equally strident insistence that she is forcing fantasy to succumb to the "real, cool and solid" material of daily life in *Shirley*. Both ladies protest too much that they are not writing Gothic romances, and their reactions away from the "reality" they drably and narrowly define are equally fierce. Still, it may be significant that George Eliot does not attack Gothic novels in her scathing review of trashy female fiction, "Silly Novels by Lady Novelists," *Westminster Review* (October 1856), 66:442–61.

10. Bernard J. Paris' "un-conversion" is a significant event in the critical history of this difficult novel. In *Experiments in Life: George Eliot's Quest for Values* (Detroit: Wayne State University Press, 1965), Paris graphed the novels by reading them as illustrative demonstrations of George Eliot's humanistic philosophy. But in "The Inner Conflicts of Maggie Tulliver: A Horneyan Analysis," *Centennial Review* (1969), 13:166–99, he abandons the attempt to extrapolate rational values out of *The Mill on the Floss*, praising instead the vividness with which the experience of being Maggie is dramatized despite the surrounding moral incoherence. But the Horneyan frame within which he tries to evaluate Maggie seems untrue to a novel which offers no "healthy" choices through which she can define herself. Critics of this novel are forced always to remember that there is "no master key" which will unlock the meaning of the action for us, including psychology in a deranged mode. For more schematic Freudian analyses of the novel, see David Smith, " 'In their death they were not divided': The Form of Illicit Passion in *The Mill on the Floss*," *Literature and Psychology* (1965), 15:144–62; and Michael Steig, "Anality in *The Mill on the Floss*," *Novel* (1971), 5:42–53.

11. For general discussions of the relationship between witchcraft, animism, and nature worship, see especially Jules Michelet, *Satanism and Witchcraft*, A. R. Alinson, trans. (New York: Citadel Press, 1965); and Pennethorne Hughes, *Witchcraft*, 2nd ed. (Baltimore: Penguin Books, 1970). Michelet's discussion of the witch as healer seems almost exactly dramatized in the Raveloe villagers' terrified reaction to Silas Marner's application of healing herbs.

12. In discussing a novel which contains two definite allusions to Dante's *Inferno*

and many atmospheric and emotional suggestions of it, it might be revealing to remember that in canto 13 of the *Inferno,* Dante transforms his suicides into wailing, bleeding trees. Suicide is a frequent cause of vampirism in legend, though not in vampire literature.

13. In her next speech, Mrs. Tulliver brings in the motif of Maggie as "a Bedlam creatur'," which recurs throughout the novel. Uncle Pullet relates her brown skin to her possible craziness on p. 334. Demonism and psychosis have worn similar faces throughout history, legend, and literature, as we can see in *Jane Eyre* when the raging Bertha Mason appears to Jane as "the foul German spectre—the Vampyre." This "crazy" motif colors our last image of Maggie, riding through the flood with wild eyes and streaming hair, a weird mélange of Beorl's Virgin of the Flood, Defoe's witch in the water, and Millais' Ophelia.

14. Robert Kiely, *The Romantic Novel in England* (Cambridge, Mass: Harvard University Press, 1972), pp. 252, 117.

15. John Hagan cites Bernard J. Paris, Reva Stump, and George Levine as the chief exponents of this view in "A Reinterpretation of *The Mill on the Floss,*" PMLA (1972), 87:53–63. See Paris, *Experiments in Life;* Reva Stump, *Movement and Vision in George Eliot's Novels* (Seattle: University of Washington Press, 1959); and George Levine, "Intelligence as Deception: *The Mill on the Floss,*" PMLA (1965), 80:402–9.

16. This "book-to-window" motif is reminiscent of *Wuthering Heights,* in which Alpine Gothic extremes are consummately transplanted in the Yorkshire countryside. Like Maggie, Catherine and Heathcliff are always flinging books about and pining toward the window. There is an important difference here between the lovely heroine of this "autobiographical" novel and its ugly, determined author, whose omnivorous course of study while she was living with her father had little in common with Maggie's erratic and undisciplined reading. George Eliot seems quite aware that Maggie is not sufficiently strong and steely—not enough like Tom, in fact—to make an alternative religion of work and ambition, as Mary Ann Evans apparently did.

17. George Eliot, *Writings of George Eliot,* 25 vols. (New York: AMS Press, 1970), 2:311.

15. SECRET PERFORMANCES: GEORGE ELIOT AND THE ART OF ACTING

1. Matilda Betham-Edwards, *Mid-Victorian Memories* (London: John Murray, 1919), p. 39. Future references to this edition will appear in the text.

2. 1869; quoted in Gordon S. Haight, *George Eliot: A Biography* (Oxford: Oxford University Press, 1968), p. 417. Future references to Haight's biography will appear in the text.

3. See Christopher Kent, "Image and Reality: The Actress and Society," in Martha Vicinus, ed., *A Widening Sphere: Changing Roles of Victorian Women* (Bloomington and London: Indiana University Press, 1977), pp. 94–116; and Michael Baker, *The Rise of the Victorian Actor* (London: Croom Helm, 1978), pp. 95–108. Sally Mitchell's *The Fallen Angel: Chastity, Class, and Women's Reading, 1835–1880* (Bowling Green, Ohio: Bowling Green University Press, 1981) discusses the impact of the aggressive, competitive actress heroines in novels of the 1870s as they supersede the martyred and self-effacing governess.

4. George Bernard Shaw, *Platform and Pulpit,* Dan H. Laurence, ed. (London: Rupert Hart-Davis, 1962), p. 22.

5. George Eliot, *Daniel Deronda* (1876; reprint, Middlesex, Eng.: Penguin English Library, 1967), pp. 691–92.

6. For another perspective on Alcharisi as a triumph of autobiographical self-assertion on George Eliot's part, see my "Artists and Mothers: A False Alliance," *Women and Literature* (Spring 1978), 6:13–14.

7. Haight, *George Eliot*, p. 5, quoting John W. Cross, *George Eliot's Life as Related in Her Letters and Journals*.

8. George Eliot, *The George Eliot Letters*, Gordon S. Haight, ed., 9 vols. New Haven, Conn.: Yale University Press, 1954–78), 1:284. Hereafter cited in the text as GEL.

9. George Bernard Shaw, "Duse and Bernhardt," in *Dramatic Opinions and Essays* (New York: Brentano's, 1925), pp. 141–42.

10. Ellen Moers, *Literary Women: The Great Writers* (New York: Doubleday, 1976), pp. 192–200.

11. George Eliot, *Adam Bede* (1859; reprint, Boston: Houghton Mifflin, Riverside Editions, 1968), p. 21. Future references to this edition will appear in the text.

12. George Eliot, *Middlemarch* (1871–72; reprint, Boston: Houghton Mifflin, Riverside Editions, 1956), p. 549. Future references to this edition will appear in the text.

13. Patricia Beer, in *Reader, I Married Him: A Study of the Women Characters of Jane Austen, Charlotte Brontë, Elizabeth Gaskell and George Eliot* (New York: Barnes & Noble, 1974), pp. 197–200, and Sandra M. Gilbert and Susan Gubar, *The Madwoman in the Attic: The Woman Writer and the Nineteenth-Century Literary Imagination* (New Haven, Conn: Yale University Press, 1979), pp. 499–520, discuss the resonance of Laure in *Middlemarch* and its marriages. Both books, however, find her more significant as murderess than as actress.

14. Beer, in *Reader, I Married Him*, pp. 188–89, discusses the subtle, provocative affinities between Rosamond and Dorothea as wives.

16. ELLEN TERRY'S VICTORIAN MARRIAGE

1. Roger Manvell, *Ellen Terry* (New York: Putnam, 1968), p. 297.

2. Ellen Terry, "Stray Memories," *The New Review* (April 1891), 23:503, 504.

3. Ellen Terry, *Four Lectures on Shakespeare* (London: Martin Hopkinson, 1932), p. 151.

4. Bram Stoker, *Personal Reminiscences of Henry Irving*, 2 vols. (New York and London: Macmillan, 1906), 2:68.

5. Christopher St. John, ed., *Ellen Terry and Bernard Shaw: A Correspondence* (New York: Putnam, 1931), p. 217.

6. St. John, *A Correspondence*, p. 247.

7. Ellen Terry, *Ellen Terry's Memoir*, with preface, notes, and additional biographical material by Edith Craig and Christopher St. John (1932; reprint, New York: Benjamin Blom, 1969), p. 127.

8. William Archer, *Henry Irving, Actor and Manager: A Critical Study* (London: Field & Tuer, c. 1900), p. 100.

9. Clement Scott, *Ellen Terry* (New York: Frederick A. Stokes, 1900), pp. 68–69.

10. Jane Austen, *Pride and Prejudice* (1813; reprint, Norton, 1966), p. 256.

11. Quoted in Terry, *Memoir*, p. 248.

12. Virginia Woolf, *Between the Acts* (1941; reprint, New York: Harcourt Brace Jovanovich, 1969), p. 153.

13. Christopher St. John, *Ellen Terry* (London: Bodley Head, 1907), p. 43.

14. Terry, *Memoir*, p. 215.

Index